Changing the Scientific Study of Religion: Beyond Freud?

Jacob A. Belzen
Editor

Changing the Scientific Study of Religion: Beyond Freud?

Theoretical, Empirical and Clinical Studies from Psychoanalytic Perspectives

Springer

Editor
Prof. Jacob A. Belzen
University of Amsterdam
Faculty of Humanities
Oude Turfmarkt 147
1012 GC Amsterdam
Netherlands
belzen@hum.uva.nl

ISBN 978-94-007-9142-8 ISBN 978-90-481-2540-1 (eBook)
DOI 10.1007/978-90-481-2540-1
Springer Dordrecht Heidelberg London New York

Softcover re-print of the Hardcover 1st edition 2009

Printed on acid-free paper

Springer is part of Springer Science+Business Media (www.springer.com)

Contents

Introduction

Past Freud – Beyond Freud?

On Progress in the Psychoanalytic Psychology of Religion

Jacob A. Belzen

In 1907 Freud published his first article on religion, thereby inaugurating the psychoanalytic psychology of religion, a part of the psychology of religion that until now has inspired more contributions than any other approach and which is even often identified with the psychology of religion as a whole by the wider public. (To give just a small indication merely of the quantitative importance of the psychoanalytic school: more than a third of the unsurpassed survey of 'classic and contemporary views' in the psychology of religion compiled by Wulff (1997a) is devoted to psychodynamic approaches.) The psychoanalytic psychology of religion has become so encompassing that it is now usual to distinguish several factions; these cannot all be discussed here. And since quite a few historical surveys are now available (Wulff, 1997a; Vandermeersch and Westerink, 2007) this introduction will take a different course: more or less inspired by viewpoints from the theory of science, it will pose the critical-sounding question whether and to what extent progress has taken place during one century of the psychoanalytic psychology of religion.

To answer that question comprehensively would take a full book (or maybe a series of books) dealing with the entire history of the psychoanalytic psychology of religion. The framework of an introductory chapter allows for no more than some explorations. We will, as it were, take a walk through a wide field, and as we go along point to some features in the landscape that may or even should be discussed for the purposes of more detailed research. To get a view of what the psychoanalytic psychology of religion has attained I will critically examine five points of possible progress: (1) there is a purer understanding of what Freud has said about religion; (2) there is a clearer view of the reach of the approach initiated by him; (3) this approach has been made more precise in some respects; (4) the psychoanalytic psychology of religion has recently found corroboration from an unexpected source; (5) a remarkable proliferation of psychoanalytic viewpoints has taken place in the study of religion.

J.A. Belzen
University of Amsterdam, Amsterdam, Netherlands
e-mail: belzen@hum.uva.nl

Among other things, I will discuss the idea that religion is projection, an idea that is often alleged to have originated in psychoanalysis (cf.Vandermeersch and Westerink, 2007, p. 159). Only recently the editor of an excellent volume on religion and psychoanalysis summarized Freud's psychology of religion as follows: "religion is made up of nothing but fantasy and a projection of our wishes and fears into the heavens" (Black, 2006, p. 63). We will see if and to what measure this is correct. But again, in doing so I do not intend to offer a narrative history of the idea of "religion as projection." Nor will a historical survey be offered of the whole field that stretches between the poles "psychoanalysis" and "religion." I will merely attempt to extend the question about the progress in the psychoanalytic psychology of religion in such a way as to apply it to the aforementioned idea as well: for example, what are the present views on the idea of religion as projection; is it a valid idea, and if so, in what sense; if not, in what other way should it be understood – if it is to be taken seriously at all? The answer to these questions will turn out to be fairly representative of the answers to similar questions that may more generally be asked after 100 years of work in the psychology of religion.

Freud on Religion

Shortcomings in the Freud Reception

To Freud, father of both psychoanalysis and the psychoanalytic psychology of religion, are attributed quite a number of critical interpretations of religion: according to Freud, religion is no more than wishful thinking, projection, illusion, neurosis and what not (Banks, 1973, p. 402). While this article does not aim to give yet another explanation of Freud's exact opinions on these points, it is important to note – as is usual in these sorts of cases – that matters are far more complicated than the one-liners, even those popular among psychologists (of religion), suggest. To give just one example: in his very first article on the psychology of religion, from 1907, Freud nowhere claims that religion "as such" is a neurosis, a pathological affliction or morbid product of anyone's mental functioning (Freud, 1907/1941). What he does say, is, briefly, the following: on the grounds of the rigidity characteristic of both neurotic behavior and religious rituals he draws a methodical comparison between the two. He does not equate them; on the contrary, in this very article can be found the statement that religiosity, the being involved in religion at the level of the individual, may well prevent a neurosis from developing. Nor does Freud say anywhere in his numerous other publications that being religious might or should be equated with being neurotic, or even count as an indication of the latter. If we look at his case studies of individual pathologies we will find that there, too, Freud does not consider a patient's religiosity a pathological phenomenon. In his study of a seventeenth-century case of "possession," for example, Freud does not declare the person involved to be ill because he is religious, not even because he considers himself possessed (Freud, 1923/1973). Freud does show that the painter Haitzmann was a severe neurotic and that his neurosis manifested itself in, among other things, his way of being religious. Comparing Freud's texts on religion and neurosis may well lead to the following conclusion: being religious may promote a person's individual mental functioning and may help prohibit a neurosis, even though in individual cases the psychological structuring of the religiosity still needs to be examined.[1]

To avoid misunderstanding, and in all fairness, it must be immediately added that even though Freud would not have denied this last proposition, he never actually wrote it down in this literal form. The picture that emerges from Freud's published work and scattered remarks on religion is definitely not that of someone intent on writing with sympathy about religion, nor of someone who takes the trouble to treat it as carefully as possible. In fact the opposite is the case: nowhere does Freud hide his opinion that he is not at all enthusiastic about religion; he even thinks that what is promulgated by religion is simply wrong and untrue. Religion proclaims things about reality that science has shown to be wrong; in Freud's view it is science, not religion, that gives us reliable knowledge. (And he places so much confidence in science, in human rationality, that he goes so far as to call it "our god," Freud, 1927/1948.) We must therefore make a sharp distinction between Freud's opinions on religion at, let's say, the macro and micro levels, between his views on religion as system of practices and (above all) convictions, and his views on religion at the level of the individual. We might term the former his ontological (or if you like, religious) views, the latter his scientific-psychological views. As far as the former are concerned, Freud regarded religion as wrong. He did not "believe" in the content of religion. In the case of the latter Freud limited himself to making pronouncements about the role of individual religiosity as a part of a person's whole psychodynamics. One should not lose sight of these nuances: for Freud, the fact that somebody is religious does not mean that that person is mentally ill or deranged in any way. Even when an individual has bizarre religious views or demonstrates bizarre faith practices, this does not mean that being religious as such is "insane" or that religion as such is madness (or even nonsense). But, as Freud would say, neither should one draw the opposite conclusion: the fact that faith enables somebody to deal with life may be a good thing, but it is no indication of its value or its truth. In Freud's eyes (natural) science has proved to be the only reliable road to truth; things incompatible with that science are wrong and doomed to disappear. For that reason Freud – like Comte, the founder of positivism, before him – thought that religion was an outdated stage in humanity's development, a stage whose origin and role are explicable but which is now, thanks to science, "superseded" and ready to be left behind. Just as children may have many neurotic features that they, as it were, "automatically" grow out of, religion is a phase that humankind will outgrow;

[1] One also finds this view in the most recent literature. Pargament, one of the best-known modern researchers in the field, arrived at the conclusion: "Questions about the general efficacy of religion should give way to the more difficult but more appropriate question, How helpful or harmful are particular forms of religious expression for particular people dealing with particular situations in particular social contexts according to particular criteria of helpfulness or harmfulness?" (2002, p. 168).

not overcoming it would certainly constitute something like a neurosis at the level of humanity as a whole. Or put in still other words: religion is wrong, according to Freud, even though at the individual level it may well be that the religious life should be valued positively in its psychological respect, since a person may find in religion strength, comfort, social embedment, inspiration and much more. (And conversely, it must be repeated, one should not draw any invalid conclusions from this: the fact that faith gives strength, etc., is wonderful, but it would be even better to derive such strength from science, which is so much superior to any form of religion whatsoever. Despite all the nuances that can be found in Freud's work on religion, his basic attitude is negative: he did not "believe" in religion, yet he did believe in science.)[2]

The critical reader may wonder whether, even according to Freud's own criteria, "believing in science" might not be psychodynamically structured in the same way as someone else's "believing in god" (or whatever form of religion is involved). In other words: is not the whole account of religion mutatis mutandis applicable to science as well? Basically this is indeed the case. When Freud remarks about religion that it is an "illusion" (Freud, 1927/1948) he does not primarily mean by that that it is nonsense, something in flat contradiction to for example intersubjectively verifiable "facts." Freud calls faith an illusion because it typically has the character of the wishes of which in part it is a consequence. Because wishes are at the basis of faith, it is an illusion, not because it is deception or untruth. The critic will immediately reply: could not the same be true of scientific accounts of things? Freud admitted this: in principle, scientific views could also be based on a wish, which would be responsible for the similar illusory nature of scientific knowledge. But this would only be the case "in principle." According to Freud's positivistic and fairly outdated views on science, wishes play no part in it; science is a purely rational process (and astonishingly many philosophers of science still cling to a similar viewpoint and reject as nonsensical such disciplines as the history of science and even more so the sociology and psychology of science ...). But even in Freud's book in which he calls religion an illusion (Freud, 1927/1948), his reasoning is more nuanced than is suggested by the well-known one-liners that pretend to sum up his opinion. In any case one returns to the same point: it is not as a psychologist that Freud objects so much to religion (in his view it is not a delusion) but rather as a "thinking person," somebody with a certain (irreligious, even antireligious) take on life and the world. That religion contains "illusion" is not a final counterargument. "Illusion" can be found everywhere except in science, and therefore science is superior to all other ways of thinking; science will progress beyond all of them, including religion. Freud was an unflinching adherent of scientism.

[2] His followers would rather quickly lose sight of these nuances: while Jung and his school would develop a great interest in religion, an interest that, though positive, also led to a contamination of religion and psychology (Vandermeersch, 1974/1991), the first generations of "Freudians" would be largely antireligious, sometimes so violently (or often without nuance) that patients who adhered to some form of religious practice were regarded as insufficiently (psycho)analyzed. But later on things changed, cf. later.

Religion as Projection?

If we were to take the trouble to present a precise exegesis, our findings would be confirmed regarding the idea of "religion as projection": Freud himself is much more nuanced than he is generally said to be. A few remarks about this will suffice. Contrary to what authors such as Black (2006), whom we already quoted, but also Banks (1973) maintain, Freud nowhere said that religion *tout court* was (a matter of) projection. That thesis should rather be ascribed to Feuerbach: according to the Feuerbach of *Das Wesen des Christentums*, god is an objectified externalization of the essence of human nature (Feuerbach, 1841/1957). Freud nowhere says this or anything even remotely similar. In only one place does Freud talk about projection in a context that has to do with religion. But it must immediately be added that the relevant chapter from *Zur Psychopathologie des Alltagslebens* (Freud, 1901/1962, pp. 287–288) deals with superstition, and that Freud talks about "myths" literally, not about religion as such. (Freud discussed religion many times in other places, but without using the notion of projection to analyze it.) The line from Feuerbach to Freud, if such can be identified, has often been presented as if Freud had provided an empirical–psychological foundation for the thesis on the essence of religion already put forth by Feuerbach. It may well be asked, however, whether this view is correct and whether Freud himself saw it that way too.

For a start, projection is one of those concepts from psychoanalysis that have remained unclear (Laplanche and Pontalis, 1972); Freud had already admitted this and expressed his intention to devote a special study to it (Freud, 1911/1964, p. 66), which however never appeared. In general one would probably have to deny that religion is a matter of projection. Despite the obscurity of the concept it can still be maintained that projection is a mental operation in which the subject denies "something" of himself (qualities, feelings, wishes) and ascribes it to someone or something else. (The best known example is hate: one denies the hate in oneself and ascribes it to others, which in an extreme form can be perceived in paranoia, for example, but equally in non-clinical situations such as prejudices, conflicts, discrimination, etc.) To say, for instance, that in the individual image of god various qualities of the subject's own father are projected onto god, then this is wrongly formulated: according to the psychoanalytic conceptual framework, what one means is not projection but *transference*. In any case, religion as an extraordinarily complex and multiform element of culture cannot be called a projection; god might possibly be regarded as a projection but is not designated as such by Freud. As already indicated, Freud merely links (outdated) myths to projection, but only very casually, in an early publication and in a way that is hardly technical-psychoanalytical yet.

Next, one should keep in mind here the nuance – ambivalence would be another good term – in Freud's text itself. With his psychoanalysis Freud developed a sound form of individual psychology (psychology dealing with individuals) that has been widely accepted in many different types of clinical practice and care. (Although psychoanalysis as a treatment is no longer found very often, it remains true that modern psychotherapy and clinical psychology, in all their diverse forms, would be unthinkable without the many different insights and techniques derived from psychoanalysis.) Freud, however, was at least equally interested in questions that far surpass the level of the individual, questions concerning art and literature, society and culture. Though many introductions to psychoanalysis fail to mention it and many psychoanalysts are ignorant of it, Freud was an important theoretician of culture. (It is therefore striking that nowadays his theories are taught more extensively at faculties of letters, humanities and the like than at those of psychology and psychiatry.) His views on culture (including religion at the level of culture) have always remained controversial, however; many consider it a category mistake when a psychoanalyst (who is judged to be competent merely at the level of individual clinical problems) airs his opinions on phenomena at a macro level, the level of society, history and culture. There is no need for us to discuss that methodological issue here. We merely wish to establish that Freud operated at both levels, that he did so far from naively (he clearly indicates, for instance, that a psychoanalytic account can always only offer a partial perspective on such things as religion as a cultural phenomenon, which he then nevertheless often presented as the last word on the matter) and that he initiated an endless stream of commentaries and reflections in this field. (Freud was for many years the most often quoted humanities scholar.) It also needs to be established that his culture-theoretical views have often been contradicted, even by sympathizers. Let us keep in mind the fact that Freud, a brilliant clinician and courageous theoretician, attempted again and again, on the basis of his authority in the field of individual psychology, to discuss phenomena located at a higher level than that of the individual, more or less successfully.

If one studies "Freud and religion" (or "Freud on religion") – provided one knows how to master the gigantic quantities of secondary literature that have accumulated over the years[3] – the same conclusion is reached again and again: with all the contradictions, redefinitions of the subject and changes in outlook that characterize his work, Freud is usually much more nuanced in his psychological statements on religion than most of his strictest adherents.[4] As a consequence, in the first decades after Freud's death the debate on "religion and psychoanalysis" immediately became less profound: nothing of the things we suggestively posed at the beginning (religion as neurosis, as illusion, as projection) can be found verbatim in Freud,[5] but they are notions that in a vulgarized form have greatly stimulated the Western psychological critique of religion. Freud was a reductionist as regards religion. He was very critical of religion, he foresaw its end, but nowhere did he reduce it to a psychic mechanism. He did believe, though, that all psychic mechanisms (including pathological derangements) can play a part in religious action and experience (and also

[3] Some years ago an application was even made to the American Academy of Religion to set up a section on "Freud and religion" as a more or less autonomous field of academic research.

[4] Freud for example never demanded that psychoanalysts be non-religious, although this become an unwritten rule among psychoanalysts after his death. He never suggested to his friend, the pastor and psychoanalyst Pfister, to either give up his faith or look for a different occupation. He did believe, however, that after psychoanalysis faith would disappear in most believers (Freud & Pfister, 1963).

[5] It is therefore striking to read how Banks (1973) in his "reappraisal" keeps on referring to Freud's projection theory of religion, while being unable to produce any textual evidence for it.

in its products, such as images of god, dogmas etc.). But this is hardly going to be contradicted by enlightened Westerners nowadays: that psychic mechanisms play a role in religious action and experience, as in all human action and experience, is almost a pleonasm.

The Range of the Psychological Perspective

As said, this chapter is not intended as one more explanation of Freud's pronouncements on religion; these have merely been some introductory remarks. What we are really concerned with is the question whether progress has been made, for instance concerning the idea of 'religion as projection' – what is the present situation? Happily, the answer can be brief: after Freud there was no progress for decades. If we may believe the American Bailey (1988), who seems to have studied the matter closely, it was only in the Netherlands that something worth mentioning was put forward on this matter, and this was during the so-called projection debate. We cannot hope to give a complete history of this debate (some aspects have already been treated by Breevaart, 2005; and Belzen, 2007), but we do want to see whether psychological theory has made any progress. So the context of that debate can only be briefly touched on here. After the appearance of Simon Vestdijk's *De Toekomst der Religie* ("The future of religion," 1947/1992) a storm of protest burst forth in the Netherlands and a (not in all respects scrupulous) discussion arose. The oft-reprinted book was, however, an "essay," as the subtitle says, not a scientific exposition. Some of the central claims of the essay were later put on a more academic foundation by Fokke Sierksma (1956/1980). This proved to be a book of exceptional scientific quality that almost nobody was able to respond to substantively. According to Fortmann, the first professor of the psychology of religion in the Netherlands, the theory of "religion as projection" was so important and contained so much explosive material which in a vulgarized form could only lead to religious doubt and even apostasy, that Vestdijk and Sierksma deserved a "good answer" (Fortmann, 1957, p. 7). Let us therefore see what important things can be found in that scientific *pièce de résistance* of the projection debate, Sierksma's *De Religieuze Projectie* ("The religious projection," 1956/1980). If it is really as crucial as Bailey maintains, a survey of its contents may be in order – since it is hardly known outside the Netherlands.

The (Dutch) Projection Debate

In his wide-ranging monograph, Sierksma takes up Vestdijk's thesis that people place the ideal of the "eternal" man outside themselves. The term used here, also by Vestdijk himself, is "projection," a term seemingly derived from Freud. But is this right? And what exactly is meant by it? What is projection and how does it operate? These have proven to be complicated questions, right up to the present day (cf. Neuser and Kriebel, 1992). Sierksma went in search of an answer and uncovered quite a few meanings of the term.

In his search for clarification he involves not only psychology and philosophical anthropology but also various data from cultural anthropology and biology (or, if you like, animal psychology). The following account of his ideas is impermissibly brief but contains at least the main outlines. Sierksma finds that the human being wants to "find out the truth"; that humans are probably the only beings on our planet who know, or at least think they knows, of a distinction between real and unreal, between objective and subjective. Human beings realize that what they perceive might not be reality as it is. Every animal, including man, lives in a fragmentary "Merkwelt," to use Von Uexküll's terminology: some things get perceived, others do not. An infinite number of stimuli – an "Ausschnitt" – is made of the world-as-such, which is the animal's own world. So the animal adapts to the world, but just as much it adapts the world to itself. The goal of particularly the last-mentioned, subjectivizing function of perception (the "projection") is to give organization and stability to a world that otherwise would remain a chaos, a function that is vital in the struggle for life. There is, however, an essential difference between the human being and the other animals: the animal lives centrically, the human "ex-centrically" (philosopher Plessner's term), the animal has no self-consciousness, man does; the human can place herself beside and opposite herself, can know *that* in perception she organizes the world in a certain way.[6]

Man must cope in the world, trying to master it with the tools designed by him. In an analogous way he tries indirectly, by means of projection, to master that part of the world that will not be conquered. When for example an "Eskimo-man"[7] knows he is threatened by famine, he projects a goddess at the bottom of the sea who keeps the seals prisoner. The unity of word and image plays a significant part in this: the word, too, is an indirect tool of the mind to get a grip on the world. When the tool reaches its limit, man uses the power of the "word-image." By means of word and tool man thus tries to complete himself and to gain control of the world.

Sierksma also discusses the distinction between consciousness and the unconscious. He points out that the external and internal world are stabilized in the same

---

[6] This point is central to Sierksma's argument, a point he finds confirmed by many scientists and thinkers: "[Man] objectifies *and* he subjectifies. He transcends himself, but he cannot cut himself loose from himself. That is the paradoxical situation of the homo proiiciens. The paradox of the being that simultaneously lives centrically and excentrically is reflected in the paradox [...] that [man] lives by appearance and reality. In appearance he finds reality, in reality he again and again discovers appearance. However one approaches man, one always encounters a paradox. The anatomist Bolk finds a grown-up fetus. The biologist Portmann finds a bird that is nidicolous and nidifugous at the same time. Sartre finds the paradox of the *en-soi* and *pour-soi*. One can continue: Nietzsche, Gehlen, Jaspers, all who do not limit themselves in a short-sighted specialty to one aspect or one fragment of man, end up with man as paradox incarnate. It may therefore be considered an advantage and a confirmation of the thesis proposed here about human projection, that it too, issuing from a comparative approach to projecting man, encounters an irreducible paradox: man with projection *and* theory of knowledge, between appearance and reality, subjectifying-*and*-objectifying" (Sierksma, 1956/1980, pp. 26–27).

[7] In this brief presentation of Sierksma's arguments I have of course retained the latter's own terminology, including his use of masculine personal pronouns to refer to human beings in general.

way. One might think that the projecting of one's own feelings and desires on others destabilizes the outside world, but in fact what takes place is a restoration of the disturbed balanced in the inner world. Projection here therefore serves as a defense mechanism (of which, by the way, there are more than psychoanalysis has described) that is meant to prevent man from being overrun by the forces of his inner world. For the psychology of religion, the main thing is to distinguish outer and inner world, since there are many religious projection phenomena that essentially serve as a defense against dangers from outside, as in many "primitive religions," while in much spirituality projection arises as a defense against man's inadequacy vis-à-vis his inner world. But in both cases it is the inner world's subjectivity that compensates for a lack of objectifying distance. In both cases the projection is the result of human limitation and inadequacy.

Although in the early part of the book Sierksma occasionally clarifies something by using an example from the religious domain, not until the fourth and last chapter does religion itself become the subject. He proves to be a proponent of a so-called functional definition of religion. There have been so many attempts to define religion in terms of a certain content that it is best to decide that it is in principle indefinable. According to Sierksma, the only scientifically tenable minimal definition is therefore that in religion there is an awareness "that there is something" (Sierksma, 1956/1980, p. 31). This awareness, that there is something that nevertheless eludes us, which we cannot get in our grip, is a necessary consequence of the correlation of the sphere of human life and the life form: in the ex-centric structure man has become his own mysterious background, and parallel to that his world has obtained a background for him. Man does not perceive signals but sees things that have a hidden back. To man it is obvious that an object (let's say a cup) is more than what we can perceive of it, that it has a back, depth. We consider this obvious because our ex-centric life form has its correlate in an ex-centric world: man himself has depth and so the world has depth. As he always did when referring to man's ex-centric structure, Sierksma relies on Plessner, who pointed out that "[a]ls Ich, das die volle Rückwendung des lebendigen Systems zu sich ermöglicht, steht der Mensch nicht mehr im Hier-Jetzt, sondern 'hinter' ihm, hinter sich selbst, ortlos im Nichts, geht er im Nichts auf, im raumzeithaften Nirgendwo-Nirgendwann" (Plessner, 1928, p. 292). This mysterious ego (the transcendental ego), that can objectify our other ego and makes us conscious of ourselves, cannot itself be objectified. In religion it is made into an absolute, it becomes a transcendent quantity, hypostatized metaphysically (Sierksma, 1956/1980, p. 167), *eo ipso* it becomes a Thou, with whom the mystic wishes to become one. Sierksma respects the mystic and the Buddhist: they at least do not remain totally naive in the face of the inevitable projection. Though a mystic projects as well, he regards the inner world as in principle and absolutely superior to the outer world; he can more easily recognize and undo his projection. The non-mystic, however, bases himself precisely on that outer world: when he constitutes that by subjectifying, he complements it with a piece of inner world, although for lack of something better.

Sierksma had published an impressive work. It is tragic that it received so little substantive response. At the time of the "projection debate" the book's arguments were hardly discussed. People talked about Sierksma personally, his style, his supposed atheism, but there was no attempt to refute him. Such an attempt was only undertaken some years later by Han Fortmann, a priest and phenomenologically oriented psychologist, but it cannot be regarded as successful (cf. Belzen, 2007). Without entering into the history of the projection debate or the (non-)reception of Sierksma's *magnum opus*, let me just say that large parts of Fortmann's four-volume *Als Ziende de Onzienlijke* ("As if seeing the unseeable One", 1964–1968) do not deal with the projection issue at all, and that Fortmann greatly changed his views during the years he worked on it. After starting out by launching a frontal attack on every notion of "projection" (as a phenomenologist he wanted to demonstrate that there is no such thing as projection), at the end of his work he indicated that he was no longer so convinced of the things he had initially proposed; in any case he recognized that it was wrong to deny the existence of empirical forms of projection. Since Fortmann's book, Dutch and other European psychologists of religion have shown remarkably little interest in the projection problem. The genius of European psychology of religion since the Second World War, the Belgian Vergote, indicated in his first major work that he would not discuss the matter and the Dutchman Faber only dealt with it in 1985 but devoted not a word to Sierksma's contribution (Vergote, 1966/1967; Faber, 1985). The non-appearance of a translation has caused the work to be totally ignored abroad. The aforementioned American Bailey was the only one to "discover" the work as part of his research into the projection problem and was very impressed; he even initiated a translation, but it had little influence. Only Harvey (1995) treats Sierksma and places him on equal footing with Nietzsche, Feuerbach, Freud, and later Guthrie and Becker.

Increased Modesty

There is something else, however, that at first view can be seen as a form of progress, partly as a result of the projection debate: a clearer view has developed of the range and thus the limitations of the psychological (including psychoanalytic) perspective. When psychology originated in its modern, self-consciously empirical form (around 1880) there was euphoria in many different fields: it was supposed that uncovering psychological "laws" would trace and reveal man's involvement in all things human (which would include forms of culture, such as religious culture). Great things were expected of psychology, among other things in the sciences of religion, which, after their "initiation" by the German Müller and the Dutchman Tiele, had begun to collect various, mainly historical, data about several forms of religion but were still lacking a systematic, analytical perspective (Molendijk, 2005; Sharpe, 1986). Psychology appeared to offer the solution: a science seemed to be developing that, with its knowledge of the human mind, could explain how and why religions are as they are, why they arise, exist and perish. The first practitioners of the psychology of religion too were full of enthusiasm and almost without exception overrated the reach of their perspective. The first monograph that carried "psychology of religion" in the title, though merely based on a very deficient questionnaire,[8] pretended to be able to draw conclusions about "religion" as such instead of (and more correctly) about the religiosity of those questioned (Starbuck, 1899). James, Wundt, Girgensohn: they all believed they could approach "religion" as it is, though with the help of entirely different types of psychology. Gradually, however, the awareness grew that the psychological viewpoint is only one of many, which, legitimate though it is, always needs to be complemented by other viewpoints (not even excluding theological ones). (In a way Freud had already set a good example here: he emphasized repeatedly the merely partial character of the psychoanalytic viewpoint, but his way of phrasing was usually such as to convey the impression, after reading his expositions, that this was apparently the last word on the matter ...)

The Dutchman Sierksma's study of religious projection was consequently not an example of empirical psychological research but a true study into foundations. It therefore moves in the direction of philosophy, and Sierksma does indeed sound more like a philosophical anthropologist than a psychologist when he proclaims his views on religion as projection. He is no longer interested in projection as an empirical mental process (however this is to be understood) but in an ontological structure typical of man as such. He no longer talks about projection in the sense that Freud gave to this concept: the placing outside of man of something subjective (wishes, instincts, feelings) and reifying it in some way (if only by ascribing it to others).[9] Sierksma really talks about the theory of knowledge: he describes how necessary it is for human beings (or at least those few intelligent people who reflect on this) to perceive the world in a certain inevitable way while at the same time realizing *that* they perceive in a certain way. Projection is a normal part of human perception and plays a part in religion, among other things. Religion is a certain type of interpretation of reality. Religions exist because man, necessarily, projects. (And there are even forms of religion where the projective character of the religious perception is recognized as such; Sierksma regards Buddhism as an example of this.)

There is also a second sense in which Sierksma strolls far beyond the borders of psychology: rather than explain the functioning of perception (a central topic in psychology), and of projection as part of that perception, religious or not, he takes up the question of why religion as such exists – a question which most psychologists of religion had meanwhile stated lay completely outside their competence. As Wulff, too, notes in his survey of the major theories in the psychology of religion (1997a, p. 15), most psychologists of religion no longer talk about religion as

---

[8] As such, however, this was a novelty in the sciences of religion; I do not mean to repudiate Starbuck's originality!

[9] With his theoretical reflections, Sierksma moved in the same direction as that in which the later Feuerbach had moved, according to Harvey (1995). In 1851 Feuerbach supposedly defended the view that man, driven by feelings, fears and desires, abstracts certain qualities from his surroundings and personifies these (or, as in the case of monotheism, unites these abstractions and personifies them). Also the later Feuerbach is no longer concerned with placing outside man something that is said to be present only in man himself, but with finding an inevitable modality of human perception, a "grid" as Harvey calls it, that is imposed on us in perception and that makes us see the world as we see it.

a macro phenomenon, at the level of culture, but only about the religious functioning of individuals. A psychologist of religion such as Vergote, who pays a great deal of attention to his discipline's foundations, does not deny in so many words that human-psychological processes have influenced the various historically grown religious *Lebensformen* (in Wittgenstein's sense), but he does exclude the issue of the human-psychological part in the rise of culture and religion. With the cultural anthropologist Evans-Pritchard (1965) he contends that the origin of culture cannot be scientifically examined: on the one hand the historical knowledge needed for this is lacking, and on the other culture and religion are nowhere found *in statu nascendi*. Those who make claims about origin or genesis base themselves on knowledge of what they have been able to study (which is precisely not that origin or genesis) and put forward inadequately validated theoretical presuppositions (Vergote, 1983/1984, p. 19). We will come back to this at the end of these reflections. Let us first look at some "innovations" in psychoanalysis in general.

The Psychoanalytic Approaches Made More Precise

In psychoanalysis itself a number of developments have taken place since Freud of which it is not unambiguously clear that they have been instances of progress. They are assessed in rather diverging ways by the adherents of the various psychoanalytic schools. For example, the Lacanians are as a rule very critical of the development of "ego psychology" (of which the so-called object relation theories are descendents), and most psychoanalysts tend to regard Kohut's so-called self-psychology not as an innovation within psychoanalysis but as a departure from it. But apart from the question whether these developments involved the use of more effective forms of psychoanalysis than Freud's, in their applications within the psychology of religion later authors have at least been able to give greater precision to the methodology. Two examples must suffice. The development set in motion by Jacques Lacan (which Lacan said was a "retour à Freud," the wish to understand afresh what Freud had meant to say instead of what the American psycho-culture in particular had made of it) has stimulated some important reflective work on the foundations of psychoanalysis (cf. among others Laplanche, 1987; Vergote, 1997/2002). A psychologist of religion from this tradition such as Vergote emphasizes strongly, following Lacan's attention to the symbolic order, that a child comes into contact with a specific historically and culturally determined form of some particular religion and that it develops a certain relation to it. When he enters into that relationship (whatever its nature), the human being brings with him his subjectivity, and that is why, for example, the image that the individual has of a god (a god with whom the individual becomes acquainted in any tradition whatsoever) always carries, besides features of a certain religious tradition, traces of the individual's father and mother as well. This constitutes a clear correction to some of Freud's statements: whereas Freud believed that one's personal image of god would derive from the father image, Vergote found through extensive research, carried out in different cultures, that motherly qualities also characterize individual images of god (Vergote and Tamayo, 1981).

The object relation approach introduced into psychoanalysis by Winnicott has produced quite an array of publications that are often more positive about religion than Freud's followers from the first half century of psychoanalytic psychology of religion (Jones, 1991; for a brief survey, cf. Meissner, 2000). One study from this tradition, now considered a classic, is that by Rizzuto (1979). Like Vergote's findings her conclusions correct Freud's statement quoted above: "god" is always more than an exalted father. Strictly refraining from making judgments about the ontological truth content of any view of "god" whatsoever, Rizzuto consistently distinguishes between god as represented in certain religious traditions and the individual's image of god. Psychoanalysis deals with the last only, where it uncovers traces not only of the biographical father but also of many others of importance to the individual. (And when Rizzuto speaks of the "birth of the living god," she does not mean god-in-himself, or god as represented by a certain tradition, but the god as experienced by an individual; she too, therefore, speaks of the formation and functioning of a personal relation to some culturally given concept of god.)

Aside: these psychoanalytic psychologists of religion (unlike psychoanalytic psychologists of religion, of course, who hardly talk about images of god, projection and the like) no longer address these problems in terms of projection – which is understandable, because it is not primarily projection but transference that is involved, as we noted earlier. We also saw earlier that they do not ask about the existence of "religion," of some religious tradition as such. Rather they reject Freud's attempts to make statements about religion at the cultural level, as a cultural system of symbolic actions and interpretations. Still, one may ask whether they do not thereby abandon a question that psychology may contribute to answering. We will briefly go into this, prompted by some recent developments that, at least in methodological respect, seem to provide a remarkable corroboration of the psychoanalytic viewpoint.

Halfway Assessment: Progress?

But let us first note that at the level of psychological theorizing about projection there has been no advance beyond what Freud had already proposed since Sierksma. Like Freud himself, Sierksma wants to go further than psychology's instruments allow: Freud arrives at this value judgment on religion as such on the basis of his positivistic and scientistic worldview. Sierksma becomes an epistemologist who connects the existence of religion with the nature of human perception. Insofar as psychologists of religion such as Vergote and Rizzuto are able to improve on Freud, they do not do so in the area of projection but in specifying which subjective factors play a part in forming the individual's image of god.

One might think, therefore, that if there has been any progress since Freud, it consists of a better understanding and use of the perspective he developed.

Psychoanalytic insights would be applicable in a more limited way than Freud himself believed (they ought not to be applied at the level of culture) and they should be used with more precision (the individual's image of god does not only bear the marks of the autobiographical father, as Freud formulated it). Seen in this light, and given the fact that Sierksma was unable to advance the theory of projection as a psychological mechanism, one would do better to speak of a relapse than of progress with the latter: for Sierksma started to consider religion again as a cultural rather than a more limited individual phenomenon. Bailey would then be wrong in suggesting that we take Sierksma seriously where projection and the psychoanalytic critique of religion are concerned.

The strange fact is, however, that these attempts by Feuerbach, Freud and Sierksma to discuss religion at the cultural level as well, which in this interpretation are to be rejected, have recently received support from unexpected quarters. I will mention three approaches and point out the paradox that some of the things we considered wrong in Freud are now being attempted again by modern scientists, although they often have no knowledge of his work and sometimes even think they are doing something original.

Unexpected Corroboration

In past years several publications have provided remarkable corroborations of a number of methodological insights from the psychoanalytic psychology of religion. The striking thing is that these corroborations originate from or are akin to approaches in psychology and the social sciences that usually have no relation to psychoanalysis and even consider themselves to be approaches of a totally different nature ("genuinely scientific," as they also employ experimental research), and therefore generally know nothing of the psychoanalytic psychology of religion. We are talking about disciplines such as neurobiology, cognitive science and evolutionary psychology. Only a few authors so far have been able to build bridges between their disciplines and the psychoanalytic tradition.

Psychoanalysis and neurobiology. A rare example of an author who knows how to integrate different perspectives is Mel Faber, whose own background is in yet another scientific field. As a professor of literature, Faber, in a fascinating set of arguments, tries to connect psychoanalysis and neurobiology. His monograph is too rich in viewpoints to summarize in a few sentences. One of his main goals is to show that the attention given by psychoanalysis to early childhood is justified and is confirmed by recent neurobiological research: the child's Ur-experiences lead to certain structures (synapses) at the physiological level that give structure to perception and provide inspiration for religion.

During the course of the early period the basic biological situation of asking and receiving between caregiver and offspring is internalized synaptically into the mind-brain of the developing child to become a rooted perceptual-neurological response to subsequent events (an attractor state). Over and over again, thousands of times, for years, the needful child asks and receives through the ministering interventions of the all-powerful parental provider. Mnemonic development among humans is such that virtually all of this previous, foundational interaction is fated to go "underground," to pass into the unconscious realm through the advent of what neurobiology terms infantile amnesia. Accordingly, and in reference to religious experience, one remembers the early period *implicitly* when one is *primed* to do so by a wide variety of inward or external cues, including most notably (1) supplication, the theological instructions for which draw directly upon the asking and receiving of the basic biological situation, and (2) crisis, in many forms such as physical danger and personal setback (loss), which awaken implicit mnemonic longings for intervention by the succoring caregiver who is now projectively present as the benign Parent-God of religious narrative. (Faber, 2004, pp. 181–182)

According to Faber projection plays a major part in perception, not as something supposedly pathological but as rooted in our earliest childhood: the relations and experiences from those days give us a bias to perceive in a certain manner. So it's entirely logical that human beings transfer onto the concept of a god (endowed to them by some religious tradition) the images of, experiences with and feelings toward the "gods" who were their parents and/or first caregivers. Religiosity is therefore not a neurosis, nor is religion nonsense. Faber may be much more nuanced than Freud (he is not, for instance, prone to scientism) but *au fond* he is very close to him: just like Freud he says he is not able or allowed to judge the truth claims of religion (whether a "god" exists outside and independent of the concept of god as constituted by human transfer and furnished by a religious tradition is a question about which psychology has nothing to say), but he also makes it clear that personally he is just as much an atheist as Freud.

Cognitive science. Recently a number of anthropologists started to take aspects of psychology seriously, especially aspects of cognitive and evolutionary psychology. From an anthropological or general social-scientific perspective many questions can naturally be asked about religion as a cultural phenomenon: why is religion so important to so many people, why are there so many forms, why are people prepared to give their all for their religion, why does religion continue to exist when there are much more efficient ways of thinking about the world, etc.? The anthropologist Boyer (2001) answers by referring to the human mind: the way the human mind works is responsible for religion. Natural selection has prepared the human mind to take in certain types of information and treat it in a certain way; evolution as it were has equipped the mind with predispositions. Boyer does not say that everybody is or becomes religious, merely that a person can become religious only in a certain almost predictable way; and if a person does function religiously, this will happen in a certain way (a way that is similar to that of others – variation is much smaller than the phenomenal level of the lived religions would lead one to suspect).[10]

[10] A small group of scientists of religion is forming under the inspiration of authors such as Boyer. Like him, they read parts of cognitive psychology and are apparently very impressed with the scientific research going on there, complete with experiments and statistical analysis. Scientists of

Not being a psychologist, Boyer is not so interested in the way religious meaning arises and is structured in individuals or groups; he is concerned with the much more fundamental question of religion as such (unlike Faber he does not give any final value judgments on this).

Evolutionary psychology. More interesting, certainly more innovative, are the attempts by some of these anthropologists to include evolutionary psychology in their arguments. Guthrie (1993, 2001), for example, explains religion from an evolutionary perspective: people are genetically equipped with a certain cognitive bias, namely to interpret ambiguous things and events as if they were of great importance. Of great importance is what is alive, and in particular what is human. So we tend to think of our surroundings as "alive," as animate, as analogous to ourselves. If we make mistakes in this (for instance mistake a branch for a snake) we don't lose much, but if we are right we may gain everything, such as our own life. Gods, demons and similar "supernatural" entities are in Guthrie's view at the end of a spectrum of human-like beings that we think we perceive in the world. Just like Boyer, Guthrie contends against various more or less popularized views of "religion," such as functional explanations of religion's existence. One cannot explain its origin from an effect (such as the comfort, the worldview, the legitimation of morality, etc., that religion can offer). The origin is thought to be due to a more primitive tendency to over-evaluate ambiguous phenomena in a certain way. This tendency has been very useful, even necessary, in the course of evolution, and has therefore become stronger through natural selection. Religion is therefore animism and anthropomorphism, of an intuitive nature at that, which means spontaneous and independent of external tutelage.

The evolutionary perspective in itself does not seem to be psychological; rather, evolutionary theory offers a framework in which psychological descriptions and explanations can be incorporated. Various mechanisms, which are also recognized in psychoanalysis, reveal themselves as the outcome of humanity's long history

---

religion usually only learn about the older theories of Freud and Jung during their education but not about the flood of research and studies that have appeared since then both within and outside psychoanalysis. Scientists of religion such as Whitehouse (2004; Whitehouse & McCauley, 2005) are apparently happy to have "finally" found a form of psychology that is scientific and may assist them in their own research. But the level of this work is often still disappointingly trivial. Take for instance the hypothesis put forward in Andresen (2001) that brain processes are of crucial importance to religion. With all respect: doesn't that sound simple? Is not blood circulation crucial as well? If one then demonstrates extensively that in children with autistic disorders or with dysfunctions of the prefrontal brain lobes no "normal" representations of god are being found, what has one proved? What else does that teach us about "religion"? A bit more knowledge of the ideas in the psychology of religion, and of social-scientific methodology in general, would have been useful to these cognitive scientists of religion (N.B. they are by training scientists of religion). The "central assumption of the cognitive science of religion" must sound highly trivial to the ears of psychologists (of religion): "all religious thought is constrained by cognition" (in Whitehouse & McCauley 2005, p. 188). This is definitely not a new insight, nor is it a methodological improvement on the psychology from the days of Freud, James, Wundt and other founders. (They could have read the same thing in the scholastic philosophers: *omne quod recipitur, recipitur secumdum modum recipientis*.) See also the thesis, proposed with much aplomb, that religion is as it is because the human mind is as it is (Slone, 2004).

(an example is the so-called attachment systems, cf. Kirkpatrick (2005), but one could just as easily try to prove this for repression, projection, transference and the other mechanisms designated by psychoanalysis). The diverse religious activities and experiences that are found cross-culturally and cross-temporally turn out to be byproducts of these psychological mechanisms and systems, which have evolved to serve completely different evolutionary functions. One must note that the authors who follow this line of reasoning do not explain religious phenomena with the help of psychology but with the help of an evolutionary viewpoint, and maybe that's where the problem also lies: they explain too much from too few premises, they leave aside various cultural-historical particulars, since these can all be subsumed under adaptation and selection. Consequently, they no longer give explanations at the levels at which psychology and the social sciences operate. In other words, although they affirm and incorporate several forms of psychology including psychoanalysis, they make no contributions to them and do not bring about progress at the level of psychological theory. They do of course, and even preferably, speak of religion at the level of culture (and even the history of mankind), but they refrain from making statements about the ontological truth claims of particular religions.

These modern scientists of religion therefore demonstrate a tendency that we previously criticized in Freud and that later psychologists of religion believed they had rectified: there is a desire again to discuss "religion" as such, not merely individual religious experiences and actions but also religion as a cultural phenomenon, as a phenomenon at the macro level. And not because, as anthropologists or scientists of religion at the macro level, such authors might indeed employ other approaches than psychology. but on the basis of that very psychology! So what was criticized in Freud is precisely what is practiced by these researchers of religion. Barrett (2004) for instance wrote a small book provocatively titled *Why Would Anyone Believe in God?* Briefly stated, his argument comes down to this: on account of their biological equipment people have, across cultures, structurally the same cognitive tools. Without being aware of it they all use certain "mental tools" which make them think about the world in a specific way. With this mental equipment people also think about god and gods. The postulate of a god who is supposedly omniscient, omnipotent, immortal, etc., is accommodated to the structure of human thought, can therefore very easily be disseminated and barely wiped out.

Proliferation of Psychoanalytic Viewpoints

Those who are happy to see attention being given to the sciences of religion, or more broadly to the scientific exploration and analysis of religious phenomena, and to the psychic dimension of these phenomena, will regard it as progress that psychological viewpoints have been adopted by many researchers who are certainly not primarily known to be psychologists of religion. Of the various psychological approaches, psychoanalysis in particular has made its way into the heart of theology, the science of religion and religious studies.

Perhaps this is only an illustration of a certain trend. It is a peculiar phenomenon at any rate: even though many have vilified psychoanalysis since its inception as being unscientific, it has had more influence on scores of scientific areas and on the thinking of the Western intelligentsia, and can be found in more of the common parlance and cultural stereotypes, than any other field of knowledge. Not only has psychoanalysis had a great impact on psychology, but it has also left its mark on "harder" sciences such as medicine (besides the obvious psychiatry, other fields that can be mentioned are psychosomatics and more far-reaching holistic approaches), while its influence in the social sciences and humanities, at the present time in particular, is especially widespread. Psychoanalytical (or at least Freudian) ideas can be found in sociology, anthropology, philosophy, literature, art and cultural studies (film studies, dramaturgy) and many other disciplines. (A sampling would produce an abundance of bibliographical references and would distract us from the actual theme, but above all it would be unnecessary: the fact is sufficiently known.) The phenomenon of this impressive proliferation of psychoanalytical ideas is simply remarkable; nothing comparable can be seen in the other branches of psychology. The explanation cannot be that these other branches require longer training (analytical training, including teaching analysis, requires many years of education and usually presupposes preliminary university training), are more difficult to learn (most psychological theories, certainly the more recent, are definitely simpler than psychoanalytical theories) or can only be practiced within a certain research setting (psychoanalysis also takes its most important data from a closed setting, and many instruments used in psychological research [interviews, questionnaires, observation] are not developed by psychologists and are also used in other disciplines, sometimes even in market "research").

The answer to the question why psychoanalysis is so widespread does not have to be attempted here. It is enough to point out the fact. As indicated, however, the phenomenon as such cannot be regarded as progress in the theoretical sense. What we are talking about here, after all, are applications of psychoanalysis. Its actual development takes place on the basis of observations made during patient treatment; reflections on these observations lead to new theories or to the transformation of existing theories. The question of progress should be answered at this level. Anyone who distrusts psychoanalysis as such will probably not be convinced of its worth or correctness by its application in the social sciences or the humanities. Anyone who thinks it is a good idea to recognize the psychic dimension in numerous cultural phenomena will probably be favorably disposed to it *a priori* (and in principle to other psychologies that lend themselves to cultural analysis). The fact remains that psychoanalysis, more than any other psychological theory, can also be found in theology and religious studies – as a conversational partner or, to a lesser degree, as an analytical instrument (cf. for example Winer and Anderson, 2007; Black, 2006; Merkur, 2005; Jonte-Pace, 2003).

Whether psychoanalysis (or any psychological approach) has ever achieved substantive progress by being applied in the exploration and analysis of religious phenomena is to be doubted, but cannot be discussed here. Nor need we answer the question whether the integration of psychological viewpoints in research of religious phenomena is not first and foremost a sort of epiphenomenon with, or example of, the enormous proliferation of psychology in general in some Western countries (and so, somewhat maliciously formulated, a following of a certain fashion). (The answer would moreover depend on one's assessment of (the dissemination of) psychology in general and of psychological analysis or religious phenomena as such.) We do, however, wish to note that the proliferation of psychology (and the accompanying protopsychologization of quite a number of everyday phenomena[11]) has been an important precondition and accompaniment of the turn toward experience that has taken place in sections of the sciences of religion in the Western world during the twentieth century.

Before Closing

At the end of this introduction we must now return to and answer the questions with which we started out: what is the upshot of one century of psychoanalytic psychology of religion? Has there been progress? What has become of the idea that religion is projection, for example?

As our discussion so far has made clear, no unambiguous answer can be given. Every brief answer could be, would even have to be, provided with critical comments. The answers will differ according to the opinion one has on a number of other matters. If one believes, for example, that psychoanalysis is not really a scientific psychology (because psychoanalysts don't perform experimental research, for instance) one will not have a high opinion of the application of psychoanalytic viewpoints in research into religion. If one thinks that a human-sciences approach is irrelevant for theology and the science of religion as such, one will leave psychoanalytic contributions unread. But even those who are more positive about psychology of religion may become somewhat disappointed after looking more closely at certain concepts of psychoanalysis. Current psychoanalysis has hardly anything more to say about projection, for example, than it did in Freud's own time. And concerning the oft-heard idea that religion is projection, matters turn out to be rather different from what they had seemed at first sight. Though Freud was negative about religion, he did not regard it as projection; he would have agreed, however, if somebody had said that projection plays a big part in religion. But after one has recovered from the possible shock caused by the imposition of a psychological perspective on religious phenomena, one may find that the notion that projection can have a role in religion is really rather trivial. Of course projection can play a part, just as all other psychic mechanisms can. Religion is human reality. It shares fully in all the

[11] Note the "psychologizing" way in which people in the West now express themselves when talking about themselves, their lives and relationships. Psychological jargon has, sometimes in a highly misunderstood way, entered into the general language of social intercourse (people talk about "complexes" from which they suffer, about "subconscious" reasons; they say "what went through your mind when ...," they tell how they feel, etc.).

vicissitudes of human life, influences them and is influenced by them, so it is no surprise that religious life contains everything that psychology studies more generally. Of course religious functioning is *also* a matter of projection, repression, fantasy, attachment and coping (to name only a few of the psychological constructs that some psychologists of religion have emphasized: van der Lans, 1988; Kirkpatrick, 1992; Pargament, 1997). *All* human affairs play a part, after all. To quote a well-known summary of clinical psychological research on religion: religion can be anything with regard to mental health and psychopathology: a cause of mental illness, but also a prophylactic, a therapy, a medium through which a disorder becomes manifest, etc. (Spilka et al., 2003).

Another matter is whether religion is nothing but a matter of projection, fantasy, attachment, coping, etc. Such a reductionist view is rather naive and in any case was not defended by Freud. Certainly, he did say some ugly things about religion, thought it was outdated, did not believe in it, and occasionally produced a sweeping statement, but in general he clearly saw that religion as a complex cultural phenomenon cannot be explained on the basis of any psychological perspective (and certainly not by appealing to a single psychic mechanism). As far as individual religiosity is concerned, he never said it was pathological as such. Freud proves to be more nuanced than many who refer to him seem to realize; one is better off reading Freud himself than his many followers. So has there been no progress since Freud? Again, the answer depends on the views one has in many other areas of life. If one believes that the developments that have taken place in the world of psychoanalysis since Freud are instances of progress, then of course analyses of religious phenomena that are based thereon will appear to be more adequate than those of Freud himself. (A follower of this opinion would have to consider, however, that (a) those different schools are in conflict with each other, and (b) publications in the psychology of religion by an author from a certain school may be rejected by other authors from the same school; see, for example, how critical Meissner (2000) and Faber (2002) are of publications like the one by Jones, 1991.)

There may have been progress since Freud on those issues where his statements were really too sweeping. That god even psychologically, as individual representation, proves to be other and more than an exalted father was seen at the time of Vergote's and Rizzuto's publications, among others, as an important correction and complement. However, whether it constitutes a theoretical improvement of the viewpoint inaugurated by Freud is questionable. For most other "corrections" of Freud's statements on the psychology of religion it is true that Freud himself would probably not have denied them. He made clear that his reflections on religion do not constitute an integral part of psychoanalysis, and he freely allowed others to use the same psychoanalytic theories and concepts to reach entirely different conclusions in the psychology of religion from the ones he had drawn. In this respect a psychoanalytic author's private convictions about religion, if she has such convictions, prove to be of greater importance to her conclusions than any form of psychoanalysis used by her. Psychoanalysis was initially clearly critical of religion. Later there were quite a number of religious persons who studied it and became experts in it, and who produced psychoanalytic publications that were much more positive about religion than those of Freud and his first followers. (Well-known authors like Vergote, Meissner, Jones and Scharfenberg all became priests in their respective churches.) To the extent that their familiarity with and possible sympathy for what they studied enabled such authors to do greater justice to the objects of their research, this is certainly a form of progress in the psychoanalytic psychology of religion. (Insofar as it produced nothing better than apologies, it probably wasn't.)

It is remarkable that a certain purification of the psychoanalytic perspective now seems to be regarded as an advantage rather than a disadvantage. It will probably be necessary to reevaluate the wish to limit the authority of psychology to analyzing individual religiosity, which would render psychology unqualified to deal with religion as a cultural phenomenon. There is after all a psychological dimension to products of religious activity at the cultural level such as dogmas, rituals and symbolism in general. As the cognitive science of religion promulgates rather bravely, religion will never be able to be or to function as anything other than what can be processed by the human mind. This insight, however, might also be extended in a historical direction: then as now, the existence and growth of various forms of religion will have depended on what the human mind could facilitate. So there seems to be even more reason to try to establish a link between history and psychology as approaches in the sciences of religion than has been considered so far (cf. Belzen, 1997). Of course, the findings of such a combination of history and psychology will always provide a merely partial view on reality as research object, as is the case with all scientific research. In any case, it seems to become possible again – via a detour and certainly with greater modesty than was sometimes demonstrated in the history of the psychoanalytic psychology of religion – to use psychoanalysis for making claims about religion at the level of culture.

The merely moderate optimism about the substantive progress achieved since Freud should not be judged too negatively. If one looks at the state of affairs in other areas of psychology, similar conclusions will be reached. When modern, scientific psychology was created, a large number of psychologies were developed by pioneers such as Wundt, Janet, James and Freud. Their "grand theories" have led to an endless stream of research and publications, but whether we have progressed much beyond initial insights and intuitions is still an open question, and one that psychologists don't usually ask themselves. Driven by the obligation to grow and expand that characterizes the academic world nowadays, maybe they don't get round to these questions. But when sometimes they ask them, their conclusions are mostly in line with what has been stated here about psychoanalysis and the psychoanalytic psychology of religion (cf. for example Gibson, 1985; Gleitman, 1985; Wulff, 1997b). It speaks volumes that the founders of psychology, almost without exception, are still able to inspire and to provide food for discussion (as has probably been the case with Freud more than with any other of the others).

Finally – A Preview

Psychoanalysis has now been integrated in various ways into research on religious phenomena, into reflections on religion and even in theological publications. Again: those who find it important to study and reflect on the human, empirical-psychological dimension of religion will very probably consider this a kind of progress. Like psychology in general, psychoanalysis has at least contributed to making human reality the subject of greater scientific attention, and the same is true in the scientific study of religion. The papers in the present volume testify to this trend, first – in a section entirely written by practicing psychoanalysts – by demonstrating the transformations in the psychoanalytic approach to religion, and second – in a section with papers authored by scholars on religion – by showing the impact psychoanalysis has had within disciplines different from the scientific study of religion.

Section one documents the changes in the way contemporary psychoanalysis deals with religion, in a twofold way. The classic object of psychoanalysis and the place where all psychoanalytic theory is developed, altered and corroborated, is the clinical setting. While one may doubt whether the way present psychoanalysts deal with the religiosity of their patients is different from Freud's approach, it is almost certainly different from the approaches of many who came after Freud or even practiced during the days of Freud. A neglectful or even deprecating approach to religiosity has given way to a more neutrally benevolent attitude – as should characterize every response to all and everything that patients bring up during analysis. In exploring the place of religiosity, or rather of religious thoughts, feelings, fantasies, acts and activities, etc., within the larger psychic household of the patient, many psychoanalysts nowadays will neither endorse nor attack religion. (Although, as noted above, it must be admitted that most of those who try to do justice to individual religiosity are personally positively inclined towards religion.) In the case-studies by Rizzuto, Meissner and Corveleyn, we observe psychoanalysts at work in their *proprium*, so to speak: in the clinical approach to individual psychic functioning.

Psychiatrist Ana-María Rizzuto discusses the history of psychoanalytic dealings with religion in the twentieth century based on her own experiences within this history. She starts by returning to Freud's bold analogy between the rituals of obsessional neurotics and religious behaviors. Freud wanted to understand "the psychological processes of religious life." His followers primarily applied his ideas to the cultural manifestations of religion, a part of which came to be known as applied psychoanalysis. Very few, however, continued Freud's efforts to understand the psychical processes of religious life in their analysands. According to Rizzuto's judgment, the arrival of postmodernism prompted a significant change. Religion became an unwelcome term while spirituality became fashionable, which she interprets as Western culture having moved its center from the divinity to the self. The new psychoanalytic schools focused on the self, and intersubjective experiences joined the postmodern trend by becoming interested in spirituality. With a clinical case Rizzuto illustrates the connections between parental imagos and the divinity, as

Freud had suggested, while at the same time signaling that the self needs a context for its meaningful existence.

A professor of clinical psychiatry, William W. Meissner discusses the technical differences separating the approach to the religiously committed patient by analysts with irreligious, agnostic or atheistic convictions (usually following the anti-religious attitudes of Freud), from the approach to these same patients by analysts who are neutral with regard to the validity of religious beliefs. He points out that while the older view saw neurotic elements as inherent aspects of religious beliefs, a religiously neutral or even accepting view would see them as neurotic contaminants or distortions of religious beliefs that can be analyzed without necessary detriment to the religious beliefs themselves. Thus, both attacks on or pressure to abandon religious beliefs as neurotic and efforts to foster or promote religious attitudes would amount to forms of countertransference enactment. The optimal stance of the analyst with respect to the patient's religious views is based on the therapeutic alliance, especially analytic neutrality – neither attacking nor promoting religiously oriented attitudes, but focusing specifically on the exploration and understanding of neurotic manifestations to enable the patient to establish a more autonomous and productive approach to religious matters, whether to embrace a more mature and adaptive approach to religious beliefs or the opposite. Meissner discusses these issues in relation to the analysis of a religiously committed but conflicted analysand.

A third chapter based on clinical work is authored by psychologist Jozef Corveleyn. His approach to the theme of religious delusion is comparative: he characterizes the religious delusion in a well known case of psychosis (the "Schreber" case, also discussed by Freud) by comparing religious delusion in the so-called hysterical psychosis. Corveleyn argues that Canetti's viewpoint on Schreber's delusion as politically motivated is wrong, and that Schreber's delusion is an essentially religious one. He defines, explains and illustrates the hysterical religious delusion with the help of an extensive case study from his own work in a psychiatric hospital. Corveleyn shows that the psychotic religious delusion differs from the hysterical one mainly in terms of three structural characteristics: the religious content in Schreber's evolution can be considered an attempt to re-construct his lost world; religion is used by Schreber as a absolute truth system; and, although Schreber's delusion can be considered a reconstruction of his world, its ultimate effect is not a real restoration of his contact with the common social world.

Following these clinically based chapters, the first section of this volume turns to theory. It testifies to the increasingly positive attention being paid to religiosity as discussed by Rizzuto, Meissner and Corveleyn by showing how present psychoanalytic theoreticians take up the issues of religion and spirituality. Historian of religion Dan Merkur asserts that most psychoanalytic publications on mysticism have followed Freud in treating mystical experiences as transient manifestations of infantile solipsism. He then makes the controversial claim that quite a number of psychoanalytic authors have been or are mystics themselves, however, and these authors would have treated the mystical as something much more central to human psychology in any case. To prove his point, Merkur briefly reviews the work of quite a number of well-known psychoanalytic theoreticians.

Philosopher Paul Moyaert concludes this first section of the book by focusing on the post-Freudian criticism that Freud would have neglected the vitalizing power of religion. He argues, however, that the critics limit their impact by focusing on Freud's one-sided emphasis on the Oedipus. According to Moyaert, a strong interest in the pre-Oedipal is not sufficient to valorize the power of religion; it is the bodily drives that need to be placed in the heart of a new discussion about Freud's negative understanding of religion. To understand why post-Freudians criticize Freud, Moyaert shows that his notion of religion is based on repression, social adaptation and moral education. What Freud missed is the ecstatic power of religion. This Moyaert illustrates with an uncommon but nevertheless well-known Christian prayer: *The Adoration of the Crucified.* This prayer is the opposite of a contemplative calming down of the drives and has no anesthetic effect. It belongs to the Dionysian dimension of religion. This example makes clear why a critic of Freud needs to focus on the drives: where else can religion find the force to vitalize life if it not by mobilizing the drives? This prayer reanimates a specific constellation of partial drives, i.e. drives organized in a masochistic scenario. In his third section Moyaert analyses what happens to these masochistic drives when an individual cultivates the Christian prayer. His example is intellectually provocative because it helps to describe the vicissitudes of the drives in religion. Freud called religion sublimation, but as post-Freudians have emphasized he never succeeded in elaborating a satisfying theory of sublimation. The example Moyaert is analyzing gives a clear idea of a successful sublimation of drives in religion. And what else is a fertile sublimation than a transformation that does not destroy the natural *élan* of drives, but rather increases and intensifies their power? In perversion the scope of masochism remains limited to the sexual; in sublimation the scope is broadened to other domains of life. Drives put their personal stamp on someone's religious way of life. The final question Moyaert addresses is why Freud didn't recognize the power of religion. Moyaert argues that the cause has to be found in Freud's inadequate notion of pleasure and in his wrong ideas of the pleasure principle. Freud associated pleasure with satisfaction or evacuation of tension. But, according to Moyaert, pleasure can better be defined as an unhindered expression of an activity.

Section two of the present volume demonstrates some of the changes psychoanalysis has brought about in classical areas of the scientific study of religion such as mythology, anthropology, ethnography and philosophy of religion. The sections opens with a chapter by sociologist Michael Carroll, who shows that although Freud himself saw myths (like dreams, literary texts, etc.) as reflecting the disguised fulfillment of repressed wishes, the study of myth was not central to his own work. Even so, the psychoanalytic study of myth can now be counted as one of many established approaches to the study of myth. As Carroll points out, for most commentators, the core divide among psychoanalytic investigators studying myth is the divide between Freud and Jung. Freud's original work on myth has given rise to at least three separate subtraditions which proceed, in turn, from (1) Freud's original wish fulfillment argument, (2) from ego psychology and (3) from the object relations tradition. The Jungian tradition, by contrast, is much the same today as it was when first presented by Jung himself in the early twentieth century. According to Carroll, this means that the psychoanalytic interpretation of a particular myth is tightly bound to a larger theoretical structure that has implications which go far beyond the study of myth. This fact would have limited the influence of psychoanalysis among those studying myth. His essay concludes by considering a final puzzle: the fact that the Jungian approach to myth has long been far more popular with the educated public than any of the Freudian approaches to myth. One likely reason for this is the fact that Jung's approach to myth promises the general public easy access to a type of "unchurched mysticism" that is popular in modern secularizing societies.

The next chapter takes a historical approach as well. It critically discusses the developments in the psychoanalytic study of Buddhism. This "dialogue," as Parsons prefers to name it, is dealt with in three sections: 1880–1944; 1944–1970; 1970–2007. Each of them proceeds by offering a brief summary of the socio-historical context of the era under consideration, followed by a critical examination of the major figures, analyses, debates, and developments. In general, Parsons sees the first era as being the most undeveloped and reductionistic. The second era exhibits more extensive cross-fertilization and mutually respectful dialogue, with an adaptive approach being featured. The current era Parsons evaluates as significantly more sophisticated, with the major figures in the dialogue evincing interdisciplinary sensitivity, existential awareness, and a willingness among the psychoanalytically inclined to champion the Buddhist claim for a truly spiritual, transcendent dimension to the human personality.

The authors of two following chapters continue to discuss specific religious traditions, only this time drawing on their own original empirical work. After presenting an historical and critical overview of the major psychoanalytic studies of Hinduism to date, focusing on intra-psychic developments in Indian men as informed by, and reflected in, Hindu culture and family life, Daniel Meckel identifies three hermeneutical dimensions of the major writings: the scientific-explanatory, the cultural interpretive, and the religious-integrative. He presents several major works in historical sequence and supplements them by psychological case studies from his own ethnographic research. Meckel makes a strong argument for a dialectical approach to studying the inner worlds of Hindu's, one that stresses the ongoing and dynamic interaction of psyche, culture and religious experience.

The anthropologist René Devisch presents his profound and rich argumentation in four steps. Before addressing the topic of the multilayered function and meaning of the father figure in the religious perspectives of the Yaka of southwest Congo in Africa, he explores some relevant theoretical avenues offered by both the social anthropological and the significant post-Freudian francophone literature in the traditions of Devereux and Lacan. These readings demonstrate a recent psychoanalytically acknowledgeable attention to a local people's particular intercorporeal, intersubjective and transworldly shaping of self, unconscious fantasy, emotion and social commitment. Conversely, such attention echoes the anthropologist's very flexible observational participation in the life of the host community, in a manner evocative of the transferential process that develops between a psychoanalyst and an analysand. Section 2 sets out Devisch's own combination of a culture-sensitive, endogenous anthropological approach and aspectual psychoanalytically informed interpretation of the domain of the religious among the Yaka. Apart from the missionary and post-missionary sphere of influence, the Yaka religious composing with the life world comprises a four-part framework, without, however, any reference to some personalized Divinity or single Supreme Being. Section 3 focuses primarily on the bilineal kinship structure of the extended family among the Yaka. Patrilineal descent as determinative of a person's social identity is combined with the matrilineal filiation of physical life and individual destiny. Devisch argues that it is the maternal uncle, and not the father, who in the name of matrilineal filiation, authoritatively gives witness to the religiously enforced Order of the Ethical Law and the local version of the incest prohibition as the minimal intersubjective ordering. In Section 4 he summarises the glaring difference among the Yaka between encompassing, religiously-tuned and phallogocentric symbolization processes on the one hand, and on the other the more fragmentary and diverse augural sensibility to transworldly matrixial *signifiance* or emerging meaning production.

The final two chapters demonstrate the impact of psychoanalysis since Freud in the field of the philosophy of religion. First, James DiCenso explores psychoanalytic resources for understanding human development involving self-reflection, increased ethical capacity, and other-directedness. He does this by tracing a line of thought in the history of philosophy that moves from concern with the objects of religion (God, the soul, etc.) to questions of self-knowledge and ethical advancement. Freud is shown to share some of these broad humanistic ethical concerns with the European philosophical tradition, while also questioning the rationalist and disembodied worldviews usually assumed by that tradition. DiCenso then moves to a discussion of post-Freudian theorists such as Lacan, Foucault, Ricoeur and Kristeva, who build upon the more differentiated, dynamic, and inter-personal psychoanalytic model. Under the rubric of "the subject," they articulate a dynamic model of self-reflection in line with Freud's work, while also more explicitly articulating an overall framework for ethical or spiritual development (as for example in Foucault's model of "care of the self" as a spiritual project). In this way they contribute to a psychology of religion that is not so much concerned with interpreting existing traditions, as articulating a spiritual potentiality for reflective capacity leading to greater other-directedness.

Finally, Diane Jonte-Pace asserts that although the year 2007 marked the centennial of Freud's first analysis of religion, his short essay *Mourning and Melancholia*, published about a decade later, provided the framework for interpretations of religion and culture that have proved more valuable in contemporary thinking. In her chapter she examines the work of French feminist psychoanalyst Julia Kristeva. After a brief introduction to Kristeva's life, career, and theory, Jonte-Pace argues that Kristeva's earlier work focused on mourning and that her later work turned to melancholia. The early work showed how traditional monotheisms structure and symbolize death and loss, while the later work showed how cultures and individuals experience melancholia when religion cannot provide the framing narratives for loss. Jonte-Pace also argues that Kristeva revises Freudian notions of melancholia as pathological, showing that melancholia can sometimes be adaptive: in particular, she discusses the study of biblical and religious texts as a constructive and creative way of engaging with postmodern, post-religious melancholia.

Largely withholding any claims about theoretical progress that psychoanalytic approaches to religion might have achieved, the chapters present a rich illustration of the claim that psychoanalysis since Freud has been transformed by and has transformed itself the scientific study of religion. Because of the study of religion, psychoanalysis has been transformed in its dealings with patients and their religiosity, and it conceptualizes and evaluates religion and religious phenomena differently than Freud and the first generations of his followers. In addition, psychoanalysis has transformed the way in which other scholarly disciplines on religion approach their subjects. Whether and in what sense, transformations as these constitute progress in the psychoanalytic psychology of religion or in any study of religion, is perhaps better assessed by more independent observers than the authors of the following chapters. A truly interdisciplinary enterprise, psychoanalysis reaches out to other disciplines, provokes discussion and seeks both collaboration and objections. And so, hopefully, does the present volume.

References

Andresen, J. (Ed.) (2001). *Religion in mind: Cognitive perspectives on religious belief, ritual, and experience*. Cambridge: Cambridge University Press.

Bailey, L. W. (1988). Religious projection: A new European tour. *Religious Studies Review, 14*, 207–211.

Banks, R. (1973). Religion as projection: A re-appraisal of Freud's theory. *Religious Studies, 9*, 401–426.

Barrett, J. L. (2004). *Why would anyone believe in God*. Walnut Creek, CA: Altamira.

Belzen, J. A. (1997). The historicocultural approach in the psychology of religion: Perspectives for interdisciplinary research. *Journal for the Scientific Study of Religion, 36*(3), 358–371.

Belzen, J. A. (2007). *Psychologie en het raadsel van de religie: Beschouwingen bij een eeuw godsdienstpsychologie in Nederland* [Psychology and the riddle of religion: Reflections on a century of psychology of religion in the Netherlands]. Amsterdam: Boom.

Black, D. M. (2006). The case for a contemplative position. In D. M. Black (Ed.), *Psychoanalysis and religion in the 21st century: Competitors or collaborators?* (pp. 63–79). London/New York: Routledge.

Boyer, P. (2001). *Religion explained: The evolutionary origins of religious thought*. New York: Basic Books.

Breevaart, J. O. van de (2005). *Authority in question: Analysis of a polemical controversy on religion in The Netherlands, 1948–1998*. Delft: Eburon.

Evans-Pritchard, E. E. (1965). *Theories of primitive religion*. Oxford: Clarendon Press.

Faber, H. (1985). Een nieuwe kijk op projectie als godsdienstig verschijnsel [A new view of projection as religious phenomenon]. *Nederlands Theologisch Tijdschrift, 39*, 110–127.

Faber, M. D. (2002). *The magic of prayer: An introduction to the psychology of faith*. Westport, CT/London: Praeger.

Faber, M. D. (2004). *The psychological roots of religious belief: Searching for angels and the parent-god*. Amherst, NY: Prometheus.

Feuerbach, L. (1841/1957). *The essence of Christianity*. New York: Harper & Row.

Feuerbach, L. (1851/1967). *Lectures on the essence of religion*. New York: Harper & Row.

Fortmann, H. M. M. (1957). *Aan de mens nabij: Over de situatie der godsdienstpsychologie en haar reden van bestaan* [Close to man: On the situation of the psychology of religion and the reason for its existence]. Nijmegen/Utrecht: Dekker & Van de Vegt.

Fortmann, H. M. M. (1964–1968). *Als ziende de Onzienlijke: Een cultuurpsychologische studie over de religieuze waarneming en de zogenaamde religieuze projectie. Vols. I–IV* [Like seeing the Unseeable: A cultural-psychological study on religious observation and so-called religious projection]. Bussum: Paul Brand.

Freud, S. (1901/1962). *The psychopathology of everyday life.* (*The standard edition of the complete psychological works of Sigmund Freud.* Vol. 6). London: Hogarth.

Freud, S. (1907/1941). Zwangshandlungen und Religionsübungen. In *Gesammelte Werke, chronologisch geordnet.* Band VII (pp. 129–139). London: Imago.

Freud, S. (1911/1964). Psycho-analytic notes on an autobiographical account of a case of paranoia (Dementia paranoides). In *The standard edition of the complete psychological works of Sigmund Freud.* Vol. 12 (pp. 3–82). London: Hogarth.

Freud, S. (1923/1973). Eine Teufelsneurose im siebzehnten Jahrhundert. In *Freud – Studienausgabe*. Band VII (pp. 283–319). Frankfurt: Fischer.

Freud, S. (1927/1948). Die Zukunft einer Illusion. In *Gesammelte Werke, chronologisch geordnet.* Band XIV (pp. 325–380). London: Imago.

Freud, S. & Pfister O. (1963). *Briefe 1909–1939* (Hrsg. E.L. Freud & H. Meng). Frankfurt am Main: Fischer.

Gibson, J. J. (1985). Conclusions from a century of research on sense perception. In S. Koch & D. E. Leary (Eds.), *A century of psychology as science* (pp. 224–230). New York: McGraw-Hill.

Gleitman, H. (1985). Some trends in the study of cognition. In S. Koch & D. E. Leary (Eds.), *A century of psychology as science* (pp. 420–436). New York: McGraw-Hill.

Guthrie, S. E. (1993). *Faces in the clouds: A new theory of religion.* New York: Oxford University Press.

Guthrie, S. E. (2001). Why gods? A cognitive theory. In J. Andresen (Ed.), *Religion in mind: Cognitive perspectives on religious belief, ritual, and experience* (pp. 94–111). Cambridge: Cambridge University Press.

Harvey, V. A. (1995). *Feuerbach and the interpretation of religion*. Cambridge: Cambridge University Press.

Jones, J. W. (1991). *Contemporary psychoanalysis and religion: Transference and transcendence.* New Haven, CT: Yale University Press.

Jonte-Pace, D. (2003). *Teaching Freud.* New York: Oxford University Press/American Academy of Religion.

Kirkpatrick, L. A. (1992). An attachment-theoretical approach to the psychology of religion. *International Journal for the Psychology of Religion*, *2*, 3–28.

Kirkpatrick, L. A. (2005). *Attachment, evolution and the psychology of religion.* New York/London: Guilford.

Lans, J. M. van der (1988). Geloven: Een kwestie van fantasie [Believing: A matter of fantasy]. In A. G. Weiler (Ed.), *Een nieuw christelijk mensbeeld* (pp. 69–83). Baarn: Ambo.

Laplanche, J. (1987). *Nouveaux fondements pour la psychanalyse*. Paris: PUF.

Laplanche, J. & Pontalis, J. B. (1972). *Das Vokabular der Psychoanalyse*. Frankfurt a.M.: Suhrkamp.

Meissner, W. W. (2000). Psychoanalysis and religion: Current perspectives. In J. K. Boehnlein (Ed.), *Psychiatry and religion: The convergence of spirit and mind* (pp. 53–69). Washington, DC/London: American Psychiatric Press.

Merkur, D. (2005). *Psychoanalytic approaches to myth: Freud and the Freudians.* New York/London: Routledge.

Molendijk, A. L. (2005). *The emergence of the science of religion in The Netherlands.* Leiden: Brill.

Neuser, J. & Kriebel, R. (Eds.) (1992). *Projektion: Grenzprobleme zwischen innerer und äußerer Realität.* Göttingen: Hogrefe.

Pargament, K. I. (1997). *The psychology of religion and coping: Theory, research, practice.* New York/ London: Guilford Press.
Pargament, K. I. (2002). The bitter and the sweet: An evaluation of the costs and benefits of religiousness. *Psychological Inquiry, 13*, 168–181.
Plessner, H. (1928). *Die Stufen des Organischen und der Mensch: Einleitung in die philosophische Anthropologie*. Berlin: De Gruyter.
Rizzuto, A. M. (1979). *The birth of the living God: A psychoanalytic study*. Chicago, IL: University of Chicago Press.
Sharpe, E. J. (1986). *Comparative religion: A history*. La Salle, IL: Open Court.
Sierksma, F. (1956/1980). *De religieuze projectie: Een anthropologische en psychologische studie over de projectie-verschijnselen in de godsdiensten* [The religious projection: An anthropological and psychological study of projection phenomena in the religions]. Groningen: Konstapel.
Slone, D. J. (2004). *Theological incorrectness: Why religious people believe what they shouldn't.* New York: Oxford University Press.
Spilka, B., Hood, R. W., Hunsberger, B. & Gorsuch, R. (2003). *The psychology of religion: An empirical approach* (3rd ed.). New York: Guilford.
Starbuck, E. D. (1899). *The psychology of religion: An empirical study of the growth of religious consciousness*. New York: Scribner.
Vandermeersch, P. (1974/1991). *Unresolved questions in the Freud/Jung debate on psychosis, sexual identity and religion*. Leuven: Leuven University Press.
Vandermeersch, P. & Westerink, H. (2007). *Godsdienstpsychologie in cultuurhistorisch perspectief* [Psychology of religion in a cultural-historical framework]. Amsterdam: Boom.
Vergote, A. (1966/1967). *Godsdienstpsychologie* [Psychology of religion]. Tielt: Lannoo.
Vergote, A. (1983/1984). *Religie, geloof en ongeloof: Psychologische studie* [Religion, belief and disbelief: A psychological study]. Antwerp/Amsterdam: De Nederlandsche Boekhandel.
Vergote, A. (1997/2002). *De sublimatie: Een uitweg uit Freuds impasses* [Sublimation: A way out of Freud's impasses]. Amsterdam: SUN.
Vergote, A. & Tamayo, A. (1981). *The parental figures and the representation of God: A psychological and cross-cultural study*. Leuven/The Hague: Leuven University Press/Mouton Publishers.
Vestdijk, S. (1947/1992). *De toekomst der religie: Essay* [The future of religion: An essay] (6th ed.). Amsterdam: Meulenhoff.
Whitehouse, H. (2004). *Modes of religiosity: A cognitive theory of religious transmission*. Walnut Creek, CA: Altamir.
Whitehouse, H. & McCauley, R. N. (Eds.) (2005). *Mind and religion: Psychological and cognitive foundations of religiosity*. Walnut Creek, CA: Altamir.
Winer, J. & Anderson, J. (Eds.) (2007). *Spirituality and religion. Psychoanalytic perspectives. (The annual of psychoanalysis, XXXIV–XXXV.)* Cattskill, NY: Mental Health Resources.
Wulff, D. M. (1997a). *Psychology of religion: Classic and contemporary* (2nd ed.). New York: Wiley.
Wulff, D. M. (1997b). A century of psychology of religion: Where does it leave us today? In J. A. Belzen & O. Wikström (Eds.), *Taking a step back: Assessments of the psychology of religion* (pp. 183–198). Stockholm/Uppsala: Almqvist & Wiksell Intern./Acta Universitatis Upsaliensis (Psychologia et Sociologia Religionum).

Part I
Changes in Psychoanalytic Research on Religiosity: Clinical and Theoretical Studies

One Hundred Years After Freud Declared That Religion Was a Universal Obsessional Neurosis

Ana-María Rizzuto

On March 2, 1907 Freud presented a lecture on religion to the Vienna Psycho-Analytical Society. He had written it on February as his requested contribution to the new journal *Zeitschrift für Religonpsychologie*, that published it in April of that year in the first issue of its first volume. It represented Freud's first approach to the psychology of religion based on the clinical observation that there were remarkable similarities between obsessive and religious ceremonies. He noted

> The resemblance, however, seems to me to be more than a superficial one, so that an insight into the origin of neurotic ceremonial may embolden us to draw inferences by analogy about the psychological processes of religious life. (Freud, 1907, p. 117) (my italics)

The analogy compares the external compulsory ceremonial acts of obsessive patients with religious ceremonies. Freud does not fail to notice that religious ritual is public and has significance and meaning. However, he had already discovered that analysis also unveils private historical meanings and symbols even in the bizarre obsessive rituals of neurotics. He also observed that many practitioners of religious rituals were not familiar with their meaning. Both, obsessive private and religious public ceremonial activities are related to guilt and are motivated by the need to avoid harm and to find protection when confronted with unacceptable instinctual wishes. Freud concluded

> In view of these similarities and analogies one might venture to regard obsessional neurosis as a pathological counterpart of the formation of religion, and to describe that neurosis as an individual religiosity and religion as a universal obsessional neurosis. (1907, pp. 126–127)

The originality of Freud's proposal does not rest so much on its conclusions but in the bold analogical thinking that brought together accepted and approved private and social religious behaviors and the apparently absurd rituals of obsessive patients. Once the comparison had been made it could not be discarded. Religious

A.-M. Rizzuto
Psychoanalytic Institute of New England, East, Cambridge, MA, USA
e-mail: arizzuto@massmed.org

J.A. Belzen (ed.), *Changing the Scientific Study of Religion: Beyond Freud?*

people had to take notice of the challenge. The paper was only the beginning of Freud's incursion into the understanding of the psychodynamic processes involved in religious practices and beliefs and in the historical roots of religion at the dawn of civilization. Freud's paper inaugurated a new approach to the study of religion. James (James, 1902/1929) had offered a phenomenological description of religious experiences, but had not searched for the motivations that contributed to their particular form and meaning. Academic psychology of religion was interested in measurements of isolated aspects of religious phenomena that offered "impeccable 'studies of nothing very much' " (Spence, 1994, p. 23, as quoted by Corveleyn and Luyten, 2005, p. 87). Theoreticians of religion had offered complex speculations about the phenomenon of religion with minimal reference to the concrete psychic processes of the religious individual. Freud's innovative attention to the intrapsychic organization of religious behavior and experience did not influence until much later the outlook of the discipline. For many years Freud's observations about the dynamic processes involved in religious activities were ignored. Paloutzian affirmed that "the science of psychology has paid only sporadic attention to the psychological processes underlying human religiousness. In fact, for much of the twentieth century, academic psychology did not address it" (Paloutzian and Park, 2005, p. 3).

Freud's clinical contributions, in particular his observations and theorizing about the Wolf Man introduced another aspect of his understanding of personal religion. He traced the psychodynamic origination of God in the affections between the father and the child in his patient's minds:

> His extravagant love of his father, which had made the repression necessary, found its way at length to an ideal sublimation. As Christ, he could love his father, who was now called God, with a fervour which had sought in vain to discharge itself so long as his father had been a mortal. (Freud, 1918, p. 115)

Freud was convinced that the child's imago of the actual father and the relationship with him were the source for the formation of the representation of God in the internal world of the child: "God himself is after all only an exaltation of this picture of a father as he is represented in the mind of early childhood" (Freud, 1914, p. 243).

Freud also linked the emergence of religion in *primeval human history* to the relationship of the sons to their father. In Freud's narrative the brothers born to the primitive and powerful male came together and killed and devoured the father. This action was followed by individual identification with him and the selection of a totem animal "as a natural and obvious substitute for their father" (Freud, 1913, p. 144). The totem animal barely hid the representation of the loved and feared father. When Moses presented to the people the idea of the Israelite single God, the affects linked to the father were revived: "Admiration, awe and thankfulness (...) The conviction of its irresistibility, the submission to his will, could not have been more unquestioning in the helpless and intimidated son of the father of the horde (...) A rapture of devotion to God was thus the first reaction to the return of the great father" (Freud, 1939, pp. 133–134).

The collective life of primeval man and the domestic life of ordinary children demonstrated to Freud's satisfaction the unavoidable connection between the libidinal and affectionate *relationship* between the father and the child and the formation by the latter of a *relationship* with the transformed internal imago of the father seeing now as God. The vicissitudes of the relationship with the father affected the person's relationship with God. Freud did not consider the significance of the child's primary relationship to the mother and the maternal imago as a source for conception of the divinity.

These are in a nutshell Freud's ideas about the religious life of human beings. We may ask what were his significant contributions to the psychology of religion? First, he made it explicit that all religion, primeval or of the single individual, stemmed from the *emotional relationship* to a deeply invested primary object, the father. Second, he saw the child's and the adult's *internal representation* of the divinity and the affects attached to it as the dynamic transformation in the course of phylogenetic or ontogenic development of that primary relationship. Third, he understood religious practices as dynamic, defensive, and transiently adaptive means of handling unacceptable and yet deeply meaningful feelings in relation to the father. Fourth, Freud demonstrated with his psychodynamic approach that religion is what it means: a way of re-linking with a very significant emotional object, the father. The originality of his conception rests on the fact that he, for the first time in the history of the psychology of religion, offered clinical evidence about the *internal psychical processes* that contribute to the formation and maintenance of a relationship with and internally conceived and socially sanctioned divine being.

In 1927 Freud wrote the *Future of an Illusion*. He asserted that religion is the great illusion of human beings who cannot face what Freud considered an incontrovertible fact of life: we are not the darlings of an attentive divine being but people who have to face "their insignificance in the machinery of the universe" (Freud, 1927, p. 49). He calls for and 'education to reality' because "Men cannot remain children forever; they must in the end go out into 'hostile life' (...) Need I confess to you that the sole purpose of my book is to point out the necessity for this forward step?" (ibid.). Freud called for a new psychoanalytic man, free from his neurotic infantile longings for divine parental protection and from the necessary submission to the will of the divinity found in the religious individual. Such a man could be capable of dealing with reality as it is and of bringing about the demise of religion. Predicting the moment when religion becomes obsolete he said to the believer

> There is nothing left for you but to despair of everything, of civilization and the future of mankind. From that bondage I am, we [psychoanalysts] are free. Since we are prepared to renounce a good part of our infantile wishes, we can bear it if a few of our expectations turn out to be illusions. (Freud, 1927, p. 54)

Freud's dramatic claim had one lasting effect. It evoked an spontaneous self-censorship that prompted analyst to leave aside whatever religion they had at the moment they decided to become Freud's followers. Who would dare to show Freud or his colleagues that he was still clinging to the infantile imago of his father/God? Such attitude, modulated today by a broader understanding of cultural and personal issues, persists in many institutes. It is not an overt assertion but a tacit understanding that analysts are neither religious nor 'really' interested in religion. The best evidence I am able to offer is a type of event that repeated itself until recently when

I was invited to lecture about my work at a psychoanalytic society. At the time of the reception after the lecture, two or three analyst asked to speak with me privately. They wanted to share with me a religious experience they had had in the past. They regularly ended our conversation with a variation of this sentence: "I did not tell this experience to my analyst." They had censored themselves during their analysis because they had felt that their religious experience was not acceptable 'analytic material'. This situation is changing rapidly in the opposite direction. Religion and psychoanalysis in the last few years is becoming a frequent theme of meetings and symposia.

The other effect did not come from this injunction to be free of religion, but from Freud's masterful clinical observations and his theoretical understanding of the significance of early childhood experiences for the future of the emotional and religious life of the individual. Leaving private religion aside did not stop analyst from theorizing about it and its dynamics. Most of Freud's followers remained faithful to his interpretative approach but rather than listening to their patients religious concerns (self-censorship might had been at work) they preferred to apply Freud's concepts to religious dogma, mythology, religious practices, ritual, and similar cultural phenomena. These studies came to be known as 'applied psychoanalysis'. In his comprehensive review of the psychoanalytic literature on religion, Beit-Hallahmi noticed that "Of 600 psychoanalytic studies listed in this book less than 10% have for a topic individual religious experiences" (Beit-Hallahmi and Argyle, 1975, p. 10). I believe that even today psychoanalysts whose own religious experiences were not analyzed and who did not have a course about the psychodynamics of religious experiences at their institute are not prepared or inclined to attend to the religious aspects of their patient's experience.

Few of Freud's followers looked at God experiences from another angle. Helene Deutsch considered the connection between God and the self: "In the state of ecstasy the idea of God that was projected outside is taken back into the ego again, but there is no conflict between ego and superego or between self and God, because self and God are both self" (Deutsch, 1989, p. 719). Eduardo Weiss connected a patient's perception of the omnipotence of the father to the eye of God: "From a father so vividly imagined (or hallucinated) the subject's own inner life cannot remain hidden; in this way too the feeling of being seen by the 'eye of God' may arise" (Weiss, 1932, p. 454). Ostow and Scharfstein claim that "we are subject to a nearly irresistible need to believe" (Ostow and Scharfstein, 1954/1969, p. 159). They insist that "Our psyche demands that the internal and external chaos be resolved into intelligibility" by some conception of God. "If we consciously repudiate God, we usually replace Him by a less adequate psychic substitute that continues to fill the same psychic role" (p. 152). These ideas found no followers or analysts that would listen in detail to their patients to prove or disprove them.

Freud's theories finally reached the field of psychology in the second part of the twentieth century and "led to a revolution in the study of religion in general and in the psychology of religion in particular" (Beit-Hallahmi, 1997, p. 12). According to Beit-Hallahmi, psychoanalysis is "the most, and the only, comprehensive theoretical approach to the psychology of religion (...) Despite its deficiencies, it is a good theory of religion not only for cases of high ego-involvement, but for explaining cultural commitments and the universal readiness for supernaturalism" (ibid.). In short, Freud's great contribution to the psychology of religion consisted in integrating the religious private experience of an individual into the dynamic fabric of his developmental life and his evolving desires, fears, and feelings, thus connecting personal history to the type of religious experience the person could or would have. The seeds of *private* religious experience lies within the psyche of those who encountered religion in their culture.

Psychoanalysis and Religion After Freud

Freud's followers did not consider that they had to analyze the religious experiences of their patients unless they appeared as part of overt symptoms or in the persistent associations of the patient. The vast majority of publications focused on "applied psychoanalysis": origins of religion, conversion, mythology, ritual, mysticism, psychodynamic interpretations of Jewish, Christian, and anthropological practices. Their papers gathered observations about the phenomena at hand and offered psychoanalytic interpretations of their meaning for the culture or the individual. Most of them relied on classical interpretations of drive, desire and defense against it, need for the affection and protection of the father or, at times, return to the mother, to give meaning to particular religious experiences. Very few papers had clinical examples and those that had them pointed to exceptional symptoms in unusual patients.

The emergence of object relations theory in Britain opened the door for a new way of looking at religious experiences. Object relations did not deny the existence of drives but insisted that the deep infantile need for the person of the mother and of the parents dominates the developmental process. The infant's needs are specific and must be adequately met for the formation of child's normal psychic structures. The conditions for psychic development go beyond the infant's intrapsychic desires and defenses and its physical need for food and physical care. The object-relation analysts believe that what a child needs is an actual good mother. Winnicott was the British analyst that made this point very explicit. An apt mother is capable of mirroring, holding, and handling her child as himself, thus providing the baby with a sense of being himself. A particular phenomenon occurs during these interactions. The reality of the maternal action is at the service not only of feeding or caring for the baby, but also of giving the child the possibility of creating the breast s/he finds in the mouth. In Winnicott's words "The mother (...) affords the infant the opportunity for the *illusion* that her breast is part of the infant. It is, as it were, under the baby's magical control (...) A subjective phenomenon develops in the baby, which we call the mother's breast. The mother places the actual breast just there were the infant is ready to create, and at the right moment" (Winnicott, 1953/1971, p. 11). Winnicott called such experiences *transitional phenomena*, which he considered to be his response to the concern about "what is objectively perceived and what is subjectively conceived of" (ibid.). There is a ground rule that applies to such phenomena: "We will never ask the question: 'Did you conceive of this or was it presented to you from without?' The important point is that no decision on this point is expected. The question is not to be formulated" (ibid., p. 12). Winnicott concludes

> This intermediary area of experience, unchallenged in respect of its belonging to inner or external (shared) reality, constitutes the greater part of the infant's experience, and throughout life is retained in the intense experiencing that belongs to the arts and to religion and to imaginative living, and to creative scientific work. (Winnicott, 1953/1971, p. 14)

Winnicott's concept of transitional phenomena and illusion opened new possibilities for the psychoanalytic understanding of religion. Freud's was convinced that religious beliefs about non-experiential transcendent beings and realms conflicted with the reality principle and called for the renunciation of the obsolete and illusory consolation offered by a paternal imago transformed into a divinity. With Winnicott's concept about the transitional space where religion could exist there was no longer a need to pit, as Freud had done, the truth of reality testing with the God created by the child and persisting in the adult. It was possible to assume that the God that had been created by the child could also have been found in some form in the culture or in another dimension of being. Psychoanalytic authors used Winnicott's concept to understand the psychodynamics of religious beliefs and to created their own integration of religious experiences and belief into psychoanalysis. Paul W. Pruyser published *Between Belief and Unbelief* (Pruyser, 1974); I wrote *The Birth of the Living God. A Psychoanalytic Study* (Rizzuto, 1979) and Meissner included the Winnicottian notion of illusion in his theoretical understanding of religion in *Psychoanalysis and Religious Experience* (Meissner, 1984). The possibility to take a fresh look at the psychoanalytic understanding of religion was there. Psychoanalysis could examine religious experiences and theorize about them without having to consider the actual existence of a transcendent God, a task that exceeds its epistemological level of theoretical competence. Psychoanalysts could now accept that the religious experience of a patient who believed in the actual existence of God did not represent an indicator of faulty reality testing or necessarily indicate an abnormal clinging to a parental figure.

In the course of a few years, however, the terms 'illusion', 'transitional space' and 'religion' suffered notable alterations, an evolution of meaning that deeply affected the understanding of religious experience. Several factors contributed to the evolution of the term 'religion'. Culturally, the influence of empiricism and modern science changed the perception of nature from a sacred reality to a machinery to be explored, dominated, and used (Nasr, 1996). Modernism belief in progress achieved by human means and political liberalism placed the center of attention on the individual and his freedom. The theological side of modernism encompassed "a tendency in theology to accommodate traditional religious teachings to contemporary thought and especially to devalue supernatural elements" (Merriam Webster's Collegiate Dictionary, 2003). In the 1960s the Protestant theologians J.J. Altizer and G. Vahanian proclaimed the 'death of God.' The communist movement crushed religious institutions and believers in three continents. The Jewish Holocaust raised the question about God's absence or even existence. Postmodernism rejected authorities of any type and, together with it, all large conceptual narratives and metanarratives that make life appear neatly organized. The use of the atomic bomb in Japan confronted everybody with the actual possibility of the destruction of the earth by human action. There was not need to wait for God to end the world. We could do it. All these cultural factors converge on one consequence: It is not God who is in charge of life. We are and there is no religious metanarrative to cling to. This is just the obverse of a religion based on the conviction about the actual existence of a divinity and the believer's relationship to a caring divine providence. This description presents the overarching spirit of contemporary culture as the context in which believers of all types must structure their experiences about any reality that transcends the limitations of their beings. 'Spirituality' and spiritualities emerged as the cultural phenomena of this historical circumstance that could offer some guidance to those who felt the stirrings of a need for something transcendent to relate to. Spirituality is subject-centered. The individual seeks to find a meaningful relationship with universal realities or a divine being without the restrictions imposed by external religious practices.

The complex cultural factors that I have listed above converged to progressively replace the word religion and to place spirituality on its stead. The shift signals a psychological and cultural change of great significance. Religion is concerned with the relationship to a God whose existence is taken for granted. Spirituality is concerned with the self and its subjective and experiential wellbeing in the complex postmodern world. "Spirituality seeks modes of relatedness with sacred realities that suit the individual's and the community's experiences of them" (Rizzuto, 2005, p. 32). Psychoanalysts would soon joint the new cultural trend by linking the needs of the self to the search for a suitable spirituality.

In the 1970s, the psychoanalytic contributions of Heinz Kohut placed the formation and the experiences of the self at the center of psychoanalytic theorizing and technique. His approach diluted the childhood Oedipal drama, which in Freud's theorizing was the corner stone for the transformation of a de-sexualized paternal representation into a God representation. Soon after Kohut published his ideas, schools of self psychology formed, expanded his work, and spurred other subjectively oriented psychoanalytic approaches. In brief, psychoanalysts became aware of the significance of the formation and transformation of the self as the result of the adequate responses of others not only during development but also during the psychoanalytic process.

Followers of Sullivan's (Sullivan, 1953) interpersonal theories become psychoanalysts and they wished to integrate his approach into main stream analysis. In the 1980s the interpersonal or relational approach (Greenberg and Mitchell, 1983) emerge within psychoanalysis. Soon after, intersubjectivity appeared not only as a new concept but as the foundation for a technical approach that favored the subjectivity of the patient and of the analyst as key to therapeutic work (Stolorow, 1987). The new approaches focused on the *experience* of the analysand and of the analyst during the analytic encounter as the instruments to give meaning to the here and now of the shared analytic moment. They favored the analyst's empathic immersion in the subjective experience of the analysand and required that s/he resigns any authority as the person who knows best. There is no true objectivity in the analytic process but only the progressive discovery of what type of event is happening in the here and now of the analytic encounter. The classic analytic approach paid attention to postulated drives and preformed unconscious fantasies related to them. Drives and unconscious fantasies, because of their nonconscious nature, *transcend* the here and now of the manifest aspect of the encounter and necessitated intense analytic work to bring them to the conscious surface of the analysand's experience. The new theories transformed psychoanalytic work into an *immanent* process between two individuals working together. The hidden power of unconscious motives that transcend and influence conscious relational moves and individual desires became subsumed within the here and now relational experiences between patient and analyst. The relational selves of analysand and analyst are in charge. No unconscious motivations transcend their relational intentions.

The new view of psychoanalysis opened the way for exploring religion from a psychoanalytic point of view by focusing on subjective experiences of some transcendent nature without the need for a transcendent object. For some analysts located at the far end of this approach, religion as a concept and a praxis no longer required belief in a transcendent existing object, a divine being or even some objective truth. Organized religion is out of the question and is substituted by so called "natural religion" (Hinshewood, 1999). As Blass points out

> the psychoanalytically ideal religion becomes more of a personal, self-determined mysticism, devoid of history, ritual, authority, obligation and mediation. Experience becomes central and truth, in the original sense of corresponding to something real, is no longer particularly relevant. (Blass, 2004, p. 624)

Blass notices that this present psychoanalytic conception of religion opposes traditional religious believers whose faith is based on the reality of a supernatural divine being (ibid., p. 625). Some psychoanalyst go as far as to consider the psychoanalytic encounter as a form of mature religious experience (Symington, 1994), even prayer (Eigen, 1998). For Eigen

> God could be anything (...) to blank oneself out and be totally open to whatever currents pulse this way or that (...) whether you're into body, or emotion (...) Taoist or Buddhist, whatever, it feels good. (Eigen, in Blass, 2004, p. 619)

Eigen represents the extreme of the analysts who make subjective experience almost divine. Such stance borders in a hedonistic subjectivity that lacks any reference to external reality.

In the latest book on religion and psychoanalysis published by The New Library of Psychoanalysis in London, Jeffrey B. Rubin, a psychoanalyst interested in Buddhism and practicing privately in New York, describes his own adolescent *spiritual transforming experience* (Rubin, 2006). It happened at the last moments of a basketball game when his team put in his hands the only possibility of winning by placing the ball in the basket. Just before doing it, he entered into a great calm and sensed that time had slowed down. He scored the point and his team won the game. He described his experience of that moment as transformative:

> Before those last five seconds of the game I would have called my childhood irreligious. While my teammates were celebrating ... I was preoccupied with the tantalizing glimpse I

> had of another domain of being, what I would later term spirituality or the sacred, in which I was opened to the moment without a sense of time, un-self-conscious but acutely aware, highly focused and engaged yet relaxed and without fear.
>
> What I experienced at the end of that game became a defining moment in my life. I knew directly and viscerally that there was a radically different way of *relating* to the world. The vice-like grip of ambition, victory, competitiveness and succeeding at all costs – the divinities I worshipped until the last five seconds of that game – was loosened. ... it was now clear to me that surrendering to and flowing with life is no less important than planning and goal-directed behavior. (Rubin, 2006, p. 134) (my italics)

Rubin's description of his experience corresponds to well known illustrations of encounters with a reality that transcends the self, described by Maslow (Maslow, 1976) as peak-experiences and by Velasco (Velasco, 1999) as non-religious mystical experiences. Rubin believes that "we may be witnessing a return of the spiritually repressed in contemporary psychoanalysis" (Rubin, 2006, p. 137) as indicated by the "profusion of analysands and analysts who are exploring spiritual practice and the increasing number of articles on psychoanalysis and spirituality" (ibid.). Rubin favors this evolution of psychoanalysis because it gives the self a *context* for its existence in the awareness of a realm of life that transcends the self and to which is worth surrendering. At the present time "The individual, in a secular world, is a god-term – the ultimate ground of being and source of meaning" (ibid., p. 136). The spiritual attitude, instead offers something different:

> In this being-at-oneness one experiences the world from a more inclusive perspective in which self and other are seen as mutually interpenetrating facets of the universe rather than as polar oppositions. (ibid., p. 137)

Freud would have read Rubin's description as a modern version of the oceanic feeling "a feeling of an indissoluble bond, of being one with the external world as a whole" (Freud, 1930, p. 65). Freud could not accept it as a primary feeling, claimed that he could not find such feeling within himself, and suggested that psychoan alyst should find a genetic explanation for such feeling. Obviously, Freud lived in a scientific culture where scholars *believed* that it was possible for science to find explanations for every feeling and had a great conviction about the power of the individual. The postmodern culture encounters a beleaguered human self, isolated, bereft of meaning, entrapped by the cultural 'divinities' (as Rubin describes them) of a competitive and materialistic society. Such self needs *a context to be* and modern spiritualities seem to have something to offer to those who have grown "irreligious" or who have left behind for their own dynamic reasons the religion of their childhood.

Rubin, even when he believes that spirituality is a basic dimension of being human, agrees with Freud when he suggest that its manifestations should be explored psychoanalytically,

> A psychoanalysis of spirit would attend to the hidden motivations and secondary gains of the spiritual quest as well as its exalted dimensions. Psychoanalysis could show that spirituality, like all human experiences, serves multiple functions ranging from the adaptive and transformative to the defensive and psychopathological. ... I have observed a variety of pathologies of spirit including using the spiritual quest to narcissistically inflate oneself,

> evade subjectivity, deny emotional losses, shield oneself from the painful vicissitudes of everyday experience and neglect ethical responsibility. (Rubin, 2006, p. 140)

We witness in Rubin's writings the positive view of spirituality as a human realm of experience and the need to examine it as a normal part of the analytic process. Many other authors, including myself, have made a similar suggestion about the analysis of religious experiences. In these approaches religion and spirituality are seeing as complex personal realities structured by developmental, object related, dynamic, and cultural phenomena that, as a composite, exceed the field of competence of psychoanalysis. The analyst can theorize about the psychic factors that converge in the formation of a particular religious or spiritual experience in an individual but cannot, as Freud attempted to do, offer an exclusive psychoanalytic *explanation* of religion or spirituality. Their cultural components are too complex to be *reduced* to an exclusive psychoanalytic interpretation.

The presentation of an actual analytic case may facilitate the understanding of the complex object-related, developmental, narcissistic, conflictual, dynamic, and realistic factors contributing to the subjective organization of particular religious thoughts, feelings, fears and wishes. The complexity and richness of each analytic moment precludes attributing to one particular factor any causal effect. They all combine in complex dynamic organizations of the patient's inner experience to bring about a particular moment of religious self-appraisal and feeling. Gathering a large number of detailed case histories, in which religious and spiritual experiences are accepted as part of the analytic process, may help us all to understand in a more systematic way the dynamic process contributing to the emergence of particular modes of organizing religious and spiritual conceptions, feelings, and desires.

Clinical Presentation

I will now present fragments of the analysis of a competent Jewish professional woman, Rachel, who asked me to help her with her confusion about herself, her difficulties in relating to others, and a vague but profound feeling of being lost. The presentation aims at illustrating that: (1) as Freud suggested, religion and the representation of God it implies, involve the never ending process of elaborating the representation of primary internal objects in relation to the individual, and (2) as Rubin proposes, spirituality represents the person's search for a *psychic context* and an *actual* space to be and to continue to become oneself as an involved participant in the larger universe when an internally represented divinity is either not available or suitable for belief.

Rachel was the second child of a professional father and a stay-at-home mother. The mother was dedicated to the children and the home and to helping her husband in his professional life. The patient had a very conflicted relationship with her mother. She felt that the mother did not let her be. During Rachel's adolescence, the mother developed a curable cancer. At the time of the diagnosis, she accused Rachel of having caused her disease. The father was attentive to her and she felt close to him. Yet, he never protected her from her mother. He always sided with his wife. Rachel had always been a very good student and never had manifest social difficulties; on the contrary, Rachel was well regarded by her peers. She was a highly moral person committed to serving others. There was no indication of any psychotic or borderline functioning in her. Rachel's suffering was private, without obvious visible symptoms. The family practiced reformed Judaism, only occasionally attended temple services, but always participated in the temple's celebration of the High Holidays. When the patient consulted me, in her early 30s, she had not attended services for many years. She had declared herself a non-believer in early adolescence. That is the time when the girl reaches sexual maturity and becomes fully aware that she is like her mother. Tyson and Tyson point out that "Whether consciously or preconsciously, this reminder revives unresolved mother–child wishes and conflicts from all developmental levels" (Tyson and Tyson, 1990, p. 272). In Rachel's case, rejecting God at this point, appears as manifestation of her struggle to separate from her mother, whose representation as an internal object, as we soon shall learn, had been used by Rachel to form a very conflicted God-representation.

The clinical material I will present belongs to the last 3 years of a 6-year analysis. The initial years of analysis had helped her to settle in analysis, to feel comfortable with me, and to let me see and know her. In short, she had accepted me after we had worked through many of her fears about my 'dangerous' intentions and the possibility that I would harm, humiliate or drop her. We were in the late middle phase of analysis when patients frequently bring to the hour thoughts and feelings that they would have suppressed before.

The clinical material starts at a moment of significant change. The patient had kept her distance from her parents. They lived in another city and she had visited them infrequently. She spoke with them on the phone with some regularity but had not allowed them to visit her in her home for 8 years. As a result of her analytic work, Rachel had accepted the parents' offer to visit her at her home. She expected with great anxiety a disastrous visit. She anticipated that her mother's criticism of her place and of her would cause her to feel overwhelming feelings of humiliation and disappointment. What she feared more than anything else was her mother's habitual attitude and behavior with her. During a conversation, the mother would suddenly absent herself emotionally from the dialogue and withdraw her eyes from the patient. Each time the mother acted in this manner, Rachel felt totally abandoned and experienced a feeling of sinking into deep waters and drowning. Nonetheless, she was determined to use the visit to understand herself in relation to her parents and to understand them in the light of what she had already discovered about herself in the analysis.

Two analytic hours prior to her parents' visit, Rachel spoke explicitly and for the first time about her wish to murder her parents. She had read in the paper about a boy who had murdered his brother. She questioned whether the adolescent's murder of his brother could be related to an unbearable fear of being murdered by his brother. She reflected that maybe she too was afraid of being killed by her parents.

During the visit she caught herself rejecting anything her mother was saying. A relative made her aware that she constantly dismissed her mother and suggested to her that she make an effort to change her attitude during the visit. She reflected about her behavior and made an effort to observe herself and to be more attentive to her parents. She found that they were kinder than she had expected them to be. She discovered that she was dealing with two versions of her parents: (1) the actual parents that visited her who did behave in some of the ways she had predicted they would, but who also did the best they could to be gracious to her and (2) the parents within herself, as she felt them to be. During the hours following the visit she examined her experience. She said that she was becoming conscious that there was a discrepancy between her actual parents and the parents she experienced within herself. It had to do with her beliefs. Belief systems, she said, come as a package. If you believe in God, you also believe in the devil. She questioned how do you stop believing what you believe. She said:

> I believe that my mother is like the devil, capable of infinite evil. That is the mother within me. Always harmful, always destructive of me. Never capable of seeing me. But I cannot stop believing. I have made my parents into gods, I have idealized them, made them so big! But I have made them also into devils, evil people capable of infinite evil. I would like to stop believing that, but I cannot. May be I have to bring them to earth, bring them to proportion.

Three weeks later she described how she felt that she was becoming much more aware of herself and her circumstances. She talked overtly about her affectionate feelings for her father and even acknowledged that maybe as a young girl she might have wanted to have a miraculous child with him. The next day she had a very elaborate dream with three main parts. In the first part she was in a professional meeting with women like her, walking alone towards a very distant place, perhaps Alaska. In the second part some workers had taken all the leaves from the street trees and were burning them. They were progressively diminishing in the way in which spinach diminishes in size when you cook it. In the third part there was a woman in a boat, rowing towards a high place in a river. When the patient saw the woman in the dream, she though that she was rowing towards God. This was the first time in 4 years of analysis that the patient mentioned God as part of a dream. We did not analyzed all the aspects of the dream, but we took notice that Rachel was in a long journey, that the leaves that clouded her vision were shrinking, and that, whoever that woman was, she was searching for God.

Five months later she pondered about the power religion has on people and the power that it bestows on them. It helps them to defend themselves in public relations to further their cases. She said: "The crucifixion, the resurrection, heaven, the Virgin Mary, those are like motherhood. No one can complain about them. No one can say a thing about that." She was dealing with issues of motherhood herself. In a few weeks she learned that she would never be able to have children because of a uterine condition. She was terribly pained but was able to deal with it. Her mother called her, but could not show any empathy for her daughter's pain. For the first time in her life, Rachel was able overtly to be angry with her mother without fearing that she would be destroyed. She directly asked her mother: "Are you trying to support me or are you trying to say that you don't like me to have children?" It was a truly new action on her part. To stand apart from her mother and hold her own ground. She described how her mother had always wanted to rule the universe and had considered herself the owner of womanhood. She commented further about her mother's attitude and shortly thereafter used for the first time the colloquial exclamation "Oh God!" in phrases such as: "Oh God! She is so narrow-minded!" "Oh God, that is the way she is!" I questioned in my mind if her getting angry at her mother was bringing about some internal separation in Rachel's inner world between her maternal representation and that of her God, obviously linked in her to her mother's representation. In the hour, however, I attended to her affect. I said to her that by focusing on her mother, she seemed to be distracting herself from the depth of her sorrow about not being able to become a mother. She defended herself saying that other people suffer more than her. I said that she was behaving like those who do not allow themselves to complain because there are children starving in Africa. She accepted the comparison and said that she was afraid of *sinking* into her pain. She continued:

> Oh God! I want so badly to leave my mother behind! I pray to God that my mother would die before me so that I would not have to die with her around me. That would be unbearable. I couldn't tolerate being so vulnerable and having her around me. I pray to God that she would die first.

This hour contains her first confrontation of her mother and her first explicit prayer during analysis. The two events were truly new. First, she manifests her recently acquired capacity to stand up to her mother, be angry with her, and not feel totally abandon or taken over by a *sinking*, *drowning* feeling. Second, her mother had diminished her godly and demonic power. The mother had been described as wanting to rule over the world but now it was God who had the power to decide when she should die. The patient had addressed her wishes to such God. In brief, the internal maternal representation had conceded the place of ruler to a God higher that her. We witness here the end result of a process of transformation in which God, whoever she/he might have been in Rachel's internal reality, had become the supreme ruler of life and death. A certain personal God representation had emerged in Rachel's private experience that is somehow different from the maternal representation. Such God, supposedly existing and capable of action, can be addressed by Rachel to help her to be protected from her mother's actions. God is now the ruler of the world not Rachel's internal mother. From the psychodynamic point of view, I dare to say, that this moment showed (1) Rachel's first indication of a belated adolescent separation from her mother, and (2) her first elaboration of a God-representation that is not directly subsumed within her maternal or parental representation.

Four months later, in April, Rachel talked about how much she needed a structure where she could be. She could not see herself unless she had a structure in which she could locate herself. During her growing up years, when her mother in looking at her beheld her, she did experience that she existed. Yet, when her mother "dropped" her from her sight she felt she did not exist. She referred to that issue again in an hour in August after she had had a satisfying and meaningful conversation with her parents on the telephone about the death of a relative who was a parental figure to her. She talked again about her need for a context in which to exist. (Perhaps, after beginning to separate from her mother, Rachel was searching for what Rubin [2006,

p. 137] described, a world in "which self and other are seen as mutually interpenetrating facets of the universe"). She said that she did not like religious people. She herself did not believe in religion, yet through all ages religion has sustained people. She needed something to give her a context. May be a sort of a black box. A black box is what scientists use to talk about the unknown reality they have to figure out. She did not know what to think about God or the afterlife. She immediately associated to several cases of murder and I reminded her that some time earlier she had discovered she herself had some murderous feelings toward her parents. Rachel recalled again that her mother had accused her of wanting to kill her by causing her cancer. I had the impression that Rachel connect God with some primal murder on her or her mother's part. Freud too had connected the murderous wishes of primitive man and the Oedipal child to the formation of the God representation. She associated about her role as a peacemaker in the family and in the world. I interpreted that she was afraid that she would in fact kill her mother if she separated psychically from her. She reflected that her mother only saw her when she made herself to be a person who existed *for* her mother. Rachel commented that she did not know if she believed in the after life but that what she needed was *protection* at the moment she was talking. The hour illustrated the psychic move between the separation from a painfully invested maternal object that cannot offer secure existence to Rachel and the search for some black-box-type of being or reality capable of offering her a meaningful context for her existence. She feared that finding such being might required the psychic or actual murdering of her mother, who, in her perception, had made herself the ruler of the world and of Rachel's existence. This hour illustrates some aspects of the emergence of a psychical conception of and need for a god. When the developing child has had profoundly ambivalent relationship with a maternal object who has not offered him/her the sense of having the right to exist on its own right, it is the *experience* with the therapist of having such a right that conditions the analytic work necessary for transforming ego-dystonic parental object representations into less malignant parental representations. Potentially, the newly emerging transformation of the early objects could offer some ego-syntonic facets capable of forming some acceptable aspects of an ego-syntonic God representation.

Rachel had experienced at this point in her analysis that she existed for me as herself. That my eyes beheld her as herself first, not as the person I needed her to be for my own needs. I did not need to be killed for her to acquire a life of her own. She could be herself and be *with* me at the same time. She could also be without me. Rachel had already mentioned that one day she wanted to terminate her analysis and I had responded that whenever she felt she was getting ready we could discuss it because she was free to go.

In September she went home to celebrate the High Holidays, Rosh Hashanah and Yom Kippur with her family for the first time in years. She wanted to reconnect with the rabbi she had met as a child in a summer camp and revive the good feelings she had had at the camp. Rachel's experience during the services was complex. She could not accept the rituals and beliefs of her congregation but she felt a need to pray for a very close friend who had died a traumatic death in Israel when they were there together as part of an exchange program. She cried deeply while talking about her friend and her prayer for her. Nevertheless, she made no explicit reference to God.

In October she had an amazing experience. She had been offered a high position in her field. Her feelings of being small, insignificant, and inarticulate returned. Using analytic self-exploration she tried to convinced herself that those were only feelings not the reality of who she was. She had already met with some high-ranking interviewers and was in the way of meeting the next one. She was walking along a corridor and found herself facing a mirror. She saw her image and was amazed to find that she looked like an adult woman. She commented that it was not that she expected to see a child but that she could not imagine to see herself with her own eyes as she actually was. In fact she found herself to be an attractive woman. When we examined her experiences she commented: "When I was feeling small and insignificant I was looking at myself in my own mind with dead eyes, eyes that had no feeling and no life. When I saw the image in the mirror I realized that I was looking at myself in the mirror with living eyes, alive, bright, perceptive." I said softly: "You had a change of eyes." She nodded vigorously. We both understood that she had left behind her mother's eyes and had began to look at herself with her own eyes. I wondered silently, how much of her "alive, bright, and perceptive eyes" were modeled on her interaction with me and her identification with my seeing her as herself and helping her to do the same. The exchange left her feeling adult and in charge of her life. Finally, Rachel had been able to perceive and to be herself on her own right, not as the person whose life and existence depended on her mothers unreliable eyes. Her psychic life was becoming her own self-sustaining and self-assessing life. Rachel had acquired a center for her sense of self from which she could live, feel, and act as an independent being. That center recognize her as adult woman with and attractive body. Her mother no longer dominated her view of herself. Her mother was no longer the sole owner of womanhood.

In February, at the time of her menstrual period, she recalled the experience of her first menstruation. She remember how, at the time, she felt that her mother would not make room for her as a woman. She said that her mother was like the God of the Hebrew Bible. I said that such God always insisted in saying that he was the only God and that no one should have another God. Rachel began to cry and said that she was desperately trying to get from under the power of such God. She was trying to become polytheistic. The problem was that she did not know who she was and therefore was unable to select knew gods. In the end, she said reflectively that she could not move away from the God of the Hebrew Bible. It is worth noticing that she consciously dropped her Jewish practices at the beginning of her adolescence. At the time of this hour she was unable to deal with the question about an existing God. It was too frightening to her.

In May, Rachel became fully aware of the depth of her anger with her mother and her hatred of her. We were revisiting her worst feelings. She recognized again the wishes to kill her mother and also to kill me. I repeated the earlier interpretation that she had always felt that she could not have any autonomy without killing her mother as a result of leaving her behind. Now, the feelings were also directed at me. If she became angry with me or left me, she would kill me. At that point she described her experience during Rosh Hashanah and Yom Kippur. She recalled the part of the service in which you have to repent to be inscribed in the book of the living. Her voice became very ironic, an unusual tone for her. She said: "Never mention God's decision to get rid of you!" She concluded in a softer tone: "Maybe, if I get angry with you [God and analyst in one package], you would erase me from the book of the living." This was the first time she spoke about God as an existing being intent on doing away with her. It was easy to see the continuity between the mother capable of "infinite evil", God, and myself. None of us wanted her as a living being. The great difference rested in the fact that, in analysis, she was talking from herself to me about the kind of things that I might have wanted to do to her. The terror of not existing that had deeply inhibited her life, had been transformed into a dialogue between us, a dialogue to make sense of her and of her suffering.

In July she had a dream in which she was in a room with me and we were talking as friends talk to each other. In the dream, I suggested that we look together at a movie. In her associations she talked about not having a religion and not believing that here is a godhead that rules the universe. For her a personal and direct relationship with another actual person is more important. Yet, it frightened her to put all her eggs in one basket because she became so deeply involved in her relationship with the other person. She used religious words: she adored, worshiped, idolized the other person. I began to think about Moses and the story of the golden calf. She continued saying that she idolized the people she loved. Finally, I said that her way of talking reminded me of Moses and the golden calf, a true idol made by human hands. Rachel said that I had made an import point. She made idols of the people she loved.

In the middle of September, Rachel experienced a moment of unbearable pain. She wanted to make love and made some gestures towards her lover, but her move was not accepted. She sunk into despair feeling deeply unwanted. She said: "The whole world has no room for me; there is only room for the person who works, but no one cares for me as myself." For the first time she spoke about committing suicide. This episode took place at the time of Rosh Hashanah. Rachel had decided to attend the temple's religious services in her local community. She said that, in spite of the depth and beauty of the prayers she could not pray. Finally, Rachel said: "I wish I could believe in God. I do not. There is something in me that does not permit me to believe that there is a God there for whom I can be."

By late November, Rachel turned a corner. For the first time she looked at her entire life. She visited her parents, old friends, people from the past to rediscover who she had been and who she was now. One of her dear friends told her that she had to be like Moses, who listened to God and did things he thought he was unable to do. Rachel commented that no matter how hard she tried she could not imagine God, produce a picture of God. She concluded: "It must have to do with my parents, with my need to reject their religion." Besides, she said, she was suspicious of people, like some nuns she had known who were very good but in her opinion they were hiding behind God. She did not want that. She wanted to face the world herself, to have her own strength to do what she had to do. However, Rachel felt she needed a mentor to guide her because she believed there was a connection between her mother and God and she was afraid. Still, she had a need for a higher authority, for a way of relating to the world at large, for a 'presence' to find a way of being herself in the world. That 'presence' would make all the difference in the world for her.

By the end of December, Rachel was feeling free in her mind. It was a new freedom because in the past she had always being busy attending to her mother in her mind, as a burdensome presence. She had lost the preoccupation with her mother and it was truly a great feeling of peace and freedom. She mentioned a fantasy she had. She, like the biblical Jacob, was fighting with an angel. In the fantasy she saw the ladder, and fought with the angel and managed to come out of the fight unscathed. She had the feeling that it was a very important fantasy. She had always been afraid of falling from ladders. It had to do with being dropped from her mother's attention. Then she reflected: "I am not sure I can call God mother. Maybe it is mother-god. It is something of that nature. It was my mother that I fought like Jacob and I too managed to win and to overpower the angel."

Rachel experienced several significant changes during this period of her life. For the first time, she was able to swim because she was no longer afraid of sinking into the water; she felt she had made a new contact with her body; the physical contact and the fighting in the fantasy gave her a new experience of her own body. I too noticed that a major change had taken place in our relationship. I felt that she was really present with me during the hour. I noticed my own change of voice: I was addressing her in a free, relaxed, direct and personal manner, as a full adult who responded in kind. We were now two adults committed to working together, not afraid of each other and capable of genuine collaboration.

By late January Rachel was looking back at her affective life. This time she was reviewing her love relationships and how she had been so psychically absent during the sexual act. In her earlier life she had participated in sexual intercourse because that was what she was supposed to do at her age. However, she had now become aware that she had not been present to herself or to her partner during their sexual engagement. She returned to the question of God. She had a need to believe, perhaps in God, perhaps in a transcendent reality. Yet, in a certain manner she did not want to believe. What she needed was a reality bigger than herself and she wished she could find one.

By the middle of May we were immerse in the termination of the treatment. She reviewed once more her predicament with her mother and concluded: "My mother was unwilling to reflect me as a person because then I would have been myself. My father always saw me as a person and we could have a relationship." The father, however, had always side with the mother and did not protect her when there were overt conflicts. Their good relationship was separate and in parallel with that of the mother and not one of partaking of an integrated family group.

She reflected about our work together:

> What made the difference in our work together is not so much what you have said to me but the way you have been with me. You made room for me. You let me be in my own way. You had respect for me. That respect made all the difference in the world. Waiting for me to have my own experience meant to me that there was something there in me that you could count on for me to do what I had to do. You did not trample the structures within me (...)

> By respecting my structures and letting me have my own experiences you have made room for me and forced me to use my own structures to become myself.

I have narrated with only a few comments, the psychic struggles and difficulties Rachel had to confront in order to wrestle with a mother who gave her physical life but who could not reliably respond to her as a psychical person on her own right. Rachel's maternal representation was too fraught with images of terrifying abandonment, rejection, and competitive feelings to become available for transformation into a believable representation of the divinity. Yet, as Rachel herself said it was her mother-god she fought in Jacob's style in her fantasy.

Commentary

Rachel's painful struggle helps to understand the delicate and subtle psychic elaboration we all need to go through for us to be capable of searching for a sacred reality. The feeling of being lost in the world brought Rachel to analysis. At the time of termination she had found, recognized, and felt herself bodily and psychically as the woman she actually was. That woman was still in an active search for a reality that transcendent her everyday comfort, a broader reality in which she could locate herself. The process that brought her to be lost in the world and to become irreligious after her adolescent rejection of her Jewish God, involved her difficulties in dealing with the maternal eyes and the person of the mother as the being that could bestow psychic existence to her. Rachel's struggle with her mother clearly reveals that the mother had occupied all along the psychic space that she could have used to create/find a believable God. The conflict with what she finally called mother-god made that impossible. It was too dangerous for Rachel to enter into any spiritual commerce with a divinity capable of infinite evil and of erasing her from the book of the living. Her Jacob-like fantasy of overpowering mother-god, allowed her to obtain a measure of freedom and to be able to swim without fearing that the waters would drawn her. Yet, her maternal representation was too powerful and too close to a possible representation of the Hebrew divinity for Rachel to have any inclination to bestow more reality to it than a passing hopeful prayer and a certain acknowledgement that God has power over life and death, including the death of her mother. Belief in the actual existence of a God that was still deeply connected in her mind to the early psychic representation of a mother capable of infinite evil could only bring her fear and trembling. She could not do it at that point in her life. I have presented in Chapter 8 of my book *The Birth of the Living God. A Psychoanalytic Study* (Rizzuto, 1979, pp. 130–148), the case of a man who saw God as an enigma because he too was too terrified of his psychic conception of God based on the representation of a terrifying father.

Yet, Rachel experientially knew that she could not live making idols of the people she loved. She felt and knew that she needed a transcendent space, a certain black hole, a reality beyond her own self to give full meaning to the self she had found in analysis. Her search now was not for a religion but for a spiritual realm of being to which she could feel connected. She was not content to be, or to have friends who were, as Rubin suggests, individuals that took the place of a god, as "the ultimate ground of being and source of meaning" for herself (Rubin, 2006, p. 136).

To sum up: Rachel case illustrates the great importance of the maternal object to form an enduring representation of a divinity capable of a genuine connection to the self, a representation loaded with powerful primary affects. Rachel's psychic fixation on her mother and the distortions that it brought to her self-experience made no room for transforming the representation of God under the influence of her relationship to her father or other people who cared for her. Freud's notion that the relationship to God follows the vicissitudes of the relation to the father, apply in Rachel's case to the relationship with the mother. Freud was right: a parental representation is used to form the representation of God. Freud was wrong: the first parent used to form that representation is the mother, not the father. Her paternal representation appeared transiently linked to the dream of the woman who was rowing towards God never to reappear in the analysis again in any connection with religious or spiritual issues. The impossibility of using the maternal representation to create a transcendent divinity or space for being did not obliterate Rachel's need for a reality that transcends her self, a place for that self to have a context for the simple act of being. I hope that her articulate words and transformation in analysis illustrates the profound connections between being a self, a particular type of self with a personal journey into the act of being, and the need for a believable divinity or some sacred reality. For Rachel, belief in the actual existence of the Jewish God could only bring to her fear and trembling. She could not do it at that point in her life. Yet, she was acutely aware that having become an alive self was not enough. As Rubin, Rachel needed to find a way of *relating* to a larger reality because she knew that idols and idolized relationships did not respond to her need. She terminated her analysis open to a spiritual search she had began at the moment she felt free from the oppressive power of her internal mother.

Was Rachel's spiritual search for a larger reality at the end of her analysis a regression or a progression? Was she still searching for a less dangerous and more inclusive mother, a universal matrix in which to exist? My answer is yes and no. Yes, her search had regressive components. Rachel was searching for a symbolic reality, a maternal holding environment, a domain of being in which she could continue some aspects of her analytic experience. I would consider such type of 'regression' the symbolic elaboration of an ever present maternal need we all have, a need to be held by a reality that lets us be and exist without being terrified of being annihilated. Without such symbolic elaboration, regardless of how tacitly we may have it or how many different forms it make take, be it sustaining internal objects, private convictions, religious, spiritual or cultural beliefs, psychic life is not possible. And, no, it was also a progression. Rachel had become a fully functional and content enough self. She had psychically integrated herself into her relationships, her activities, and her world. Her search for a transcendent reality, might have been her taking up again her early adolescent development when all children ask profound philosophical and religious questions and find a need to create a certain unitary view of the world. That period in her life was disrupted by the conflict with a mother that did not make the questions possible because she fully occupied the psychic space available for the questions. Rachel was again asking the question about *something in reality* that could give contextual meaning to her existence. Her *inner reality* did not have a benign enough divine representation to offer such meaning.

References

Beit-Hallahmi, B. & Argyle, M. (1975). God as a father projection: The theory and the evidence. *British Journal of Medical Psychology*, *48*, 71–75.

Beit-Hallahmi, B. (1997). *The psychology of religious behavior, belief & experience*. London/New York: Routledge.

Blass, R. B. (2004). Beyond illusion: Psychoanalysis and the question of religious truth. *International Journal of Psychoanalysis*, *85*, 615–634.

Corveleyn, J. & Luyten, P. (2005). Psychodynamic psychologies and religion. In R. F. Paloutzian & C. Park (Eds.), *Handbook of the psychology of religion and spirituality* (pp. 80–100). New York/London: Guilford.

Deutsch, H. (1989). On satisfaction, happiness and ecstasy. *International Journal of Psychoanalysis*, *70*, 715–723.

Eigen, M. (1998). *The psychoanalytic mystic*. New York: Free Association Books.

Freud, S. (1907). Obssessive actions and religious practices. In J. Strachey (Ed.), *The standard edition of the complete psychological works of Sigmund Freud*, *Vol. 9* (pp. 115–128). London: Hogarth.

Freud, S. (1913). Totem and taboo. In J. Strachey (Ed.), *The standard edition of the complete psychological works of Sigmund Freud*, *Vol.* 13 (pp. 1–161). London: Hogarth.

Freud, S. (1914). Some reflections on schoolboy psychology. In J. Strachey (Ed.), *The standard edition of the complete psychological works of Sigmund Freud*, *Vol. 13* (pp. 239–244). London: Hogarth.

Freud, S. (1918). From the history of an infantile neurosis. In J. Strachey (Ed.), *The standard edition of the complete psychological works of Sigmund Freud*, *Vol. 17* (pp. 1–122). London: Hogarth.

Freud, S. (1927). The future of an illusion. In J. Strachey (Ed.), *The standard edition of the complete psychological works of Sigmund Freud*. *Vol. 21* (pp. 1–56). London: Hogarth.

Freud, S. (1930). Civilization and its discontents. In J. Strachey (Ed.), *The standard edition of the complete psychological works of Sigmund Freud*, *Vol. 21* (pp. 59–145). London: Hogarth.

Freud, S. (1939). Moses and Monotheism. In J. Strachey (Ed.), *The standard edition of the complete psychological works of Sigmund Freud*, *Vol. 23*. London: Hogarth.

Greenberg, J. R. & Mitchell, S. A. (1983). *Object relations in psychoanalytic theory*. Cambridge, MA: Harvard University Press.

Hinshewood, R. D. (1999). Foreword. In S. M. Stein (Ed.), *Beyond belief: Psychotherapy and religion* (pp. xv–xix). London: Karnac.

James, W. (1902/1929). *The varieties of religious experience*. New York: Modern Library.

Maslow, A. H. (1976). *Religions, values, and peak-experiences*. Harmondsworth/New York: Penguin.

Meissner, W. (1984). *Psychoanalysis and religious experience*. New Haven, CT/London: Yale University Press.

Merriam-Webster's Collegiate Dictionary (2003). (Eleventh Edition). Springfield, MA: Merriam-Webster.

Nasr, S. H. (1996). *Religion and the order of nature*. New York/Oxford: Oxford University Press.

Ostow, M. & Scharfstein, B.-A. (1954/1969). *The need to believe: The psychology of religion*. New York: International Universities Press.

Paloutzian, R. F. & Park, C. L. (2005). *Handbook of the psychology of religion and spirituality*. New York/London: Guilford.

Pruyser, P. W. (1974). *Between belief and unbelief*. New York: Harper & Row.

Rizzuto, A.-M. (1979). *The birth of the living god: A psychoanalytic study*. Chicago, IL: University of Chicago Press.

Rizzuto, A.-M. (2005). Psychoanalytic considerations about spiritually oriented psychotherapy. In L. Sperry & E. P. Shafranske (Eds.), *Spiritually oriented psychotherapy* (pp. 31–50). Washington, DC: American Psychological Association.

Rubin, J. B. (2006). Psychoanalysis and spirituality. In D. M. Black (Ed.), *Psychoanalysis and religion in the 21st century* (pp. 132–153). New York: Routledge.

Spence, D. (1994). The failure to ask the hard questions. In P. F. Talley, H. H. Strupp & S. F. Butler (Eds.), *Psychotherapy research and practice: Bridging the gap* (pp. 19–38). New York: Basic Books.

Stolorow, R. (1987). *Psychoanalytic treatment: An intersubjective approach*. Hillsdale, NJ: Analytic Press.

Sullivan, H. S. (1953). *The interpersonal theory in psychiatry*. New York: Norton.

Symington, N. (1994). *Emotion and spirit: Questioning the claims of psychoanalysis and religion*. London: Karnac.

Tyson, P. & Tyson, R. L. (1990). *Psychoanalytic theories of development: An integration*. New Haven, CT/London: Yale University Press.

Velasco, J. M. (1999). *El fenómeno místico: Estudio comparado*. Madrid: Trotta.

Weiss, E. (1932). Regression and progression in the super-ego. *International Journal of Psychoanalysis*, *13*, 499–478.

Winnicott, D. W. (1953/1971). Transitional objects and transitional phenomena. In *Playing and reality* (pp. 1–25). New York: Basic Books.

Religious Conflicts in Psychoanalysis – A Case Study

Changing Views of the Nature and Meaning of Religious Beliefs in the Analytic Process

William W. Meissner

The history of the relation between and mutual influence of psychoanalysis and religion has undergone a somewhat checkered history. Freud's rather biased, prejudicial, agnostic and antireligious perspectives have subsequently proven to be ill-founded and by-and-large misleading (Meissner, 1984). The subsequent developments in this field have moved in the direction of separating the wheat from the chaff in the freudian account of religion and defining what is authentically psychoanalytic as opposed to religious prejudices and misconceptions. More current trends in the practical dealing with religious issues and conflicts in the psychoanalytic process have tended to be more open and accepting of the patient's religious beliefs and orientations, while at the same time remaining attuned to the role of unconscious determinants and neurotic resolutions that may be playing a role in influencing the patient's religious views and/or practices. In this sense, the analyst remains open to and accepting of the patient's belief system, while seeking to identify, explore, understand, and interpret – and thus hopefully help the patient to resolve – the neurotic influences that can distort the patient's religious stance and pervert what should be a source of strength and psychic support of a given religious system into a burdensome, often guilt-inducing, and personally undermining set of convictions.[1]

So stated the therapeutic task is not always without its vicissitudes. Some religious belief systems incorporate varieties and degrees of such unconsciously determined and decidedly pathological concepts and formulations that little more room is left for the development of a more mature and psychologically adaptive religious orientation. In such cases, the analysand may have to choose between psychologically more mature and adaptive resolutions discovered in the analytic

[1] Among the advocates of a more open and religiously accepting orientation, I would include Jones (1991, 1996), Pruyser (1968), Rizzuto (1979), Sorenson (2004), Spero (1992), Spezzano and Gargiulo (1997), and Vergote (1978/1988) among others.

W.W. Meissner
Boston College, Chestnut Hill, MA, USA
e-mail: meissner@bc.edu

J.A. Belzen (ed.), *Changing the Scientific Study of Religion: Beyond Freud?*

process and the less mature and neurotically determined beliefs and practices of his espoused religious belief system. Often this discrimination is neither simple nor easy. It cannot be made in any simple or straightforward way by an appeal to evidences based on the cold, hard light of reality as known in naturalistic or scientific terms. The reason for this is that the analysand's belief system is not sustained by such evidences but by the faith commitment he makes to his credo. We might read this as a contradiction between the analysand's psychic reality (i.e., the belief system) in opposition to the material reality of a secularized world view – as would Freud (1927/1961). But, as I have argued elsewhere (Meissner, 2000, 2001), the connotations of psychic reality may well extend to include both frameworks equally well. The basis of this discrimination, then, would rest not on the opposition of belief versus reality, but on the determination of what in the religious belief system can be regarded as relatively reasonable, mature, adaptive, and promoting psychological health, integrity, and spiritual identity as opposed to elements that reflect unconscious and neurotic underpinnings that do more to distort and undermine authentic religious perspectives than not. Even if religious beliefs are not based on real and naturalistic evidences, the religious belief system cannot all the same legitimately and validly incorporate contradictory or illogical tenets.[2] The issue for the patient is whether and to what extent he can sustain his authentic religious belief and commitment in the face of the erosion or abandonment of less mature and neurotic elements within the belief system.

The analyst's stance in this relationship is a far cry from that recommended by Freud. Rather than presuming that the religious belief is through-and-through neurotic and infantile and therefore is best dispensed with, as might many analysts following in Freud's footsteps, the analyst views the patient's religious orientation as open to the distorting influence of unconscious motives, as would be the case for any other aspect of the patient's life activity or involvement. The analytic task is not to help the patient abandon his religious viewpoint and involvement, but to enable the patient to discriminate what is positive, reasonable, mature and adaptive in his religious outlook as opposed to what is conflictual, neurotic, maladaptive or simply untrue. The direction in this effort is toward enabling the patient to attain a more mature religious orientation that can further strengthen and facilitate his religious commitment, should that be his inclination or desire. Within this perspective, then, were the analyst to insert his or her preconceived ideas or attitudes toward religion into the interaction with the patient – whether negative, agnostic, or atheistic, or on the other hand positive, believing, and religiously oriented – this would have to be regarded as a form of countertransference acting out. Analysts of an earlier era who would have taken it on themselves to disabuse the patient of his naïve and infantile religious beliefs would have certainly been subject to this indictment.

I will present an analytic case in which some of these issues found expression within the analysis. Hopefully, discussion of the analytic expression of these issues as they arose in the analytic process and as they were responded to by the analyst,

[2] The argument is far more complex than I am indicating here. See my further discussion of these issues in Meissner (1992, 1996a).

can further illumine the manner in which changing views of the nature and meaning of religious beliefs can find expression within the analytic process itself.

The Analysand

First, let me tell you something about this patient. When he first contacted me, he was engaged in a psychological Ph.D. training program. He had completed his master's degree in clinical psychology and was continuing his graduate studies, working toward a Ph.D. in clinical psychology. He sought analytic treatment on the advice and urging of his clinical mentors, on the presumption that an effective analysis would help him overcome some of the inhibitions, conflicts and character problems that seemed to limit his effectiveness in doing psychotherapy. He also had long had a personal interest in psychoanalysis, had read a fair amount of analytic literature, and was strongly motivated to undertake an analysis.

Carl, as I will call him, was the youngest son in a comparatively well-to-do family in which there were two older brothers, one older sister, and a younger sister. His relation with his siblings was benign if somewhat distant. One brother was a physician who practiced in their home town, another was a successful businessman; the older sister was happily married, but the younger sister less happily so, constantly complaining to their mother and sometimes to my patient about her rather ineffectual husband. Carl had developed an interest in psychology from his teenage years, and had read widely in psychoanalysis. He ambitioned a position as a prestigious psychologist and professor at some famous American university. It was these ambitions that had drawn him to Boston, where he imagined such institutions and opportunities abounded.

Carl portrayed himself as a miserable, unhappy, fearful, even terrorized child. The cause of this unhappiness was his father. The father was a minor official in a small provincial Southern town, and as such was generally accorded respect and status in the community. But he was not a popular figure since he tended to be harsh and judgmental in many of his public actions. At home he was a terror. The relationship between Carl's father and mother was a disaster. The father had a drinking problem, and typically would arrive home late in the evening, after a bout of drinking at a local bar. He would be drunk and belligerent, shouting and throwing things, even breaking furniture. His rage was directed primarily at his wife toward whom he directed his abuse – both verbally in the most insulting, demeaning and obscene terms, and physically, at times hitting her and beating her. This scenario was repeated countless times over the course of Carl's growing up. He recounted episodes, especially when he was quite young, when he and his mother would hear the father coming and run out of the house to escape the assault, staying out of the house for hours until the father would finally quiet down and fall asleep. On other occasions, he recalled episodes in which his mother would run out of the house and disappear, while he quivered in fear and terror in his bed, listening to his father's raging. He did not know where his mother had gone, did not know whether she would return, and felt terrorized, vulnerable, lying in paralyzed fear of his father's rage and with a sense of abandonment and loss of the protective presence of his mother.

Needless to say, there was not much positive in what Carl had to say about his father. The prevailing affects were hatred, repulsion, studied and defensive indifference, and at times an intense denial of any meaningful relationship with his father. The picture was not totally negative: reluctantly and in somewhat fragmented fashion he would grudgingly acknowledge a certain amount of admiration and envy of his father's strength and power to dominate and terrorize others, qualities he secretly wished for himself but vigorously repressed and denied. Positive elements were even harder to come by. There were rare occasions when the father had engaged him in some positive nonthreatening way – once the father took him to the movies, on another occasion they went to the beach together. These stood out as exceptions to the dominant themes of hatred and rejection.

On other occasions, Carl had expected severe punishment from the father for some minor transgression, but the father had reacted with benign understanding – as when Carl had dropped and broken the father's favorite drinking mug. Carl had expected an enraged beating, but the father only smiled and treated it as an unintended accident. In any case, the prevailing portrait of the father was of a vindictive, rageful, demanding, and punitive tyrant. The father was demanding of both wife and children. For example, he had certain preferences for special dishes to be prepared according to his wishes. If such a dish were not up to his expectations, he would hurl the dish on the floor and storm out of the room, leaving his wife to clean up the mess. Other examples abounded, quite enough to substantiate Carl's childhood fears and the antipathy and fear he felt toward his father.

His mother provided the opposite side to this coin. She demonstrated the opposite masochistic counterpoint to the father's sadistic brutality and imperious demandingness. She was portrayed by Carl as long-suffering and patient, undemanding and self-sacrificing, especially for her children. In his position as the youngest son, Carl felt himself to be his mother's favorite child. In the face of the threat and terror in relation to his father, he clung desperately to his dependence on his mother, not only as the only stable and reliable figure in his environment, but as though his very life depended on maintaining his position as her special and favored child. This pattern prevailed not only throughout his childhood, but persisted well into his adult years and became a central issue in the course of his analysis. As might be expected, his school experience was marked by a rather severe early period of school phobia in which any device that would enable him to avoid going to school and allow him to stay home with his mother was brought into play. This pattern was only broken by his being sent to a regional high school where he had to struggle with separation from his mother and rather severe bouts of homesickness.

The impress of these strongly etched parental figures on Carl's development was marked. The predominant configuration in his character was reflective of his identification with his mother. From this perspective he presented himself as self-effacing, submissive, obsequious, undemanding, and self-devaluing. From this perspective his typical stance was somewhat depressive and reflective of diminished and readily deflated self-esteem. Although he was the oldest and most advanced member of his seminar group, he saw himself as knowing less than the others, not measuring up, constantly seeking the approval of his mentors and instructors – clearly reflecting the model of his position as his mother's favorite son.

In contrast to this self-depleting and self-diminishing posture, the opposite side of his personality came to light only gradually and reluctantly, that is the side deriving from identification with his hated and rejected father. There were early indicators in which he would attempt to adopt the father's imperious ways with his mother, demanding certain special treatment and favors from her. One telling incident brought these elements into dramatic focus. One hot day he came home from school feeling thirsty. He found his mother working in her vegetable garden and demanded that she get him something to drink. She asked him to wait a minute until she had finished howing one section. He became enraged, and like a smaller replica of his father started tearing up the plants in a fit of pique and rage. His mother stood back without interfering while this temper tantrum ran its course – we speculated later whether she may have taken some pleasure in this performance of dominance and self-assertion so clearly cast in the mold of his father.

Other revealing episodes came to light during the analysis, particularly in relation to his interactions with his clients and with his wife. With his clients he expected them to conform to his expectations and to respond positively and appreciatively to his interventions. When they did not, he would become coldly indifferent and distanced, or would respond angrily, blaming them for not measuring up to his demands. He felt he was being measured and judged according to the performance of his clients, so that their failure to measure up to his demands meant that he would be judged poorly and thus lose any chance to become the favored student of his teachers. In relation to his wife, the same issues played themselves out. When he came home, the self-effacing and meek mouse of a man would close the front door and be instantly transformed into a frightening tiger. He was demanding, expecting dinner to be on the table waiting for him, expecting his wife to prepare certain dishes according to his wishes, and so on. He tended to treat her in a demanding and devaluing manner, reflecting the devaluing attitude toward women prevailing in his Southern culture which he had witnessed being enacted by his father on countless occasions. If he were not satisfied, he would become enraged, sometimes break dishes and even stomp out of the house and eat at a MacDonald's. At other times, he would storm out of the dining room and sulk in his study for the rest of the evening.

The problem, of course, was that his wife refused to accept such high-handed treatment and protested vigorously. She would not retreat into the submissive and accepting posture of his mother and this resulted in a fair degree of marital turmoil. Like his father, he would rage at her and insult her with obscene epithets, and a few times even hit her. These episodes were followed by paroxysms of regret, guilt, and self-accusation, all the more so in that they brought home to him the extent to which he had become a replica of his father, especially those aspects of the father that he so hated and rejected. The realization of the strength and degree of identification with his father was severely disturbing and painful for him, and puzzling in the extreme since he so detested and condemned the same behavior as he had known it in his father. To have to acknowledge the same behavior in himself was perplexing and seemingly contradictory to his conscious sense of himself and to his ego ideal.

All this took place in a context heavily overburdened with religious implications. As might be anticipated, the father was agnostic and irreligious. During Carl's childhood and during most of adult life the father had nothing to do with religion and never went to church. In his final years, however, he had been forced to retire because of the inroads of his alcoholism, and his health became failing and fragile. Under such circumstances he became increasingly physically dependent on his wife and more subject to her influence.

In contrast, she had always been a devout religious believer and was intensely devoted to religious practices. As Carl recounted, she would regularly arise early in the morning and spend the first few hours meditating and praying. She would then prepare the family breakfast and then go to church. This was a daily routine in addition to which she spent many hours reading and reflecting on the Bible. When Carl was younger, she would frequently take him with her to church. She constantly encouraged him to pray and read the Bible and to do good works. He tried to emulate her religious fervor, but without much success. He did not like church and found it boring. He did not know how to pray and did not understand why anyone would want to pray. Stirring in this brew, there were more subtle and largely unacknowledged components reflecting his identification with his antireligious father caught up in conflictual irresolution with his desires to please his mother and remain in her favor by measuring up to her religious ideals.

An interesting twist to the story is that the father, in his terminal condition of depleted health and dependence, became more interested in and accepting of religion. He would accompany his wife to church, and became softer and more forgiving in his attitudes. Carl marveled at this transformation, attributing it to the power of his mother's influence that was neither dominating nor forceful, but finally won out in the end, converting the father to accepting and adopting her view of life and the meaning of religion. The effect on Carl, as we shall see, was to mitigate his antireligious tendencies and to reinforce his conviction that the road to salvation lie along the mother's path, thus confirming the importance of remaining in her good graces, maintaining his position as her favorite, specifically in terms of aligning himself with her religious convictions and ideals.

The Analysis

The analysis began more or less conventionally. Carl seemed to take to the couch easily and had no difficulty in expressing himself. There was even so a palpable degree of anxiety and an apparent desire to please the analyst and measure up to his own image of what was expected of a good analytic patient. The role of transference was thus evident from the very beginning of the analysis, probably reflecting a fair degree of transference anticipation even before the analysis began. The transference continued to deepen as the analytic process developed – these transference components would emerge in relation to his religious concerns and can be considered more economically in that context.

Religious Concerns and Conflicts

His religious interests and concerns began to emerge only after the first few months of analysis, when it seems that he had become comfortable enough to bring them up. By that time he had become aware that I was a Jesuit priest and was uncertain whether I would reflect the same model of orthodoxy and religious severity that he had associated with Jesuits in his own Southern Baptist religious upbringing. His first mention of his interest in religious matters came after about 6 months when he expressed his wish to take some courses at the Harvard Divinity School. He talked about his longstanding interest in religion and his wish to deepen his involvement in the church. His comment was revealing:

> I feel inferior and behind in everything, but a lot less than I used to feel. But I keep comparing myself. I wonder if my interest in the Divinity School is just to impress people or whether it's a genuine interest. I want to know more about God like I want to know more about my father. I don't feel connected with God: that's the way I felt with my father. I never felt I had father. I envy people who have good relationship with their fathers.

While earlier analytic attitudes might have viewed this admission as fertile ground for neurotic enactments, a more accepting orientation would regard this as an important and legitimate area of his life experience and would seek to know more about the meaning of these involvements and their underlying motivation. The analyst would hear this expression of interest non-judgmentally, as simply no more than an interesting fact about the patient's life. At the same time Carl was pointing directly to the relation between his image of God and that of his father. The yearning to know God is thus connected with the frustrated yearning to know his father better in the hope of finding the father of his frustrated and denied hopes. These first glimmerings of the connection between his view of God and his father were fertile material for further exploration and inquiry as the analysis progressed.

This line of thought seemed to reflect deeper concerns. As he expressed it:

> I want to strike roots. I'm looking for connections. [Do you have any thoughts about your turning to religion? (This response was intended as nonjudgmental and oriented toward advancing the inquiry. Does he have any further thoughts about his appeal to religion? In fact, he did.)][3] I know you're a priest, but don't know if that influences me. I was always interested in religion, but I was always scared to get close to it. Religion is related to feelings about death – they're constantly there but I avoid them. I have a fear of thinking about religion and God and death. I live on the surface: religion could be source of strength, but makes me feel tense and awkward and anxious. I just peak in the door and then run away. I

[3] In these quotations, comments by the analyst will be enclosed in brackets [...]. Similarly additional explanatory comments will be enclosed in parentheses (...).

don't want to face death, but I don't want to live on the surface either. I guess it's progress that now I can at least look at the door and even look inside. [Your mother is the religious one in family? (This was the analyst's first move in the direction of opening the door to possible transference implications of his religious adherence.)] My father was opposed to her going to church, but later he used go with her. Before he died, he even went on his own. That was important for her: she believes he went to heaven. My mother was always a central figure in church and was an Elder. My father was only on the edge when he died: he never read the Bible. I want to get inside and belong; I'm tired of being on the periphery.

This can be heard as a profoundly meaningful expression of his religious concerns, together with clear suggestions of the transferential overlay relating these concerns to conflicts arising from opposing religious orientations and convictions of both parents. The question is – what motivations underlie these respective religious configurations and what do they have to do with transference determinants?

Soon after he continued:

I'm questioning my religious commitment. I want to change my constantly comparing myself with others. It creates a constant pressure to do better. And I worry about everyone's feelings about me. I'm so self-conscious. I want more self-content. I feel foolish and stupid, and I don't appreciate what I have. I'm constantly looking for credit, waiting for an invitation on a silver platter. I shouldn't expect be the favorite all the time. [What makes that so important? (The issue, of course, is his narcissism which plays a dominant role in his self-feeling and his behavior, including especially his religious behavior.)] If I'm not the favorite I don't have anything to give, but give me some credit then I can function, especially with authority figures. I feel far below them and small. It's like a magic ball: if I have it I can do anything, but without it nothing. [How come so much depends on such slight input?] I always feel I'm not as good or don't know as much as others. I'm not as pure, not as good, as I want to be.

He continued to express his doubts:

I'm not sure about prayer. [How do you mean?] It feels like a cloud between me and God. It affects my believing in prayer: it feels dark and gloomy and fearful. I feel anger and want to rebel. That feels like the other side of my fear: I'm afraid of judgment. That's scary – no way to hide. I still hold a grudge, and I don't acknowledge His existence fully. I'm passive–aggressive. That makes me wonder about faith, and makes me feel vulnerable. My relations to you and God are difficult: I wish the steps toward God were clearer. [Are you waiting for Him to acknowledge you? (The question has a point – that he was always waiting for some acknowledgement from his father.)] I want to be sure He acknowledges my existence and importance: that's so much in my father's image. It isn't clear how important I am to my mother, but with my father it's dark and cloudy. His judgment was that I was a bad boy. [It sounds like any judgment means something bad for you?] I'm not going share that with you. I'm stubborn; if you want it you'll have to get it. But what can you do? (My pen drops.) I'm looking for signs that you're inattentive: that puts me in a dilemma with you and God. With the pastor I can hold a grudge; but when I apply that to you and God it seems silly. I still look for clues to justify my withholding.

The father transference is at this point dominant, and is applied to both God and the analyst. The problem for the religious patient is whether there is a God who has religious meaning and relevance beyond the transference images.

At the same time, other elements were stirring that pointed in the direction of a more maternal component of his image of God. As he commented: "I have some magical wish, that God will protect me and help me with my life. [Do you want to make a deal with God?] More like a bargain: I'd become God's special favorite, and I'd have a sense of participating in God's world." The motif of being the special favorite in relation to God echoed the same theme in relation to his mother. Being her favorite son and the beneficiary of her favors and privileged treatment were cornerstones of his self-image and the adherent ties of dependency on his mother. It is hardly surprising that these heavily invested narcissistic fantasies were transferred wholesale to his fantasied and wish-impregnated imagery of God. His portrayal of God in colors reminiscent of his mother was reflected in his wishes to be passively given to and taken care of by God. As he reflected on his place in the church: "I expect others to lead me and give me a special place. I wait passively and keep outside: I want to be called in ... [It seems you want things to be given to you on a silver platter? (The silver platter was his imagery.)] That's right: the pattern is striking ... The worst situation is when the pastor asks me to lead prayers. [What details?] I get almost phobic: attention is on me and I'm on center stage. I'm afraid of making a mistake. I feel weak in my faith."

Not long after, he continued:

> I want to pray more too. [Those are all things your mother would approve?] That's true, but for whom am I doing it? It perpetuates my bond with my mother. [Also wouldn't it be opposite to what your father did?] My mother would be very happy to hear this. But it's really my decision; she isn't part of it. But it turns out to be what she'd approve of. [Funny thing about that?] All my brothers and sisters are regular churchgoers. My mother's influence is powerful; I tried to get away from it but now I surrender. I commit myself to religion: it's a way to discipline myself and my wild inner self. [Is that the part of you like your father?] Yes, he was rough and a boxer and brilliant. [So you feel suffocated and want run from your mother's influence, but then you turn around and embrace what she'd approve?] I'm trying be a nice boy, but I want to be different. I have to be compliant – I'll settle for that.

And somewhat later he reflected: "I'm afraid God will forget and abandon me, and I'll be left in darkness. I want God to lift me up. Why does He put me through all this? Why doesn't he lift me to heaven and give me credit? Then I'd be sure God loves me – I knew my mother loved me because she gave me favors." This seems to suggest how extensively his religious concerns and commitments were motivated by his pervasive desire to be the favorite in his mother's eyes and to behave in ways that would win her approval. The question, however, remained whether and to what extent there was any real religious investment here – if his dependence on his mother and his wish to please her were withdrawn or mitigated, what would be left of his religious investment? Embracing God in these terms as dictated by his maternal transference was as much a distortion in his religious outlook as was his antipathy and rebellious attitude toward God that reflected his father transference. Ultimately, the God of authentic religious belief is not a transference figure.

He was not slow to express his religious concerns and conflicts. Early in the analysis he observed:

> I have religious concerns: I want to commit myself to Christ; I want to have more faith and be born again, But there's a struggle in my mind, I'm not comfortable about faith. I never really believed, but I still go to church. At times I find consolation and strength in church, but going to church tires me out. We spend all day Sunday at church, and that

> leaves no time for my work. (His church was a minor Baptist sect in which long services and other church related activities kept the members occupied for most of the day on Sundays.) [You mentioned a struggle?] I have wish to give myself up, to surrender to God and God's will. It's painful process to be a good believer. I just have to work at it and read the Bible more.

At the same time, he complained that he could not afford the time for Bible study. There was a realistic dimension to this complaint, since the demands on his time were considerable, but there was also an element of protest against the demands of his religious commitment – even religion did not come easily and without demands for effort and work. At one point, the smoldering ambivalence and resentment flared forth:

> I thought about looking at the Bible and Playboy. I was on the toilet shitting: that requires time and I have to do it every day. But I have unconscious motives: it's a smelly place. I shit on the Bible and women. I feel a deep anger, more primitive and like rage, against God and women. They represent sexuality. [Like you have to decide between the Bible and Playboy, like opposite sides of your mother?] Or my mother vs. my father: both sides in conflict. In my mother the religious side dominates: one side would kill the other rather than grow together. [Was it that you tried to follow that pattern?] I think of the Bible and rebelling against God. I don't give a shit; that's covered by my compliant behavior and reading the Bible, but I have so many raw feelings.

The faith question was obviously contaminated with issues related to his subservient, submissive, unquestioning and blind faith as an aspect of his characterological stance more generally. But underneath, functioning at an unconscious and largely repressed level, his compliance was accompanied by a defiant rebelliousness and rejection of everything that was built into his complaint submissiveness and self-depletion. The rage and destructiveness of these feelings were more than his conscious mind and espoused self ideal could handle. The effort to repress them was only partially successful, so that under the induced regression and permissiveness of the analytic situation the resistance to them was weakened and they found a way to burst forth into the open. The analyst does not condemn the patient's faith altogether as an expression of neurotic motives, as earlier areligious approaches might, but he does recognize that the patient's faith has become permeated with a variety of both narcissistic and authoritarian conflicts and motives that will require analytic scrutiny and understanding. The analyst is as concerned and interested in the motives lying behind Carl's complaint and accommodating behavior as he is in the motives contributing to his defiant resistance and rebelliousness at so many level of his involvement with others.

These underlying conflicts came to a dramatic focus in his clinical work. At one point, he was referred a clergyman as a client. He commented:

> I was referred a minister: he's a pastor but has a lot of conflicts over religion, similar to my conflicts. I'm not sure whether I'm the right one to treat him. He's close to God and the church. [Your conflicts about religion haven't come up much here? (Carl had been avoiding the issue for some time. The question seeks to open the door to further exploration of his religious issues, indicating once again that they are welcome and legitimate issues for analytic consideration.)] I've gone to church all my life, but I never read the whole Bible. I don't know much about it: I have vague ideas about God. I just accept it all on faith. [You

> have no questions? (The analyst here is probing his unquestioning and submissive stance.)] Faith is vital, but what is it? I take it for granted if I don't think about it. But if I think about it, I start rebelling and doubting. Then I offer myself as a believer in Him: that's faith rather than psychology of faith. Christ died and was resurrected, living God. [Am I going to get a lecture in theology? (The analyst is less interested in theorizing about religion than in hearing about the patient's actual; experience.)] That's part of my struggle; it's never clear what I'm supposed to believe. [Supposed to or do believe? (Driving the point home.)] What God do I believe in? I feel so unfocused, like we're missing each other. God is up there and everywhere but I'm down here: we don't meet face-to-face. My father was too far away and my mother too close. I don't know where God is, but why do I believe in him? Why is faith necessary?

On another occasion, he commented:

> I don't know how to describe my feelings: I have different feelings about myself. The pastor preached yesterday about grace and rebirth. I am more patient with my wife and son. I believe in God because I'm weak and humble. I'm happy that I have religion, but I want to keep that private. I'm not sure of my image of God. I think of God as Michelangelo drew Him. But I feel tense in church and try to hide myself. I ran away from Him and felt fear. [How do you mean?] It was parallel with my relation to my father; it was rebellion against my mother too. I was never comfortable in church. [Were you afraid of God? (The analyst is interested in knowing more about what God means to him.)] It seems God didn't want to have anything to do with me. And I didn't want to have anything to do with Him – a distant feeling. [Like with your father? (Picking up on the patient's own statement.)] My fear comes up readily with any authority figures. It was a hidden rebellion against my father. At times I felt very disconnected and looked down on people who went to church. My father never went to church except for few months before he died: he despised churchgoers.

The lines between his judgmental, distant, violent and punitive father and the image of God as fearful, judgmental, and punitive were becoming clearer. A freudian approach to this material would regard it as fundamentally neurotic and would direct its effort to eliminating it completely – the patient would be better off, so it might say, without any religion at all. An alternate approach would view this material as expressing the neurotic distortions in the patient's understanding of God and would direct its efforts to modifying the neurotic influences on the patient's view of God, especially those related to identifiable transferential distortions coming primarily from internalizations of parental figures, and secondarily from other sources of such introjective content. Once freed from such neurotic influences – to whatever degree possible – the patient is more autonomously and relatively more freely able to come to his own understanding of God and His meaning in his personal life.

On another level, his relation to God was permeated with guilt and shame. This focused primarily on his sexual impulses, desires and behavior. As he put it:

> It feels like a stain. If I don't get enough credit it confirms my feeling that I'm bad, like original sin. I try to hide. I pray to God but it doesn't feel real (...) If I had to face God, I'd feel some guilt and sin. I would try to run and hide, and then I'd feel deserted. [What do you imagine God would feel?] I think he'd forget me. I'd prefer that; otherwise I'd have to show the real me. He'd ask if I'd done good things so I could go to heaven rather than hell. I think I'd ask for special credits because I was my mother's favorite; otherwise I wouldn't pass. [You have an interesting God: who is He? (This is equivalently a transference interpretation.)] I don't know, He's a judgmental figure and authoritarian and powerful.

And again: "My image of God parallels my attitudes to older people and my supervisors and you. I want to be pleasing to God, to be faithful and loyal, but I tend to hide. I'm still seeking my mother's favor but I run away and hide from God. I'm afraid of being picked out and found not good enough. I feel shameful about myself: He wouldn't accept me. He's glorious and holy and I'm spoiled. I have to confess my sins. I'm afraid of being thrown out, not deserving attention or favor."

I would call attention to the idea that the religiously-oriented analyst does not question or challenge the patient's belief in God which is inherently part of the patient's belief system. Nor does he do anything to induce, endorse, or promote the patient's religious attitudes. But the analyst does seek to explore, illumine, understand, and interpret the attributes and attitudes toward God that the patient contributes out his own psychic reality, and to identify them in relation to specific projective aspects on the patient's own inner world rather than as attributes of the real Godhead.[4] Here the issue for analysis is not whether there is or isn't a God existing beyond the patient's imagination, but what human attributes does the patient contribute to his God-representation and what are their sources and what motivates the patient's use of them to represent his God. His God at this point is painted largely in colors deriving from his father transference.

Prominent on his list of sins were his occasional visits to prostitutes and his wishes to have his wife perform fellatio on him. In regard to the fellatio, he felt he was forcing her to do this to please him against her wishes, so that it brought into focus all his tendencies to want to dominate, force her to do his will, to have her submit passively and compliantly to his demands, and so on. He commented: "I'm thinking of oral sex: it's stimulating and exciting for both of us, but it has a nauseous and dirty quality. It's repulsive; how can I do that? I have guilt feelings about it. It started after we saw *Deep Throat*, but it does help with my with premature ejaculation. I'm glad when it's over, but oral sex isn't OK for God or my mother." Behind this superego figure of his puritanical and disapproving mother, there lurked the image of his father who was so flagrantly sexual in his behavior, had extramarital affairs with a number of women, and even carried on a liaison with the housemaid for years right under his mother's nose.

This was another area in which his resemblance to his father was distressing and made him realize the extent to which he had identified with him. He pondered:

> How can I deal with these pleasant things? Can I give them up for God? I feel devilish. [How do you mean?] That's associated with sex, but not intercourse. Not all sex is unacceptable to God, excluding foreplay and oral sex, and if there's no manipulation. [How did you conclude that?] That's how my mother felt. It's hard to imagine that my mother had intercourse with my father, but they had eight children. I can't believe she did anything to increase his pleasure though; it was merely mechanical. [So in your view any pleasure would be sinful?] That's how I feel: only sex without pleasure is acceptable to God.

The effort to preserve an image of his mother as pure, innocent, and asexual seems apparent. But when faced with the undeniable reality, he rationalized by

[4] An important empirical study of the role of primarily parental transference images in the development and formation of the God-representation is provided in Rizzuto (1979).

distinguishing between sex-with-pleasure and sex-without-pleasure – the latter would apply to his mother and would allow her to remain sinless and close to God. Sex-with-pleasure belonged to his father who was thereby steeped in sin and rejected by God. But the conflict remained – could he surrender the pleasure like his mother, or was he basically sinful and evil since he had the same impulses and desires as his father. How could he be God's favorite if such were the case?

Along similar lines, he reflected on his mother's influence on his own religious views. She had written an autobiography at the request of the pastor, on which he commented:

> I read my mother's autobiography that she wrote for the church. Her story is very emotional, especially her agony and pain with my father. It's so vivid: how she wanted to leave so many times. I felt respect and admiration for her: she had a lot of courage, which she attributes to God's grace. Reading that my religious faith deepened. I have a special relation with her, but something in me tries to destroy that. But she's much stronger than me. [Do you have something destructive in mind?] I'm lazy and evil: that's related to my anger and anxiety and sex. Sex is something destructive. I'm not sure what I mean. I have an image of my penis: it gets small after intercourse and shrunken, like a little piglet, powerless.

And again: "I think about reading the Bible and God, but I feel blocked. I'm connected with religion through my mother, but I struggle and feel constant tension and anxiety. Why do I go church? I have rescue fantasies and magical wishes. I like going to church. That's how I look at God: I expect to be rescued." And at another point he added:

> Now I have feelings of submission and commitment to God. That makes me feel more at peace and relaxed, but I wonder about it. I'm trying to make the seed grow, but what is my motivation behind that? I don't have feeling of running away any more, but I need to understand man's relation to God (...) When I talk about religion, it takes the edge off my feelings and conflicts. [Is it also related to standing better in your mother's eyes?] Yes, that's what I want!

As the analysis progressed, he became increasingly aware of and caught up in the tension between the polarized identifications between his mother and his father. He commented:

> I thought about feeling awkward. We had a family prayer service, and I felt awkward standing before God. I want to be healthy and wholesome, but I feel conflicted. I'm easily drawn to the other side, and start looking awkward. It's easier not to look: I have feelings related to aggression and greed that I shy away from. I feel like I'm exposed to too much violence; so I shy away but eventually act out. It's a struggle between the two images: my father and my mother. wholesome vs. violent, life vs. death. But I don't want to be like my mother or my father: they're extremes. I rebel against being like my mother and don't want be like my father. But I can't find my own position.

Comments like this made much clearer the extent to which his religious involvement was caught up in the travails of his identifications with both parents, and how any effective resolution of his religious conflicts depended on the extent to which he could find his own footing in a more authentic, autonomous, and adaptive involvement not only in religion, but in his involvements more generally in his life and relationships.

On occasion he would ponder on his relation with God and what it meant. He mused:

> My faith is part of me. I'm a religious person, but I question how much God knows and loves me. I communicate through praying and reading the Bible. It's like here: how much connection do I have with you? But where and how would I meet Him? I'm also tired of His presence: I want to rebel and lead my own life. After all, where is He? It feels like dealing with the unconscious. The church was always my mother's church. [Not God's church? (This amounts to an interpretation – the question hinges on a distinction between his image of his mother and his image of God. If God is different and separate, what and who is God if not cast in the image of his mother or father?)] I still feel anxious and intimidated in church: God is there but He doesn't want to see me. He represents my father. [You wonder how much He knows and loves you? (The analyst seeks to expand the implications of his view of God in the image of his father. His shift to a father-model comes after some weakening in his view of God in the image of his mother. If God is not a reflection of his mother, Carl turns to the image of his father.)] Does he remember and recognize me as one of millions of believers? I'm convinced that he does, but I shadowbox with God too. I put my own colors into Him. God is there to accept and love and restore me. [Does that sound like your mother?] She's too weak: she can't bring me up, so she and I have to turn to God. But I also want to destroy the image of God: that comes from my feelings to my father. I distrust him, like I don't need you. I want to stand on my own. How much does He remember and think of me? [You have the same questions about me and your father?] You only know me when I'm here; otherwise you forget me. You and God and my father don't care about me. My mother cares. I need reconciliation, but I don't feel I'm good enough.

Late in the analysis, it became clearer that the more positive aspects of his attitudes and feelings toward God were gaining an edge over the negative ones. As he noted:

> I have good feelings about my relation with Christ and God. I'm feeling more convinced that He loves me. It's striking how I put all that negative stuff out of my mind. The other side is more alive and sunny and happy and carefree, not ashamed and hiding. It's like a dark and secret and scared side vs. the light. [I wonder what prevents you from accepting good opinions and feelings? (The analyst tries to broaden the implications of this shift in attitude, namely that it reflects a more general tendency to self-devalue and assume the negative.)] I always assume bad and critical opinions.

The critical question in this shift toward a more positive view of God is whether it reflects a more mature and adaptive approach as opposed to whether remnants of his infantile attachment to his mother are still at work.

The analyst would not take any satisfaction if these transferential elements had not been effectively modified. This issue crystallizes a point that never seemed to occur to Freud, and played little or no role in the attitudes of earlier analysts biased against any form of religion, namely the possibility of religious belief and adherence that was mature, realistic, adaptive and relatively autonomous. One goal of the analysis is the attainment of a more mature and autonomous stance in the patient's life and interpersonal involvements more generally. To the extent that religious issues constitute a meaningful aspect of the patient's life adjustment, one possible and important outcome is a greater degree of autonomy and maturity with regard to the patient's religious beliefs and praxis and the elimination or minimization of the infantile dependence and unrealistic wishful fantasies that may attend the patient's religious orientation.

Toward the end of the analysis, thoughts of losing me as his analyst also stirred thoughts about losing his mother. He observed:

> My mother is getting old: she will leave me rather than my leaving her (...) I would miss her. She was the only one in the world for me. My world was pitch dark; until I die she is the one and only special person for me. I'm in love with her. I imagine being with her in heaven and continuing our relation. My father still remains a stranger (...) It will be sad to lose my mother, but religion gives me hope and comfort. I'll have to leave you in time. I don't want to depend on you; I want to move on and be on my own. [Any thoughts about that?] I never have been on my own. I've always been self-conscious and intimidated and envying.

From the perspective of the analytic process, important chords are being struck here. The thought of losing his mother is saddening but not devastating, as it would certainly have been earlier – even without her he can now go on his own. Religion has taken on a supportive and consoling function, looking forward to the prospect of a heavenly reunion with his mother – a reunion that equivalently eliminates the father. This seems to be a heavily narcissistic vision of heaven beyond or without oedipal complexities or conflicts that would satisfy all his preoedipal narcissistic wishes and fantasies. If the fantasy can be displaced to the heavenly realm, the result may be to effectively resolve the conflicts on the level of worldly involvement by substituting the promise of heavenly satisfaction. On these terms, he can cast off the threatening and terrorizing influence of his father and allow for at least some degree of declaration of independence and autonomous self-reliance. At the same time, the intensity and desperate quality of his clinging dependence on his mother and his need to remain in her good graces and favor can give way in this-worldly terms to a greater sense of his own independence and responsibility for himself and his life. The loss is thus compensated by the fantasy of eternal heavenly bliss and reunion with his mother. Thus losing her looms less as a crisis and catastrophe than an occasion for sadness and mourning, and a sense of loss that is redeemed in terms of a hoped for reunion in heaven. Is this pie-in-the-sky neuroticism run wild, as the freudian view might say, or is it a reflection of the power of religious belief to sustain the believer in the face of the painful struggles and losses of human existence?[5]

---

5 The difference here can be articulated more clearly in terms of the contrast between Freud's view of illusion as neurotically determined and Winnicott's view of illusion as a transitional area of human experience that has important adaptive and life sustaining effects. The issue here is that infantile wishes and fantasies cannot be completely eliminated, but can be effectively moderated to play a diminished and even minor role in the patient's psychic economy – perhaps effected by displacement or substitution of ultimate satisfaction in heavenly terms. In Winnicott's terms, the partial satisfaction of life-sustaining desires in and through the transitional satisfactions of illusion are viewed as self-sustaining rather than as neurotically destructive. The dynamic here is also consistent with the loss complex as described in Rochlin (1965) in which the capacity to sustain and mourn loss is followed by restitutive effort and functioning in a more mature and adaptive response to psychic loss. See my more extended discussion of these issues and differentiations in Meissner (1984).

Church-Related Issues

Throughout the analysis, he maintained an active and continuous involvement in church activities, participating in various church activities and holding important positions among the church members. He was appointed a deacon and was asked at times to lead the congregation in prayer. And for an extended period he functioned as church treasurer. Consequently, he was rather closely involved in dealing with the pastor on several levels. In this context, his basic narcissistic and authority-related conflicts came into play. The pastor was the primary authority and many of my patient's conflicts were focused around the figure of the pastor and his problematic behavior. Needless to say, these vicissitudes had a powerful impact on Carl's religious struggles.

He struggled to be faithful and devoted to the church and its support. The wish was contaminated by his feelings regarding the pastor:

> I have religious interests. I give $70-a-week to church, and I want to increase it to $100. That's my offering to God, but I feel pressure of the amount. I could manage more but I feel ambivalent. The pastor is critical and controlling and narcissistic; that makes it hard to like him. My feelings to you are friendly: you're more humorous and relaxed. The pastor is just the opposite – he's tense and rigid and like an ego-maniac. Paying the tithe makes me feel like a man, but I still get anxious (...) Accepting my money means accepting me. The amount is substantial but I manage; it fits naturally into my life style. I hope if I make more I can offer more.

In fact, the church and related activities served as one of the main outlets for social engagement for himself and his family. His wife was also deeply involved in and devoted to church activities. Even so, he complained that he often felt tense and anxious in church. He thought of himself as older and different from others, and as a Ph.D. he expected respect and felt entitled to recognition and acceptance form others. As he said: "I have a nagging sense that I'm a Ph.D. psychologist and older and entitled to respect. I cling to a sense of superiority. I want them to acknowledge me, but I feel conflicted because I also want to be accepted as a person. I lose confidence in my ability and competence. I'm so easily affected by others opinions." And again: "I'm thinking about the Bible study group. I've done that for several years, but I start feeling old among those college kids. [How do you mean?] I'm the oldest deacon except for one woman. The new pastor is younger and prefers younger deacons. I resent that and feel jealous; I feel like I've been pushed aside. I used be the youngest. But now I don't feel appreciated: old feelings – who gets more love? It's a jealous competition: with the pastor I feel defeated and not good enough."

After I commented that in any of his relationships he always seemed to get caught up in issues of being special and the favorite, he added: "Even with the pastor I notice with whom he sits and talks: does he enjoy them? Am I the favorite among the deacons? Do other deacons have more trust? That puts me back: I feel easily replaced." Although a deacon, he clearly ambitioned the higher position of elder, the highest position in the church open to laymen. His brother at home had become an elder, and my patient felt that this meant that the brother had in some degree displaced him as the most favored in his mother's eyes. Becoming an elder would redeem him and regain his position as his mother's favorite. Finding favor in the pastor's eyes was closely paralleled by similar infantile wishes related to his mother. Faced with such an anxiety-provoking threat, he complained:

> If I don't perform my duties, the pastor becomes punitive and rejecting – any slight failure makes me feel I'm not good enough for him. That's a familiar feeling: I lose my favored position. I feel knocked off my throne: I felt the Reverend has replaced me as his favorite. But I was number one. I was greedy and possessive, a spoiled brat; like in tearing up my mother's garden. She promoted that, but my father was still king. My position is vulnerable and easily shaken.

These feelings were no different than his feelings in any other social situation, but it is noteworthy that they invaded his church-related connections. Even in relation with the pastor, he clung to his infantile and narcissistically invested childhood demands for special consideration and treatment – when he went to church, it seemed that he took his neurosis with him.

Some of these conflicts found expression in dreams. For example: "I had a dream. I was in a church: it looked like a Catholic Church. There was a huge congregation, and people were festive. But I felt frustrated that I couldn't participate. Then the Pope passed through. I felt like I was just mimicking the others' behavior, clapping etc. I felt anxious." He commented:

> I felt self-conscious: I couldn't be part of the crowd. We had special services at church over the weekend. I felt resistant and didn't want to go; I didn't feel I could participate. [Like in your dream?] I'm ambivalent to the Reverend: I resent him, and want to protest and rebel. His preaching is ridiculous, angry and shouting. And he never appoints me to any important tasks. But what have I done to gain his trust? [Is it possible that you communicate your ambivalence?] Clearly I do. I respect him but I don't like him: he's too intense and angry. He thinks he's the only one right. [Any connection with your dream?] I couldn't participate. [And you were in a different church?] I'm think of quitting church and going to another church. But the rebellion is from me. I want to feel the Reverend is the problem and my resentment is valid; that creates a dilemma.

The analyst is attuned here to the transference reverberations in relation to both the pastor and to the analyst – the transference paradigm seems to be the same in both. While the extra-analytic church-related context provides a testing ground for enactment of these elements, it may turn out that the therapeutic modification of these transference determinants may have to be worked out and through within the analysis and in relation to the analyst.

His resistant and rebellious feelings in relation to the pastor continued to perturb his involvement in church affairs. At first his attitude toward the pastor was expressed in terms of a personal antagonism. He complained: "I have anger at the Reverend: he demands submission to his view. He's charming only if I'm compliant. He holds a pure Calvinistic orthodox faith; everything else gets sharply criticized. [How does that affect you?] I resist his attitude: he's extremely authoritarian, but also well-meaning and caring and devoted. I resist that too; I refuse to be in his good graces." And again later: "His preaching Sunday was dogmatic and conservative: he damned everything for $1\frac{1}{2}$ hours. He had no consideration for us. That made me furious – he's a pitiful guy, harsh and vindictive. I didn't think it was worth listening to, but I sat through it, feeling immobilized and vulnerable. He was like a drunk spewing dirt. Others were angry and critical too, but I have a sense of him as invincible and overwhelming and I see myself as powerless." His negative feelings toward the pastor seemed to intensify. He proclaimed: "I'm thinking of the pastor. I don't like him as person: he's obnoxious, always talking about himself and his accomplishments. He's a showoff and dogmatic, wants us listen like children and give him undivided attention and obedience. I feel resistant and repulsed: I don't want to give him anything. That's the opposite of complying. I feel anger; I don't even want to look at him." And further: "I realize that I don't like the pastor: he's obnoxious and narcissistic and controlling. I don't like him but we need each other; we have to coexist. That makes me feel powerless; I have anger and have to bite my tongue. [What comes to mind about the anger? (The analyst is interested in knowing more about what is motivating the anger, particularly any transference implications.)] He's an impossible guy, manipulative and exhibitionistic, always trying to impress. He infuriates me. [How so?] I think of my father. The Reverend is authoritarian and controlling."

He later reflected with some greater degree of insight on how his self-demeaning and submissive behavior played a role in his dealing with the pastor. He commented:

> I also tend to make myself a loser – I keep myself small and humiliated, inferior and defeated; I deprive myself of chances to be successful. I have the same problem with the pastor: he's narcissistic and wants to be the ultimate authority. He demands submission and that makes me feel irritated and angry. [Is it that you cast the situation in terms of power and submission, superior and inferior?] The pastor is ugly and self-centered and I feel contempt. I'm ambivalent: with him and you I put myself in a disadvantageous position, but I still feel envious and jealous.

He was able to see that he tended to squeeze people into a dominant-submissive mold, as he was doing with the pastor. He found this distressing because he saw in the pastor elements of authoritarian and narcissistic attitudes that he found increasingly despicable and ego-dystonic in himself.

Gradually his difficulties and conflicts with the pastor continued to surface. In the face of the pastor's narcissism and self-righteousness, my patient found himself wanting to rebel against and reject the pastor. He referred to looking at the pastor in this context: "If he looks at me it means liking, and I'd have to return the liking. That would mean acceptance and approval, and I don't want to give him that idea. It would mean giving in and becoming an obedient disciple and being at the mercy of his power. I wouldn't get any similar attention or affection from him." The struggle and conflict over giving-in versus rejecting dominated his relation with the pastor, and found its echoes in relation to his analyst – or perhaps the revivification of these aspects of his relation with his father in the analysis spilled over into his contacts with the pastor.

As it turned out, some of the pastor's activities proved to be suspect and his apparent misbehavior, both in dealing with women and in managing church finances, met with increasing disapproval not only by my patient, but by other church members as well. As he reported:

> There are complaints about pastor: it's getting out of hand. The deacons are upset and are planning a meeting to see what we can do. It's not just my distortion. I don't know why I feel so withdrawn and rebellious, but I don't express myself. I feel like my voice isn't heard and doesn't deserve to be heard; but also I want to lash out. I think he needs to be confronted. He's not like my father, but my father never learned to communicate either. Perhaps the pastor can turn around. I wished that would happen with my father: it was such a relief when he went to sleep, but I wanted to destroy and kill him.

It was interesting that reality and the patient's transference fantasies came to clash in this context – in my patient's mind the misbehavior of the pastor was amalgamated with the memories of his father's failures, and seemed to elicit the same combination of wishful repentance and reform along with intense hatred and murderous wishes.

This situation became a crisis within the church and members of the church governing board, of which my patient was a member, had to take up the allegations of the pastor's misconduct. This was difficult for my patient to consider, since it so violated his wishes to conceive of everything related to the church as good, pure and innocent. His response was complicated by his wish to gain acceptance from the pastor, to placate him by complying with his wishes, and thus to curry favor. As he explained: "If I felt I was his favorite, I might continue to do whatever he asked. I would just give in and go along with whatever he wanted. But I'm afraid how he'd react: he might say he didn't need me and I was no good." Assuming that the pastor represented a powerful and important authority figure in my patient's eyes, his inclination to comply and submit himself on whatever terms is perfectly consistent with his responses to authority figures of whatever stripe, including his analyst.

As the church crisis progressed, it became a form of personal crisis for my patient. As he reflected:

> We had another meeting about the pastor. He puts himself on the level of Christ, but he has problems dealing with women and money. He's just corrupt. He's insulting and manipulative and authoritarian. I'm the church treasurer, and he says I'm not good enough and have no faith. [What feelings?] I get irritated: he says that to get his way, as though he knows everything and what's best. He uses his power and authority. In our church a pastor is like a king, but he damages my self-esteem. [I seem to remember that not long ago you wanted to increase your contribution to the church.] Now I wonder about my motivation. I have a conflict between participating as a church member and my personal feelings. The pastor wanted to make me an ordained deacon, but if I did that I'd put myself at the mercy of his influence. I started to contribute more, but then withheld it when this controversy started. The financial problem is only the tip of the iceberg. I have shifted my attitude. We're all so meek and good: that's how I was raised, but you can't just give in and accept things. But I don't want my personal feelings to distort how I respond, but Sunday I felt tired and disillusioned. I feel like quitting and going to another church.

Carl reported further on the actions of the governing board:

> I met with the pastor and deacons. He has become a dictator and just can't listen: he wants to run things his way, and there's no communication or participation. There's also a problem with his handling of funds: he keeps the books secret. He's cut off from other Baptist churches and never invites anyone in to speak. But he was finally able to listen, and at the end he cried and prayed for forgiveness. He has led people on the wrong path, but we all felt moved and touched. We'll see if he follows through. But I was able to say what I wanted. I need to learn how to assert myself and participate. I want to stand on my own feet,

> but that means taking responsibility. That's scary. It's easy to fall back to a dependent and passive position, but then I feel miserable and whine. I don't want to be a slave. I struggle between rebelling and feeling burdened vs. trying to learn something; but that's my choice. There really is no pressure, but I do it as if it were someone else's choice and was imposed on me.

We can hear glimmerings of an emerging autonomy here, perhaps abetted and supported by his fellow deacons and board members, but detectible nonetheless. This could be seen as another diminishing or stripping away of his infantile dependence and submissive subjection to this powerful religious authority figure, and the adoption of a more realistic, autonomous, and adaptive posture.

Subsequently, the board asked for the pastor's resignation. As my patient commented: "The problem at the church goes on: we voted to ask the pastor to resign. In our church, an ordained minister is God's messenger and untouchable. The idea of analyzing that is overwhelming. It's difficult for me to get an overview of the case: when I'm with him or reading his material, I get distracted easily." And further: "I get so frustrated with the pastor. He's clever and holds his ground. He presents me with tough issues: I tend to pull back and give up, take the easy way out. That's my cowardice; I feel frustrated with myself. I know what's right, but I want to retreat. Let him have what he wants. It makes me think of my expectations for an immediate response from my mother: if she didn't give me what I wanted I'd have a temper tantrum. I cover that up but it's still there deep inside." It seems that for Carl a judgment against the pastor was equivalent to a judgment against himself. But he also realized that the pastor had severe character problems that were hurtful to others – an acknowledgement that did not come easily since it ran so radically against his idealizing wishes and wishful fantasies.

The process of discharging the wayward pastor and choosing his replacement required some degree of independent judgment and autonomous action. It was difficult for him to meet this challenge and he found himself retreating to his customary defensive and self-depleting posture. He reported:

> We voted on a new pastor. I had some demands and negative reactions. It may not work out. We had a discussion with many opinions, and then I started feeling confused. I took a back seat and was quiet – it felt like my penis had shrunk. [What was going on?] My opinion got shrunk in with all those other opinions. I wanted to encompass the others, propose a bigger idea that would be better than the others. But that was a formidable task so I gave up. I felt repelled by any reasons, and felt pushed aside. [You make it sound like if you're not number-one you don't want to play at all?] It's partly that, but I never participated in my whole life. It's something deeper – I never volunteer in class or group situations. Then I feel left out and unimportant, and feel not as good as others. But when others express their thoughts, I feel contempt that they think they know something. [Perhaps we can turn that around: are you afraid they'll have contempt for your thoughts?] Right, I'm sensitive to any narcissism or self-importance: I feel irritated and contemptuous, so I keep a low profile.

As the problem with the pastor was evolving, he complained at one point:

> I'm in a struggle with the pastor. He's going to hold services just for his followers and will take the name of our church with him. The general congregation voted against him and requested that he resign. I get caught in the middle. He's an ordained pastor and authority. But I have a conflict in my faith. I vacillate and I want to withdraw and give in. I have

doubts about what to do. He's so self-serving, but we can't put up with that. Such incredible misconduct, but what is God's will? I feel like he's too powerful and invincible and I'm too weak. [Does that bring anything to mind?] I'm like a little boy who can't get what he wants. I was at the mercy of my father, too weak to fight. It's just like home: we were abused and couldn't get away. [Do you see the pastor with such power?] 1,000 times over; he has God's power. [So whatever he does is the same as God's power?] That's what I was taught to believe, but that's not the case. [That sounds a little confusing: is it or isn't it?] I am confused. The pastor isn't Jesus Christ, but I attribute absolute power to him. [I find that curious. You're a psychologist and his behavior sounds pathological, but you don't seem to want to acknowledge that? (The analyst's question challenges Carl's submissive and authoritarian stance. From a more objective and realistic perspective, he is professionally qualified to evaluate the pastor's misbehavior but holds back from doing so. He opts for a submissive, self-effacing and self-devaluing course of action rationalizing it in the name of religious motifs.)] I'm cloudy about the issues: I confuse faith and authority and power. It's like I'm fighting against myself.

Religion Versus Psychology/Psychoanalysis

In the course of his training, he had developed an interest in the relation between psychology-and-psychiatry and religion, and was thinking of joining a discussion group on that topic. While this seemed to reflect a longstanding interest, it undoubtedly resonated with issues related to his involvement with me, especially since he knew this was one of the areas of my interest and writing. The question was stirring whether this could be an independent interest that he could claim as his own, or was it in some sense a reflection of his wish to be close to me, to please me, and to submissively establish a bond with me that would put him in my good graces and give him a favored position in relation to me. Along the way, he hinted that he wished to keep his religious feelings private, that is keep them separate and outside of the analysis. It seemed clear that as the analysis deepened, he was experiencing a more intense pull toward greater autonomy, which was related to the wish to extricate himself from his clinging dependency on his mother, which lay at the root of his feelings of inadequacy, weakness, helplessness, and the need to be given special favors and consideration. Correspondingly, greater autonomy also connoted freeing himself from his terrorized, vulnerable, and self-devaluing view of himself that was connected with his relation with his father. The struggle between these internalizations in his inner world were not only drawing into question his concept of himself as a person and what kind of person he wanted to be and could be, but also had reverberations for how he saw himself in relation to God and what implications the possibility of greater autonomy might have for his future relation to God. In drawing him toward greater autonomy, psychoanalysis was on one hand helping him to free himself from his neurotic entanglements with his parents, but on the other hand was posing problems in his religious orientation and his status in the eyes of God. If he were not the terrorized, helpless and vulnerable victim-child or the special, privileged and favored child of a loving and protecting God, what was he? And what was he in God's eyes?

A few months later, he hinted that he was experiencing some conflict between the help he felt he was getting in analysis and the help he anticipated from religion – was there a sense in which there was a choice between analysis and religion? He reflected:

> God could be the analyst of my soul. I'm thinking of soul and mind – I'm not clear about the difference. I could have that. [You mean God's guidance?] For the rest of my life I would be guided and protected. [What thoughts about that?] I think of God as helping: He has a giant hand, like in Michelangelo's painting, God touching Adam's hand. I need that kind of help. He would show me the way; I'd be enlightened, so I wouldn't be so totally dependent. [You make God sound like a perfect supervisor? (The analyst here begins to pick up on the fantasy aspects of the patient's God-image.)] (He laughs) Supervisors are limited, but God is infinite and could always give to me (. . .) But God is farther away, so it comes down to myself. I think of my father: he had big hands, but he never held my hand. I don't remember touching him.

The big hands provide a link between the image of the wished-for but unavailable and remote father and God – God's touch would provide life, power, and enlightenment. The analyst does not confront or challenge the fantasy, but looks for ways to deepen or expand it in the interest of understanding the connection with the father more fully.

One difficulty was that, as he saw it, psychoanalysis required him to become more aggressive and assertive in contrast to what he felt was required by religion. Clearly, extracting himself from his infantile dependence on his mother called for a degree of aggressive effort and self-assertion in the interest of establishing a firmer footing in a sense of authentic autonomy and thus overcoming the obstacle to his own personal growth and maturity posed by his continuing attachment and dependence in her.[6] This in itself was threatening insofar as it posed the possibility of his having to live his life on his own terms and without the self-sustaining fantasies of maternal approval and specialness. But, in addition, even that moderate degree of aggressive action was overshadowed by the imagery of his brutal, violent and terrorizing father. This added fear of becoming like the despised and violent figure of his father further added to his repulsion and dread of losing his seemingly life-sustaining dependence on his mother and in addition losing his standing and hope of salvation in continuing his childlike and passive dependence on his Mother-God. This proved to be one of the strongest resistances to his engagement and effective involvement in the analytic process.

He continued to be bothered by the opposition he assumed between psychoanalysis and religion. His difficulties were complicated by his relation with me. He knew that I was a priest, that I had written on the relation between psychoanalysis and religion (Meissner, 1984) and on the problem of the psychology of grace (Meissner, 1987). To an extent, he felt this made his interest in psychoanalysis and religion legitimate, but part of him resisted any compliant acceptance in this area. He resisted reading my books and opposed that to reading the Bible – better to read the

[6] For further elaboration of this view of aggression as motivation, rather than as drive, see Rizzuto et al. (2004).

Bible than anything in psychoanalysis. But he didn't read the Bible much either – as he noted: "I'm fascinated with the Bible. I want to know God better but don't even read the Bible; so I turn my interest and enthusiasm into a burden." As he put it, "I know you wrote a book on grace. [What thoughts?] It made me feel that it's OK to be interested in that, that it's not so far-fetched. But my rebelliousness comes to mind: I'm a compliant rebel." His rebellious attitude continued well into the later stages of the analysis; he complained:

> I feel constricted. I don't want to be bound by the theory of psychoanalysis. I want to be free from that, I mean the problem of religion and psychoanalysis – trying to find a place for psychoanalysis (...) But I am interested in religion and psychoanalysis, fascinating areas. [Perhaps you'd rather talk about religion and psychoanalysis than problems of your behavior? (This suggests that, whatever his interests in psychoanalysis and religion and whatever conceptual problems they posed for him, more immediate issues related to his maladaptive behavior were more pressing. My question here suggests that he may have been using the psychoanalysis vs. religion matter as a diversion from dealing with his more immediate issues and was thus a form of resistance.)] That's a problem. Intimidation is pervasive: I'm intimidated by any authority. I even see you that way.

The transference dimension is manifest here, both in relation to analysis as reflected in his view of the analyst as powerful authority figure and, as we have seen above, in relation to God as infinitely powerful and judgmental. In both areas, the figure of the father looms large as the source of this transferential content.

Late in the analysis, he complained that his longstanding interest in the relation between religion and psychoanalysis had diminished and been eroded to a degree by his analysis. In this sense, his analysis had been a disappointment. He complained:

> Psychoanalysis has become a monster. I'm interested in other areas like religion. Analysis takes on too much importance. I used to see the analyst as an overwhelming authority, but that's gone down a lot. That was part of my transference neurosis. [You seem to have a problem reconciling psychoanalysis with religion? (The analyst is interested in sustaining the inquiry rather than in confronting or interpreting.)] My view of God has gone down too. Christ's message was love and hope. I wanted to see God as gracious rather than judging and vindictive. I inherited my mother's faith but that's too narrow. [Do you make psychoanalysis your father's territory? (In other words, has he dichotomized religion as his mother's territory and psychoanalysis as his father's? This would imply a split in which the respective transference figures would be cast – God in the image of his mother and the analyst in the image of his father.)] I think of old men and books, stern eyes, and God; you're one of the old guys.

At the same time his interest and enthusiasm for psychology had waned. As he complained: "I don't like my work. All I have is fear, no fun or enthusiasm. I hate it, but feel I should enjoy it. I feel guilty. I'd much rather do what I like, like reading and studying the Bible. I wouldn't regret giving up psychology (...) I identify with my mother: religion is important to me. In church I feel restored and held. I find hope in prayer: God is the ultimate analyst, but I never see him." It seemed as though the tension he felt between psychoanalysis and religion, operating more narrowly as a displacement for his transference-related conflicts, casting the analyst in an oppositional position to God, also embraced his more general feeling between what he saw as a nonreligious and scientific orientation, as he knew it in his psychological work, and belief in and faithful adherence to God.

At this point, he was also seeing more clearly the inadequacy and limitations in his mother's self-sacrificing and masochistic stance. Despite this, he wanted to cast his lot with his mother's religious orientation, but that was suspect too. The problem seemed to be – how could he relate to God if he did not follow in his mother's submissive and intensely devotional footsteps? Unfortunately psychoanalysis was not offering him any resolution of this problem, but was leaving it to him to find his own solution to the difficulty. His well-worn paths of adaptation were failing him. If he could not play the favored and special child so that the analyst would help him out and show him what path to follow, and if he could not in turn play the role of the terrorized, vulnerable and helpless victim who was forced to submit to the analyst's demands and expectations, he had to find some other resolution of his difficulties. If these patterns of introjective self-organization and their projective derivatives (Meissner, 1981) which he used to paint his portrait of the image of God were proving less effective and meaningful, where else was he to turn? The dilemma was clear enough; as he put it: "I need to clarify my relation to Christ and the church. [Are you reluctant to examine that?] It's difficult talking about that here. I feel a tension between here and church, between psychoanalysis and religion. I feel a definite growth in my faith: it feels more personalized. I can see God through Christ and the Bible, but psychoanalysis is so different and opposite. My view of God is colored by my neurotic conflicts. [How do you apply that to yourself?] My view of God is colored by my views of my father and my mother."

Close to termination, he commented further: "I thought about wanting to rebel against God, but I really believe in and trust God. I could tell Him any feelings, and He would understand. My father's influence was extrinsic and fearful; my mother's influence was intrinsic but guilt-ridden. [It seems you've been tossed on waves of fear and guilt all your life?] Yes!" I concluded that one outcome of the analysis was that the degree of insight he had achieved had resulted in an at least partial stripping away, or diminishing, of the intense transferential elements that had contaminated his image of and understanding of God, and had allowed him to gain a more authentic and autonomous relationship with the God he could now love and worship.

Discussion

Clinical experience has taught us that religious beliefs and religiously oriented activities are as open to and vulnerable to the effects of infantile and neurotic motivations as any segment of human activity. The appreciation of the role of such neurotic elements in the religious behavior of his patients led Freud to conclude that religion itself was a neurotic manifestation, formulated in his perspective according to the model of an obsessional neurosis (Freud, 1907/1959). Religious behaviors were in this perspective nothing more than symptomatic actions that required analytic cure – so that one goal of analysis was to eliminate these neurotically determined behaviors from the patient's life. Rethinking of this basic freudian paradigm in the last score of years and more has led to a more religiously accepting and open orientation to the understanding of religious phenomena. While the areligious analyst, basing his approach on his own antireligious and agnostic or atheistic persuasions, would direct his attention to the supposed neurotic determinants of the patient's religious orientation, the aim of his and the patient's exploration and understanding would be to expose the neurotic nature of any religious beliefs and to enable the patient to resolve the underlying neurotic issues and thus eliminate the symptomatic needs and behavior. To the extent that this approach might play a role in the analytic process it would, in my view, constitute a form of countertransference enactment – in which the analyst's prejudicial view of religion is imposed on the analysand from whom compliant acceptance of an irreligious perspective would be preferred.

As I have noted above, the analyst, while accepting the patient's religious orientation, employs the same processes and therapeutic techniques in the analytic process, but with a very different orientation and purpose. He also looks for the neurotic determinants in the patient's religious behavior, but he sees them, not as constituting the essence of the religious behavior itself, but as neurotic elements that can contaminate and distort the patient's potentially more authentic and mature religious adaptation. The therapeutic objective, then, is not undermining or abandoning the religious orientation, but helping the patient to discover and understand the role of such neurotic influences and their origins, and thus potentiate the patient's capacity to adopt a more meaningful and mature religious orientation and to establish a more mature and realistic relationship with a more gracious and loving God whom the patient is free to love and worship. Underlying this more religiously accepting approach, there is a basic acceptance of the authenticity and truth-value of the patient's belief system, including the real existence of such a God and the ultimate form of mature and relatively autonomous dependence on such a Godhead. This means accepting the idea that forms of religious belief and behavior can exist that do not derive exclusively from infantile needs and dependencies and that belief systems and their existential content draw their validity from revelatory and faith-based contexts that lie beyond the scope of analytic inquiry and meaning. These assumptions do not rest easy in the world-view of the areligious analyst.

But it should be emphasized that countertransference traps are readily available on the other side of a more religiously accepting approach. If the analyst's imposition or interpretive intervention in support of his antireligious views amounts to a countertransference enactment, so also would the similar advancement of the analyst's own religious persuasions. The sauce here is as good for the goose as the proverbial gander. In terms of preferred analytic technique, the analyst is not interested in promoting a religious outlook in the patient; rather his interest lies in the direction of a persistent inquiry into the manner and origins of the neurotic dispositions and entanglements that are reflected in the patient's religious behaviors. The operative supposition is that the clarification and understanding of these issues and their therapeutic resolution would enable the patient to gain a more mature and authentic stance with respect to matters religious, if he so chooses. The ultimate choice and decision in these matters, as in other matters of therapeutic relevance, lies in the patient's hands. The analytic process seeks no more than to enable the patient to free himself from neurotic entanglements and thus be empowered to make his own self-determining choices about his own identity and life patterns – including what he wishes to believe and what kind of religious life he wishes to follow or not. The analyst can and should have nothing to say about that.

From a technical point of view, my own view is that, in regard to religious issues just as much as with any other important issues in the patient's life, the analyst is well advised to avoid these transference and countertransference traps. They arise inevitably and provide the meat of the analytic process. But the analyst's best approach is not to allow himself to get caught up in these aspects of the process, but to preserve his more neutral analytic stance and keep as well as he can to the path of analytic inquiry. I have in previous writings sought to articulate this basic stance within the analysis in terms of the therapeutic alliance (Meissner, 1996b). The point I wish to make in this context is that the optimal approach for the analyst in working with the patient on religious issues is to maintain the stance of the alliance with all its component elements. In this way, the transference and countertransference traps I have discussed can be avoided and the patient left free to find his own meaningful and adaptive path to a more mature religious outlook – whether that find expression in greater faith and belief, or not.

References

Freud, S. (1907/1959). Obsessive actions and religious practices. In *The standard edition of the complete psychological works of Sigmund Freud. Vol. 9* (pp. 115–127). London: Hogarth.

Freud, S. (1927/1961). The future of an illusion. In *The standard edition of the complete psychological works of Sigmund Freud. Vol. 21* (pp. 1–56). London: Hogarth.

Jones, J. W. (1991). *Contemporary psychoanalysis and religion: Transference and transcendence*. New Haven, CT: Yale University Press.

Jones, J. W. (1996). *Religion and psychology: Psychoanalysis, feminism, and theology*. New Haven, CT: Yale University Press.

Meissner, W. W. (1981). *Internalization in psychoanalysis*. New York: International Universities Press (Psychological Issues, Monograph 50).

Meissner, W. W. (1984). *Psychoanalysis and religious experience*. New Haven, CT: Yale University Press.

Meissner, W. W. (1987). *Life and faith: Psychological perspectives on religious experience*. Washington, DC: Georgetown University Press.

Meissner, W. W. (1992). The pathology of belief systems. *Psychoanalysis and Contemporary Thought*, *15*, 99–128.

Meissner, W. W. (1996a). The pathology of beliefs and the beliefs of pathology. In E. P. Shafranske (Ed.), *Religion and the clinical practice of psychology* (pp. 241–267). Washington, DC: American Psychological Association.

Meissner, W. W. (1996b). *The therapeutic alliance*. New Haven, CT: Yale University Press.

Meissner, W. W. (2000). Reflections on psychic reality. *International Journal of Psychoanalysis*, *81*, 1117–1138.

Meissner, W. W. (2001). Psychic reality in the psychoanalytic process. *Journal of the American Psychoanalytic Association*, *49*, 855–890.

Pruyser, P. W. (1968). *A dynamic psychology of religion*. New York: Harper & Row.

Rizzuto, A.-M. (1979). *The birth of the living god: A psychoanalytic study*. Chicago, IL: University of Chicago Press.

Rizzuto, A.-M., Meissner, W. W., & Buie, D. H. (2004). *The dynamics of human aggression: Theoretical foundations, clinical applications*. New York: Brunner-Routledge.

Rochlin, G. (1965). *Griefs and discontents: The forces of change*. Boston, MA: Little, Brown & Co.

Sorenson, R. L. (2004). *Minding spirituality*. Hillsdale, NJ: Analytic Press.

Spero, M. H. (1992). *Religious objects as psychological structures: A critical integration of object relations theory, psychotherapy, and Judaism*. Chicago, IL: University of Chicago Press.

Spezzano, C. & Gargiulo, G. J. (1997). *Soul on the couch: Spirituality, religion, and morality in contemporary psychoanalysis*. Hillsdale, NJ: Analytic Press.

Vergote, A. (1978/1988). *Guilt and desire: Religious attitudes and their pathological derivatives*. New Haven, CT: Yale University Press.

Religious Delusion in Psychosis and Hysteria*

Jozef Corveleyn

Introduction

In the 1890s, Daniel Paul Schreber (b. 1842, in Leipzig) was the "Senatspräsident"[1] in the Kingdom of Saxony, one of the highest positions in the juridical system of the kingdom. He came from a very well-known medical family in the capital which had links with the leading players in European academic and cultural life. His father, Moritz Schreber, was a renowned doctor who wrote popular books about remedial gymnastics and educational discipline to promote the health of young children. He was an advocate for the creation of green open spaces in workers' neighbourhoods, play areas for children and parcels of land to allow the workers to do some gardening, the so-called "Schreber Gardens." Daniel Paul suffered from psychological illness (excessive fatigue, depression and hypochondria) after a defeat in a political election in 1884. He was successfully treated with sleep therapy by Professor Dr. Flechsig, the Director of the University psychiatric hospital in Leipzig. He became seriously ill for a second time, manifestly psychotic, in 1893, just after he had been appointed to the above-mentioned highest position in the magistracy. This psychosis lasted for a long time, and was first treated in Leipzig, but after a few months he was transferred to a hospital in the country. It began with a radical experience of alienation, followed by hypochondriac delusional imaginings which gave rise to considerable anxiety. In a third phase he developed a religious delusion of grandeur, whose outlines were broadly as follows. He was the sole remaining true

* This text was originally published in French, in D. Devreese, Z. Lothane & J. Schotte (Eds.) (1998), *Schreber revisité* (pp. 185–209). Leuven (Belgium): Leuven University Press (Figures of the Unconscious, hors serie). The English text is a revised version.

[1] This is President of the highest court, directly appointed by the King. "He was to preside over a five-judge panel in the Third Civilsenat of the Dresden Oberlandesgericht" (Lothane, 1992 p. 41), i.e. "the presiding judge of the Royal Superior Appellate Court in Dresden" (Idem).

J. Corveleyn
KU Leuven, Leuven, Belgium, e-mail: jozef.corveleyn@psy.kuleuven.be

J.A. Belzen (ed.), *Changing the Scientific Study of Religion: Beyond Freud?*

man on earth, the one chosen by God. At the same time he deduced from his physical feelings that he was going to gradually undergo a change of sex (transsexual delusion). As a result he would soon, through fertilisation by sunbeams sent to him by God, be the origin of a new race of mankind. As soon as this delusional "reconstruction" became firmly established in his experience, he began to interpret his entire cultural environment, the political context of the time (the gradual unification of the German states and small kingdoms at the instigation of Bismarck) and the struggle between Protestants and Catholics, in terms of his experience. His entire thought became a beautiful and reasonably coherent construct. This also brought him peace of mind and enabled him to make use of his undoubtedly great intellectual talents once again. It was in this context of recovery that he began to rebel against his incarceration in psychiatric care. He had been taken into compulsory care at the beginning of his second psychosis. He was denied all civil rights, on the grounds of "madness" (Verrücktheit). As a good lawyer he wanted to show the doctors, the lawyers and indeed to the whole population that he was indeed in possession of all his rational faculties and consequently that there was no reason to keep him in confinement. He systematically wrote down his psychotic experiences and his delusions. He arranged them into logically structured chapters and wrote the necessary introductions and appendices for the voluminous text, as well as an open letter to his former doctor, Dr. Flechsig. The whole document is structured as an extensive legal pleading. In 1902 he was discharged from psychiatric care and his "Entmündigung" (loss of civil rights) was reversed. He published all his texts and documents as a book in 1903. This publication is known in English as *Memoirs of My Nervous Illness*, which is a bad translation of *Denkwürdigkeiten eines Nervenkranken.*[2] *Denkwürdigkeiten* is not "memoirs," it indicates much more than memories; *Denkwürdigkeiten* are thoughtful ideas, important events and reflections about these. Lothane (1992, p. 7) proposes the following complete translation of the title: "Great Thoughts of a Nervous Patient with Postscripts and an Addendum Concerning the Question: 'Under what Premises Can a Person Considered Insane be Detained in an Asylum Against His Own Declared Will?'."

This publication was brought to the attention of Freud by, among others, Carl Gustav Jung, who was engaged in an in-depth study of the problems of psychosis in the context of his job at the clinic in Zürich. The text was discussed in the Viennese circle, Freud made contact with Schreber's latest doctor and, propelled by the growing interest in psychosis in psychoanalytical circles, he set about an in-depth analysis of the content of Schreber's text. In this way he developed his first comprehensive study on the specificity of psychosis in comparison with the neurotic and psychosomatic conditions that were better known to him. Freud published his study in 1911 (Freud, 1911). In this study he established for the first time a clear link between the schizophrenic psychosis and early stages of psychosexual development, partly supported by the early work of Karl Abraham and Carl Gustav Jung. In

---

[2] German: *Denkwürdigkeiten eines Nervenkranken nebst Nachträge und einem Anhang über die Frage: "Unter welchem Voraussetzungen darf eine für geisteskrank erachtete Person gegen ihren erkläriten Willen in eine Heilanstalt festgehalten werden?"*, Leipzig:Mutze, 1903.

this text he also established a link (which was later disputed) between the paranoid aspects of a psychotic delusion and latent homosexuality. What is more, in a move that was very significant for psychoanalytical psychopathology, he demonstrated that the most striking symptoms of psychosis, namely delusions and hallucinations, do not constitute the disease itself, but are indications of the patient's attempts to recover from his illness by reconstructing the world from which he has become alienated. This is: the delusion as an attempt at healing. At the core of the psychosis lies the deep alienation from the world which normally is ordered on an inter-subjective basis.

In this essay I would like to approach the Schreber case from the perspective of the problem of religious delusion. It is a comparative study: I will try to outline the specific characteristics of a religious delusion in psychosis (Schreber's psychosis) more clearly by comparing it with another form of religious delusion, namely the religious delusion that often occurs in the context of hysterical psychosis.

This comparative study is significant in two ways. First of all, comparing these two types of delusion may contribute to a clear differential psychopathological description of and a better psychodynamic insight into psychosis. What is more, this comparison may be fruitful for the so-called 'clinical psychology of religion'. This branch of psychology covers two areas of work. On the one hand it studies the possible interaction (positive or negative) between religiosity and mental health, specifically within the wider field of psycho-therapeutic practice. On the other hand it seeks to make a theoretical clinical and psychopathological study of religious behaviour. This study on religious delusion fits into this second part of clinical psychology of religion. Exceptional or pathological forms of religiosity are studied here, first of all of course to know them better in themselves, but also to improve the differential diagnosis. The question here is how exceptional religious behaviour can be distinguished from deviant religious behaviour and, more general, how so-called "normal" religious behaviour can be distinguished from "deviant" religious behaviour, taking the social context into account. An in-depth knowledge of the various deviant forms of religious behaviour may give us greater insights into the so-called normal structures of religious faith and unbelief.

The theoretical foundation of this questioning can be referred to by a metaphor, the so-called 'crystal principle' (Schotte, 1981, 1994). This principle refers to the metaphor used by Freud in one of his attempts to specify the relationship between what is normal and what is pathological. This metaphor was first put into words in the 31st lesson of his *Introduction to psychoanalysis*:

> we know that pathology, by enlarging psychological processes and, as it were, making them more severe, is capable of drawing to our attention the normal processes that would otherwise remain hidden. Where pathology shows us a fault-line, perhaps there is normally only an ordinary dividing-line. If a crystal is thrown to the ground, it will break into pieces, not in a random way, but according to specific fault-lines which, although they are invisible, have been predetermined by the structure of the crystal. This broken structure is the structure of people with psychological illness. (Freud, 1933/1971, p. 80)

Let us return, however, to the distinction between normal and deviant behaviours in the religious domain. In terms of psychological practice, a differential diagnosis is highly important. This is so both for individual psychotherapy and for the necessary preventive and psychosocial actions in the context of extraordinary and sometimes deviant forms of religiosity (e.g. sectarianism, occultism and satanism). The latter forms do not only occur in American society (Richardson, 1980, 1984, 1985; Bromley & Richardson, 1983; Richardson, Best & Bromley 1991), but are gradually also conquering the Old Continent. We are thinking here of the collective suicide in Jonestown, Guyana (1978; Richardson, 1980), and the disaster in the sectarian community led by David Koresh, in Texas in 1983. It is clear that, in the face of these phenomena, not only sociological or criminological but also psychodynamic and psychopathological distinctions and predictive criteria are urgently needed (see West, 1993).

Schreber's Delusion – Paradigm of a Psychotic Religious Delusion

Before I try to carry out a comparative study between a psychotic and a non-psychotic (in this case a hysterical) religious delusion, I want to demonstrate how, in my opinion, the Schreberian delusion is essentially a *religious* delusion, and is in fact a *paradigm par excellence* of such a delusion. In this way I am strongly opposing the assertion defended by Elias Canetti in his well-known essay *Crowds and Power* dating from 1960, in which he represents Schreber's delusion as an example of a *political* delusion.

In this work, in which he carries out a very penetrating socio-psychological analysis of the interaction between the power of the leader and the human "crowd," Canetti characterises Schreber's delusion as the paradigm of the thinking of the potentate, the autocratic and absolute leader, the dictator and therefore as the (delusional) paradigm of the political discourse. Canetti's hypothesis was as follows: this delusion "which apparently demonstrates an outdated view of the world [...] is, in reality, the exact model of political power which is fed by the crowd and is built on it" (Canetti, 1976, p. 500; see also p. 503). A little later, he goes into more detail about this: "[in Schreber's delusion], the religious aspects are permeated with the political aspect and inextricably bound to it. The Saviour of the World and the Master of the World are one and the same person. The desire for power lies at the heart of this entire discourse" (p. 508).

To support his view Canetti refers to three themes which, in his opinion, are typical of the dictator's discourse.

First comes the theme of *position* ("Stellung"). In this author's opinion, this is the central theme in the Schreberian discourse. With the term "position" Canetti means the way in which Schreber situates himself in the world (the cosmos), in relation to people and in relation to God. For Schreber it is "the position itself which is most important, and it cannot be great or eternal enough" (Canetti, 1976, p. 494). Canetti refers specifically here to the chapters of the *Denkwürdigkeiten* which deal with the world order and with the "economy" of nerves. Schreber specifically states that this world order is a principle that stands above all other principles, a principle to which even God is obliged to submit completely. The only exception to this is Schreber himself. If he is not superior, then he is in any case extraordinary in this world order. He is unique, a superman, the soul who is distinguished from all the other souls who form a single undifferentiated crowd. In this context the "fact" of the imperfect nature of God is emphasised. After all, God has allowed himself to be tempted and drawn into a plot against the innocent Schreber; in this way he has been incorporated into the crowd of souls ... Can it not be seen in this aspect of the delusion that Schreber has reserved for himself the place of "primus," the one who is unique in comparison with everything and everyone? This is paradigmatically the perfect position of the Master, the absolute ruler or dictator: alone against everyone and superior to the uniformity of the crowd.

The second theme which is emphasised by Canetti to strengthen his hypothesis is that of the *plot* and the *conspiracy*: the plot, in existence for generations, of the Flechsigs against the Schrebers, the plot of Dr. Flechsig against this particular Schreber, and God's involvement in all this. But he, Daniel-Paul, has scented the plot. As a good 'dictator' – as Canetti emphasises – he has brought to light the secret plans and dark machinations of the others, he has unmasked and accused them, he has *seen* everything. Once again, as in the previous theme, the President occupies the position of sole subject, the central point within the undifferentiated crowd of "people." The emphasis on this same aspect of claiming a difference or a psychologically (unique) 'position' can be found in the description by Alphonse De Waelhens of the paranoid world, in his important study of the Duc de Saint-Simon [Duke of Saint-Simon] (De Waelhens, 1981; see Corveleyn, 1984b).

The third and last theme emphasised by Canetti to support his view of the essentially political nature of the Schreberian discourse, is that of *surviving the general catastrophe*. He refers to the fantasy, which is nurtured by Schreber, that he will be the sole survivor of a universal disaster which will destroy all of humanity, so that he becomes the 'Saviour' who will found a new human race. From this perspective Canetti thinks that he is able to emphasise the paradigmatic function of the paranoid discourse to gain an understanding of the psychology of the absolute "leader." I quote: "The deepest desire of every person who wields power is to be the last survivor. The person who wields power, the dictator, kills everyone in order to avoid his own confrontation with death" (Canetti, 1976, p. 502).

The importance of these three themes cannot be denied, and it is clear that these three aspects of the *content* of the delusion have a paradigmatic value, forming part of a discourse which is at least coloured by paranoia, for a psychological insight into the "man in power." This, however, does not constitute proof that the Schreberian delusion is entirely, or at least primarily, a political rather than a religious delusion. It cannot be asserted, as Canetti does, that the reference to religion in this delusion is only a "harmonic" and a secondary characteristic. The additional argument which he puts forward, namely the reference to Schreber's direct involvement in the political life of his country, does not in my opinion make his interpretation any more convincing.

Canetti's argument is actually based mainly on an analysis of the content, which can be compared with the direct reading and interpretation of the manifest content of a dream (or a symptom or delusion), something which was sharply criticised by Freud. There are two pathways that can be used to circumvent this obstacle. The first was suggested by Freud himself: the study of "the dream-work" (*Traumarbeit*), the dreamer's "work" when sleeping, which can be detected in therapy by the study of free association. Dream-work distorts *content* from the unconscious (latent content) into elements of a discourse (manifest content) which are acceptable to the subject's conscious ego. The second pathway is the one that is followed by certain phenomenologists (see e.g. Rümke, 1954/1981, pp. 201–202) who primarily emphasise the importance of analysing the *form* of the discourse. They use the analysis of the "literary genre" of the text, following the example of the Biblical exegetes. This is expressed in the characteristics of the "surface" of the discourse being studied. Let us follow this path to discover the true content of Schreber's text.

I will now set aside for a moment the rich content of President Schreber's delusion. It is multi-faceted and it is impossible to give precedence to one aspect of its content over another, purely on the basis of the selection of quotations or on the basis of a summary. It is always possible to make different selections, as a result of which the number of interpretations will increase. The risk of working arbitrarily is reduced if one first considers carefully the form of the discourse. The most important formal aspect of a discourse is the way in which the author presents *himself* in his discourse, namely as the active subject of the discourse (the subject of the enonciation). And then there are the details that he provides on the specific attitude which he encourages his reader to take. Whom is he addressing? For what purpose is he writing his text? What is he ultimately seeking to achieve? Who is his (real and/or imaginary) audience?

It is clear that Schreber presents himself as the bearer of a religious message. The whole text, it is true, has an evident legal slant (see Devreese, 1989, 1996), but that does not change the fact that his pleading as a whole is strongly characterised by a religious perspective. To add force to this assertion, I refer to what Schreber himself has written, and specifically to the last-minute texts, as it were, namely the texts which he added to his book after the final editing of his entire pleading. These texts are, as it were, intended to reveal the author's viewpoint. Here I am referring to the *Vorwort* ("Foreword") and the *Open Letter to Flechsig*, which were written in December 1902 and March 1903 respectively, largely after he wrote the *corpus* of the book.

I will begin with the *Vorwort*, which follows immediately after the title page and is therefore the first introduction to the author. Even in the first paragraph Schreber warns the reader: he says that he was not considering the possibility of publication when he began writing and adds that he is aware of the objections that may arise to this publication (due to "respect for persons still living,"Schreber, 1903/1973, p. iii). Nevertheless, he has decided to publish the *Denkwürdigkeiten* because he thinks that "his work is valuable to science and for the knowledge of certain *religious* truths," and because he hopes that the publication of these truths will "give professionals in this field the opportunity to make observations of his body and his fate" (ibid.,

p. iii, emphasis ours).[3] The author also states that this publication serves a general and public interest ("allgemeines Interesse," p. v), although certain errors may have crept into his discourse. In his opinion, this public interest is founded on his relationship with God. The importance of his fate and his testimony about it is therefore religious in origin. At the end of the *Vorwort* the author once again emphasises the central themes of his book: "the essence and priorities of God, the immortality of the soul, etc." (ibid., p. v). To emphasise the importance of the truths that he wishes to explain even more strongly, he also adds at the end of this introduction that he "does not have to change anything in the chapters that follow: I, II, XVIII and XIX" (ibid.), chapters whose titles leave no doubt whatsoever about the religious nature of his activity as an author. The titles of the four chapters are as follows: I. God and immortality; II. A crisis in God's kingdoms? The murder of souls; XVIII. God and the Processes of Creation; XIX. Continuation of XVIII: The omnipotence of God and the freedom of the human will.[4]

This religious concern is equally clear in the *Open Letter* which is addressed to the psychiatrist who treated him at the beginning of his illness, namely Dr. Flechsig. His extensive text, the corpus of the book, begins after this open letter. I would also like to point out here that this *Open Letter* is the last text he wrote, just before he handed the book to the publisher. The text begins with a clear request to Flechsig to subject the book to a "favourable investigation" ("wohlwollende Prüfung", ibid., p. vii). Schreber continues by apologising to Flechsig: "Your name will be mentioned several times in my book, particularly in the early chapters, and it is quite possible that you may be annoyed by this" ("Ihre Empfindlichkeit berühren", ibid.); "indeed I am very afraid of this, but I can do nothing about it without jeopardising the comprehensibility of my work." (ibid.). He then makes clear the aim that he is seeking to achieve, an aim that justifies the publication in the face of all possible subjective or personal objections: "my aim through my work is to achieve the following end [*Zweck*]: to increase the knowledge of the truth in an exalted field, namely the field of religion".[5] For him this is an intimate conviction: the publication of his experiences is in fact a pressing duty, literally a religious duty. I notice

[3] Complete German text: "Dabei habe ich mir die Bedenken nicht verhehlt, die einer Veröffentlichung entgegenzustehen scheinen: es handelt sich namentlich um die Rücksicht auf einzelne noch lebende Personen. Auf der anderen Seite bin ich der Meinung, dass es für die Wissenschaft und für die Erkenntnis religiöser Wahrheiten von Wert sein könnte, wenn noch bei meinen Lebzeiten irgendwelche Beobachtungen von berufener Seite an meinem Körper und meinen persönlichen Schicksalen zu ermöglichen wären." (Schreber, 1903/1973, p. iii). I use here and in the citations that will follow in the footnotes, the page numbers of the original German edition which can be found in the current re-editions of the text.

[4] Titles in German: I. Gott und Unsterblichkeit; II. Eine Krisis der Gottesreiche? Seelenmord; XVIII. Gott und die Schöpfungsvorgänge; XIX. Fortsetzung des Vorigen. Göttliche Allmacht und menschliche Willensfreiheit.

[5] "Jedenfalls liegt mir die Absicht eines Angriffs auf Ihre Ehre durch-aus fern, wie ich denn überhaupt gegen keinen Menschen irgendeinen persönlichen Groll hege, sondern mit meiner Arbeit nur den Zweck verfolge, die Erkenntnis der Wahrheit auf einem hochwichtigen, dem religiösen Gebiete, zu fördern" (Schreber, 1903/1973, p. vii, Schreber underlines).

here that he never refers to the political or religious context when he is speaking about what drives and motivates him to carry out this whole work.

After he has clarified the essentially religious nature of his mission as an author, by addressing first the general public in the *Vorwort*, then his doctor, Dr. Flechsig, in the *Open letter*, Schreber turns in the actual *Einleitung* to his wife and his family. From the very first sentence he mentions one of the most important reasons for publishing his book: before he returns home he considers it "necessary" to inform his wife and those who will be with him of the reason for the "visible eccentricities" of his behaviour; he will only be able to do this by giving them "some idea of his *religious* ideas" (emphasis mine).[6] He then adds a footnote in which he explains once again his purpose in this statement, which is intended primarily for his wife. He warns the readers who may be amazed at this highly personal and even private message, at the beginning of a book: after all, he is convinced that what follows will also be of interest to a wider public ("für weitere Kreise", ibid.). And, as if he is seeking to apologise, he explains that he has left the introduction as it stands "because the first occasion [for this book] was my wife's orientation concerning my personal experiences and my *religious* ideas" (emphasis mine).[7]

The Hysterical Religious Delusion

To understand the specific nature of the psychotic religious delusion better, I will consider it here alongside a different form of religious delusion, namely the hysterical delusion. The specific nature of each of these forms of delusion will be made clear by elucidating the fundamental differences between them in terms of both structure and function.

[6] "Da ich den Entschluss gefasst habe, in absehbarer Zukunft meine Entlassung aus der Anstalt zu beantragen, um wieder unter gesiteten Menschen und in häuslicher Gemeinschaft mit meiner Frau zu leben, so wird es notwendig sein, denjenigen Personen, die dann meine Umgebung bilden werden, wenigstens einen ungefähren Begriff von meinen religiösen Vorstellungen zu geben, damit sie die manchen scheinbaren Absonderlichkeiten meines Verhaltens wenn auch nicht vollständig begreifen, so doch mindestens von der Notwendigkeit, die mir diese Absonderlichkeiten aufzwingt, eine Ahnung erhalten" (Schreber, 1903/1973, p. 1).

[7] (ibid., footnote): "Vorbemerkung. Im weiteren Fortgang der Beschäftigung mit der gegenwärtigen Arbeit ist mir der Gedanke gekommen, dass dieselbe doch vielleicht auch für weitere Kreise Interesse haben könnte. Nichtsdestoweniger habe ich es bei dem Eingang gelassen, da die Orientierung meiner Frau über meine persönlichen Erlebnisse und religiösen Vorstellungen nun einmal die erste Veranlassung zu derselben gewesen ist" (Schreber, 1903/1973, footnote on p. 1; The first underlining is Schreber's, the second is mine).

A Clinical Example

Marie, aged 42, tells us when she is first admitted to the clinic about her fears of an impending global catastrophe. This disaster can only be prevented if the "world" listens carefully to her message: it is a message of love. This is all about her love for God, her love with God and the need for everyone to start to love one another and to love God, after the example of this new love which is given by her, Marie, on the instructions of the Lord.

This is a 'passionate' love, a love between her and God which has now lasted for 2 years. During the first interviews she expands on the specific features of this long history. Let us begin by saying that she sees this love as the result of her being chosen. She behaves, both in her conversations with me or with the other care personnel, and in her daily life, as if she is perpetually in direct contact with God – and more specifically with the person of Jesus Christ, a relationship which is both loving and harmonious and also passionate. During the day she regularly stays in bed, where she yields to the burning and intensely erotic love of Jesus. She says that she is possessed by him. When she lies in the arms of her divine Lover, as she later confides in us, she enjoys all the pleasures of physical love, while simultaneously exchanging all kinds of intimacies, spiritual and other confidences with Him. Marie does not keep this possession a secret from those living with her or from the staff: she does not talk to them, but she yields unashamedly to her love, in the presence of the "public": the nurses and her three room-mates. As soon as she is in bed, she withdraws completely into herself, and shortly afterwards she twists herself into all kinds of contortions and she can be heard moaning, laughing, talking etc.

During the first interviews she tells the story of this love-relationship with Jesus. She was originally German but married a French-speaking Belgian who worked for a company close to her village during the time of their engagement. When they came to live in Belgium, they made their home in the Dutch-speaking part of the country. In order to integrate effectively she quickly learned Dutch. During our interviews she speaks all three languages, but when she speaks about God and her love for Christ, she speaks German, which is the language of affectivity for her. She explains how this relationship has gradually developed. Even in Germany, before moving to Belgium, she was disappointed in her marriage which had been childless; on the other hand she became more and more annoyed by her "depressing civil-servant-husband." Thus, a short time after her arrival in Belgium, she began a love-affair – which, she emphasises, was quite healthy – with her singing teacher, a man who was 20 years older than she and had many admirers. She was very satisfied by this relationship.

During the time when she was beginning to feel disappointed with her marriage (Germany), she began to be interested in the religion of her youth, with strong encouragement from one of her brothers who was living in the atmosphere of a very pious reading and praying group. Nevertheless, she dates the beginning of her love-relationship with God back to a moment of ecstasy during one of her long walks in the Black Forest.

I would like to look here at the religious atmosphere that was passed on to her by her brother, and then offer a few quotations from her religious discourse. Her brother mainly gave her folk piety books to read. These are works by one Jakob Lorber, a very simple man who formerly lived in Southern Germany and wrote or dictated his prophecies and visions. These books mainly describe the day-to-day life of Jesus. During his ecstasies he took part, to some extent, in this "simple life, full of love, of the man of Nazareth." He therefore thinks that he is a direct witness of the childhood of Jesus, he sees him playing with his friends, he sees him growing up and witnesses his conversations with all kinds of people etc. After spending some time in this ecstatic state, Lorber tells those around him what he has "experienced" and "seen" during his visionary journey through the Holy Land and, like a reporter, presents some highly visual reports of it.[8] Our patient had eagerly read all the books that her brother gave her and had mentally begun to live in this slightly unreal atmosphere, although during the first stage of the process she did not lose her realistic contact with the world that surrounded her. Her reading of Lorber taught her "how God loved his children most."[9] Here are her comments: "I was sorry for all my sins and He gave me the power that he gives to every person, namely Love for him and Faith in Him." For her this was a real religious rebirth.

In this atmosphere – with all the sensitivity which is characteristic for her – she seeks for closer contact with "The Transcendent" in an encounter with the wide countryside around her. Particularly in the interplay between the sun and the clouds she says that she sees signs, not only of the presence of God in general, but above all of His personal and unique presence for her.

While walking in the Black Forest one day she has an ecstatic experience of the quasi-mystical type (an experience of a direct meeting with God):

> I was walking along and I looked up at the sky; on my left I saw a large cloud with waves that looked like hills; one of those hills was shining with a kind of holy aura around it ['einen heiligen Schein']. I saw for myself that it was an angel, or God himself, who lived there. I continued my walk without losing sight of that cloud. Suddenly that cloud with its holy aura began to rise. I said to myself: 'Now I must stay, now I must see it.' I stood still and the cloud rose majestically in front of me; I knew that it had been sent for me by God. Tears ran down my cheeks; I was deeply moved. I murmured words of thanks to God.

---

[8] It is very difficult to find exact data about this author and, above all, about the (small) piety movement that he has founded. Anyway, I can quote some of his works that have been read by the patient: *Das jenseitige Kinderreich: Mitteilungen über die geistigen Lebensverhältnisse der frühversorbenen Kinder im Jenseits, Durch das innere Wort empfangen* (Bietigheim: Lorber-Verlag, 1956); *Jesus-Worte zur Meditation: aus der Neuoffenbarung empfangen* (Bietigheim: Lorber-Verlag, s.d.); *L'enfance de Jésus: l'évangile de Jacques* (trans. V. Secretan; Genève: Helios, 1984). I refer also to some prophecies in the strict sense of the word: *Naturgeheimnisse: Das Naturgeschehen und sein geistiger Hintergrund nach den Offenbarungen* (Württemberg: Lorber, 1968); *Heilung und Gesundheitspflege in geistiger Schau: Textauswahl aus den Werken der Neuoffenberung* (Text-auswahl durch Jakob Lorber e.a.; mit einem Vorwort von Erich Heinze, 2. neu bearb. und erw. Aufl., Bietigheim, Lorber-Verlag, 1980). There is even a book of a more "theological" nature: *Johannes das grosse Evangelium, empfangen vom Herrn durch Jakob Lorber und Leopold Engel* (7. Aufl., Württemberg: Lorber, 1981–1987).

[9] I translate his words form German, as litterally as possible.

> The cloud then began to sparkle even more and suddenly a brightly illuminated altar appeared in the cloud, with a lot of white light. Then I said to myself: 'The angel – or God – is going to appear.' My heart was beating very hard; I tried to calm it by placing my hand on it; but it carried on beating like that." This first moment of ecstasy is interrupted by something that she describes as comical: "I suddenly became aware that I had a piece of chewing-gum in my mouth, and I thought: 'I cannot appear before God with chewing-gum in my mouth!'" So I spat it out ... and the vision disappeared ...

During another walk, some time later, she felt that she was directly touched by a sunbeam. "It was God forgiving all my sins and I was so happy, I felt so grateful to Him that the tears once again rolled down my cheeks. I thanked the Lord for His love and His grace, and my tears of love and joy ['Liebesfreudeträne'] continued to flow."

During the same period her husband became increasingly concerned as he observed that his wife was becoming more and more absorbed in this religious experience. He started off by teasing her, but eventually he begins to object aggressively whenever he notices the way that she is becoming completely lost in her dreams. "But I continued with God. Do you know, for a person who loves God with his heart and has felt His love, even only once, that love grows constantly and becomes a feeling so wonderful that one would like to leave this passing world and in fact even to die of love ['und am liebsten von Liebe sterben möchte']."

Marie also allowed me to read her diary. It covers the whole period from the beginning of her privileged religious experience to the moment of her admission to hospital. From the detailed descriptions set out in it one can clearly see that it was only after 6 months of intensifying religious life that it began to limit her daily life to such an extent that any realistic relationship with those around her ultimately became impossible. After about 10 months the transition was complete. Now I will illustrate two steps by using a few quotations from her diary.

Marie situates the beginning of the erotic and passionate phase of her intimate relationship with Jesus Christ 6 months after her first 'mystical' experience. One night, when she was unable to sleep, He comes to visit her for the first time.

> I turned to Jesus and began talking to him: He had to place his right hand on my heart and his left hand on my head so that I would fall into a 'sleep of delight' [or ecstasy; translation of 'Endzückungsschlaf' (sic 'en*d*-' = end, instead of 'en*t*-zückung')].[10] As soon as he did that, a light breeze blew through me; my whole body was illuminated from the inside; and it became brighter and brighter. It was such a wonderful feeling ['wonneartiges Gefühl'] that I believed I was already in heaven. I murmured words of gratitude, breathed very deeply and eventually fell into a sleep of pure delight ['schlief wohlwonnig'].

Every day, she continues, she receives similar proofs of the fact that Jesus has chosen her. She complains that she is unable to pass on these divine signs to her husband: "He does not believe in God and I cannot show him the signs that I *see*." In relation to this episode, which is recorded in part of her diary, the husband relates (hetero-anamnesis) that it was approximately from that time that Marie refused almost all

[10] This slip of the pen (en*d*- instead of en*t*-) could be interpreted as referring to the "end" of (her) life. This could be the expression of an unconscious death wish, related to her passionate love of Jesus: see some quotations below in the text that support this hypothesis.

intimate contact with him. The reason that she gave is that God has provided sexual contact with a view to reproduction; and since they are not capable of that, such contact is forbidden to her. Nevertheless, she could tolerate her husband approaching her if he allowed her to transform her love for God into an earthly but exalted love for him, her husband. "Then she saw me, or I took her in my arms, she thought I was her god." Contrary to what one might imagine at first sight, her husband was not very pleased about this. In fact she was not coming to him as a person, but tolerated his presence insofar as she could project her erotic-religious fantasies onto him.

About 10 months after that first "visit" from Jesus in her bed, Marie finally and completely turns away from her husband and those around her. Thus, after about 1 year of growing "mystical" fervour, Marie is living entirely within her delusion. The husband also comments that recently she has also refused to talk to him, or to allow him to touch, help or even come close to her. "I lost all contact with her on 25 December 19xx," which was precisely 1 month before she was admitted to hospital. He waited until January before taking his wife to hospital; he gave the following reason for this: "On 22 January she declared to me that she had been married to God since the 14th, that she had sexual contact with Him, that she had to save the world, that God was always at her side but that I could not see him." In Marie's diary we find the following story about an event in November:

> For three nights I have been in permanent meditation and I have received light and love from the Lord. This loves comes to me in gusts which become increasingly intense and provide me with a happiness that becomes more and more extreme. Sometimes I shed tears of pure love for Him. My deepest desire is to die to this world and ultimately to come to our holy father [sic] Jesus Christ. I can hardly describe the feeling of joy that Jesus creates when he loves you in your heart. During the last few nights the Lord with His light came into my body and sent me a gentle breeze so that I would answer him with my love. In this way, two rays of flame met each other. I can feel and perceive that fire, it is like an intoxicating rush [double meaning of the German word: 'ein Rauschen']. Usually I hold Jesus in my arms and love Him in my heart. In any case, as soon as I call Him by name, He is there with his movements..., I have noticed that I fall into an ecstasy of love after an hour of meditation and receiving the light. This means that my heart burns so fiercely and my body floats up so high that it takes on a bent form. Then I fall back in my bed because my heart cannot bear any more love. At that moment I have an incredibly strong longing for release: the death of the body.

Several similar erotic–mystic experiences can be found in the diary for the months of November and December.

Theoretical and Clinical Framework

The Concept of Hysterical Delusion or Psychosis

The concepts of hysterical delusion or hysterical psychosis have long been the subject of controversy in the history of psychopathology. I studied this history in detail elsewhere,[11] but I will limit myself here to a brief summary. Contrary to Maleval's suggestion that the old notion of hysterical "madness" should be used, to make a distinction between this form of delusion and a 'real' psychosis, namely schizophrenia, I prefer continuing to use the term hysterical psychosis to avoid adding to the confusion of nomenclature and terminology which already exists in the field of psychopathology (see e.g. Maleval, 1978a, b; and Maleval & Champanier, 1977). In fact, in the Anglo-Saxon literature those authors who wish to distinguish these hysterical disorders from the field of schizophrenia also use the term *hysterical psychosis* (see Corveleyn, 1981).

Historical Overview

Three periods can be identified in the history of the concept of hysterical psychosis. Here I will use the distinctions that I used in an earlier study (Corveleyn, 1981).

The concept of hysterical psychosis was *generally recognised* in psychiatric literature from the second half of the nineteenth century. This concept was used to refer to the psychological illness (called hysterical "madness," "delusion" or "psychosis") that could affect a hysterical person. We should remember that at this time hysteria was understood to be a neurological condition: a real disease of the neuronal system (central and/or peripheral, of the physiological or functional type), hence the terms neuropathy or *neurosis* were meant literally. This "somatic" disease was characterised by a symptomatology in which physical "stigmata" were in first place, and which are still classified under the label of hysteria, although there are now different conceptual reasons for this (see Israël, 1977). Hysterical madness or hysterical *psychosis* was a complication of the underlying *neurosis*, with serious psychological disturbances: dramatic changes could be seen in the character, and above all disturbances in the hysterical person's connection with reality (disturbances of perception: hallucinations and disturbances in thinking and behaviour: deliria (a distinction was made between *délire des actes* – "delusion of action" and *délire de la pensée* – "delusion of thinking"). These concepts were particularly in vogue in the writings of the *aliénistes*, the psychiatrists in the great psychiatric institutions in France (such as Morel) and much less so in the works of university neuro-psychiatrists who wanted to win respect for their science in the medical world, among other things by neurologising and anatomising every psychopathological phenomenon.

The second period begins at the end of the nineteenth century and lasts approximately until the 1960s. This was the period in which the concept *disappeared* or was brushed aside. During this phase there were two influences that played a crucial role. First, on the side of academic neuro-psychiatry, there was a new emphasis on an integrated neurological understanding of the whole area of hysteria, associated with a refusal to take seriously all the psychological disturbances reported

[11] See for some parts of this history: Maleval & Champanier, (1977) and Maleval, (1979, 1981); I have reconstructed this history more completely in my doctoral dissertation (Corveleyn, 1981).

by the *aliénistes* in the context of this neuropathy. Second, the very influential book, published by Bleuler (1911/1950) on "schizophrenia," further pushed away the older concepts for psychosis-related phenomena, by absorbing them all in the concept of schizophrenia. One might say that the concept of schizophrenia served as a kind of vacuum cleaner: almost all phenomena which were suspected to be capable of being labelled as psychotic, in the sense of an alienation from the social world, were somehow incorporated in the increasingly wide-ranging category of "schizophrenias."

It was only from the 1960s that the concept of hysterical psychosis was *restored to its proper place*. This concept can be seen emerging among a number of authors with a mainly clinical background. It is therefore not in the great academic manuals of psychopathology but in the writings of psychoanalytical psychotherapists (e.g. Pankow, 1973 – see Corveleyn, 1984a) or phenomenological psychiatrists (e.g. Hugenholtz, 1946) that the old concept came to be used again. This was also the time when the concept of *borderline disorders* was born (see Knight, 1953). In each case, what took place was the description of the specific characteristics of a psychotic pathology – in the descriptive sense of dysregulation of the relationship between the subject and the common reality – in relation to the schizophrenic structure. This specific character is expressed mainly in the course of the delusion and in the opportunities that exist for psychotherapy (see e.g. Pankow, 1973; Maleval, 1978a, b and 1980).

Pragmatic Definition

One thing that clearly emerges in the tortuous history that I have just briefly described is that in most of the writings the same operational and pragmatic definition of hysterical psychosis is found, albeit with connotations specific to an individual author. I will offer a kind of snapshot of these definitions here, using contemporary psychopathological descriptive language.

In hysterical psychosis what is involved is an underlying hysterical problem in which certain psychological factors bring the subject to a break in his current connection with the common reality. This break is expressed in the delusion and/or in hallucinations. The delusion sometimes has quite a systematised appearance, and sometimes a paranoid "colour" with grandiose thoughts can even be detected. Erotic and religious themes are frequently in the foreground. Due to these phenomena of delusion and hallucination the clinician may be misled into making an incorrect diagnosis of schizophrenia: the similarity between hysterical psychosis and schizophrenia is certainly closest during the acute phases. In the context of a differential diagnosis, contemporary authors stress that the hysterical psychosis is specifically characterised by two types of phenomena. On the one hand they mention a quite rapid recovery, after the initial phase of the delusion, of a personal and authentic contact between carers and the psychotic subject. As regards countertransference, one does not see the so-called "praecox Gefühl" (Rümke, 1941/1981) but the possibility of a real relationship of "sympathy" (Mitleiden) can clearly be seen: a dynamic transference which contributes quite quickly to the therapeutic process known as "working through."

On the other hand the specific characteristics of the delusion are also mentioned (which were first set out in a systematic way in Maleval & Champanier, 1977). This delusion demonstrates a high level of adaptability to the sociological or psychological details of the patient's current surroundings. In the context of psychotherapy, it can also be seen that the hysterical patient, unlike the schizophrenic, can establish a connection after the initial phase of the delusion between different elements of the content of the delusion and elements from his personal history. Here I must emphasise that this is a link which is experienced subjectively and is relevant to the subject himself. It is not a link that can only be seen by the psychotherapist or the observer, as is almost always the case when discussing the schizophrenic delusion. A hysterical psychosis is also characterised by a more or less sudden onset. The various authors also always emphasise the episodic nature of hysterical psychosis. In prognostic terms, a full recovery is usually expected. Some authors, however – including Freud, in the few comments that he makes on hysterical psychosis in his *Studien über Hysterie* (Studies of Hysteria, 1985) – point out that in some cases the hysterical psychosis may become chronic and degenerate in the direction of schizophrenia.

Psychodynamic Characteristics

To complete the picture we can quote some other important characteristics of the hysterical psychosis which are mainly emphasised in psychoanalytical writings (see Pankow, 1973; Maleval, 1981; Corveleyn, 1981; Jeanneau, 1990). The characteristics in question clearly indicate the distinction between the hysterical psychosis and schizophrenia: they concern the onset of the delusion and the mechanism of symptom formation that can be psychodynamically described and understood.

1. As regards the *onset* of the hysterical psychosis, it can be said that a traumatic episode (e.g. a painful disappointment, a betrayal or an unbridled realisation of sexual desires) can be found in the area of the subject's affective and love-life, an episode which activates repressed representations of an infantile nature. Hence, in Marie's case, we find a deep disappointment in the area of her intimate relationships (lack of sexual gratification, a husband who is an unimaginative civil servant, and above all the narcissistic pain of a childless marriage), which brings old, repressed oedipal desires back to life. Here one might consider Marie's search for an idealised father in the figure of God and her confusion between the significance of the father and the erotic relationship with the Son: "My deepest desire is to die to this world and ultimately to come to our holy Father, Jesus Christ." It is not only the aspects of deprivation or psychological pain which have a traumatising effect: the experience of unexpected fulfilment of a desire may also act as the trauma that can precipitate a hysterical psychosis. In this case, as

Maleval says, what is involved is the "fantasmatic virtual realisation of an oedipal wish," or "to put it less precisely, but with greater certainty, the coincidence of a fantasy and the reality" (Maleval, 1978a, pp. 696–697; see also Maleval, 1981). I quote from the testimony of Maleval's patient, which illustrates well this second traumatic possibility. Speaking of her love-relationship and her relationship with her analyst, she says: "The thing that deters me is that X *loves me too much*, and *you loved me too much too*, sometimes I could see that you had an erection when I arrived. I was always thinking of you when I was with him, and I feel the same love for you. X is too free, and he has no sexual complexes. *The thing that worries me is that he wants to give me the maximum pleasure* [...] Everything was allowed [...] it was too much [...] my analysis was over [...] We did everything that I wanted. [...] *I had a feeling of perfection, and it was worse than death*" (Maleval, 1978a, pp. 696, 697; emphasis mine). Maleval quite rightly says: "She is not in the emptiness of rejection of the Name of the Father, which would bring her to the place of trying to bridge the gap; on the contrary, suddenly she encounters excess, the fullness, 'perfection'. In other words: she misses her lack..." (ibid., p. 697).

2. To understand the failure of the relationship between the schizophrenic subject and the world and to understand the accompanying process of the development of symptoms, we can use – according to psychoanalytical language – the mechanism of *Verwerfung* (rejection), or foreclosure, or projection. In the case of hysterical psychosis, the model of displacement (or total failure of displacement) and of the dream is enough to shed light on the mechanism creating the break between the subject and his world and also the development of the symptoms of delusion. In my earlier study (1981) I showed that the process of hysterical psychosis can be understood by using two references that can be taken from the first works of Freud on "*Abwehrneuropsychosen*" and on dreams: the mechanism whereby what has been repressed returns in the case of a hysterical attack (Freud, 1895), and the concept of wish-fulfilment (*Wunsch-Erfüllung*) as in dreams and so-called "hallucinatory psychosis or confusion" (*halluzinatorische Psychose* or *halluzinatorische Verworrenheit* in Freud, 1894), or what he calls "amentia" (see Freud, 1917, p. 420). I would like to propose the following "formula":

   i. The traumatic event consists of a seriously and narcissistically painful disappointment for the subject which, due to its affective impact, causes a reactivation – initially "silently" – of repressed oedipal representations. The traumatic event may, however, also be a kind of surprise attack on the subject's normal defence mechanisms through an encounter with experiences of wish-fulfilment. This overwhelming of defences also gives rise to a reactivation of what has been repressed.
   ii. The hysterical-psychotic delusion does not occur immediately. On the contrary, the trauma is followed by a period of varying length during which the subject generally invests less and less in the world around him and simultaneously invests the pulsional energy which is released in this way in the

intermediate world of his preconscious, the world of imaginary representations, that part of his psyche that is closest to the unconscious: a reservoir of representations that can 'transport' that which has been repressed. As Freud says, in the context of his theory on the emergence of neurosis, the libido undergoes an *introversion* which can be very far-reaching and can draw the neurotic person into a situation of derealisation. Freud makes the following comment on the mechanism of introversion: "The libido turns away from reality, which due to unrelenting frustration [Versagung] has lost its value for the subject. It then turns to the *fantasy life* [das Phantasieleben] in which *new representations of desire [neue Wunschbildungen] are created and in which it brings back to life traces of old, forgotten wish-representations*" (Freud, 1912, pp. 323–324, emphasis mine). Let us now return to our case study. We saw that Marie, in response to a disappointing love-life, had embarked on an extra-marital relationship and had renewed her interest in the religion of her youth. Gradually she comes to find more personal gratification in that religion. This new way of investing her interest does, it is true, have an impact on her day-to-day behaviour, but for several months it does not immediately and comprehensively undermine her contact with her family and social environment. Nevertheless, it is evident that the process of introversion is translated into a growing psychological absorption with the pious world of her "master" Jakob Lorber. It can be said that the introversion operates in two directions during this period. On the one hand the introversion allows her to devote herself to wishful oedipal representations in an "innocent" way: she can approach her idealised father (God) and find a certain gratification of her desire for his love. On the other hand the respectability and sublimating character of religion paradoxically collaborates in the work of repression that must inevitably be intensified when approaching the old, oedipal conflictual material more closely. The investment in the religious world therefore contributes towards this work of repression by significantly reinforcing the counter-cathexis (*Gegenbesetzung*). Tender affection for Jesus and devoting attention to his private life are – both in terms of subjective experience and censorship – a very long way from forbidden oedipal desires, although they are psychologically very close to them.

iii. It is noticeable that the break with reality, the radical alienation (alienatio), takes place in one sense in the same area where the increased repression has occurred. The *religious delusion* emerges in the patient's first "mystical" experience: her experience of election by and union with God. It all seems as though this experience of "real" gratification comes too close to the repressed fantasies and destroys the intense efforts at repression from the previous phase. From this time onwards this patient is no longer "Marie, aged 42, married to …", but she is the "fiancée of Jesus." From a psychoanalytical perspective, one can use the term "*de-identification*" to refer to this step into delusion. Nevertheless I must stress that this provisional suspension of the repression is not complete; the repressed desires do not appear plainly, without any treatment or psychological elaboration: it is not the oedipal desires *an sich* which appear on the scene of the delusion. As in the dream, the latent content undergoes a certain transformation which makes them more or less permissible to censorship, which apparently continues to carry out a part of its function. However, as in the dream, the subject is cut off from any effective relationship with the environment: as in the dream the hallucinatory content, i.e. the internal aspects of the psyche, are experienced as ontologically real. To account for this replacement of the common reality by the psychic reality, we can then find help from Maleval and his mechanism of projection: "Since the hysterical delusion is the projection into reality of repressed elements – and not rejected elements [as in schizophrenia] – one might just as well speak of the return of that which has been repressed to the world of the subject's experience" (Maleval, 1978a, p. 714).

The Comparison Between the Psychotic Religious Delusion (Schreber) and the Hysterical Religious Delusion (The Case of Marie)

When studying the *content* we can only establish a large number of similarities between these forms of religious discourse. In both delusions we therefore find ideas about a global catastrophe and Messianic thoughts, ideas of grandeur and imaginings about a privileged relationship with God. I have already pointed out earlier that this thematic similarity can mislead the clinician during the acute phase of a hysterical delusion, since he will certainly be struck by the deep alienation, sometimes the agitation and the confusion of these patients.

Studying these two forms of psychosis more carefully the difference is quickly revealed, even at the first level, in the way in which they appear and the mode of self-expression. I am referring here to the very different *style* and *atmosphere* in the two forms of delusion. In Schreber, negative feelings and negative psychological attitudes are predominant: suspicion, confrontation, competition with other people and even with God, while in Marie's discourse about God and her relationship with the world there is only one concern: love for God and an intimate bond with Jesus. In her words she *defends* her love and her divine lover before other people, but in fact she is certain of it "in her heart": she is *in* the love of God-the-Father-Son. In her case there is no trace of the carefully constructed and patiently written pleading of President Schreber. Many pages in his texts speak about God; Marie also cannot stop talking about God. In Schreber's case it is as if the knowledge of God and the uncovering of His secrets are his only aims, while Marie is barely concerned with the essence or the theological knowledge of God: her only aim is to perpetuate her unification with God, Who gives her an undeserved and almost intolerable joy (*jouissance*), and she does not allow her pleasurable experiences to be disturbed by questions from the catechism or by metaphysical questions. For Schreber, on the other hand, knowledge is the main aim, or to put it more accurately, it is a safe asset after so many years of suffering. Having wanted to know in the past, he now wants to show his knowledge to his doctors and to the whole of humanity; he wants to prove that he is right, because he knows. Finally I would like to draw attention to the difference in the image of God. On the one hand we have a distant, haughty God, a very mighty God, a strict judge and a jealous rival, which we do not see at all in Marie's case. She naturally recognises the greatness of God in nature, but that does not deter her; quite the contrary; she is comforted by God showing himself in such visible and material ways. In this way she is assured of His personal attention and His love. The only dimension of God that interests her, one might say, is a God who provides shelter, protection and warm care.

Let us now look more closely at some more structural characteristics.

The Place of Religion in Delusion

The articulation of the religious dimension in these two pathologies is very different. In Schreber's case the reference to God is not present at the beginning of the psychosis; it is not the first expression of it. As far as the evolution of his disease can be reconstructed on the basis of the documents that have been discovered (for the publication, see mainly Devreese et al., 1986; Devreese, 1996, 2003; and Lothane, 1992 and 2004; see also Prado de Oliveira, 1997) and from the report that he gives in his *Denkwürdigkeiten*, the religious element arrives at a relatively late stage, i.e. after the negative phase of the loss of vital contact with the world and hypochondria. This religious element then begins to play an important part in the patient's efforts to reconstruct a world in which he can live, a reconstruction which reaches its climax in the writing of his book. It is only in this *end-product* that the reference to God is there from the beginning. It serves as a support to the whole construction.

So, how is it for our patient now? She was certainly experiencing psychological suffering and neurotic disturbances long before the delusion emerged. We cannot, however, find any traces of "psychosis" in her earlier life: reduced attention to everyday reality, yes, but no real break in her connection with the world. Here we must observe that the break occurs on the basis of her increasingly intense preoccupation with religion. The religious element is therefore present at the beginning of the psychosis; this element is, as it were, the language of this psychosis; it is the essential form in which it is expressed. We should not forget here what I have already emphasised: in the path followed by Schreber, God appears on the scene when he is at a low point in relation to the fundamental questions of his existence, while Marie is not disturbed by existential or metaphysical questions, but by a fundamental confusion in her relational life.

Religion as a System of Truth

Schreber treats religion mainly as a monolithic system of absolute Truth. He wants to control it by describing it extensively, as if it were a datum set before him. He is looking for a *firm and unshakeable construction*. Marie, on the other hand, is not concerned with the Truth. She does not care about arguments, demonstrations or proofs. During her first weeks in the hospital, when she abandons herself completely to her delusion, she does not once, in all our many conversations, present any discourse intended to prove to me the correctness of her ideas about God, but tells a *story* about the history of her relationship with Him. Indeed this story does initially have a monomaniac and highly repetitive character: it is as though she can do nothing about it and simply confides in me her past and her current divine amorous adventures. She does boast about it, but she is not seeking to surprise me or convince me of anything. It is true, she is God's chosen one! As time goes on, her discourse begins to evolve. References appear increasingly frequently in her stories to her unhappy personal history, as if a second line of narrative is slipping into the fabric of her delirious discourse. Thus, gradually, the psychotherapeutic task of working through the delusional representations can begin.

From a typological perspective it can be said that the hysterical delusional discourse is the discourse of a *witness-participant*, while the Schreberian discourse is that of a *prophet-seer*. Right from the beginning of his text, Schreber assumes the position of the possessor of the truth. It is as if he, in contrast to the pleading style of his "dossier-book" does not wish or need to convince his interlocutor of the facts of the case. He, Schreber, *knows* and he limits himself to demonstrating what he knows, which is the simple truth. He may be willing to make an effort to explain it to us, but no more than that. He is speaking about a knowledge that naturally belongs to him: he knows God, His projects, His mistakes, His attitudes, His intentions ... and furthermore he knows everything about the cosmos and about humanity. It is from this knowledge and this superior position as possessor of the Truth that he writes his book: he says as much in the passage of the *Vorwort* which we have studied (see note 1). This clearly comes back in one of the added texts in the *Appendix*. "Comes back" is not really the correct term, since it becomes clear here that he held this position with some conviction long before writing his *Vorwort*, in December 1902. I am referring to the letter of February 1901, which he himself introduced as the sixth appendix and in which he gives the Directors of the hospital in which he is being cared for the reasons for the publication of his *Denkwürdigkeiten*. At a certain moment he says that he hopes that Dr. Flechsig will also take a scientific interest in his *Denkwürdigkeiten*, so that he is able to repress his personal sensitivities; "otherwise," he adds, "I will accept the risk of a condemnation for slander [...] due to the great importance that I attach to the distribution of my work, in view of my hopes of enriching science and clarifying religious problems".[12]

---

[12] The complete text: "Für den entgegengesetzten Fall ist das Gewicht, das ich auf Bekanntgabe meiner Arbeit mit Rücksicht auf die davon verhoffte Bereicherung der Wissenschaft und Klärung

I cannot avoid thinking here of the description of the "paranoid character" by De Waelhens (see mainly De Waelhens, 1981; also in De Waelhens, 1972 and in De Waelhens & Ver Eecke, 2001). He gave the most precise analyses of this in his last book on "Le duc de Saint-Simon," which I have already mentioned above. Here De Waelhens emphasises, as do other authors, the specific character of the relationship to the knowledge which is specific to the paranoid subject: he has the position of a seer and as absolute master of the truth. According to De Waelhens, two characteristics are of essential importance: the metaphor of "seeing" or of the gaze, which defines the type of knowledge being referred to here, and the subjectively experienced obvious absence of any sense of doubt or even of the possibility of error. With his perspective the paranoid person sees and discovers, without any hindrance, what is and what is *true*. "Like the gaze of God, his gaze is also infallible. No doubt can ever disturb him. For himself he does not know any form of ambiguity, duality of perspective or uncertainty..." (De Waelhens, 1981, p. 227). In other words, "he embraces everything, there is no risk or fear of error in him, (...) he *is* seeing and knowing, seeing what he knows and knowing what he sees" (ibid., p. 203). The truth therefore does not need to be sought or discussed with others, his "fellow men" who are seeking it. The paranoid person *sees through* the truth and he therefore does not need the opinions of others. He knows and the others must simply listen. "In the most extreme case, the other is deprived of his own discourse" (ibid., p. 239). Flechsig may perhaps have some objections or personal feelings, but these are of no consequence to THE truth: there is no doubting his truth – him, Schreber – and therefore it must be disseminated at all costs. What De Waelhens says about Saint Simon can be perfectly well applied to Schreber: "He only wants, using all the means possible, to lift the veil which still, particularly in the eyes of other people, conceals a truth which is already clear and which he will unveil to those whom it concerns and indeed to everyone" (ibid., p. 232).

As regards the *certainty* with which Schreber believes that he is in the truth, I refer back to the text of the *Introduction* to the *Denkwürdigkeiten*, a text in which he sets out his position in this matter very clearly. His only aim, he says, is to inform people about his knowledge of supernatural things, a knowledge that he has accumulated over 6 years. Of course, so he adds "I cannot count upon full understanding [he underlines this], since these are things that cannot be expressed in any human language, things that go beyond the capacity of human understanding" (Schreber, 1903/1973, pp. 1, 2). He is therefore the only "person" who stands above the crowd. In a rhetorical gesture he admits that he should not dare to assert that he knows everything, nor to enjoy an unshakeable certainty, but then immediately adds that he "has no doubt come much closer to the truth than any other person to whom no divine revelation has been given."[13]

religiöser Ansichten lege, eine so grosse, dass ich selbst die Gefahr einer Bestrafung wegen Beleidigung [...] auf mich nehmen würde" (Schreber, 1903/1973, p. 341).

[13] The complete text is as follows: "Auf volles Verständnis kann ich von vornherein nicht rechnen, da es sich dabei zum Teil um Dinge handelt, die sich in menschlicher Sprache überhaupt nicht aus-drücken lassen, weil sie über das menschliche Begriffsvermögen hinausgehen. (...) Ich

Delusion – Reconstruction and Communication

Let us return to our clinical example. Of course Marie's religious delusion is an expression of her alienation. At the same time, however, this personal delusion is also a language that allows her to connect with society: as regards her own subjective experience, this no doubt gives her a significant amount of emotional comfort; it is a way of expressing herself and of communicating with those around her. During the psychotherapeutic sessions I was able to observe that she was turning to the other with this language, questioning him and questioning herself. It was her way of gaining access to intersubjectivity. If we characterise the hysterical delusion as an attempt to reconstruct the world, as Freud does in the case of the psychotic delusion, then we can place this reconstruction on two levels: on the one hand there is the reconstruction of the internal psychological world in and through the delusion, and on the other hand a slow recovery of the possibility of intersubjective interaction takes place during the course of the delusion.

One of the most frequently quoted passages from Freud's text on Schreber is no doubt the one in which he characterises the delusion as an attempt at healing (*Heilungsversuch*) and reconstruction (see Freud, 1911, p. 308). It is very important to understand this text in its context. Freud is not saying that the psychotic delusion is a recovery in the sense of a return to a *status quo ante*; the recovery he is speaking of is what follows the silent (*stumm*) process of the first phase of psychosis, namely the "withdrawal of the libido from the loved people and things," which is subjectively experienced as a "global catastrophe." Freud states that this withdrawal "is the actual process of repression," (*der eigentliche Verdrängungsvorgang*, ibid.) and that what is correspondingly experienced in subjective terms must be understood as "the projection of the internal catastrophe." He further explains: "his subjective world [that of the psychotic person] has collapsed because he has withdrawn his love from it," to which he adds in a footnote that "perhaps not only the withdrawal of the libido is involved, but also the withdrawal of his interest, hence the withdrawal of the investments that are made by the ego" (ibid. p. 307). It is clear that the actual psychotic "disease" for Freud is the first, silent phase, and that the delusion is the tumultuous (*lärmend*) process of an attempt at healing; this attempt "may succeed to a greater or lesser extent, but never entirely" (ibid., p. 308).

Schreber's book is therefore a "reconstruction." It is, in any case, the result of long psychological work: the long process of a reinvestment that, according to Schreber himself, took about 6 years ("for about six years," Schreber, 1903/1973, p. 1). The book is the end-product of this work. Every reader of the *Denkwürdigkeiten* must admit that this book is a huge achievement. In it one can see the results of the huge effort that Schreber has made to reconstruct his inner world. Nevertheless, we cannot say that this reconstruction has resulted in a true recovery of his

---

bin eben auch nur ein Mensch und daher an die Grenzen menschlicher Erkenntnis gebunden; nur soviel beruht für mich ausser Zweifel, dass ich der Wahrheit unendlich viel nähergekommen bin, als alle anderen Menschen, denen göttliche Offenbarungen nich zuteil geworden sind." (Schreber, 1903/1973, pp. 1–2).

communication with the social world to which he belongs. Here, once again, the attempt at healing is only partly successful. It must be admitted that Schreber is turning to society in his book and that ultimately with this "pleading" in which he defends his case, he does achieve a remarkable social result: the recovery of his civil rights. However, this openness to the social world does not mean a true reintegration in society, either objectively (see the continuation of his story) or in terms of his own subjective experience of it. He does not succeed in seeing himself in context, as a "fellow man," as an equal to other men. This is very noticeable when one studies Schreber's texts in which he indirectly describes his position *vis-à-vis* the Christian community: the use of religious language in his work of reconstruction no doubt expresses his efforts to restore his links with the community; at the same time this language serves to explain to that community the special place which he occupies in relation to it: he is not "within it," like the others, but he is outside it; he is himself, as the person who knows, outside of ordinary existence, superior to it because of the truth which he knows from the inside out.

Let us go through a few texts in which this is clearly expressed. "I am not seeking to say in this way that I recognise all the articles of christian faith as true, as theological orthodoxy does. On the contrary, I am convinced that some of those points are clearly counter-truths or are at least only partly true..." (ibid., p. 3). Later on Schreber approaches the Christian faith in the opposite sense: "On the other hand I can give a more complete explanation of certain points in the Christian faith on the basis of my personal experiences, for example demonstrating how some miracles are possible..."[14]

Here we see the two aspects which have already been referred to above: on the one hand Schreber comes back into contact with human society through religious language, but on the other he distances himself from it through the way in which he uses this means of communication. From this perspective, we cannot fail to recognise that despite all his attempts at reconstruction, President Schreber remains as lonely at the end of the journey as he was at the beginning. This clearly shows that the psychotic experience is not, as Ronald Laing imagines it (1967), equivalent to a journey of discovery through which the psychotic subject can truly know the whole cosmos better than ordinary mortals and reintegrate himself more authentically in human society.

[14] "Damit will ich keineswegs gesagt haben, dass ich alle christlichen Glaubenssätze im Sinne unserer recht-gläubigen Theologie als wahr anerkenne. Im Gegenteil hab ich sicheren Grund anzunehmen, dass einige derselben bestimmt unwahr oder nur in grosser Beschränkung wahr sind..." (Schreber, 1903/1973, p. 3). And a little bit further, in a footnote: "Auf der anderen Seite bin ich in der Lage, für einige christliche Glaubenssätze auf Grund des von mir selbst Erlebten eine Nähere Erklärung, wie dergleichen Dinge im Wege göttlicher Wunder möglich sind, zu geben" (ibid., p. 4).

References

Bleuler, E. (1911/1950). *Dementia praecox or the group of schizophrenias*. Translated by Joseph Zinkin. Foreword by Nolan D.C. Lewis. New York: International Universities Press.

Bromley, D. & Richardson, J. T. (Eds.) (1983). *The brainwashing/deprogramming controversy*. New York: Edwin Mellen Press.

Canetti, E. (1976). *Massa en macht* [Crowds and power]. Translated in Dutch by Jenny Tuin. Amsterdam: Athenaeum/Polak & Van Gennep. English version, e.g.: New York: Farrar, Straus and Giroux, 1984.

Corveleyn, J. (1981). *Religieuze themata in de hysterische psychose: Onderzoek naar de eigenheid van het ziektebeeld in de literatuur en psychodynamische analyse van een religieuze waan*. [Religious themes in hysterical psychosis: The specificity of the clinical entity and psychodynamic analysis of a religious delusion]. 2 vols. (Unpublished doctoral dissertation in psychology, Leuven (Belgium): Katholieke Universiteit Leuven.)

Corveleyn, J. (1984a). De hysterische psychose in het oeuvre van Gisela Pankow [Hysterical psychosis in the works of Gisela Pankow]. *Psychoanalyse*, *2*, 47–56.

Corveleyn, J. (1984b). Het gepassioneerde betoog: Alphonse De Waelhens over le Duc de Saint-Simon [The passionate discourse: Alphonse De Waelhens about the Duke of Saint-Simon]. *Tijdschrift voor Filosofie*, *46*, 57–82.

Devreese, D. (1989). *De waan lezen: Een hermeneutisch-psychoanalytische ontleding van de paranoïde waan van D.P. Schreber* [Reading the delusion: A hermeneutical and psychoanalytical analysis of the paranoid delusion of D.P. Schreber]. 2 vols. (Unpublished doctoral dissertation in psychology, Leuven (Belgium): Katholieke Universiteit Leuven.)

Devreese, D. (1996). Anatomy of soul murder: Family romance and structure of delusions in the Memoirs of D.P. Schreber. *The Psychoanalytic Review*, *88*, 709–734, 913–927.

Devreese, D. (2003). *L'acte manqué paranoïaque: Le délire de Schreber, entre les quatre discours universitaires et dans l'histoire allemande de Luther à Bismarck*. Paris: L'Harmattan.

Devreese, D., Israels, H. & Quackelbeen, J. (1986). *Schreber inédit: Poèmes de circonstance et autres écrits du président Schreber, avec les notes autographes de l'asile de Leipzig-Dösen, et la publication intégrale de son dossier personnel retrouvé aux archives du ministère de la Justice de l'ancien royaume de Saxe*. Paris: Seuil.

De Waelhens, A. (1972). *La psychose: Essai d'interprétation analytique et existentiale*. Leuven-Paris: Nauwelaerts.

De Waelhens, A. (1981). *Le duc de Saint-Simon: Immuable comme Dieu et d'une suite enragée*. Bruxelles: Editions des Facultés Universitaires Saint-Louis.

De Waelhens, A., & Ver Eecke, W. (2001). *Phenomenology and Lacan on schizophrenia, after the decade of the brain*. Leuven (Belgium): Leuven University Press.

Freud, S. (1894/1973). Die Abwehr-Neuropsychosen: Versuch einer psychologischen Theorie der akquirierten Husterie, vieler Phobien und Zwangsvorstellungen und gewisser halluzinatorischer Psychosen. In A. Freud (Ed.), *Gesammelte Werke: Chronologisch geordnet*. Vol. I (pp. 57–74). London: Imago/Frankfurt: Fischer.

Freud, S. (1895/1973). Studien über Hysterie. In A. Freud (Ed.), *Gesammelte Werke: Chronologisch geordnet*. Vol. I (pp. 77–312). London: Imago/Frankfurt: Fischer.

Freud, S. (1911/1973). Psychoanalytische Bemerkungen über einen autobiographisch beschriebenen Fall von Paranoia (Dementia paranoides). In A. Freud (Ed.), *Gesammelte Werke: Chronologisch geordnet*. Vol. VIII I (pp. 239–320). London: Imago/Frankfurt: Fischer.

Freud, S. (1912/1973). Ueber neurotische Erkrankungstypen. In A. Freud (Ed.), *Gesammelte Werke: Chronologisch geordnet*. Vol. VIII (pp. 321–330). London: Imago/Frankfurt: Fischer.

Freud, S. (1917/1973). Metapsychologische Ergänzung zur Traumlehre. In A. Freud (Ed.), *Gesammelte Werke: Chronologisch geordnet*. Vol. X (pp. 411–426). London: Imago/Frankfurt: Fischer.

Freud, S. (1933/1971). *Nouvelles conférences sur la psychanalyse*. Paris: Gallimard.

Hugenholtz, P. (1946). Psychogene psychosen [Psychogenic psychoses]. In L. van der Horst, *Anthropologische Psychiatrie*. Deel II: Bijzonder Gedeelte: *Randpsychosen* (pp. 373–478). Amsterdam: Van Holkema & Warendorf.

Israël, L. (1977). *L'hystérique, le sexe et le médecin*. Paris: Masson.

Jeanneau, A. (1990). *Les délires non psychotiques*. Paris: Presses Universitaires de France.

Knight, R. P. (1953). Borderline states. *Bulletin of the Menninger Clinic*, *XVII*, 1–12, 139–150.

Laing, R. D. (1967). *The politics of experience and the bird of paradise*. Harmondsworth: Penguin.

Lothane, Z. (1992). *In defense of Schreber: Soul murder and psychiatry*. Hillsdale, NJ/London: Analytic Press.

Lothane, Z. (2004). *Seelenmord und Psychiatrie: Zur Rehabilitierung Schrebers*. Giessen: Psychosozial Verlag.

Maleval, J.-C. (1978a). Le délire hystérique n'est pas un délire dissocié. *Evolution Psychiatrique*, *43*, 691–739.

Maleval, J.-C. (1978b). Schizophrénie et folie hystérique. *L'Information Psychiatrique*, *54*, 743–765.

Maleval, J.-C. (1979). L'escamotage de la folie hystérique. *Psychiatries*, *3*(38), 53–75.

Maleval, J.-C. (1980). La déstructuration de l'image du corps dans les névroses et les psychoses, I et II. *Evolution Psychiatrique*, *45*, 91–129, 493–515.

Maleval, J.-C. (1981). *Folies hystériques et psychoses dissociatives*. Paris: Payot.

Maleval, J.-C. & Champanier, J.-P. (1977). Pour une réhabilitation de la folie hystérique. *Annales Médico-Psychologiques*, *135*, 229–272.

Pankow, G. (1973). L'image du corps dans la psychose hystérique. *Revue Française de Psychanalyse*, *37*, 415–438.

Prado de Oliveira, E. (1997). *Freud et Schreber: Les sources écrites du délire, entre psychose et culture*. Paris: Erès.

Richardson, J. T. (1980). People's temple and Jonestown: A corrective comparison and critique. *Journal for the Scientific Study of Religion*, *19*, 239–255.

Richardson, J. T. (1984). Psychotherapy and new religions in a pluralistic society. *American Psychologist*, *39*, 237–251.

Richardson, J. T. (1985). Psychological and psychiatric studies of new religions. In L. B. Brown (Ed.), *Advances in the psychology of religion*. Vol. II (pp. 209–223). New York: Pergamon Press.

Richardson, J. T., Best, J. & Bromley, D. G. (Eds.) (1991). *The satanism scare*. New York: Aldine de Gruyter.

Rümke, H. C. (1941/1981). Het kernsymptoom der schizofrenie en het 'praecox- gevoel' [The core symptom of schizophrenia and the 'praecox feeling']. In H. C. Rümke, *Vorm en inhoud* (pp. 63–70). Utrecht: Bohn, Scheltema & Holkema.

Rümke, H. C. (1954/1981). Een bloeiende psychiatrie in gevaar [A blossoming psychiatry is in danger]. In H. C. Rümke, *Vorm en inhoud* (pp. 188–208). Utrecht: Bohn, Scheltema & Holkema.

Schotte, J. (1981). *Analyse du destin comme pathoanalyse: Cours 1980–1981*. Louvain: Archives Szondi, Université Catholique de Louvain.

Schotte, J. (1994). Sporen: Voor een anthropopsychiatrie [Traces: In the direction of an 'antropopsychiatry']. In P. Nijs (Ed.), *De mens... in samenspraak, in tegenspraak...* Festschrift for Prof. Dr. Jacques Schotte (pp. 15–48). Leuven: Peeters.

Schreber, D. P. (1903/1973). *Denkwürdigheiten eines Nervenkranken nebst Nachträgen und einem Anhang über die Frage: "Unter welchen Voraussetzungen darf eine für geisteskrank erachtete Person gegen ihren erklärten Willen in einer Heilanstalt festgehalten werden?"* (Ed. S. M. Weber). Frankfurt a. Main: Ullstein.

West, L. J. (1993). A psychiatric overview of cult-related phenomena. *Journal of the American Academy of Psychoanalysis*, *21*, 1–19.

Psychoanalytic Contributions on the Mystical

Dan Merkur

The existence of clinical psychoanalysts who were or are mystics has largely escaped academic notice. Neither are their views well understood within the profession, where mystics are rare and mystical ways of thinking have generally been scorned and ignored. Previous scholarship on my topic is confined to a literature review in Michael Eigen's (1998) major statement of his own position, a few pages and a scholarly article by Jones (2001, 2002), and several chapters in Sayers' (2003) introductory survey of psychoanalysis, religion, and mysticism. The roster of psychoanalytic mystics nevertheless includes many eminent analysts from several major schools within psychoanalysis: Otto Rank (1884–1939), Erich Fromm (1900–1980), Marion Milner (1900–1998), D. W. Winnicott (1896–1971), Heinz Kohut (1913–1981), Hans W. Loewald (1906–1993), Wilfred R. Bion (1897–1979), and, among living writers, James S. Grotstein, Neville Symington, and Michael Eigen.

Mysticism is, of course, an enormous and poorly defined topic among both scholars and clinicians. Until the 1970s, it was widely but erroneously assumed that all mystical experiences were one and the same (for example, Heiler, 1932). The current consensus instead recognizes the diversity of mystical experiences (Almond, 1982). For social scientific purposes, I have elsewhere reflected recent textbooks in comparative mysticism by suggesting that "mysticism may be defined for contemporary purposes as a practice of religious ecstasies (that is, of religious experiences during alternate states of consciousness), together with whatever ideologies, ethics, rites, myths, legends, magics, and so forth, are related to the ecstasies" (Merkur, 2002, p. 10270). None of the psychoanalytic mystics were consistent with older definitions of mysticism that typically concerned introverted, solipsistic states and devaluations of the world of sense perception. The psychoanalytic mystics have instead been unanimous in following the "Outward Way" (Otto, 1932/1970) of

D. Merkur
University of Toronto, Toronto, ON, Canada
e-mail: dan_merkur@yahoo.ca

J.A. Belzen (ed.), *Changing the Scientific Study of Religion: Beyond Freud?*

"extrovertive mysticism" (Stace, 1960), which apperceives the world of physical reality in any of a variety of unitive ways.

The psychoanalytic mystics were none of them theologians or philosophers of religion. None had expertise in the psychology of religion. Neither did they adhere to a strict, academically defensible definition of mysticism. Most of what they discussed concerned the vicissitudes of unitive experience and thinking; but some also addressed the undifferentiated, the numinous, and/or the transcendent. For convenience, I use the historian Michel de Certeau's term *la mystique*, "the mystical," which de Certeau contrasted with *le mysticisme*, "mysticism." De Certeau's translator proposed the noun "mystics" in parallel with physics, mathematics, ethics, and aesthetics (de Certeau, 1982/1992); but Kripal (2007) suggests that we refer instead *la mystique*, "the mystical." My suggestion that "the mystical" is an imprecise umbrella term is intended to reflect common usage. Psychoanalytic patients are similarly unschooled and imprecise in their uses of such terms as religious, spiritual, mystical, transcendent, and so forth. It is consequently appropriate for clinical purposes to be inclusive of the views of the psychoanalytic mystics, rather than to fuss academically about definitions and categories.

Only Milner, Grotstein, Symington, and Eigen openly called themselves mystics. Fromm discussed his practice of meditation, praised mysticism, but did not label himself a mystic. Winnicott (1971/1974, p. 123) wrote that his views were like those of mystics except that he applied his interiorism to the world of sense perception. Rank, Kohut, and Bion were silent regarding their private convictions, but they wrote in praise of mysticism so very knowingly that their allegiances are transparent. Lastly, Loewald discussed the proximity of his views to existentialism but would have been surprised to hear the term "mystical" applied to himself (Ana-Maria Rizzuto, 2007, Personal Communication). From the standpoint of the academic study of comparative mysticism, all ten theoreticians may nevertheless be regarded as mystics. Historically, they can be seen as a distinctive movement or trend within the history of mysticism that compares, for example, with American Transcendentalism. Highly individual voices that bear a family resemblance among themselves, they differed in common manners from previous trends in the history of mysticism. None conformed with an existing religious institution and its historical mysticism. All were extrovertive mystics, for whom the unification of all things proceeds in the world of sense perception, and not as an introverted withdrawal from the world. Most privileged interpersonal relations – the unions of love and fellowship – as the most mature and desirable types of union. As analysts, all practiced "evenly hovering attention" while listening to their patients, which Fromm, Bion, Grotstein, Symington, and Eigen explicitly recognized as a type of meditation. None of the psychoanalytic mystics advocated the kinds of "concentrative meditation" (Goleman 1977) that intravertive mystics employ. Neither did the psychoanalytic mystics privilege dissociative states (Ostow and Scharfstein, 1954; Furst et al., 1976), with their consequences for derealization and depersonalization.

The psychoanalytic mystics were divided in their opinions regarding the relation of psychoanalysis to mysticism. Commenting on his study, *The Future of an Illusion* (1927/1961), Freud had recommended: "He who occupies himself with science arrives at agnosticism" (Sterba, 1978, p. 178). Although Rank endorsed Nietzsche's metaphysics and Fromm described himself as an atheist, Milner, Winnicott, Kohut, and Loewald conformed with Freud's example and limited themselves to agnostic discussions of the mystical. Bion, Grotstein, Symington, and Eigen have instead espoused panentheism – all things are in and of God – and they have conceptualized clinical psychoanalysis as a mystical practice. Leavy (1995) argued, however, for the continuing importance of separating psychological work from mystical faith-claims.

> It think it is important to pursue this examination in a literally agnostic way, neither presuming nor excluding the divine origins of the mystics' experiences. If the religious believe cannot allow this bracketing of faith, i.e. a suspension of judgement on its 'reality,' then he would do well to avoid any psychoanalytic consideration at all. And if the skeptical psychoanalyst cannot allow that the faith of the mystics be taken seriously enough to bracket it, he might also better abandon the quest. (p. 354)

Where methodological agnosticism permits psychoanalysts of all persuasions to aspire to a consensus, the accommodation of faith-claims within psychoanalysis leads rapidly to the divisiveness of religious dogmatism. We have already seen, for example, an Orthodox Jewish psychoanalysis (Spero, 1992) and a Protestant Christian psychoanalysis (Sorenson, 2004) that are necessarily unacceptable to analysts and patients whose faith-claims are otherwise. The axiomatic presuppositions of Bion, Grotstein, Symington, and Eigen present similar problems.

In the space of this article, it will not be possible to offer more than a rapid survey of literature that fills two metres of shelf space. The theoretical views reflect differences in data, in ideas of what mysticism is, and in approaches to formulation. The approaches converge in many respects, but a thorough-going synthesis is not to be expected.

Mystical Experience as a Transient Anomaly

The modern study of mysticism had its origin with Catholic and Anglican responses to Charcot's claim that the hysterics of the Saltpetrière could produce all of the miracles of the saints (Knowles, 1967/1979); but apologetics were soon followed by psychological studies (James, 1902/1958; Underhill, 1910/1955) and a revival of interest in the practice of mysticism among lay people. As late as 1914, it was still possible for a psychoanalyst to use the term "mysticism" when referring to spiritual alchemy (Silberer, 1914/1971); but the *Zeitgeist* was already in process of change. The publication in 1913 of Karl Jaspers's *Allgemeine Psychopathologie* (1913/1963) brought international attention to Søren Kierkegaard's theory that every child's psychological development replicates the fall of Adam. Kierkegaard suggested that Adam was created in natural union with animal life, but his acquisition of the knowledge of good and evil provided him with moral responsibility, selfhood, and transcendence of nature, including his body. In the same year, the American psychoanalyst Trigant Burrow (1914, 1917, 1918) advanced an analytic variant of Kierkegaard's theory that replaced Kierkegaard's idea of union in the sense of community or fellowship with animal life, with the different idea of mystical union.

Burrow characterized neonatal mentality as an unthinking, precognitive process that he named "primary identification." After Burrow lectured but before he went to press, Freud (1914/1957) published his own ideas about neonatal experience. Freud similarly proposed a developmental progression from mystical to rational thinking, but his concepts of primary and secondary narcissism located both phases within consciousness.

In 1919 (English translation, 1933), Sandor Ferenczi proposed the theory that genitality, the adult drive to coitus, is symbolically a return to the condition of the foetus in the womb. The concept of intrauterine regression was promptly taken up by psychoanalytic writers on mysticism, most famously by Alexander (1931) in a 1922 congress paper (see also Moxon, 1920; Schroeder, 1922; Carver, 1924; Rank, 1929/1993). In 1927, after Rank's ideas about the trauma of separation from the mother had been attacked as a threat to the hegemony of Freud's theory of the Oedipus complex, Helene Deutsch interpreted mystical union as a fusion of the ego with the superego. Three years later, in a discussion of the "oceanic feeling," Freud (1930/1961) re-asserted his interpretation of mysticism as a persistence of the neonatal state of the ego. Little further was added for over two decades. In the 1950s, the analysis of the symbolism in mystical experiences that occur spontaneously in mania led to theories of regressions to falling asleep after satiated nursing (Lewin, 1951; Greenacre, 1958/1971; Linn and Schwarz, 1958). When direct infant observation established that newborns communicate with their mothers (Gaensbauer, 1982; Lichtenberg, 1983; Stern, 1983, 1985), the theory of neonatal solipsism was abandoned (Kernberg, 1991), and mystical experiences were interpreted as regressions to wishful fantasies of mother–child fusion that compensate for the disappointment of separation during the second year of life (Pine, 1981, 1986, 1990; Meissner, 1992). Mystical experiences have generally been considered pathological (Ostow and Scharfstein, 1954; Furst et al., 1976); but formulations since the 1960s have tended increasingly to diagnose regression in the service of the ego (Deikman, 1966a, b; Prince and Savage, 1966; Allison, 1968; Fauteux, 1994, 1997; Meissner, 1999).

The psychoanalytic mainstream has regularly assumed that mystical ecstasies are anomalous experiences. The common assumption has been unaffected by differences of opinion as to whether the infantile solipsism underlying mystical experiences are intrauterine, neonatal, a fantasy of fusion with the breast, pathological, or in the service of the ego. The shared assumption unwittingly perpetuates the Christian belief that mystical union is discontinuous with the rest of life. Whether mystical experience is seen as supernatural grace intervening within the soul's nature, or infantile solipsism interrupting a more mature psychic organization, it has been treated as an anomaly, as something apart from the rest of psychology that can safely be ignored for most practical purposes.

The Mystical as a Developmental Line

The psychoanalytic mystics have consistently taken the fundamentally different position that mystical experiences are not anomalous and unimportant, but are part of something much more central to human psychology. Paul Federn (1926, 1932, 1952), who linked mental ego-feeling to ecstasies and suggested that it antedates body ego-feeling, also suggested that primary narcissism persists unconsciously, changing and developing throughout life. Federn's conceptualization of the legacy of primary narcissism as a developmental line, a biologically driven trajectory of healthy growth and maturation, constituted a paradigm shift not only for the psychoanalytic theory of mysticism, but in the general history of mysticism. The world's major mystical traditions often discuss mystical development as progress in achieving mystical experiences of the type or types that particular traditions privilege. Development in this context consists of the acquisition of a cognitive skill set, a learning to have mystical experiences (Bharati, 1976; Brown and Engler, 1984). The psychoanalytic mystics have instead conceptualized mystical development in terms of epigenetic maturation. For example, my own previous efforts (Merkur, 1998, 1999), written in ignorance of most of the publications that I review in this article, conceptualized different varieties of mystical experiences with reference to the Freud-Abraham stages of psychosexual development, as the latter have been refined and extended into adulthood by ego psychologists.

Otto Rank

The first extensive contributions on the mystical in psychoanalysis were offered by two analysts who were expelled from the psychoanalytic establishment, Otto Rank and Erich Fromm. After two decades of close collaboration with Freud, Rank struck an independent course when, in *The Trauma of Birth* (1929), he rejected Freud's (1920/1955) theory of the death instinct and accounted for its clinical evidence by postulating that birth is traumatic. On first publication in German in 1924, Rank (1929) attributed the trauma to the infant's physical separation from the mother at birth, but he was speaking of psychological separation, as we today think, by the late 1920s. Although Freud, who was then newly diagnosed with cancer, initially liked the book, Karl Abraham and Ernest Jones spin-doctored its emphasis on the mother trauma as an abandonment of the Oedipus complex; and Freud, fearful for the Oedipus theory after his death, supported their reading. In the sequel, Freud lived another 15 years, but Rank, deeply wounded, left the psychoanalytic movement. Rank's post-psychoanalytic writings went unmentioned in "orthodox" Freudian publications, but his original ideas contributed to the interpersonal, existential, and relational approaches to psychoanalysis.

Rank's (1930/1998, 1932a, b, 1941, 1968, 1996) post-Freudian practice, which he called "will therapy," inaugurated a paradigm shift in the understanding of the mystical. Mysticism was not a question of rare, transient experiences that were unconnected with the major trends of psychic life. The psyche was mystical from birth to adulthood. Rank started with Nietzsche's model of a Dionysian, mystical unconsciousness and an Apollinian, rational consciousness or ego. For Rank, the process of "individualization" from primal unity was the central human dilemma. The solipsism of the unconscious was the same for everyone. Individuality was a matter of the ego. Will, which was located in the ego, originated as a counter-force, a repression of primal unity, and only secondarily became a positive force, a will that was not engaged in repression but was free to progress upon its own. The ego's establishment of an ego ideal provided direction for its further growth, as well as both fear and guilt. Each emotion was paradoxical. There was fear to individuate, but fear also pertained to the failure to achieve and individuate. There were both guilt over having individuated, and guilt over the failure to individuate. Rank's "will therapy" used the psychoanalytic situation to promote regression to and resolution of the birth trauma, as means to reduce inhibition by fear and guilt. Once will was firmly individuated, it had access to the vitalism of the unconscious in the form of mystical experiences and, more importantly, artistic and other creativity. Artistry was a sort of applied mysticism, a unity of artist and artwork or artifact that imposes an individuated will on external reality. In Rank's understanding of the human, there is no not being mystical. There is only being mystical inefficiently; and therapy's address of psychopathology seeks to correct morbid forms of the mystical.

Erich Fromm

Where Rank believed that creativity was mystical and "beyond psychology," Fromm regarded psychoanalysis as a therapy of repressedness that could additionally be practiced to "transtherapeutic" and mystical ends. Fromm (1941) asserted that individuation from neonatal oneness is fearful and leads to "mechanisms of escape from freedom" that are pathological vicissitudes of union. Authoritarianism depends on a sado-masochistic symbiosis of leader and follower. Conformism finds union in the group; while destructiveness destroys the object that is unavailable for union. Fromm (1947) argued that ethics have a mystical basis in the personality, in that self-love and love for others coincide, as do self-hate and hate for others. He then contrasted rational and irrational authority, rational and irrational ethics, and the psychic processes of conscience and the superego, respectively. Rational ethics are exclusively concerned with human welfare, which involves a "productive orientation" of the personality toward both love and work. Fromm (1950) next contrasted humanistic and authoritarian religion, treated the negative theology and/or metaphysics of the mystics as humanistic, and described the mystical in terms of wonderment, concern for relatedness, and oneness in self, others, and the all. He argued that psychoanalysis was a humanistic religion, a path of individuation that pursued the goals of the mystics. In a study of dreams, Fromm (1951, p. 33) suggested that "we are not only less reasonable and less decent in our dreams but (...) we are also more intelligent, wiser, and capable of better judgment." To the Freudian understanding of dream symbolism he added a new category, the universal symbol, which was an unconscious evaluation whose projection transformed phenomena into symbols. For example, people in a desert tend to evaluate the sun one way, in an Arctic climate another, so that meaning does not inhere in the sun (as phenomenologists and Jungians maintain), but in the universal values that are unconsciously projected onto the sun. The capacity to manifest universal symbols imparts a higher wisdom to dreams. Fromm's (1955) use of existential terms and concepts increased markedly after he articulated his theory of universal symbols, presumably because he saw self, reason, love, life, death, and other "transcendental" quiddities not existentially as inherently meaningful phenomena, but psychoanalytically as universal symbols. Taking up the problem of capitalism, Fromm (1955) proposed that the investment of part of oneself in an external thing, which then rules over oneself, is a form of symbiosis, a pathological type of oneness. In Marxist terms, it is an alienation not only of the worker from the work, but of the person from anything that may healthfully be done productively. In prophetic terms, it is an idolatry; and in clinical psychoanalysis, it is the transference. Fromm (1956) maintained that mature loving union between two people was the optimal form of oneness that is possible for human beings; immature love, consisting of a symbiotic fusion, was again a pathological vicissitude of the mystical.

Fromm's (1962) therapeutic procedures placed the cultivation of a reciprocal I–Thou relationship at the center of the analysis and interpreted any deviation from a wholesome rapport as a transference. He regarded the analyst not as a participant observer, but as an observant participant. Fromm (1980, 1991, 1992, 1994a) privileged the interpretation of dreams and the patient's coming to awareness of his or her suffering. He discouraged the daydreaming and infantilization that ego psychologists promoted in their handling of free association. An analysis was completed when the patient had learned to self-analyze properly. Fromm et al. (1960, 1994a, b) recommended Zen meditation and mindfulness meditation as valuable, optional adjuncts to psychoanalysis, for both analysts and patients. He considered reality to be ultimately paradoxical in a dialectical (Hegelian) fashion. He compared satori with psychoanalytic insight – implicitly, with his sort of mystical psychoanalytic insight. He also recognized that biblical monotheism served paradoxically to promote individuation. "Obedience to God is also the negation of submission to man" (Fromm, 1966, p. 73). In passing remarks on psychedelic mysticism, Fromm, 1973, pp. 247–248, 1994b, pp. 78–79) noted that genuine mystical experiences do not of themselves produce mystical character transformations. Neither do they avoid narcissistic appropriations of mystical experience. Where Rank was a Romantic, imagining the mystical creative personality as a rare individual, Fromm was a Utopian who saw the mystical in all manner of common, everyday experiences that were readily accessed by all of humanity.

Marion Milner

Marion Milner was a mystically inclined amateur painter who published two books about her artistic process, under the pseudonym Joanna Field, before her work as an education psychologist led to her training as a psychoanalyst. Her first book reported her discovery that "an internal gesture of standing back and watching" (Field, 1934/1986, p. 101) might bring on more valuable creativity than she could produce through an effort of will. There was something more at work in her, something unconscious, than she had realized. After book reviews remarked that her self-reports included mystical experiences, she embraced the term. In her second book (Field, 1937/1986), she developed the idea that creativity could endow objects, both those she happened to see and those that she created as an artist, with meanings that originated in "the inner attitudes and movements of the spirit" (p. 167). She set herself the task of learning to know "the mysterious force by which one is lived, the 'not-self', which was yet also in me" (p. 179). She knew that psychoanalysis worked with "storm-giving images, and others (...) that brought panics and confusions," but she was equally concerned with "peace-giving images, which seemed to be no less powerful" (p. 192). She recognized that access to her unconscious creativity required an "internal gesture of submission" (p. 207). At this time, she began analysis with Sylvia Paine and befriended D. W. Winnicott. Her third book (Field, 1957), was published after her qualification as a psychoanalyst and years of exchanging ideas with Winnicott. The book discussed artistic creativity as a union of the artist and the artwork, during which "the imaginative realities of the inner world" are imparted to "the tangible realities of the external world" (p. 9). The integrity of a successful artwork, and its seeming autonomy from the artist who created it, attested to "a rhythm and pattern and integrated wholeness" (p. 80) that Milner attributed to the unconscious. She concluded that creativity originates in "moments when there is a temporary fusion of inner and outer, an undoing of the split between self and not-self, seer and seen" (p. 190). In a foreword to the second edition of the book, Anna Freud noted parallels between the creative and psychoanalytic processes. Milner's (1987) collected psychoanalytic articles include technical elaborations of her views on the mystical.

D. W. Winnicott

Winnicott's (1945/1992, 1948/1992) ideas about babies fantasizing the breast before discovering it, which results in the illusion that they have created it, had inspired Milner's thesis that creativity in the arts and also in science and technology, proceeds by imposing an illusion on external reality. Winnicott (1951/1989, 1953, 1971), in his turn, extended Milner's thesis into a general theory that culture in its entirely, including our most scientific knowledge of reality, is precisely the same sort of creative illusion – and has its paradigmatic example in a child's Teddy bear. It is an objective, inanimate thing that paradoxically has living, subjective meaning, and there is no knowledge of reality that is not equally paradoxical, equally an illusion born of the coincidence of subjectivity and objective reality.

Anton Ehrenzweig

Another friend of Milner, Anton Ehrenzweig, was a university level art teacher who was deeply engaged in Kleinian object relations theory. He published two books on the theory of creative illusion. Ehrenzweig's (1953) first book argued that Gestalt psychologists' division of consciousness into the figure and ground of attention had implications for depth psychology. He suggested that the vagueness of the conscious ground was consistent with unconscious perception, in being less differentiated, as is consistent with the demonstrable perceptions of children. Creativity accesses comparatively undifferentiated perceptions that are made unconsciously while consciousness is occupied with the figure of attention. In his second book, Ehrenzweig (1967) recognized that artists and musicians routinely cultivate the ability to attend to both the figure and the ground simultaneously. This de-differentiation of attention is also practiced by psychoanalysts as "evenly hovering attention." The creative surrender to conscious de-differentiation enables unconscious perceptions to manifest despite their comparative undifferentiation. Ehrenzweig postulated a stratification within the unconscious that reflected a developmental sequence of increasing differentiation that is laid down during the child's passage from primary narcissism through the (Kleinian) stages of psychosexual development. All art is ultimately mystical; mysticism is creativity at its core.

Both Ehrenzweig and most writers who have cited his ideas failed to appreciate that the de-differentiation of consciousness to become comparatively undifferentiated differs from unitive experiences. Where de-differentiation suspends use of Gestalts, allowing simpler and more basic Gestalts to come into play, unitive experiences involve discrete ideas of unity that function apperceptually as Gestalts that unify sense data. Undifferentiation is a watchful, uncritical state, lacking many ideas of normal consciousness. For example, a visual field may be reduced to areas of color, devoid of ideas that identify the objects that have the colors. Union is a state that involves ideas of unity or unification, for example, the concept that a variety of perceptible objects are united in having color. De-differentiation and union can coincide, but vary independently.

More on Winnicott

Winnicott's (1965, 1971, 1975/1992) theories of early ego development may be understood as further contributions to the psychoanalysis of the mystical. Like Rank and Fromm, Winnicott saw individuation from neonatal solipsism as a major developmental challenge. Winnicott's theorizing began with the clinical fact that analysis of aggression will arrive a patient at the guilt, remorse, and wish to make reparation that Melanie Klein termed the depressive position. Winnicott described it as a "capacity for concern" and agreed with Klein regarding its onset in health around age 8 months. He also cited it as evidence that children are innately good. Winnicott then proceeded to coordinate Freud's and Klein's ideas about early ego development. The realistic awareness of self and other that Freud had named secondary narcissism was the condition of relations, in Klein's terms, between whole objects. Winnicott spoke of the achievement of "unit status" as the condition for the capacity for concern. Addressing Freud's concept of primary narcissism, Winnicott famously maintained that "there is no such thing as a baby." There is always both the baby and a caretaker. Infantile solipsism consists of the infant plus the environment, including the maternal care that the infant experiences as part of its self. Primary narcissism is paradoxically an object relation, a solipsistic experience of self that resolves analytically into the baby and its "environmental mother." Dovetailing with Ehrenzweig's ideas of undifferentiated perception, Winnicott suggested that the baby begins with an "unintegrated" sense of self and incrementally builds up memories of different experiences that gradually coalesce into a coherent sense of bodily self. The achievement of an integrated sense of self coincides with the capacity to become anxious at the prospect of disintegration.

In between the "environment–individual set-up" of the neonate and "unit status" of the capacity for concern was a "transitional stage" of development. Transitional phenomena were exemplified by the Teddy bear and included creative illusions as a class. All were experienced solipsistically as subjectively perceived objects. They were subject to "object-relating" that involved an unconcern that was pre-ruth rather than ruthless. When objects had unit status and were perceived objectively, Winnicott referred instead to "object usage" that manifested a capacity for concern. Pathogenic development during the solipsistic developmental stages produced pathology of the self. People experienced inauthenticity or meaningless or otherwise felt that their self was unreal or false. A true self, by contrast, found meaning through creativity. The therapeutic shift from a false self to a true self was conceptualized by existentialism as self-actualization, but was seen by Winnicott as an unconscious object relation between the infant and environmental mother components within the sense of self. A lifelong legacy of infantile solipsism was an incommunicado element at the core of the personality, which manifested, among other manners, in the mental orgasms of mystical ecstasies. Also related to the infant–mother dyad were the capacity to be alone and the capacity to believe-in whatever might be the object of belief. Winnicott followed Michael Balint (1937/1952, 1969/1992) in postulating a naturally occurring healing process that could be facilitated clinically by promoting a regression to the developmental stage prior to the occurrence of trauma. Winnicott regarded the therapeutic process as a regression prior to the onset of the false self, in order to gain access to the primary creativity at the core of the true self.

Heinz Kohut

Kohut (1971, 1977, 1978a, b, 1984, 1990, 1991) founded his system of self psychology on a redefinition of narcissism. Where Freud had discussed the devotion of psychosexual desire toward objects that could include the self, Kohut discussed the devotion of self-love ("narcissistic cathexis") toward both the self and other objects, in parallel with object-love ("object cathexis") toward others. In this way, he postulated that narcissism formed a developmental line that paralleled the line that led from primary to secondary narcissism. The narcissistic developmental line led from "archaic narcissism" to "mature narcissism" without interruption of its narcissism. Developmentally prior to archaic narcissism was a state of disintegration that was to be avoided. The ever-present threat of its recurrence provoked anxiety and rage. Archaic narcissism was Kohut's term for infantile solipsism. Narcissism then divided into the "grandiose self" and idealized objects. Other people were experienced as "selfobjects" whose existence was appreciated only in so far as it was meaningful to the self. In Winnicott's terms, they were subjectively perceived objects. In 1966, Kohut remarked that mature narcissism involved awareness of both the finitude of the self and its participation within a greater infinity. At the end of his life, Kohut (1985) explicitly suggested that "the transformation of narcissism into the spirit of religiosity" might give rise to "a new rational religion (…) an as yet uncreated system of mystical rationality" and he called for psychoanalysis's "amalgamation with mystical modes of thinking" (pp. 70–71). Kohut designed self psychology to promote the developmental shift from the naive assumption of being the One into a realistic awareness of being one of the Many that participate in the One. It was a therapy of the mystical, but it had no aspiration to reduce repression. It was a question, in Winnicott's terms, of modifying the false self to become less socially maladaptive.

Hans W. Loewald

Marjorie Brierley (1947, 1951) introduced the concept of psychic integration when she suggested that the Christian mystical life aims at an integration of the ego and the superego, whereas psychoanalysis promotes the integration of the id together with the ego and the superego. Loewald (1978, 1980, 1988) placed integration at the center of his understanding of both human development and psychoanalysis. He ordinarily referred to integration and avoided the term "mysticism." However, Loewald (1978) included himself in his discussion of the quality of timelessness that mystical experiences share with commonplace experiences that "all of us know" (p. 64) and he traced timelessness to condensation. In recognizing that condensation can represent all time as the one eternal now, Loewald traced mystical experiences to the id. He interpreted ecstasy as a fusion of instincts, hence as regressions to the id in the service of the ego. Noting the dedifferentiation in mystical experiences, he traced their developmental origin to early infancy, but abandoned the term "primary narcissism" as an inaccurate means to discuss "the absence of subject–object differentiation." In this way, Loewald conceptualized the undifferentiation of the neonatal psyche and its use of condensation to achieve integration through unitive thinking – implicitly, two different aspects of the mystical.

Loewald cited Freud on the tendency of Eros to "bind together," accomplishing integration. He saw the ego's synthetic function as its contribution to integration. The synthetic function accomplishes a compromise between its attraction to unity and its dread of engulfment in the non-differentiation of the womb. The result is a unity that coincides with progression, a tendency to synthesize at ever more differentiated levels of organization. Oscillations between de-differentiating regression and differentiating progression proceed constantly as the means by which the psyche accomplishes integration. In representing the past from the perspective of the future, the superego integrates the temporal dimension of psychic experience. Preoedipal identifications contribute structure to the ego; oedipal identifications are internalized as the superego. Preoedipal mechanisms, such as introjection, projective identification, and splitting promote differentiation, as also do the classical defenses of neurotics. Sublimation carries instinct forward to the highest levels of differentiation, accomplishing a union of the psychic levels involved. The psyche's capacity to move back and forth among its divisions and levels, the fluidity of its access to its constituent parts, is the index of its health. Psychoanalysis promotes integration. Interpretations rid the psyche of stagnation and promote synthesis by reflecting the patient's state from the higher level of organization that belongs to the analyst. In this respect, the analyst performs a parental function, empathizing with the patient from a more mature perspective whose internalization by the patient promotes the integrative process. The parental function made psychoanalysis an asymmetrical two-person psychology.

The theory of the mystical as a developmental line reached critical mass with Loewald. Rank had located the mystical "beyond psychology," Fromm called it "transtherapeutic." Milner, Ehrenzweig, Winnicott, and Kohut connected the mystical with earliest childhood and occasional repercussions in later life. Loewald instead argued that both psychic development and psychoanalysis were integrative from top to bottom. The therapeutic process was not to be contrasted with integration. The psyche's natural healing process was the particular type of integration to which the psyche resorts when dealing with repression.

Loewald further maintained that psychoanalysis is a moral enterprise. In making the unconscious conscious, psychoanalysis calls every patient to become accountable for his or her unconscious. The call to self-knowledge is a call to responsibility for one's actions. In this connection, even guilt is an integrative force in the psyche. Morality and religiosity are normative in health; their repression, which Loewald called as severe in our time as the repression of sexuality was in Freud's era, is pathological. "Superpersonal and transcendental aspects of human existence and of unconscious and instinctual life ... can be experienced and integrated convincingly – without escapist embellishments, otherworldly consolations, and going off into the clouds – only in the concreteness of one's own personal life, including the ugliness, trivialities, and sham that go with it" (Loewald, 1980, p. 416). In his final publication, Loewald (1988) offered an implicitly mystical conception of nature. He suggested that psychoanalysis is a science that makes an objective study of subjectivity. Because subjectivity exists in nature, it necessarily belongs to nature, even if it manifests in individual consciousnesses alone.

Clinical Psychoanalysis as a Two-Person Practice of Mysticism

Loewald (1960) was responsible for persuading American ego psychologists that the image of the analyst as a neutral mirror was mistaken, and that clinical psychoanalysis is a two-way interaction between the analyst and the analysand (Bergmann, 2000, p. 61). He did not suggest, however, that the psychoanalytic process is integrative for the analyst as well as the analysand. It was Bion who first conceptualized clinical psychoanalysis not only as a therapy of the pathological vicissitudes of the mystical, but also as a two-person practice of mysticism. Unfortunately, Bion abandoned methodological agnosticism at the same time. Bion has since been followed by several writers who have similarly mixed metaphysics with their psychology. Because each has advanced a different metaphysical position, the possibility of a consensus has been precluded. Even if a school of mysticism were to emerge, metaphysical faith-claims can only be evaluated from scientific and humanistic perspectives as speculations. Methodological agnosticism remains a valuable self-discipline for mystics, as it keeps them aware of the distinction between what they know and what they speculate. It is necessary to consensual progress in research both among mystics and in the general professional community.

Wilfred R. Bion

Precisely because he was familiar with pagan and Christian Neoplatonism and the kabbalah, Bion (1962, 1963/1984, 1965/1984, 1967/1984, 1970/1984, 1989, 1994) brought both a doctrinal precision and a dogmatic bias to his metaphysics. He began with the fact that the latent contents of psychotic hallucinations and delusions are often transparent to external observers. According to Freud's theory of the dream-work, the preconscious ego devises the latent content of the dream. All that the unconscious contributes is the conversion of the latent content into symbolism. If Freud's theory were correct, the latent content of psychotic productions should be as mad as the rest of their ego functions. The latent contents are nevertheless as coherent as anyone's dreams. To account for the coherence of latent thoughts that psychotics are incapable of thinking, Bion took recourse to Plato's World of Forms. He suggested that psychotic productions are "thoughts without a thinker." They are Platonic Forms that inform their sense perceptions without the knowledge of the psychotics. The analytic task is to enable the patient to transform unthought Forms within their psyches into thoughts that they think. Bion invented the term "beta-elements" to designate unthought Forms in sense perceptions and emotions; and the terms "alpha-function" and "alpha-elements" to designate thinking and thoughts, respectively. Alpha-function included a great many cognitive activities. The most important were the dreamwork, which converts beta-elements into images than can be thought with, and abstract conceptual thinking, which converts imagery into higher order mentation.

Bion suggested that the analytic situation replicates the infant–mother dyad, in which the baby presents beta-elements to the mother, for the mother to contain and transform into alpha-elements by means of her alpha-function. Once the mother, in her state of reverie, produces the alpha-elements, she communicates them to the baby, who gradually builds up his own alpha-function on their basis. Because beta-elements are Forms that cannot be thought, their communication must always proceed unconsciously, from the unconscious of the baby or patient to the unconscious of the mother or analyst. If the communication is conscious, the elements must already have been converted to alpha-elements before they were communicated, and there is no need for the analyst to alpha-function for the patient. The type of unconscious communication that conveys Forms that are not being thought is called "projective identification" in Kleinian object relations theory. Feelings and ideas are evacuated out of a person through their placement in another person. For example, hatred that is intolerable to the patient may be felt by the analyst as the analyst's hatred of the patient. Close observation will discover that the patient unconsciously manipulated the analyst into hating the patient. Bion recommended that an analyst entertain neither memory, desire, nor understanding while listening to patients, in order to detect the unconscious effects in herself of the patient's projective identifications. Bion described the analyst's state of consciousness as a reverie.

In transforming beta-elements into alpha-elements, the analyst's alpha-function transforms sense data and emotions into knowledge and deploys knowledge in the pursuit of truth. To complete the ascension from the Many to the One, Bion proposed the term "O," abbreviating the word "origin" (Bion, 1965/1984, p. 15), to designate the ineffable God of negative theology.

> I shall use the sign O to denote that which is the ultimate reality represented by terms such as ultimate reality, absolute truth, the godhead, the infinite, the thing-in-itself. O does not fall in the domain of knowledge or learning save incidentally; it can be 'become,' but it cannot be 'known.' It is darkness and formlessness but it enters the domain K[nowledge] when it has evolved to a point where it can be known, through knowledge gained by experience, and formulated in terms derived from sensuous experience; its existence is conjectured phenomenologically. (Bion, 1970/1984, p. 26)

For Bion, O was the unknowable essence of God; and an analyst with neither memory, desire, nor understanding is engaged in faith in O, while listening to detect the patient's beta-elements in the form of the analyst's own countertransferences. Bion's O was not exclusively transcendent, however. O was simultaneously immanent as the unknowable thing-in-itself of each beta-element. O is both no-thing and all things, because all is in and of God. The process of mystical ascension, from sense data to knowledge to faith and the ineffable, in which the analyst serves as the patient's spiritual guide, is a process that transpires within O, who is God.

With his postulate of O, Bion and those who have followed him routinely transgressed the methodological boundaries of psychoanalysis. Bion's concept of O conflated the transcendent with the manifest, no-thing with all things, that of which we know and can say nothing with everything that we sense perceive and know. Bion's panentheism may be regarded as a simplistic metaphysics that was equal and opposite to the materialistic reductionism of mainstream psychoanalysis. Bion's question was "mystical or not"? The methodologically agnostic psychoanalytic mystics had instead moved the boundary line between psychology and metaphysics, by claiming large parts of the mystical as psychological. Their work could accommodate a negative theology, an O that was no-thing; but they avoided, presumably as an idolatry or impiety, the option of additionally deifying all that we sense perceive and know.

Bion's Neoplatonic psychoanalysis was dogmatic. He wrote of transformations in and of O and did not write of interpreting anything other than projective identifications. His description of both psychotic productions and sense data as beta-elements implied that sense data may be a type of hallucination. Bion was agnostic regarding the existence of physical matter. Bion (1994) wrote: "The classic psycho-analytic view supposed the mind or personality to be identical with the physical identity of a person. The object of my proposal is to do away with such a limitation and to regard the relationship between body and mind (or personality, or psyche) as one that is subject to investigation" (p. 314). He affirmed the existence of a "noösphere," a term that he took from Teilhard de Chardin (p. 313), but the existence of a material stratum to the cosmos remained an open question. "The breast, the thing in itself, is indistinguishable from an idea in the mind. The idea of a breast in the mind is, reciprocally, indistinguishable from the thing itself in the mouth.... The realization and the representation of it in the mind have not been differentiated" (Bion, 1962, pp. 57–58). It is possible that Bion held to the view, anciently maintained by the Christian Neoplatonists St Basil of Caesarea and St Gregory of Nyssa (Armstrong, 1955), that perceptible phenomena are thoughts that exist in the mind of God and have no physical existence.

Bion had no use for Milner's, Winnicott's, and Ehrenzweig's ideas about the conjunction of subjectivity and objective reality in generating the paradoxes of creative illusions. Bion's mysticism was of the exclusively inward type from which Fromm, Winnicott, Kohut, and Loewald explicitly distanced themselves. Bion was a panentheist for whom all things, including individual human psyches, exist in and of O. Continual mystical union is the invariable nature of all existence; there is no not being at one with O. We are all O, everything we do is O. The mystical project is not to achieve union, but to become aware of the divine nature of all that is. Bion's mystical practice was consequently focussed exclusively on ascending the "great chain of being" (Lovejoy, 1936/1976) which he conceptualized, in Neoplatonic fashion, as a hierarchy of types of mentation: sense data, dream images and fantasies, knowledge, faith. Bion's mysticism had only limited points of contact with earlier psychoanalytic contributions on the mystical. He showed no interest in the oceanic feeling, the vicissitudes of individuation, the processes of integration, freedom of will, moral responsibility, or creativity.

Bion's concept of alpha-function may nevertheless be counted as a major contribution to psychoanalytic theory, to which his interest in the mystical had sensitized him. Bion was attempting to formulate much the same phenomena that led Fromm to conceptualize conscience and the unconscious production of universal symbolism, Milner and Ehrenzweig to revise the theory of primary process, and Winnicott to treat the internalization of both the environmental mother and the unit status mother at the foundation of the capacity for concern. On the clinical side, Bion's advice that an analyst seek a state of reverie by listening to patients without memory, desire, or understanding, may be compared with Ehrenzweig's observation that the analyst's "evenly hovering attention" opens consciousness to de-differentiation by attending simultaneously to the figure and the ground. Both are ways of speaking of the analyst's "creative surrender" to the task of analysis.

James S. Grotstein

A Los Angeles analyst who was re-analyzed by Bion, Grotstein (1981, 1996, 1997, 2000) recognized that the coherent creativity that is sometimes apparent in the manifest content of dreams is inconsistent with Freud's theory of dreamwork. Elaborating Bion's theory of alpha-function, Grotstein speculated that dreams are intrapsychic communications between functions that he personified as the Dreamer Who Dreams the Dream and the Dreamer Who Understands the Dream. He later referred to the two personifications – in Kleinian terms, "internal objects" – as the Ineffable and Phenomenal Subjects. The Ineffable Subject creates the dream; the Phenomenal Subject receives it, much as a patient receives alpha-elements through her analyst's interpretations of her beta-elements. Grotstein further identified the Ineffable and Phenomenal Subjects as the id and the ego, respectively.

Grotstein conceptualized the Ineffable Subject as a numinous, preternatural, psychic presence whose union with the Phenomenal Subject constitutes mystical union, or the attainment of the transcendent position. Psychic presences are the phenomena that Klein and Bion regarded as internal objects, but Grotstein maintained that they do not have subjectivity, do not think, and do not have autonomy. They are recurring characters that are portrayed as autonomous, thinking subjects in the manifest contents of dreams, symptoms, and other derivatives of unconscious phantasies; but the only subjectivity in the psyche is the one subjectivity of the psyche as a whole. The Ineffable and Phenomenal Subjects is each a presence with a distinct orientation and line of development. The Ineffable Subject reasons in a mathematical fashion that Ignacio Matte-Blanco (1959) termed "symmetrical." It produces what Fromm called the paradoxical logic of mysticism. The Phenomenal Subject accomplishes asymmetrical thinking, in keeping with Aristotelian logic. The two types of thinking produce different types of content. The Ineffable Subject is solipsistic, synchronistic, and "autochthonous" – a term that Grotstein employed to refer to Winnicott's concept of creative illusion. The Phenomenal Subject engages in "alterity," the construction of an external world, with reality-testing and object relations. The two subjectivities are responsible for the paranoid–schizoid and depressive positions and proceed simultaneously as a "dual track" function.

The integration of autochthony and alterity takes form as "the transcendent position," a "state of serenity that accompanies one who (...) is able to become reconciled to the experience of pure, unadulterated Being and Happening" (Grotstein, 2000, pp. 281–282). It is an extrovertive mystical experience.

> The concept of a transcendent position does not constitute a whimsical journey into lofty, ethereal abandon, nor does it necessarily validate religion, spirituality, or the belief in God, except as a need by humans whereby they attempt to close the maw of the ineffable with an all-encompassing name. It is not in the oeuvre of W. Somerset Maugham's Larry Darrell, the protagonist in *The Razor's Edge* who sought "enlightenment" atop the Himalayas. In other words, it is not a blissful, 'autistic enclave.' O is one's reality without pretense or distortion. This reality can be a symptom, the pain of viewing beautiful autumn leaves, gazing on the mystique of Mona Lisa de la Giocanda, contemplating the horror of Ypres (for Bion), trying to remember Hiroshima, Nagasaki, Auschwitz, or Viet Nam, or resting comfortably beside one's mate trying to contemplate the exquisiteness and ineffability of the moment. (Grotstein, 2000, pp. 300–301)

Grotstein agreed with Bion that the therapeutic process involves a transformation of beta-elements, by means of alpha-function, into alpha-elements, but he innovated that the transformation is incomplete until the patient attains the transcendent position. Grotstein recognized that mystical experiences may be either ecstatic or horrific, depending on the attitude and maturity of the individual. Even dread at the numinous constituted a progress beyond the depressive position, however, toward mystical awareness. Grotstein generally replaced Bion's panentheism with a negative theology. "Since God is ineffable and inscrutable (never an object of contemplation), then the only way He can be known is through the projective attribution of some essence within us that is proximate, that is, through the ineffability of our unconscious (or, more specifically, of the Ineffable Subject of the Unconscious)" (Grotstein, 2000, p. 139). In characterizing presences as "numinous," Grotstein included Rudolf Otto's (1917/1950) concept of the numinous within the scope of the mystical. Otto's designation of God as "something more" and "wholly other" dovetails with Grotstein's concern with ineffability. At the same time, Grotstein's prose is often poetic, and he sometimes follows Bion more closely, which results in inconsistent phrasing. Grotstein (1996) acknowledged, for example, "an inherent circularity in the concept of 'O,' i.e., it is within us, around us, and beyond us (...) yet we also temporarily proceed from it, through it, and toward it" (p. 118).

Neville Symington

At one time a Catholic priest, but subsequently Tavistock trained and currently resident in Sydney, Australia, Symington (1993, 1994/1998, 2001, 2002, 2004, 2006) placed a mystical spin on Fairbairn's view of the auto-erotism of orality and anality as products of inhibited object relations. In Symington's view, all pathologies involve a retreat from object love into narcissism. The narcissistic rejection of object love is a denial not only of whomever happens to be in the narcissist's vicinity at any moment, but more generally of the concept of personhood, a "psychic object" that Symington initially termed "the lifegiver." Holding to the general view among object relations theorists that self is a construction of self-with-other, Symington (1993) maintained that "this turning away from the lifegiver is a turning against the self" (p. 41), a refusal or abandonment of part of the self. Symington argued that narcissism invariably incurs unconscious guilt over its denial of the lifegiver. The refusal affects the self even when another person happens not to be involved at the moment. The denial is a choice or, as Symington preferred to state, an "intentionality" for which the narcissist is responsible. Trauma may motivate the choice, but it nevertheless remains a choice at a very deep level of the personality.

In later writings, Symington mingled metaphysical faith-claims with his psychology of the mystical. He dispensed with the term "lifegiver" and wrote instead of "the infinite," which he identified with the god of the Hindu Upanishads: "the Absolute, the Truth, or just Reality" (Symington, 2002, p. 103). Although Symington equated the infinite with Bion's O, he had no use for Bion's causal determinism within O. Symington regarded reality as a personal God, a Thou, from which the self differentiates by virtue of its intentionality. Conscience is an intrapsychic process that represents the infinite to the self. Like Fromm, Symington contrasted conscience with the superego. Conscience invites the self to make choices. The superego, by contrast, coerces and bullies and is integral to the pathology of narcissism. Symington regarded the psychoanalytic process, with its therapeutic arrival at the depressive position, as a process of moral education – indeed, as the most refined, sophisticated, and nuanced moral education that humanity has yet devised.

Symington advocated meditation and contemplation, which he understood as sober, intellectual thinking. Contemplatives engage in rational reflection, remain in control of their own intentionality, and arrive at truths that, owing to the nature of reality, happen to be mystical. Symington contrasted contemplation with ecstasy, which involves "a cultic outside God with whom the individual self has an ecstatic encounter" (Symington, 1994/1998, p. 95). The oceanic feeling was an instance of ecstasy, a temporary madness (p. 109). An ecstatic god is a split-off part of the personality, a projective identification of the superego, and part of the syndrome of narcissism. In keeping with this contrast of contemplation and ecstasy, Symington categorized religions as "mature" or "primitive," "natural" or "revealed," respectively. "Psychoanalysis is a natural religion but not a revealed one" (Symington, 2004, p. 161). Symington's major technical innovation was to phrase interpretations in manners that avoided the superego while inviting conscience to manifest. "Any interpretation that is really effective has to bring conscience into play (...) conscience then starts to invite the person to do something" (Symington, 2001, p. 31). Because conscience manifests the infinite, the patient's therapeutic attainment of the depressive position was simultaneously a spiritual "awakening" and a "vital realization" of the mystical character of reality. It was a religious conversion.

Symington's categorical contrasts of health and pathology resulted in a series of mutual exclusions: sanity or narcissism, conscience or the superego, contemplation or ecstasy, natural religion or revealed religion. His model lacks the nuance of Bion's theory that everyone continually goes back and forth between the paranoid–schizoid and depressive positions, on which Grotstein built his dual-track function. Symington's dualism also has no place for a concern with psychic integration.

Michael Eigen

Although trained in New York during the heyday of ego psychology, Eigen found the British Independents more to his liking and appropriates "whatever hits me" (Eigen, 1998, p. 163). "If I had to situate my writings, I think I see myself as part of a budding subculture of psychoanalytic mystics" (Eigen, 1992, p. xx). Eigen is disinterested in the debate whether psychoanalysis is or ought to be mystical. "There is no reason to place artificial limits on where or how far therapy should go" (Eigen, 1998, p. 41). Eigen sees O, the numinous, the presence of God, aliveness, Light, ecstasy, *jouissance*, and non-being everywhere, all the time.

Eigen's views on the mystical are scattered throughout his writings (1986, 1992, 1993, 1995, 1996, 1998, 1999, 2001a, b, 2002, 2004–2007). His book on the topic, *The Psychoanalytic Mystic* (1998), aspires toward a systematic presentation; but he confesses, "I believe in lack of definition" (Eigen, 2007, p. 106). Finding mysticality wherever he looks, he insists on the diversity of mysticisms and ecstasies. He deplores psychoanalysts' preoccupation with the oceanic feeling as though it exhausted the topic of mystical experiencing. He rejects the theory of primary narcissism and cautions that undifferentiation can only be relative or comparative. He endorses the theory of his major analyst, Henry Elkin (1958, 1972), on the development of the self in early infancy. The newborn commences without an identity, or sense of unity, but instead experiences consciousness of a collective environment that includes the mother. When self and mother are first distinguished, they are experienced as a dual unity, an I-yet-not-I; and dual unity subsequently manifests in a host of different ways. Dual unity is the primary content of mystical experiencing, whether an impersonal union with all existence, or a personal I-Thou encounter and dialogue with God. Dual unity may also be recognized in the double perception, partly ego-centered and individualistic, and partly mystical and collective, that Fromm called a dialectic of Aristotelian and paradoxical logic, and Grotstein called a "dual track" of alterity and autochthony.

In early development, dual unity is at work when the infant first distinguishes matter and mind, as exemplified by bodily and mental ego-feelings, respectively. For Eigen's clinical purposes, the most important aspect of mind is the ideal. Where Rank, Fromm, and Winnicott were much concerned with failed individuation, Eigen's postulation of inborn relationality leads him to see pathology extensively through the lens of ideality. Infants experience omniscience of mind and the creative illusion of omnipotence of body. Splitting of materiality and ideality is, in

Eigen's view, the dominant pathology of our age. The application of ideality to the dual-unity of self and other generates a divine self and a divine other around age six months. Disappointment by the divine other, with its traumatic hurt, rage, and despair, becomes prototypical of all traumas; and consolation by the divine other, with its return to favor and joy, becomes prototypical of all ecstasies. This death-and-rebirth pattern is the basic theme of psychotherapeutic change. It has a history in religion because it exists in nature. Like Winnicott, Eigen (1993, p. 31, 2004, p. 75) maintains that a patient should be allowed to regress or to manifest a negative transference until reflexive awareness sets in. Only as the negative transference becomes ego-dystonic and recovery begins to occur spontaneously does Eigen recommend intervening with transference interpretations.

The infinity of God is the prototypical instance of ideality. Omniscience and omnipotence apply infinity to mind and body, respectively. All mental representations or imagos are ideal images. Idolatry, as discussed by Fromm, is a pathology of ideality; but there are developmentally earlier syndromes. In some cases, "one's O, one's very sense of aliveness, is off – poisoned, warped, traumatized malformed" (Eigen, 2002, p. 120). In other cases, mystical experiencing is intact but remains unintegrated within people's lives. Omniscience forecloses learning and creativity. It may also encourage intolerance, hate, and contempt.

Influenced by both Buddhist meditation and kabbalah, Eigen entertains paradoxical ideas about God. Eigen's God is firstly the biblical God, a Creator, who acts through providence and grace, and converses verbally in mystics' minds during their ecstasies (Eigen, 1998, pp. 11, 193, 2002, p. 140). Intrapsychic dialogues have sometimes been associated with prophetism and contrasted with mysticism (Heschel, 1962/1969); but Scholem (1950/1971, 1954) established that experiences of "communion" have been the rule rather than the exception throughout the history of Jewish mysticism. At the same time, Eigen's God is an appropriation of Bion's O, manifest everywhere, the very stuff of the creation. Mystical experiencing includes peak experiences but is more importantly a way of appreciating all experience, regardless of one's state of consciousness. Because the sense of presence is variable despite God's omnipresence, Eigen suggests that God is "more highly concentrated" in some places than in others (Eigen, 2007, p. 18). "There may be no end to God, but there are different God zones" (Eigen, 2001a, p. 22). The ecstasy of non-being, of Lacanian lack, is ghastly and horrific; its therapeutic transformation into a euphoric ecstasy of aliveness, of Lacanian *jouissance*, is beatific. The whole of the psychoanalytic process is a transformation of O, a journey of God, with God, through God.

Rephrasing Fairbairn's (1943/1952, p. 60) claim that "libido is essentially orientated towards objects," Eigen (1979/1993) asserts that "instincts seek an ideal imago" (p. 102). The reintegration of instinct and ideality, body and mind, is the goal of therapy. The goal can be achieved neither by reducing ideality to the body, as Freud and mainstream psychoanalysis attempted, nor by ignoring the body while addressing ideality, as both existentialism and Kohut's self psychology have done. Many of Eigen's clinical strategies aim to promote mystical experiencing – a sense of the numinous – through the psychoanalytic dialogue. Where Grotstein's conceptualizes the transcendent position as a transient achievement, Eigen aspires to a transformed personality that has ready access to *jouissance* and numinous experiences. The divergence between Grotstein and Eigen is analogous, perhaps, to aesthetic experiences that depend on occasional visits to art museums, and the continuous aesthetic experiencing of an artist at work and play. Interestingly, although most analysts refer to transient experiences when they mention the oceanic feeling, Freud (1930/1961) introduced the term in reference to continuous mystical experiencing (Parsons, 1999).

One of Eigen's (1998) case reports concerns a mystic, so taken with mystical experiences, that she neglected the remainder of her life, going from mystic state to mystic state, while suffering desolation in the intervals between them. Another patient had an abusive temper which he was able to calm by practicing meditation. However, he could not transport his experience of renewal into the remainder of his life. In both cases, Eigen addressed the dissociation of ideality without undermining the ideality itself. Eigen has developed a similar strategy for a variety of other cases. Winnicott (1963/1965) had remarked that the psychopathic "child knows in his bones that it is *hope* that is locked up in the wicked behaviour, and that *despair* is linked with compliance and false socialization" (p. 104). Applying the insight to psychopathy in adults, Eigen (1993) asserted: "It is both crude and subtly oppressive to try to undercut the patient's pathology without helping to bring to light and assimilate the capacities and tendencies that the pathology embodies" (p. 12). Eigen subsequently generalized the pattern of liberating *jouissance* from negativity and made the mystical character of the pattern explicit (p. 103)

> One of life's cruel tantalization is that there are black hole ecstasies, mutilated ecstasies, damaged and damaging ecstasies, including evil imaginings, evil dreams. Ecstasy plays in damaged keys. One keeps aiming at the ecstasy in the warp, pressing buttons to heighten it. There is a sense one can undo the warp by feeding on ecstatic twists. Can warp continue after bliss? (Eigen, 2001b, p. 17)

Eigen (2004, p. 88) is aware that his clinical strategy conforms with the pattern of the kabbalistic practice of *tikkun*, "healing," which proceeds by liberating sparks of holiness from the material shards in which they have been since the primordial, cosmogonic catastrophe.

Concluding Reflections

The psychoanalytic mainstream has treated mystical ecstasies as anomalous experiences that are transient and unimportant for most practical purposes. Working with the theory of infantile solipsism, analysts regarded mysticism as a matter of making the unconscious conscious. Because the psychoanalytic mystics credited the experiences with long-lasting importance, they studied them more closely. Their first and most basic contribution was the recognition that the mystical involves a complete line of development. Because Rank, Fromm, Winnicott, and Loewald assumed that the deepest layer of the unconscious was solipsistic, they placed the infantile sources of mystical experience at the beginning of human development. They interpreted individuation as the primary goal of both maturation and therapeutic change, and they identified failed individuation with psychopathology. Extending the same line of reasoning beyond early infancy, Kohut postulated a narcissistic line of development, which Grotstein located within a Kleinian model under the term "autochthony." However, the theory of infantile solipsism collapsed in the early 1980s, leaving psychoanalytic theories of mysticism in disarray (Harrison, 1986). What may we salvage from the wreckage?

Psychoanalytic discussions of the mystical have addressed five different phenomena.

(a) In their discussions of O, Bion, Grotstein, Symington, and Eigen have presented mystical theologies. They have conceptualized God in a variety of ways: panentheistic, transcendent, and/or immanent. These discussions are speculations, inconsistent with each other, and unhelpful departures from methodological agnosticism.
(b) Milner, Winnicott, Ehrenzweig, Grotstein, and Eigen discussed creative illusion, the infant's fantasizing the mother prior to discovering her in reality, the infant's similar endowment of the Teddy bear with personhood, and more generally all perception, all culture, and all scientific knowledge. Limited by the universality of the illusions that we project, we cannot know the real. Where Bion was uncertain whether realism was to be preferred to idealism, and limited his faith to O, it is more common to place faith in the real, whether or not one additionally places faith in the transcendent. Whether faith or, in Winnicott's term, "belief-in," is to be counted precisely as mystical, it is presupposed by all reality-testing.
(c) Grotstein and Eigen have invoked Otto's concept of "numinous" experience. Otto explicitly equated numinous experiences with religious experiences in general, and treated mystical experiences as a subcategory. For Otto, all mystical experiences are numinous; but not all numinous experiences are mystical. Grotstein and Eigen instead reflect popular usage, which extends the term "mystical" to numinous experience in general. The merits and disadvantages of both approaches await further research. There is considerable merit, however, to Grotstein's and Eigen's view that clinical psychoanalysis should routinely inculcate the achievement of a sense of the numinous, the distinctive experience of wonderment, awe, fascination, humility, immediacy, and tranquility in the face of life's mysteries (see Merkur, 1996, 2006).
(d) Ehrenzweig, Winnicott, Loewald, Bion, and Eigen have addressed the concept of undifferentiation. The organization of sense impressions into coherent perceptions involves a great deal of learning, for example, that differently colored areas within the visual field are individual objects, located at specific distances from the viewer, and so forth. Undifferentiation implies a comparative absence of ideas concerning sense impressions. Writing in advance of Ehrenzweig, Fromm did not use the term "undifferentiation," but he recommended its achievement when he advocated Zen Buddhist meditation and the "bare attending" procedure of Buddhist mindfulness meditation.

(e) All of the psychoanalytic mystics have taken concern with unitive experiences, which are many and varied in their contents (Merkur, 1998, 1999). Rather than to think in terms of unitive experiences, it is more useful to reflect on unitive thinking processes that are consistent with Loewald's emphasis on integration. Psychoanalysts have detected a series of unitive trends in the psyche, including: the synthetic function of the ego (Freud, 1919/1955; Nunberg, 1931); the over-determination and multiple function of single mental representations (Wälder, 1936); therapeutic conflict resolution through the psychic integration of the id, ego, and superego (Brierley, 1951); the developmental integration of neonatal ego nuclei into a coherent ego structure (Glover, 1968); the developmental process of separation-individuation (Mahler and Furer, 1968; Mahler et al., 1975; Mahler, 1979a, b); and, I would add, the resolution of the Oedipus complex through the introjection of the father representation within the superego (Freud, 1923/1961).

We may assume, I suggest, that the psyche commences with undifferentiated sense perceptions and gradually learns to organize them. The process of organization involves reality-testing, which has differentiation as its corollary. Organization also involves an integration of sense data into meaningful wholes. Integration is a unitive function that possibly has its basis in a discrete process of thinking. Freud's (1900/1958) concept of "condensation," to which Loewald attributed the mystical sense of timelessness, is presumably involved.

Freud traced the psyche's unitive trend to Eros, but Eros is itself shaped by the unitive trend. Lacan (1982, p. 138) remarked: "*There is something of One* (...) in the discourse of Freud, it is set forth in the concept of Eros, defined as a fusion making one out of two, that is, of Eros seen as the gradual tendency to make one out of a vast multitude." Freud (1915/1957) claimed that there is no conflict in the unconscious. "When two wishful impulses whose aims must appear to us incompatible become simultaneously active, the two impulses do not diminish each other or cancel each other out, but combine to form an intermediate aim, a compromise" (p. 186). Freud's suggestion will account in an exclusively psychological manner for the clinical evidence that is consistent with Freud's (1905/1953) extension of the concept of sexuality. Whether or not all instincts are sexual physiologically, all mental representations of instincts become psychosexual through the compromise function. This distinction permits us to abandon reified abstractions such as drive, psychic energy, and libido while retaining the psychological concepts of Eros and extended sexuality. The unconscious compromise formation is, as Lacan 1982, pp. 138–139) recognized, a metaphor. It is produced, as Freud implied, through condensation. The organization of sense impressions of the body, proprioceptions and emotions and sensory observations of instinctive bodily motions, into a teleologically oriented concept of general motivation, such as the extended concept of sexuality, is the product of a considerable task of integration, symbol-formation, and thinking. A capacity for love is inborn, but its flourishing is an achievement of its integration in every stage of human development. Love is integrative not only interpersonally, but also intrapsychically. It falls under the scope of the mystical, as Fromm rightly recognized.

Development as a whole involves lifelong processes of increasing differentiation and increasing integration. We optimally become both more knowledgeable and more wise. The successful resolution of the Oedipus complex, the achievement of universalized morality is unitive both interpersonally and intrapsychically. Moral development, including capacities for guilt, atonement, and restitution, is spontaneous, natural, and healthy. There is a discrete part of the psyche, a psychic process, that is responsible for conscience, universal symbols, sublimations, and the rationality of dreams. The ego experiences this process as another self, an internal object. The internal object's view of the ego accomplishes reflexive awareness, the function that is generally but wrongly called "self-consciousness" or "self-observation." As Eigen suggests, the self is a product of reflexive thinking, a construction. The function of reflexive awareness operates prior to its construction of a self-representation or self-image, and should be distinguished from it. Condensation, identification, and mystical timelessness, may be further applications of reflexive thinking, or perhaps owe to a separate symbol-forming process. Therapy that successfully addresses aggression, which is to say, inhibitions of moral development, produce moral transformations; but neither therapy nor the unitive consists of morality alone.

Narcissism is not a discrete line of development. Neither is autochthony. Subjectively perceived objects and selfobjects are symptoms of a wounded self, an unconscious denial of relationality; and they incur unconscious guilt. Other pathologies of the unitive include idolatry, one-sided ideality, nightmarish ecstasies, rampant materialism, and a host of other syndromes. Trauma, and the repression to which it gives rise, inhibits both differentiation and integration. The psyche's natural healing process works to integrate trauma, so that both differentiation and further integration can be resumed. When the natural healing process is unequal to its task, therapeutic intervention is appropriate. All effective therapies are integrative. Therapy is intrinsically unitive. The unitive includes much more than the therapeutic, but the therapeutic cannot be pursued apart from the unitive.

References

Alexander, F. (1931). Buddhistic training as an artificial catatonia (The biological meaning of psychic occurrences). *Psychoanalytic Review*, *18*(2), 129–145.

Allison, J. (1968). Adaptive regression and intense religious experiences. *Journal of Nervous and Mental Disease*, *145*, 452–463.

Almond, P. C. (1982). *Mystical experience and religious doctrine: An investigation of the study of mysticism in world religions*. Berlin/New York: Mouton.

Armstrong, A. H. (1955). Plotinus's doctrine of the infinite and its significance for Christian thought. *Downside Review*, *73*, 47–58.

Balint, M. (1937/1952). Early developmental states of the ego: Primary object-love. In M. Balint (Ed.), *Primary love and psycho-analytic technique* (pp. 90–108). London: Hogarth Press.

Balint, M. (1969/1992). *The basic fault: Therapeutic aspects of regression*. Evanston, IL: Northwestern University Press.

Bergmann, M. S. (2000). The Hartmann era and its contribution to psychoanalytic technique. In M. S. Bergmann (Ed.), *The Hartmann era* (pp. 1–78). New York: Other Press.
Bharati, A. (1976). *The light at the center: Context and pretext of modern mysticism*. Santa Barbara: Ross-Erikson.
Bion, W. R. (1962). *Learning from experience*. New York: Basic Books.
Bion, W. R. (1963/1984). *Elements of psycho-analysis*. London: Karnac Books.
Bion, W. R. (1965/1984). *Transformations*. London: Karnac Books.
Bion, W. R. (1967/1984). *Second thoughts: Selected papers on psycho-analysis*. London: Karnac Books.
Bion, W. R. (1970/1984). *Attention and interpretation: A scientific approach to insight in psycho-analysis and groups*. London: Karnac Books.
Bion, W. R. (1989). *Two papers: The Grid and Caesura*. London: Karnac Books.
Bion, W. R. (1994). *Cogitations* (Ed. F. Bion), 2nd ed. London: Karnac Books.
Brierley, M. (1947). Notes on psycho-analysis and integrative living. *International Journal of Psycho-Analysis*, *28*(2), 57–105.
Brierley, M. (1951). *Trends in psycho-analysis*. London: Hogarth Press/Institute of Psycho-Analysis.
Brown, D. P. & Engler, J. (1984). An outcome study of intensive mindfulness meditation. *Psychoanalytic Study of Society*, *10*, 163–225.
Burrow, T. (1914). Character and the neuroses. *Psychoanalytic Review*, *1*(2), 121–128.
Burrow, T. (1917). The genesis and meaning of "homosexuality" and its relation to the problem of introverted mental states. *Psychoanalytic Review*, *4*(3), 272–284.
Burrow, T. (1917–1918). Notes with reference to Freud, Jung and Adler. *Journal of Abnormal Psychology*, *12*, 161–167.
Carver, A. (1924). Primary identification and mysticism. *British Journal of Medical Psychology*, *4*, 102–114.
de Certeau, M. (1982/1992). *The mystic fable*. Vol. 1: *The sixteenth and seventeenth centuries* (trans. M. B. Smith). Chicago, IL/London: University of Chicago Press.
Deikman, A. J. (1966a). De-automatization and the mystic experience. *Psychiatry*, *29*, 324–338.
Deikman, A. J. (1966b). Implications of experimentally induced contemplative meditation. *Journal of Nervous and Mental Disease*, *142*(2), 101–116.
Deutsch, H. (1927/1989). On satisfaction, happiness and ecstasy (Ed. P. Roazen). *International Journal of Psycho-Analysis*, *70*, 715–723.
Ehrenzweig, A. (1953). *The psychoanalysis of artistic vision and hearing: An introduction to a theory of unconscious perception*. New York: Julian Press.
Ehrenzweig, A. (1967). *The hidden order of art: A study in the psychology of artistic imagination*. Berkeley, CA: University of California Press.
Eigen, M. (1979/1993). *The electrified tightrope* (Ed. A. Phillips). Northvale, NJ/London: Aronson.
Eigen, M. (1986). *The psychotic core*. Northvale, NJ/London: Aronson.
Eigen, M. (1992). *Coming through the whirlwind: Case studies in psychotherapy*. Wilmette, IL: Chiron.
Eigen, M. (1995). *Reshaping the self: Reflections on renewal through therapy*. Madison, CT: Psychosocial Press.
Eigen, M. (1996). *Psychic deadness*. Northvale, NJ/London: Aronson.
Eigen, M. (1998). *The psychoanalytic mystic*. Binghamton, NY: ESF.
Eigen, M. (1999). *Toxic nourishment*. London: Karnac Books.
Eigen, M. (2001a). *Damaged bonds*. London/New York: Karnac Books.
Eigen, M. (2001b). *Ecstasy*. Middletown, CT: Wesleyan University Press.
Eigen, M. (2002). *Rage*. Middletown, CT: Wesleyan University Press.
Eigen, M. (2004). *The sensitive self*. Middletown, CT: Wesleyan University Press.
Eigen, M. (2005). *Emotional storm*. Middletown, CT: Wesleyan University Press.
Eigen, M. (2006). *Lust*. Middletown, CT: Wesleyan University Press.
Eigen, M. (2007). *Feeling matters: From the Yosemite God to the annihilated self*. London/New York: Karnac Books.

Elkin, H. (1958). On the origin of the self. *Psychoanalysis and the Psychoanalytic Review, 45*(4), 57–76.
Elkin, H. (1972). On selfhood and the development of ego structures in infancy. *Psychoanalytic Review, 59*, 389–416.
Fairbairn, W. R. D. (1943/1952). The repression and the return of bad objects (with special reference to the 'war neuroses'). In W. R. D. Fairbairn, *Psychoanalytic studies of the personality* (pp. 59–81). London: Routledge & Kegan Paul.
Fauteux, K. (1994). *The recovery of self: Regression and redemption in religious experience.* New York, NY: Paulist Press.
Fauteux, K. (1997). Self-reparation in religious experience and creativity. In C. Spezzano & G. J. Gargiulo (Eds.), *Soul on the couch: Spirituality, religion, and morality in contemporary psychoanalysis* (pp. 11–41). Hillsdale, NJ: Analytic Press.
Federn, P. (1926). Some variations in ego-feeling. *International Journal of Psycho-Analysis, 7*, 434–444.
Federn, P. (1932). The reality of the death instinct, especially in melancholia: Remarks on Freud's book: "Civilization and Its Discontents." *Psychoanalytic Review, 19*, 129–151.
Federn, P. (1952). *Ego psychology and the psychoses.* New York: Basic Books.
Ferenczi, S. (1919/1933). Thalassa: A theory of genitality. *Psychoanalytic Quarterly, 2*, 361–403.
Field, J. (pseud. M. Milner) (1934/1986). *A life of one's own.* London: Virago Press.
Field, J. (pseud. M. Milner) (1937/1986). *An experiment in leisure.* London: Virago Press.
Field, J. (pseud. M. Milner) (1957). *On not being able to paint*, 2nd ed. Los Angeles, CA: Tarcher.
Freud, S. (1900/1958). *The interpretation of dreams.* In J. Strachey (Ed.), *The standard edition of the complete psychological works of Sigmund Freud* (Vols 4–5). London: Hogarth Press.
Freud, S. (1905/1953). Three essays on the theory of sexuality. In J. Strachey (Ed.), *The standard edition of the complete psychological works of Sigmund Freud* (Vol 7, pp. 130–243). London: Hogarth Press.
Freud, S. (1914/1957). On narcissism: An introduction. In: J. Strachey (Ed.), *The standard edition of the complete psychological works of Sigmund Freud* (Vol 14, pp. 78–102). London: Hogarth Press.
Freud, S. (1915/1957). The unconscious. In J. Strachey (Ed.), *The standard edition of the complete psychological works of Sigmund Freud* (Vol 14, pp. 166–204). London: Hogarth Press.
Freud, S. (1919/1955). Lines of advance in psycho-analytic therapy. In J. Strachey (Ed.), *The standard edition of the complete psychological works of Sigmund Freud* (Vol 17, pp. 159–168). London: Hogarth Press.
Freud, S. (1920/1955). Beyond the pleasure principle. In J. Strachey (Ed.), *The standard edition of the complete psychological works of Sigmund Freud* (Vol 18, pp. 7–64). London: Hogarth Press.
Freud, S. (1923/1961). The ego and the id. In J. Strachey (Ed.), *The standard edition of the complete psychological works of Sigmund Freud* (Vol 19, pp. 12–59). London: Hogarth Press.
Freud, S. (1927/1961). The future of an illusion. In J. Strachey (Ed.), *The standard edition of the complete psychological works of Sigmund Freud* (Vol 19, pp. 5–56). London: Hogarth Press.
Freud, S. (1930/1961). Civilization and its discontents. In J. Strachey (Ed.), *The standard edition of the complete psychological works of Sigmund Freud* (Vol 21, pp. 64–145). London: Hogarth Press.
Fromm, E. (1941). *Escape from freedom.* New York/Toronto: Rinehart.
Fromm, E. (1947). *Man For himself: An inquiry into the psychology of ethics.* New York/Toronto: Rinehart & Company.
Fromm, E. (1950). *Psychoanalysis and religion.* New Haven: Yale University Press.
Fromm, E. (1951). *The forgotten language: An introduction to the understanding of dreams, fairy tales and myths.* New York/Toronto: Rinehart.
Fromm, E. (1955). *The sane society.* New York/Toronto: Rinehart.
Fromm, E. (1956). *The art of loving.* New York: Harper.
Fromm, E. (1960). Psychoanalysis and Zen Buddhism. In D. T. Suzuki, E. Fromm & R. de Martino (Eds.), *Zen Buddhism and psychoanalysis* (pp. 77–141). New York: Harper.

Fromm, E. (1962). The philosophy basic to Freud's psychoanalysis. *Pastoral Psychology, 13*(121), 26–32.
Fromm, E. (1966). *You shall be as gods: A radical interpretation of the Old Testament and its tradition*. New York: Holt, Rinehart & Winston.
Fromm, E. (1973). *The anatomy of human destructiveness*. New York: Holt, Rinehart & Winston.
Fromm, E. (1980). *Greatness and limitations of Freud's thought*. New York: Harper & Row.
Fromm, E. (1991). Causes for the patient's change in analytic treatment. *Contemporary Psychoanalysis, 27*(4), 581–602.
Fromm, E. (1992). *The revision of psychoanalysis* (Ed. R. Funk). Boulder, CO: Westview Press.
Fromm, E. (1994a). *The art of listening*. New York: Continuum.
Fromm, E. (1994b). *On being human*. New York: Continuum.
Furst, S. S., Leavy, S. A., Lewis, R. C., Lubin, A. J., Ostow, M. & Zales, M. R. [Committee on Psychiatry and Religion]. (1976). *Mysticism: Spiritual quest or psychic disorder?* New York: Group for the Advancement of Psychiatry. (Group for the Advancement of Psychiatry, Volume IX, Publication No. 97, November 1976.)
Gaensbauer, T. J. (1982). The differentiation of discrete affects: A case report. *Psychoanalytic Study of the Child, 37*, 29–66.
Glover, E. (1968). *The birth of the ego: A nuclear hypothesis*. New York: International Universities Press.
Goleman, D. (1977). *The varieties of the meditative experience*. New York: Dutton.
Greenacre, P. (1958/1971). The family romance of the artist. In P. Greenacre (Ed.), *Emotional growth: Psychoanalytic studies of the gifted and great variety of other individuals* (Vol. 2, pp. 505–32). New York: International Universities Press.
Grotstein, J. S. (1981). Who is the dreamer who dreams the dream and who is the dreamer who understands it? In J. S. Grotstein (Ed.), *Do I dare disturb the universe? A memorial to Wilfred R. Bion* (pp. 357–416). Beverly Hills: Caesura Press.
Grotstein, J. S. (1996). Bion's "transformation in 'O'," the "thing-in-itself," and the "real": Toward the concept of the "transcendent position." *Journal of Melanie Klein and Object Relations, 14*(2), 109–141.
Grotstein, J. S. (1997). Integrating one-person and two-person psychologies: Autochthony and alterity in counterpoint. *Psychoanalytic Quarterly, 66*, 403–430.
Grotstein, J. S. (2000). *Who is the dreamer who dreams the dream? A study of psychic presences*. Hillsdale, NJ/London: Analytic Press.
Harrison, I. B. (1986). On "merging" and the fantasy of merging. *Psychoanalytic Study of the Child, 41*, 155–170.
Heiler, F. (1932). *Prayer: A study in the history and psychology of religion* (trans. S. McComb with J. E. Park). London: Oxford University Press.
Heschel, A. J. (1962/1969). *The Prophets*. 2 Vols. New York: Harper.
James, W. (1902/1958). *The varieties of religious experience: A study in human nature*. New York: New American Library.
Jaspers, K. (1913/1963). *General psychopathology* (trans. J. Hoenig & M. W. Hamilton). Manchester: Manchester University Press/Chicago, IL: Chicago University Press.
Jones, J. W. (2001). Hans Loewald: The psychoanalyst as mystic. *Psychoanalytic Review, 88*(6), 793–809.
Jones, J. W. (2002). *Terror and transformation: The ambiguity of religion in psychoanalytic perspective*. Hove, UK: Brunner-Routledge/New York: Taylor & Francis.
Kernberg, O. F. (1991). Some comments on early development. In S. Akhtar & H. Parens (Eds.), *Beyond the symbiotic orbit: Advances in separation-individuation theory. Essays in honor of Selma Kramer, M.D.* (pp. 103–120). Hillsdale, NJ: Analytic Press.
Knowles, D. (1967/1979). *What is mysticism?* London: Sheed & Ward.
Kohut, H. (1966). Forms and transformations of narcissism. *Journal of the American Psychoanalytic Association, 14*, 243–272.
Kohut, H. (1971). *The analysis of the self: A systematic approach to the psychoanalytic treatment of narcissistic personality disorders*. Madison, CT: International Universities Press.

Kohut, H. (1977). *The restoration of the self.* New York: International Universities Press.
Kohut, H. (1978a). *The search for the self: Selected writings of Heinz Kohut: 1950–1978* (Ed. P. H. Ornstein). Vol. 1. New York: International Universities Press.
Kohut, H. (1978b). *The search for the self: Selected writings of Heinz Kohut: 1950–1978* (Ed. P. H. Ornstein). Vol. 2. New York: International Universities Press.
Kohut, H. (1984). *How does analysis cure?* (Ed. A. Goldberg with P. Stepansky). Chicago, IL: University of Chicago Press.
Kohut, H. (1985). On leadership. In C. B. Strozier (Ed.), *Self psychology and the humanities: Reflections on a new psychoanalytic approach* (pp. 51–72). New York: Norton.
Kohut, H. (1990). *The search for the self: Selected writings of Heinz Kohut: 1978–1981.* Vol. 3 (Ed. P. H. Ornstein). Madison, CT: International Universities Press.
Kohut, H. (1991). *The search for the self: Selected writings of Heinz Kohut: 1978–1981.* Vol. 4 (Ed. P. H. Ornstein). Madison, CT: International Universities Press.
Kripal, J. J. (2007). *The serpent's gift: Gnostic reflections on the study of religion.* Chicago, IL/London: University of Chicago Press.
Lacan, J. (1982). *Feminine sexuality: Jacques Lacan and the "École freudienne"* (Ed. J. Mitchell & J. Rose; trans. J. Rose). New York: Norton/Pantheon.
Leavy, S. A. (1995). Roots of unitive experience. *Psychoanalytic Review, 82*(3), 349–370.
Lewin, B. D. (1951). *The psychoanalysis of elation.* London: Hogarth Press.
Lichtenberg, J. D. (1983). *Psychoanalysis and infant research.* Hillsdale, NJ: Analytic.
Linn, L. & Schwarz, L. W. (1958). *Psychiatry and religious experience.* New York: Random House.
Loewald, H. W. (1960), On the therapeutic action of psycho-analysis. *International Journal of Psycho-Analysis, 41*, 16–33.
Loewald, H. W. (1978). *Psychoanalysis and the history of the individual.* New Haven: Yale University Press.
Loewald, H. W. (1980). *Papers on psychoanalysis.* New Haven: Yale University Press.
Loewald, H. W. (1988). *Sublimation: Inquiries into theoretical psychoanalysis.* New Haven: Yale University Press.
Lovejoy, A. O. (1936/1976). *The great chain of being: A study of the history of an idea.* Cambridge, MA: Harvard University Press.
Mahler, M. S. (1979a). *The selected papers of Margaret S. Mahler.* Vol. 1: *Infantile psychosis and early contributions.* New York/London: Aronson.
Mahler, M. S. (1979b). *The selected papers of Margaret S. Mahler.* Vol. 2: *Separation-individuation.* New York/London: Aronson.
Mahler, M. S. & Furer, M. (1968). *On human symbiosis and the vicissitudes of individuation.* Vol. 1: *Infantile psychosis.* New York: International Universities Press.
Mahler, M. S., Pine, F. & Bergman, A. (1975). *The psychological birth of the human infant: Symbiosis and individuation.* New York: Basic Books.
Matte-Blanco, I. (1959). On introjection and the process of psychic metabolism. *International Journal of Psycho-Analysis, 40*, 1–5.
Meissner, W. W. (1992). *Ignatius of Loyola: The psychology of a saint.* New Haven: Yale University Press.
Meissner, W. W. (1999). *To the greater glory: A psychological study of Ignatian spirituality.* Milwaukee, WI: Marquette University Press.
Merkur, D. (1996). The numinous as a category of values. In T. A. Idinopulos & E. A. Yonan (Eds.), *The sacred and its scholars: Comparative methodologies for the study of primary religious data* (pp. 104–123). Leiden: Brill.
Merkur, D. (1998). *The ecstatic imagination: Psychedelic experiences and the psychoanalysis of self-actualization.* Albany, NY: State University of New York Press.
Merkur, D. (1999). *Mystical moments and unitive thinking.* Albany, NY: State University of New York Press.
Merkur, D. (2002). Mysticism. In N. J. Smelser & P. B. Baltes (Eds.), *International encyclopedia of social and behavioral sciences* (pp. 10270–10273). Oxford, UK: Pergamon.
Merkur, D. (2006). Interpreting numinous experience. *Social Analysis, 50*(2), 204–223.

Milner, M. (1987). *The suppressed madness of sane men: Forty-four years of exploring psychoanalysis*. London/New York: Tavistock.
Moxon, C. (1920). Mystical ecstasy and hysterical dream-states. *Journal of Abnormal Psychology, 15*, 329–334.
Nunberg, H. (1931). The synthetic function of the ego. *International Journal of Psycho-Analysis, 12*(2), 123–140.
Ostow, M. & Scharfstein, B.-A. (1954). *The need to believe: The Psychology of religion*. New York: International Universities Press.
Otto, R. (1917/1950). *The idea of the Holy: An inquiry into the non-rational factor in the idea of the divine and its relation to the rational*, 2nd ed. London: Oxford University Press.
Otto, R. (1932/1970). *Mysticism East and West: A comparative analysis of the nature of mysticism* (trans. B. L. Bracey & R. C. Payne). New York: Macmillan.
Parsons, W. B. (1999). *The enigma of the oceanic feeling: Revisioning the psychoanalytic theory of mysticism*. New York/Oxford: Oxford University Press.
Pine, F. (1981). In the beginning: Contributions to a psychoanalytic developmental psychology. *International Review of Psycho-Analysis, 8*, 15–33.
Pine, F. (1986). The "symbiotic phase" in light of current infancy research. *Bulletin of the Menninger Clinic, 50*(6), 564–569.
Pine, F. (1990). *Drive, ego, object, and self: A synthesis for clinical work*. New York: BasicBooks/HarperCollins.
Prince, R. & Savage, C. (1966). Mystical states and the concept of regression. *Psychedelic Review, 8*, 59–81.
Rank, O. (1929/1993). *The trauma of birth*. New York: Dover.
Rank, O. (1930/1998). *Psychology and the soul: A study of the origin, conceptual evolution, and nature of the soul* (trans. G. C. Richter & E. J. Lieberman). Baltimore, MD/London: Johns Hopkins University Press.
Rank, O. (1932a). *Art and the artist: Creative urge and personality development* (trans. C. F. Atkinson). New York/London: Norton.
Rank, O. (1932b). *Modern education: A critique of its fundamental ideas* (trans. M. Moxon). New York: Knopf.
Rank, O. (1941). *Beyond psychology*. Philadelphia, PA: Hauser.
Rank, O. (1968). *Will Therapy and Truth and Reality* (trans. J. Taft). New York: Knopf.
Rank, O. (1996). *A psychology of difference: The American lectures* (Ed. R. Kramer). Princeton, NJ: Princeton University Press.
Sayers, J. (2003). *Divine therapy: Love, mysticism and psychoanalysis*. Oxford: Oxford University Press.
Scholem, G. G. (1950/1971). *Devekut*, or communion with God. In G. G. Scholem (Ed.), *The Messianic Idea in Judaism and other essays on Jewish spirituality* (pp. 203–227). New York: Schocken Books.
Scholem, G. G. (1954). *Major trends in Jewish mysticism*, 3rd ed. New York: Schocken.
Schroeder, T. (1922). Prenatal psychisms and mystical pantheism. *International Journal of Psycho-Analysis, 3*, 445–466.
Silberer, H. (1914/1971). *Hidden symbolism of alchemy and the occult arts* (trans. S. E. Jelliffe). New York: Dover.
Sorenson, R. L. (2004). *Minding spirituality*. Hillsdale, NJ: Analytic Press.
Spero, M. H. (1992). *Religious objects as psychological structures: A critical integration of Object Relations Theory, psychotherapy, and Judaism*. Chicago, IL: University of Chicago Press.
Stace, W. T. (1960). *Mysticism and philosophy*. Philadelphia, PA/New York: Lippincott.
Sterba, R. (1978). Discussions of Sigmund Freud. *Psychoanalytic Quarterly, 47*, 173–191.
Stern, D. N. (1983). The early development of schemas of self, other, and "self with other." In *Reflections of self psychology* (Ed. J. D. Lichtenberg & S. Kaplan; pp. 49–84). Hillsdale, NJ: Analytic Press.
Stern, D. N. (1985). *The interpersonal world of the infant: A view from psychoanalysis and developmental psychology*. New York: BasicBooks.

Symington, N. (1993). *Narcissism: A new theory*. London: Karnac Books.
Symington, N. (1994/1998). *Emotion and spirit: Questioning the claims of psychoanalysis and religion*. London: Karnac Books.
Symington, N. (2001). *The spirit of sanity*. London/New York: Karnac Books.
Symington, N. (2002). *A pattern of madness*. London/New York: Karnac Books.
Symington, N. (2004). *The blind man sees: Freud's Awakening and other essays*. London/New York: Karnac Books.
Symington, N. (2006). *A healing conversation: How healing happens*. London/New York: Karnac Books.
Underhill, E. (1910/1955). *Mysticism: A study in the nature and development of man's spiritual consciousness*. New York: New American Library.
Wälder, R. (1936). The principle of multiple function: Observations on over-determination. *Psychoanalytic Quarterly*, *5*, 45–62.
Winnicott, D. W. (1945/1992). Primitive emotional development. In D. W. Winnicott (Ed.), *Through paediatrics to psycho-analysis: Collected papers* (pp. 145–156). New York: Brunner/Mazel.
Winnicott, D. W. (1948/1992). Paediatrics and psychiatry. In D. W. Winnicott (Ed.), *Through paediatrics to psycho-analysis: Collected papers* (pp. 157–173). New York: Brunner/Mazel.
Winnicott, D. W. (1951/1989). Critical notice of *On Not Being Able to Paint*, by Joanna Field. In C. Winnicott, R. Shepherd & M. Davis (Eds.), *Psycho-analytic explorations* (pp. 390–392). Cambridge, MA: Harvard University Press.
Winnicott, D. W. (1953). Transitional objects and transitional phenomena: A study of the first not-me possession. *International Journal of Psycho-Analysis*, *34*, 89–97.
Winnicott, D. W. (1963/1965). Morals and education. In D. W. Winnicott (Ed.), *The maturational processes and the facilitating environment: Studies in the theory of emotional development* (pp. 93–105). New York: International Universities Press.
Winnicott, D. W. (1965). *The maturational processes and the facilitating environment: Studies in the theory of emotional development*. New York: International Universities Press.
Winnicott, D. W. (1971/1974). *Playing and reality*. Harmondsworth: Penguin.
Winnicott, D. W. (1975/1992). *Through paediatrics to psycho-analysis: Collected papers*. New York: Brunner/Mazel.

The Adoration of the Crucified

What Freud and Post-Freudian Psychoanalysis Could Have Learned from This Christian Prayer

Paul Moyaert

One cannot understand the contributions of post-Freudian psychoanalytic studies on religion without drawing Freud into the discussion. Some psychoanalytic studies investigate the possibility of extrapolating Freud's ideas on religion. Are his religious intuitions and categories as universal as he seems to pretend? Are they appropriate for understanding religions he didn't investigate personally? ("Psychoanalysis Meets Buddhism", Parsons, this volume; "Hinduism and Psychoanalysis", Meckel, this volume; "The Paternal Metaphor Revisited in Post-Freudian French Religious Psychoanalytic Anthropology", Devisch, this volume) In addition, there are the psychoanalytic studies mainly motivated by a dissatisfaction with Freud. This dissatisfaction has many faces. One of the most important psychoanalytic critiques directly echoes the critiques of religious believers. Freud's ideas on religion are not only one-sided, but basically misrepresent religion. His ideas, according to this critique, keep religion confined to negative categories such as repression, moral discipline and social adaptation. He has no eye for the vitalizing and ecstatic forces of religion that can come to the foreground in, for example, the liturgical celebration of life and its power to deeply transform the self. And although Freud knew that religion can be inspired by mystical surrender, he never integrated this insight into a more systematic description and analysis of religion.

My contribution is based also on the idea that Freud gives an incomplete and distorted presentation of religion. However, I am not interested in giving a descriptive overview of the different aspects he neglects. Rather, I focus on one element only: the *vitalizing power* of religion. Here, I try to explore why Freud could not really understand that religion can set free forces that affirm life. Why didn't Freud grasp the vitalizing energy of religion? Why couldn't he understand religion in terms of drives expressing themselves, which is quite different from religion serving repression? Freud's ideas on religion are strongly connected with his theory of sublimation. For Freud, sublimation is a healthy alternative to a neurotic, perverse or

P. Moyaert
KU Leuven, Leuven, Belgium
e-mail: Paul.Moyaert@hiw.kuleuven.be

J.A. Belzen (ed.), *Changing the Scientific Study of Religion: Beyond Freud?*

psychotic response to the demands of the sexual drives and the restraints of human culture. In sublimation, drives can manifest their creativity, and this vital creativity is their health. Freud wants to explain how sexual drives can be transformed into non-sexual activities without loosing their natural *élan* or driving character. Religion is also a transformation of sexual drives. Though his theory of sublimation was meant to articulate the creative power of the drives, apparently Freud didn't see how religion could fall under this general idea of sublimation. For him, religion was always linked more strongly to repression than to a vital expression of drives. He doubts that religion has the flexibility necessary for a resourceful interaction with its ritual rules and doctrines and for relieving the weight of its rigid commands and prohibitions. For Freud, religion cannot overcome its own reactive character.

However, post-Freudian critics are not all that eager, in their criticism, to confront Freud's complicated theory of sublimation. They prefer to explain Freud's incomplete understanding of religion in terms of his predominant male representation of a fatherly God, a representation linked, in turn, with his view of the Oedipus complex. What Freud overlooked, goes this widespread critique, is the maternal dimension of the divine and, related to this, the pre-Oedipal relation with the mother and the oceanic sphere of a wider motherly nature. Here, the pre-Oedipal must be the cornerstone of a correction of Freud. This is indeed an important addition. But is that all a post-Freudian approach to religion needs in order to restore and to understand the ecstatic power of religion? Certainly, the one-sided emphasis on the lawgiving and forbidding father can hardly explain how or in what way the vitalizing force of religion could exist. But does a reference to the maternal object change that much in this perspective? According to me, Freud's inability to explain the vital power of religion has deeper grounds than his neglect of the pre-Oedipal. His failure is rooted, I would like to suggest, in his theory of the drives and the pleasure principle that governs them. Furthermore, Freud's theory of sublimation is precisely a theory in which his basic ideas on sexual drives and the pleasure principle are really crucial. From where else can life draw its vitality, if not from the drives? This goes for a religious life as well. Post-Freudian approaches to religion (which still want to be called psychoanalytic) cannot succeed in their plea for a more vivifying conception of religion if they do not at the same time re-examine some aspects of Freudian theory and, more specifically, as we shall see, some of his ideas on the drives and the pleasure principle. The pre-Oedipal sphere and the reference to the maternal object are not sufficient to explain the revivifying force of religion. There can be no successful move beyond Freud without a critical re-examination of his ideas about drives and pleasure. And this move beyond is necessary for elaborating (from within a psychoanalytic perspective) a non-reactive conception of religion.

To really grasp what Freud misses, I will briefly recount in the *first section* the basic points of how he understands religion. To illustrate the vitalizing power of religion, in the *second section* I use an unusual but well-known Christian prayer that still appeals to our religious imagination – *The Adoration of the Crucified* – as presented by Teresa of Avila in her autobiography. To describe this kind of prayer, I make a detour through the two most important axes of aesthetic experience, the sublime and the beautiful, as symbolized by Dionysius and Apollo. The adoration of the

Crucified is an ecstatic prayer that is made up of masochistic drives. The masochistic enjoyment one can find in this prayer is, according to me, stronger than the spiritual fruits of contemplation. Unlike prayer aimed at contemplation, adoration does not aim at reconciliation and acceptance, but rather at participation. In *section three*, I argue that post-Freudian theories must insert the notion of bodily drives into their alternative view of religion, and that the combination of an ecstatic and masochistic enjoyment (as found in the adoration of the Crucified) offers some interesting indications for a better understanding of the interaction between drives and religion. In my view, the enjoyment in masochistic prayer perfectly corresponds to the demands of a successful sublimation. In the *last section*, I examine why Freud could not understand sublimation, and in particular religious sublimation, as he wants to understand it. Sublimation according to Freud is not directed against drives, it is a transformation of them. In fact, post-Freudian psychoanalysis generally agrees that Freud did not succeed in developing the notions necessary for a non-reactive conception of religion. The cause of this failure has to be sought, ultimately, not in his ideas on religion, but in some of his ideas on the very nature of the drives and pleasure (Vergote, 1978/1988, 1997).

Freud's Narrow-Minded Vision of Religion

Freud connects religion to the frustration of drives, the imposition of moral rules, social adaptation, and the visionary picture of an all-embracing fulfillment. Which drives are repressed? Only partial sexual drives and the aggressive components of sexuality are susceptible to repression. And only drives that can be repressed are also open to sublimation. Sometimes, Freud argues that religion is rooted in the defense against anal drives. Thus, he relates religion to the repression of aggression. In the same vein, religious purification rituals are related by Freud to an archaic aversion to filth. Freud suggests that religion builds upon the effects of infantile reaction-formations, effects which are so favorable to ethics and society. In *Three Essays on Sexuality*, Freud remarks that sexual inhibitions resulting in disgust and feelings of shame (these primordial inhibitions are also called reaction-formations) are no mere cultural phenomena, but psychic dams that are spontaneously raised by the human organism.

One gets an impression from civilized children that the construction of these dams is a product of education, and no doubt education has much to do with it. But in reality this development is organically determined and fixed by heredity, and it can occasionally occur without any help at all from education. Education will not be trespassing beyond its appropriate domain if it limits itself to following the lines which have already been laid down organically and to impressing them somewhat more clearly and deeply (Freud, 1905/1978, pp. 178–179). Reaction-formations constitute the core of moral sense and they are, according to Freud, organically motivated. Upbringing and culture are here not formative principles of nature, but strengthen a tendency that already resides in human nature. There is no question here of a radical break between nature and culture, such as defended by Lacan in his theory of the symbolic order. Religion, which continues to build upon reaction-formations and consolidates their effects, works in service of repression and the frustration of drives (Freud, 1907/1978). For Freud, ethics without repression is unthinkable. Moreover, repression is for him not a singular occurrence. It is a process that continually repeats itself over and over again, and one that can never be abolished. The consequence of this is that there is no place in Freud's vocabulary for a notion such as 'virtue', since virtue implies that the suppression of drives is not the last word. According to the moral psychology of classical virtue theory, drives permit themselves to be reformed through practice and education such that transformation becomes their second nature. This is in principle excluded by Freud: there is no ethics without conflict.

Religion is also a cultural phenomenon that promotes community. It is not solely a source of frustration, but at the same time spurs socialization (Freud, 1913/1978). In later works, ranging from *The Future of an Illusion* (1927) to *Moses and Monotheism* (1939), Freud also understands religion as proceeding from human helplessness, mourning and nostalgia, the need for protection, archaic attachment, etc. Thus, religion fits in with dimensions of our *conditio humana* that cannot be reduced to reaction-formations and a repression-based ethics. Other than in *Totem and Taboo* (1913/1978), respect for the law, repression of aggression and guilt (as the price paid for the rebellion against our loving lawgiver) are no longer central. Religion has a role to play in the fulfillment of deeply human and infantile needs and in the mitigation of human suffering. In Freud's later works, the law-giving and punishing divinity seems to fade into the background and in its place there emerges a divinity more responsive to the longing for security and protection. Post-Freudian analysts have seen this change of emphasis in Freud as a welcome feminization of religion. In the end, there is some room for a more motherly divinity. The new image of God as a more considerate and understanding father finds its psychic roots in the damaged fantasy of an omnipotent and omnibenevolent parental figure. The figure of an almighty and all-embracing, care-giving divine person has its psychological origin in infantile fantasies, but covers up the cracks and flaws in these fantasies which emerge in the real confrontation with fatherly mothers and motherly fathers. Religion heals the injuries of life and feeds the nostalgic longing for a world without loss and pain. In short, religion facilitates earthly frustration by fostering in the imagination visionary images of an all-embracing fulfillment in which the unconscious and deeper self welcomes the return of reassuring incestuous desires. Thus, religion no longer exclusively stands under the sign of repression and social adaptation, but rather for compensation and restitution.

In Freud's approach to religion as a cultural phenomenon, two radically different questions constantly intertwine, and this confusion plays serious tricks on him. There is, on one hand, the question of the *origin* of a phenomenon, and, on the other hand, the question of its *function*. However, Freud understands the origin of religion in and through the functions of religion. It is obvious that religion plays a role in ethics, and thus, according to Freud, we must understand the origin of religion in moral terms. Take the consoling grace of religion. Religion that is not capable of consolation does not deserve the name. Does this imply however that religion originated in the urge for consolation? Religion can have favorable effects on society, but does this imply that religion originated in the need for socialization? Freud seems to make this argument. However, it is not that difficult to formulate an alternative view of religion. In which sense? Religion could have originated in something other than the moral, social and psychological functions it fulfills. It could have been first of all a spontaneous expression of bodily joy, a celebratory joy expressed in dance, song and prayer. Functions such as moralization and compensation could be seen as secondary effects which are a sort of limitation or even taming of a more spontaneous and generous enjoyment that was originally not grounded in these functions. It is not all that surprising that Freud never found his way towards a more joyful form of religion.

In Freud's presentation of religion, the fantasy of a future paradisiacal existence plays an important role. Freud thinks that psychoanalysis can throw some light onto cultural products, insofar as cultural phenomena resemble individual neuroses, perversions, and psychoses. All emerge from the same fabric of conflicts. Freud's theory of the unconscious can teach us something about cultural phenomena, but these in turn can teach psychoanalysis something about the unconscious. In this way, a psychoanalytic approach to cultural phenomena can be more than applied psychoanalysis. However, there exists a remarkable discrepancy between Freud's approach to different products of cultural phenomena. A cultural product such as art is treated by him as any other product of the mind and free association. He submits these to the demands of subjective truth: what do these products teach about human drives and conflicts? Religion, on the other hand, has to answer the demands of objective truth, and must go through a confrontation with scientific objectivity. However, seen from the perspective of psychoanalysis proper, Freud was not obliged to measure a religious cosmology against a scientific worldview. Here, Freud brings in the demands of the Enlightenment. This comparison is inevitably disadvantageous for religion. In relation to science, religion is for Freud a lesser form of rationality, just as children are less developed than adults and a primitive culture is less than developed than modernity. As with every right-minded Enlightenment thinker, Freud can only see religion as a lower form of scientific rationality. Moreover, religion is not just the reflection of a less rational worldview, but based on an illusion.

Frustration, *repression*, *socialization*, and *reconciliation* are the pillars of Freud's concept of religion. That is, all in all, a rather reassuring view of religion. What Freud seems to miss, according to post-Freudian analysts, is religion as a joyful and generous affirmation of life. Affirmation is stronger than acceptance and resignation. However important frustration of drives and resignation may be, a religion that only promotes acceptance will not be capable of including the full vitality of life within itself. Should a resilient religion not celebrate all the forces of life, make people sing and dance as much at deaths as at births? In Christianity, there exists a fascinating form of prayer – *The Adoration of the Crucified* – which does not fit with Freud's image as just outlined.

The Ecstatic 'Jouissance' in the Adoration of the Crucified

The Adoration of the Crucified is a form of prayer practiced by the mystics, among others. (Merkur, 2007) In Teresa of Avila, we can read a striking presentation of this prayer. "Who," asks Teresa of Avila, "can look upon our Lord, covered with wounds and bowed down under persecutions, without accepting, loving, and longing for them?" (Teresa of Avila, 1904, p. 222).[1] In the autobiography of Teresa of Avila, one can read how she encourages her fellow nuns during meditative prayer to direct their attention to the crucifixion death of Christ. For this, the soul needs the power of the imagination. But the imagination may only take the lead after it is formed through the understanding. "We now reflect on something from the passion. For instance, the Lord on the whipping post. The understanding searches for the causes of abandonment, the great sorrow and the great pains of His Majesty (...) everybody ought to begin, to progress, and to end with this form of prayer." It is much less beneficial to choose one's own sinfulness and mortality as a point of departure, because then one's own self stands once again at the center of importance. An authentic spirituality, on the other hand, is coupled with a kind of self-forgetfulness and that is something different than a narcissistic return to oneself. The attending to the Crucified liberates the Ego from itself because it is taken up in the sublime object of contemplation. Teresa describes how she initially did not succeed in collecting her thoughts and in putting herself into the very touching tableau of the suffering Christ. Gradually, however, her soul is overtaken by the image. Teresa describes how her soul is grasped by an excessive enthusiasm that takes the form of an amorous adoration of the suffering Christ. Her soul is completely outside itself and this ecstatic surrender elicits words whose masochistic tenor cannot be denied. "Who," asks Teresa of Avila, "can look upon our Lord, covered with wounds and bowed down under persecutions, without accepting, loving, and longing for them?"[2] The loving soul does not have a caring attitude here. The longing for union takes the form of a far-reaching imaginary identification with Christ – imaginary, as Lacan would have it, because it gravitates around its sublime corporeal *Gestalt*. The soul loses itself in this prayer. The *enjoyment* brings the soul beyond itself, and the surrender to this self-loss is expressed in a religious rapture that intensifies the longing for a deeper identification and unification.

[1] In my paper, I take this prayer as a prayer that can stimulate and facilitate a still deeper mystic union as has been the case for Teresa. However, this prayer can also be cultivated by believers who do not share the deeper spiritual concerns of some mystics and for them too the meditation of the Crucified can be a source of deep enjoyment.

[2] Though I am emphasizing in my paper a masochistic sensitivity, I don't claim that this sensitivity is the only one between the soul of Teresa and the Crucified. Moreover, I am not arguing that without masochistic interests a believer cannot enjoy the adoration of the Crucified. The image of the Crucified consists in a very complex scenario with different entries for different drives such as the sadistic, exhibitionistic, and voyeuristic oriented drives as well as their mutual combination. From a psychodynamic point of view, this prayer is over determined or multi-layered. Different motives and configurations of the drives are in play. To clarify my argument, it is not necessary to articulate all the levels.

This ecstatic form of prayer should be distinguished from contemplation aimed at meditation (Moyaert, 2007a, b). We have to be more precise. What happens to the soul of Teresa is that her meditation turns, unexpectedly, into an ecstatic prayer. What is the difference between rapture (ecstasy) and contemplation? Rapture is not only based on the beholding of what is sublime, but is also coupled with a far-reaching *identification* or *participation* with that which is more powerful and impressive than one's own self. Rapture is beholding mixed with participation. The distance between the self and the object of beholding diminishes. What appears on the side of the objective pole, the object of beholding, takes the lead and takes up the contemplative Ego in itself. In rapture, the Ego is filled with what is stronger than itself, and this participation causes the Ego to surpass itself. Participation fills the Ego with energy. The Ego shares in the grandeur and in the power of the *Gestalt* in which it participates. The sublime *Gestalt* of the suffering Christ communicates its force to the soul that looses its self in adoring the overwhelming greatness of that suffering. The effects of rapture upon the soul are stronger than what reconciliation and acceptance can bring about. In a fit of unconditional surrender, the soul not only falls into suffering; it also longs for suffering. In a moment of infatuation, the soul desires to participate in the suffering of Christ. The soul loses its self in the adoration, and this self-loss is at the same time a narcissistic aggrandizement. The self is aggrandized through its participation with the suffering Christ. It shares in the greatness of Christ. Participation vitalizes one's own desires and gives them a power that they do not have on their own. To be sure, ecstatic enjoyment is different from the frustration of the drives. Moreover, this form of prayer does not provide the reassuring and comforting grace of reconciliation, acceptance, and resignation. This prayer is much more powerful. The prayer urges the soul to *embrace* and to *affirm* the world and God to the extreme, even to suffering. The adoration of the Crucified does not give meaning to suffering. This prayer does not say that suffering has meaning or that it is good that people suffer. The grace received in this exciting prayer has a much more powerful and dramatic impact. It gives the soul the capacity to suffer. The suffering of Christ can give a believer who loves meditating on the Crucified the power to suffer himself. To put it in religious terms: Christ doesn't give meaning to my suffering, but gives me, through identification and participation, the strength to suffer. The deeper spiritual dimension of this prayer consists in the desire to be unified in suffering with the suffering Christ.

Rapture stands in stark contrast to contemplation. In rapture, the diminishing of the distance between the self and the *Gestalt* of beholding is central. In contemplation, the world (the self included) is approached at a some distance. The world appears as a theater. The contemplating subject takes distance from its desires and projects, and develops in the direction of a distant self without desires. In contemplation, the subject surpasses its desires. It is on the point of becoming a subject without desires, a subject purified of desires. In rapture, it's just the other way around. In rapture, the Ego is at the point of dissolving in forces that surpass the Ego. In rapture, the Ego is outside of itself, overwhelmed by what is greater than itself. In contemplation, the self stands above or outside of its desires. In contemplation, one lets loose of one's desires. In rapture, one lets go of oneself. If contemplation refers to a self without desires, rapture refers to an unfolding of forces without a personal self. Contemplation is an enjoyable death to this world. According to Schopenhauer, the enjoyment found in contemplation has the meaning of a liberation. It is the joy of being delivered from life, from its restless drives and its infinite desires. Enjoyment here consist in the contrast between the inner rest and peace of contemplation and the ephemeral, turbulent life of desires. The enjoyment of contemplation is a *negative enjoyment* because the soul enjoys its inner peace as a liberation from stimuli. This is a negative pleasure which resembles the pleasure of the Freudian Nirvana produced by the evacuation of the tension of the excited drives. The enjoyment found in rapture is the complete opposite of this negative enjoyment. It is rather the enjoyment of joining and embracing life, even in suffering. Contemplation tends towards isolation from the world; rapture, towards participation. Contemplation leads toward relativization and acceptance. The enjoyment in ecstatic delight vitalizes and stimulates. It is a less comforting, less reassuring, enjoyment. This enjoyment does not throw the subject to itself. It is not a relativization of oneself but a surrendering oneself to that which is greater than the self. Ecstatic enjoyment is animated by a kind of self-forgetfulness (Moyaert, 2007a, b).

However, the enjoyment Teresa finds in her prayer has not yet been sufficiently described. We must examine in more detail the strong impact the adoration of the *suffering* Christ has upon the drives. Adoration cannot inject energy without awakening and reactivating drives that have 'subcutaneously' animated the desire to adore. Which drives have motivated adoration and have been, in turn, animated and excited by it? As is well-known in psychoanalysis, there is a strong link between masochism and idealization, which is another term for adoration (Freud, 1905/1978, p. 150 note 1, p. 158 note 1). There is no idealization without the willingness to submit oneself to the object of adoration. Adoration does not only cause masochism; a masochistic organization of the drives is an unconscious motive for adoration.

Seen in the context of Christian meditation, this prayer certainly reinforces the connection with masochism. *The Adoration of the Crucified* is a very intimate prayer and needs an appropriate and nourishing environment to be practiced fully. Religion as an objective framework and the subjective corporeal sensibility of an individual soul interact with each other. Without a deeply *masochistic aptitude* that enables drives to experience pleasure in suffering, the faculties of the soul cannot be stirred by the image of the Crucified. In order to act upon the passions of the soul, the image of the Crucified needs masochistic tendencies and, at the same time, that image, through its embedding in a more comprehensive religious framework, gives a broader extension to the masochistic identification that it stirs up and keeps alive. The enjoyment the soul finds in meditating on the Crucified overrides the barriers of bodily aversion for what is cruel and disgusting, barriers which (as we have seen) Freud called reaction-formations (Freud, 1905/1978, pp. 151–152). It is incorrect to describe the relation the soul has with the suffering Christ with such terms as empathy, pity, or caring. The soul undergoes an exciting adoration that leads to an identification. To be sure, both processes, adoration and identification, can bear fruit on the level of morality. And in the spiritual context of mystical love, they must bear these fruits, but the moral fruits are not the core of the excitement.

The interaction between religious adoration and a masochistic organization of drives works both ways. If religion gives a broader extension to the subjective masochistic sensitivity of, for example, Teresa, her sensitivity in turn puts its stamp on her personal prayer. Masochistic enjoyment prepares and stimulates a still deeper mystical attitude of surrender. The obedience to a divine person who is greater and more powerful than one's own individuality undoubtedly can receive a strong impulse of masochism, just as every adoration and idealization profits from masochistic tendencies. At the same time, these tendencies can put their stamp upon the prayer life of some persons. Not all Christian believers and mystics are equally sensitive to this kind of praying. The fact that the soul of Teresa was set on fire by this prayer says something about her drives. A particular configuration of partial drives can individuate prayer. The principle of individuation is not found in the mind, but in the body, i.e. in the corporeal drives. Self-surrender, bordering on self-loss, does not imply that an ecstatic enjoyment has no individual character. Ecstatic self-loss also passes through the individual program or configuration of partial drives. I have to emphasize this in order to avoid an overhasty association (so often made in spiritual circles) of self-loss with an evaporation of the body and its drives. To the contrary, even the state of a spiritualized self-loss still follows the paths of individualized drives. Each self-loss is distinct and strictly individualized and this individualization comes from the particular constellation of the corporeal drives.

In *The Economic Problem of Masochism* (Freud, 1924/1978, pp. 167–168), Freud suggests a link between masochism and religion. He observes a relation between masochism and the acceptance of the fact that life is guided by a necessity or a fate that surpasses the power of the individual. This awareness extends our relationships to other authority figures and gives them a broader reach. A religious life is based on the idea of belonging to what is greater than yourself, to a horizon more powerful than the perspective of one's own individuality. Once again, the amplification of one's own limited perspective brought about by religion can profit from masochistic drives, in order to introduce this greater breadth to the human soul. In addition, the masochistic organization of the drives certainly receives an extra impulse from a contemplation permeated by adoration. In advancing from a masochistic disposition, religion can also give a greater amplification to that disposition, greater, for example, than the scope it has in a sexual perversion (Moyaert, 2002a).

Inserting the Masochistic Prayer in a Freudian Inspired View on Sublimation

Together with the post-Freudians and against Freud, we want to understand religion as force that *enhances* and *reinforces* drives. However, without reference to the drives, the strengthening force of religion cannot be understood. Religion works upon the self and has the power to deeply transform it. This transformation remains an hollow phrase if not analyzed on the level of the drives. Religion is not an overcoming of the body, but is rather, through and through, a bodily affair. Religion affects the drives that are stuff the self is made of. Prayer, too, is a libidinal affair. Believers pray with their drives. Hence, my suggestion, addressed to post-Freudian alternatives, is not to focus solely on the Freudian images of God and not to set aside Freud's struggle with sublimation. Religious images do say something of the encounter between the moving drives of the body and the divine.

According to Freud, sublimation consists in the transformation (*Umbildung*) of the aim of the sexual drives into a non-sexual aim. The aim of the drive is an action. Drives motivate the body to act. However, to understand sublimation as a metamorphosis of sexual drives is, in a Freudian perspective, still too broad. For Freud, only the *partial drives* (and these are the components of sexuality that are responsible for the perverse components of any human sexuality) are susceptible to sublimation. Aggression, too, is an element of the drives. Sublimation is not an alternative to a genital sexuality, but affects the partial drives, as in our example the masochistic disposition of the drives. Sublimation is a concept which consists of three elements. It refers to a *beginning term* (i.e. what has to be transformed), to an *end term* (i.e. the result of the transformation), and to the *relation* or the *transition* between the starting point and the product. Freud does not use only the term transformation (*umbilden*) for rendering what happens to the aim of the drives in sublimation (Moyaert, 2007a, b). He also describes the relation between the starting point and the end product with terms such as diversion (*Wendung*), turning away (*ablenken*), transposition (*umsetzen*) and exchange (*vertauschen*, *wechseln*). Freud understands the transition from the sexual to the non-sexual as a unilateral moving away from the original sexual aim, and this moving away consists in a turning away from perverse aims. Freud's term *desexualization* perfectly fits in this picture. This sketch of a unilateral moving away from the original sexual aim suggests the following interesting question. How radical does the turning away from the sexual have to be? If sublimation is a transition, one has to consider that at least *some* sublimations have to be deeply ambiguous, in the sense that for *some* sublimations it will not be crystal clear, if they have moved away far enough from their sexual origin, that they cannot also be recognized in sexually perverse expressions. The argument here is not that all sublimations are ambiguous in this sense, but that it is always possible that some sublimations are ambiguous. In other words, understanding sublimation in terms of transition implies that there is only a *gradual distinction* between perversion and sublimation.[3] Can our example of the masochistic prayer throw some light in these matters?

I take this prayer to be a successful sublimation. It differs both from a neurotic compromise-formation and from perversion, though, as we will see, the relation with perversion can be rather confusing. Neurosis does not experience enjoyment in surrender and is moreover a defense against self-abandonment and participation. In

[3] An author such as Lacan criticizes the notion of desexualisation. One reason is that this term does not remind us that some sublimations explicitly stay in touch with their perverse counterparts, so explicitly that it is not always clear if a transformation belongs to a sublimated rather than to a perverse expression of the drives (Lacan, 1992, p. 111).

his *Guilt and Desire*, Vergote (1978/1988, p. 154) sees the unrestrained freedom of Teresa's ecstatic enjoyment as a decisive criterion for distinguishing her mystical experience from one of a neurotic character. Neurosis revolves around self-control or fear of self-loss. Neurotic symptoms are a compromise between two opposing tendencies, wherein the suppressed tendencies only find some expression after being unrecognizably deformed. Clinical experience teaches that neurosis is a defense against passivity and against a body formed by masochistic drives, even though neurotic symptoms don't indicate directly they are a defense against passivity. Repression dominates any direct expression. Take, for example, the ecstatic enjoyment as described by Teresa. I am not inclined to understand this prayer as a product of the repression of a masochistic drive-configuration. These tendencies are too emphatically present for this. The prayer of Teresa is also to be distinguished from neurotic self-humiliation. The adoration of the Crucified is surrender without self-debasement. Through participation, the prayer aggrandizes the self and makes it stronger, which is quite the opposite of self-humiliation. This form of prayer does not need moralizing or the inference of sin to be appealing. To the contrary, the crucifix has a direct, sensually appealing power. The prayer is borne by a longing for unification with the suffering Christ. This identification is not motivated by an exaggerated notion of sin. The notion of sin is neither a spoilsport nor a prerequisite for self-abandonment. The soul does not long for suffering as punishment for its sins. The source of pleasure is not a neurotic self-punishment. There is a *direct chemistry* between the image of the Crucified and the admiration motivated by masochism. It's as if the not-yet-Oedipalized archaic layers of the partial drives are *directly* mobilized, as if the Oedipus complex is passed over like a way station. To summarize, the whole-hearted 'yes' of the surrender is unthinkable in neurosis. In neurosis, it is never simply 'yes', but always a tense and ambiguous 'yes and no', which poisons any generous surrender. This explains why ecstatic surrender is coupled with a less reassuring image of religion.

The prayer also differs from perversion. Perversions are a more direct sexual expression of partial drives. Compared with sexual perversion, the longing for unification with the suffering Christ brings about a *displacement* and a *widening* of the bodily enjoyment, wherein the enjoyment is not merely sexual. But is this widening and displacement not to be seen as a *defense* against sexual drives? Rabidly Freudian psychoanalysts will certainly see it that way. They will see displacement and widening as a flight response, i.e. as being motivated by negative motives. Drives are motivated to seek out other territories (displacement) and to conquer new territories (widening) because unpleasure forced them to do so. Here, there is no change without pain to be avoided. But perhaps one can see it from another point of view as well.

Widening can be understood in two senses. By widening, one can understand a movement through which a particular interest is inserted into a broader framework and thereby loses something of its self-willed partiality. In this view, religion brings about the transformation of masochism into something else, into a kind of life that no longer follows its former masochistic path. The emphasis is on the impact of a broader framework and its effects upon the particular drives that undergo the influence of that larger perspective. The framework reorients the drives. What happens is that the part hands over its influence to the whole. We can rephrase this in terms of the organ and the organism. The organism submits to the organs and the organs accept giving up their own limited perspective. The interests of the organism as a whole are reflected in the different organs. The organism dominates the organs and not the other way around. If we apply this approach to the vicissitudes of our masochistic prayer, we have the following rough sketch. As the scope of the masochistic drives is weakened, their impact becomes smaller. These drives are required to become a component in a framework that surpasses them, and that which surpasses them can no longer be described in terms of the masochistic drives. The drives loose their particularity. It's as if the masochistic attitude has evaporated within the broader framework. It is interesting to note that sublimation originally means a chemical process phenomenologically described as a direct evaporation. By submitting themselves to a broader framework, according to our sketch, drives become more mitigated. However, is this a correct description of ecstatic enjoyment? After all, this enjoyment is not a softening of masochistic drives, not even an announcement of their enfeeblement.

Widening can be understood from a different, more Nietzschean, angle as well. It can be seen as an amplification or an expansion of the limited perspective itself: an organ dominating the organism and the organism reflecting the growing influence of an organ. From this perspective, what is happening with the drives can no longer be seen as a weakening of their particularity. One organ reveals its power by penetrating the organism down to its smallest pores and fibers and in using the organism for its own partial purposes. To be sure, religion does affect the drives. But the reverse movement is just as important for the health of the drives. Masochism, in turn, can do something with religion, when it imposes its own traces and its own perspective upon religion. The image here is of the expansion of a particular perspective. Sublimation is not religion doing something with the drives, but drives doing something with religion. *Partial drives are using religion to express themselves.* They conquer religion for their own expansion. If this movement is the hard core of a successful sublimation, then sublimation is basically an expression of the drives. Organs and drives transform cultural phenomena into expressions of themselves. Religion no longer functions as a framework that demands the renunciation of the individuality of the drives, but rather the drives manifest their power and their creativity by transforming religion into an expression of their own individual perspective. Prayer can become the signature of someone's body. The difference between perversion and sublimation can be seen in the tension between a narrow and a wide expression of the partial drives. Perversion is a narrowing the scope of the drives because it reduces their expression to a sexual expression. But sexuality is only one manifestation of masochistic drives, and a rather poor one at that, because the influence of masochism doesn't reach further than the sexual body. Aren't healthy drives much more powerful? Are they not capable of inspiring and animating other territories of someone's life? If one begins by understanding drives as self-expression, then sexuality too can be an expression of them, albeit only a limited one. Sublimation again delivers the drives from this limitation and brings them once again in touch with their basic self-expressing power. In sublimation, *even* religion can become a territory for these drives, *even* prayer can be an enjoyable expression of masochism.

The hunger of the drives is not satisfied by sexuality. Drives need much more to feed their hunger, hence they conquer religion, art, and moral life as well. Creative and flowing as they are, drives can even find self-expression in an ascetic way of life. It is only in a superficial sense that the demands of asceticism seem to go against the drives of, for example, religious persons. On a deeper level, some drives look for asceticism – not in the sense that the drives want to be tamed or to be suppressed, but rather because in asceticism they welcome their real enjoyment. Drives finding their masochistic enjoyment in a ascetic way of life will at the same time impose their own enjoyment upon asceticism by exaggerating this kind of life. This exaggeration is a sign of their expansion. In this view, religion *is* no longer the partner of repression. Of course, religion brings in its own demands to which the drives are submitted. But I would rather search for the traces of sublimation where drives recognize themselves in a ascetic way of life and use asceticism for their own purposes. In sublimation, drives prove that they are creative and ingenuous enough to impose their own style and perspective on asceticism. It is obvious that, in this view, sublimation is not necessarily that reassuring. The fact that drives conquer an ascetic way of life for their own self-expression goes necessarily together with a risk of exaggeration. I have quoted here the rather 'soft' example of Teresa. However, as we all know, this type of prayer has found much more extreme and messy expressions in the Christian tradition. Angela de Folignio joyfully lapped up the water in which she had just washed the feet of lepers. The blessed Marie Allacoque ate the excrement of a sick man with no less a reward of spiritual elevation (Lacan, 1959–1960/1992, pp. 187–188; Vergote, 1978/1988, pp. 153–167). How far are we still removed from perversities? Control imposed to mitigate the risk of perversities returns religion once again to the neighborhood of the depressing picture of mere social adaptation. Where is the vitality of religion in this depressing picture? Some exaggerations run the risk of being judged perversities, and some can put the actual religious context so strongly under pressure that religion is obliged to transform its own judgments, and exaggerations, instead of being condemned as perversities, must then be seen as the manifestation of holiness. Nobody knows beforehand where exactly the distinction is to be situated. And the creativity of the drives consists in their power to transform religion.

Religion is not a medium which delivers us from the perverse components of our drives. Vital drives, after all, never give up their perspective. Masochism, for example, can inspire someone's moral engagement in a very specific way. It can reanimate someone's awareness of never having done enough. Masochism becomes more fecund in various areas of life. In this view, religion is not the transformation of masochism into manifestations wherein masochism no longer recognizes itself. To the contrary, masochism conquers religion in order to discover itself anew. This much must be clear: in this view, sublimation is not a weakening nor a repression of the drives, but rather an expression of their creativity, demonstrated by the fact that drives are capable of imposing their perspective even in contexts where one would not expect it. Along similar lines, one can understand the relationship between anorexia and holiness. Without religion, it is much more difficult for a groan of hunger not to be a symptom of sickened anorexia. But anorexia finding its way into religion can transform its own expression into a life of holy fasting. Religion, here, is not an overcoming of anorexia, but a place to cultivate it and to give it the opportunity to become more fertile on other levels than one's own body. Of course, the relationship with religion has to be described in terms of interaction. On the one hand, religion is a fertile ground that can offer a new meaning to a body already structured by anorectic drives. Religion can give a meaning to the body that the body cannot give to itself. Hence, the sociological disappearance of religion takes away from the anorectic body one of its most powerful expressions. But as seen in the tenor of my essay, it is more important to emphasize the other side of the interaction. The anorectic body imposes its own demands upon religion and obliges religion to reconsider its own evaluations. An anorectic body can use a religious context to really cultivate its own enjoyment.

By now, we are far away from Freud's picture of religion as presented in the first section of my essay.

Investigating Freud's Failure

Freud's relationship to religion is rather complex. On the one hand, our suggestion to insert masochistic prayer into Freud's theory of sublimation seems to correspond to what he had in mind in his theory of sublimation, even though our vocabulary was not completely in line with the standard Freudian one. On the other hand, we have seen in section one that Freud did not explain religion in that way. How best to understand this tension in Freud?

The psychoanalytic literature broadly agrees that Freud's theory of sublimation was not really successful (Laplanche and Pontalis 1983, pp. 431–433). In *The Language of Psycho-Analysis*, Laplanche and Pontalis (1983) did not exclude possibility of the development of a more successful theory within the limits drawn by Freud. According to these authors, the major conceptual tools for elaborating such a theory are mostly there in Freud, even though some of them have to be found in the margins. It is up to post-Freudian psychoanalysts to take advantage of their as yet uncultivated theoretical possibilities. In his seminar on sublimation, Laplanche gave a very concise diagnosis of Freud's difficulties with sublimation, but he still left the question open as to how to solve them. "Is there a non-sexual destiny of the sexual drive, a destiny that can be radically different from symptom-formation? In plain words, does that exist?" (Laplanche, 1980, p. 119). However, there is one voice in the complex psychoanalytic debate on sublimation that I wish to explore in detail and that is the point of view of Vergote. In two books written at an interval of 2 decades, Vergote discussed both Freud's ideas on sublimation and on religion. In *Guilt and Desire: Religious Attitudes and Their Pathological Derivatives* (1978/1988), Vergote, while interpreting mystical love as a sublimation of hysteria, recognized the incompleteness of Freud's ideas on sublimation. However, Vergote did not yet exclude the possibility that Freud's basic assumptions could still be used for a more successful theory of sublimation and religious sublimation (p. 158). In *La Psychanalyse à l'épreuve de la sublimation* (Vergote, 1997 – not yet translated in English), Vergote radically changed his ideas. Of course, his diagnosis did not change. As with Laplanche, he still localizes Freud's failure in his inability to really distinguish religion from symptom-formation. For Freud, sublimation is an alternative to symptom-formation. Sublimation is not a defense, but an *auto-transformation* of the drives (p. 125). But, according to Vergote's argument, Freud cannot think of sublimation the way he wants to think it. Take, for example, Freud's ideas on symbols or symbolization. He understands symbolization from the point of view of dreams and hysterical symptoms and thus *via repression*. This means that he can see in symbols only a deformation and defense against a repressed content, while symbols, claims Vergote, are basically a creative transformation (pp. 115–170). Though his diagnosis is still in agreement with most post-Freudian authors, his solution has radically changed and is quite uncommon in the psychoanalytic literature (Moyaert, 2002b). The reason for Freud's failure is to be found in some of his basic anthropological assumptions and ontological definitions. The argument is philosophical. Vergote does not argue that some Freudian notions have to be understood differently in order to develop a better theory on sublimation. (That would be a *petitio principii.*) Rather, some definitions have to be changed simply because they are wrong. In summarizing some of Vergote's arguments, the reader will come to the conclusion that the sketch I gave in section "Inserting the Masochistic Prayer in a Freudian Inspired View on Sublimation" is based on ideas much in line with Vergote's alternative. Before commenting on Vergote, I should point out that my exposé has to remain mostly a one-way communication. Though the critique really strikes at the heart of some basic Freudian insights, this does not imply that Freud could not have responded. Moreover and more importantly, given the enormous complexity of Freud there are some notions in Freud that without a doubt can be activated and developed more in line with the tenor of the critics. I cannot investigate how this can be done here, and must confine myself to some minor suggestions in need of later elaboration.

Freud's failure is due to a combination of *three misconceptions*. The first concerns Freud's conception of sexuality. This problem goes in part back to Jung, but there is a difference. For Jung, the crucial question was about the content of this term. According to Jung, Freud's understanding of sexuality was much too broad. Vergote tackles the question of how Freud understands the very *nature* of sexuality. Secondly, Freud improperly understands drives under the model of needs. And thirdly, Freud wrongly reduces pleasure to satisfaction or an evacuation of tension.

Firstly: for Freud, sublimation is a transformation of the partial *sexual* drives. Jung was the first to criticize Freud for not having clarified what he means by 'sexual'. What are the criteria for identifying a drive as sexual? Take for example the pleasure the organism finds in the stimulation and excitation of the oral instinct. It is evident that this pleasure contains more than the pacification of a stimulus. A child finds pleasure in sucking even if there is no bodily need to be satisfied. But it does not follow from this that one should need to call the pleasure of sucking itself sexual. One could instead call it an expression of Eros, rather than an archaic manifestation of sexuality. And if it is not really necessary to call the most archaic manifestations sexual, then the idea that sublimation is a metamorphosis of sexuality becomes a lot less obtrusive. To be sure, sublimation can still be associated with a transformation of sexuality, but in a Jungian vein, it would instead consist in freeing drives from their limited sexual content. Sublimation returns towards the original non-sexual or erotic power of drives. According to Vergote, this Jungian critique is only one aspect of a much more important question. Freud thinks of the sexual as a natural (biochemical) quality of drives (pp. 107–113). To be sure, drives are corporeal through and through. That much has to be affirmed repeatedly against Jung, who tends towards a spiritualization of the body. Drives put the body permanently under pressure. But, although thoroughly corporeal, the sexual cannot be reduced to a strictly biochemical quality. What Vergote wants to emphasize is the psychodynamic character of sexuality studied by Freud as no one before him. Contingent encounters and the deeply individual experiences that feed our fantasies determine which parts of our body, which activities, in which sense and with whom, will be taken up in our sexual pleasure. However, Freud undervalues the importance of his own psychodynamic approach and this comes to the fore in calling the first manifestation of the drives bluntly sexual. The fact that Freud renders his notion of sexuality more sophisticated by adding qualifications such as oral and anal, does not take away the fact that the partial drives *are* sexual. The ontological nature of a drive is ultimately explained through its biochemical substance (p. 108). Is there an alternative? The first manifestations of the most primordial drives *eroticize* the body. They make the body *susceptible to* sexual pleasure and these drives are sexualized only afterwards. The sexualization of the drives takes advantage of an earlier erotization of the body. Without this previous erotization, brought about in a great diversity of contacts and encounters, sexuality misses a lot infiltrating the different parts of the body to let them communicate with the bodies of others. In Vergote's view, the Freudian process of the transformation of sexual drives has to be understood as a return to the original erotic power of the drives.

Secondly: according to Vergote, Freud improperly understands drives under the model of needs. This argument is based on Freud's economic approach to the drives. Bodily needs must be alleviated, and they motivate the body to take actions that eliminate undesirable stimuli. An action motivated by a need is inclined to reach a point as quickly as possible where the action can reach an end. Liberation from painful excitation is the endpoint or, as Freud calls it, the aim of the instincts. Freud understands the sexual drives improperly according to this model. The aim of the sexual drives is an action that results in the *discharge* of tension and this *evacuation* is called satisfaction. That is a wrong approach to understanding what drives are. There is more pleasure in the sexual than the orgasmic release of tension. (Think, for example, of eating and drinking.) This brings us to the most important theoretical contribution.

Thirdly: What is pleasure or what is enjoyment? Freud defines pleasure as the sensation (consciousness) of a lessening of tension, or as the fulfillment of a lack, or as the recovery of a disturbed balance. To put it another way: for Freud, pleasure is identical with the disappearance of displeasure. For Freud, the pleasure principle is the motor of the drives and that implies that searching for pleasure is the same as the avoidance of displeasure. What moves the drives? Avoidance of displeasure! In this way, pleasure is defined as a negative reality. Freud, who puts pleasure in the heart of our life, in the end identifies a negative reality as the motor of our life. (What a depressing picture.) What motivates us is nothing other than the avoidance of pain. Pleasure is not the presence, but the absence of something, as if health were the same as the absence of sickness, or beauty were merely the absence of ugliness. And if pleasure, as defined by Freud, is the motor of the drives, then sublimation is in principle unthinkable. For how could sublimation be something other than a reaction against unpleasant stimuli? Freud's negative definition of pleasure lies at the bottom of his idea that all instincts do is protect the organism against an increase of stimuli.

The very nature of pleasure has been debated in philosophy since Plato and Aristotle (Van Riel, 2000). It is interesting to observe that Freud's definition is in line with Plato, who subsumed pleasure under the ontological category of becoming. Pleasure has no substance, it is only the fleeting transition from one state to another, the transition from empty to full. Freud doesn't use these terms, preferring the economic vocabulary of stimuli. But the general picture is the same: pleasure is simply the lessening of disturbing energy, or the evacuation of stimuli. However, already since Aristotle, a tradition has existed that, unlike Freud and Plato, does not think of enjoyment in terms of perceptible fluctuations of tension, but as the *perfection of an activity* (p. 99). To enjoy is not to perceive some changes in the body, but to be active. Hence enjoyment is something other than a return to a balanced rest. Enjoyment as perfection means that drives motivating to act can carry out their activity unrestrained. This is not the place to comment Aristotle's alternative in detail. I will have to render his intuition in less technical terms. To fully consecrate oneself to what one does, to not be diverted, the capacity to concentrate and to surrender yourself – these are the objective signs of enjoyment. Enjoyment is the generosity of a free action. To be thrown back into your bodily feelings and to notice what is happening with the corporeal tensions is rather a disruptive and disturbing enjoyment. Every enjoyment is instead involved in some kind of self-forgetfulness. Freud cannot fully conceive of sublimation because he starts off from an incorrectly orgasmic notion of pleasure (i.e., pleasure as sexual gratification). However, Freud knew very well that his definition of pleasure was not the only one. In the footnotes of *Three Essays on Sexuality*, Freud observes that the German term *Lust* has two meanings. It can denote the gratification, the very moment of the satisfaction that brings an end to the action. It can also denote the impulse to act in the sense of 'I should like to', 'I feel an impulse to' (Freud, 1905/1978, p. 135 note 2, p. 212 note 1). In the first sense, actions seem to be a means of reaching a point outside the activity. In the second sense, the activity itself is an autonomous source of pleasure. If the action is pleasurable in itself, then reaching an endpoint is rather secondary. Freud only complains about this double meaning, and doesn't take it as a starting point to change his own definition, wherein he reduces pleasure to a rather poor reality. His economic approach to the human organism and his ideas on the pleasure principle based on that approach prevent him from fully considering the implications of an alternative definition of pleasure. His ideas on autoeroticism too could have been an occasion to introduce a more Aristotelian conception of pleasure. Autoeroticism is Freud's term for the pleasure found in bodily actions that have freed themselves from the aim of satisfying bodily needs. It is the pleasure found in sucking (i.e. oral drives), in exploring and mastering one's own body (i.e. anal drives), in looking (i.e. voyeurism) and in flaunting (i.e. exhibitionism). This enjoyment is like play, and is purely generous, because it doesn't primarily look to self-preservation and the satisfaction of needs. However, on the one hand, Freud neutralizes this opportunity too easily by describing autoeroticism as merely fore-pleasure. The real pleasure is still the end-pleasure, the *orgasmic* satisfaction which is, after all, another term for death. For Nietzsche, it is a sign of moral sickness that instincts prefer satisfaction. On the other hand, Freud never systematically incorporated his ideas on autoeroticism into his theory of sublimation.

For Freud, pleasure is what comes at the end of an activity and is what brings an activity to its end. For him, drives look for nothing other than bringing an end to themselves as soon as possible. That is, after all, the depressing picture of people who say that the highest goal of human life is pleasure in the sense of satisfaction. This satisfaction is ultimately another name for rest, peace and death. As long as Freud's notion of drives and the pleasure principle are inextricably linked with the vocabulary of needs to be satisfied, there is hardly any place for a joyful sublimation. Concerning the notion of drives as the real motor of human life, there is a philosophical tradition with roots going back to (amongst others) Spinoza, and with branches to be found in Nietzsche, Bergson and Deleuze. This tradition does not take filling a gap or evacuating energy as the paradigm understanding of the driving force of life. In this alternative, which I can only roughly sketch, drives are basically self-expression. This notion is stronger than the self-preservation or survival of the organism. To be sure, self-preservation (according to Freud, the task of the Ego-drives) is a kind of self-expression, but it is a relatively weak conception of self-affirmation. Self-preservation emphasizes the movement of adaptation. Drives adapt themselves to their environment in order to survive. What is adaptation other than giving up some of your own interests in order to survive? Creativity, in this view, concerns an ingenuity for finding new means to survive. On the other hand, the stronger view claims that drives survive by conquering the world and imposing themselves upon their environment. Of course, there is adaptation in this too, but here, survival is not the goal but rather the consequence. Drives survive through their permanent changing and creative self-expression. There is still adaptation in play, but the effects of the adaptation evaporate due to the fact that drives make their own mark in life. Certainly, drives could not transform themselves in a infinite changing self-expression if they did not encounter obstacles that hinder their totally free movement. These obstacles force the drives to take new and different paths. For Freud drives avoid obstacles and try to overwin the obstacle in order to find rest again. In the alternative view drives look for obstacles because they need them to express themselves. An obstacle plays the role of a catalyst, an agent that furthers or advances the process of spontaneous self-transformation. To understand the drives as a power that *informs* being (i.e. imposes their form upon life) is a stronger notion of drives than the one Freud works out in his theory of the pleasure principle.

Do later Freudian speculations on Eros, in the sense of a *vital drive*, bring Freud closer to the more vitalizing conception of sublimation we are looking for? Freud's notion of Eros is intrinsically linked to his speculations on the death drive. As is well-known, for Freud (1924/1978) masochism was one of the paths that lead him to speculate on the death drive. To be sure, there are many things to be clarified here. At least one thing is clear: masochism finds pleasure in a fantasy that brings the body close to self-destruction. However, what must be emphasized is that drives enjoy that fantasy and it is for just this reason that masochism can vitalize life. Sublimation cultivates that kind of pleasure, serves the will to live and embraces it.

References

Freud, S. (1905/1978). Three essays on sexuality. In J. Strachey (Ed.), *The standard edition of the complete psychological works of Sigmund Freud. Vol. 7* (pp. 124–245). London: Hogarth.

Freud, S. (1907/1978). Obsessive actions and religious practices. In J. Strachey (Ed.), *The standard edition of the complete psychological works of Sigmund Freud. Vol. 9* (pp. 115–127). London: Hogarth.

Freud, S. (1913/1978). Totem and taboo. In J. Strachey (Ed.), *The standard edition of the complete psychological works of Sigmund Freud. Vol. 13* (pp. 1–162). London: Hogarth.

Freud, S. (1924/1978). The economic problem of masochism. In J. Strachey (Ed.), *The standard edition of the complete psychological works of Sigmund Freud. Vol. 19* (pp. 157–170). London: Hogarth.

Freud, S. (1927/1978). The future of an illusion. In J. Strachey (Ed.), *The standard edition of the complete psychological works of Sigmund Freud. Vol. 21* (pp. 5–56). London: Hogarth.

Freud, S. (1939/1978). Moses and monotheism. In J. Strachey (Ed.), *The standard edition of the complete psychological works of Sigmund Freud. Vol. 23* (pp. 3–139). London: Hogarth.

Lacan, J. (1959–1960/1992). The ethics of psycho-analysis. In J.-A. Miller (Ed.), *The seminar of Jacques Lacan. Vol. 7.* London: Routledge.

Laplanche, J. (1980). Problématiques *III: La sublimation*. Paris: Quadrige/P.U.F.

Laplanche, J. & Pontalis, J.-B. (1983). *The language of psycho-analysis*. London: The Hogart Press.

Merkur, D. (2007). *Crucified with Christ: Meditation on the Passion, mystical death, and the medieval invention of psychotherapy*. New York: SUNY.

Moyaert, P. (2002a). Mysticism: The transformation of a love consumed by desire into a love without desire. *American Catholic Philosophical Quarterly*, *76*(2), 281–294.

Moyaert, P. (2002b). *Begeren en vereren: Idealisering en sublimering*. Amsterdam: Sun.

Moyaert, P. (2007a). The image of the crucified: Art and religion between contemplation and rapture. *Janus*, *21*, 58–67.

Moyaert, P. (2007b). Can sublimation be brought about through idealization? *Ethical Perspectives: Journal of the European Ethics Network*, *14*, 53–78.

Teresa of Avila (1904). *The life of St. Teresa of Jesus, of the Order of Our Lady of Carmel. written by herself* (trans. D. Lewis, introd. & ann. B. Zimmermann). London/New York: Baker & Bros.

Van Riel, G. (2000). *Pleasure and the good life: Plato, Aristotle and the Neoplatonists*. Leiden: Brill.

Vergote, A. (1978/1988). *Guilt and desire: Religious attitudes and their pathological derivations*. New Haven, CT: Yale University Press.

Vergote, A. (1997). *La psychanalyse à l'épreuve de la sublimation*. Paris: Cerf.

Part II
Changes in the Scientific Research on Religion: Empirical and Theoretical Studies

The Psychoanalytic Study of Myth Since Freud

Pursuing the Dream*

Michael Carroll

When searching for an particularly good illustration of how Freud approached the study of myth, commentators typically cite his analysis of the story of Oedipus in *The Interpretation of Dreams* (1900/1953). And indeed, I suspect that few would disagree with Robert Segal's (2004a, p. viii) suggestion that that particular analysis was "Freud's own key analysis" when studying myth. Taken as face value, the ease with which commentators turn to this example might seem to suggest that the psychoanalytic study of myth has been a part of the psychoanalytic tradition almost from the beginning. Yet that is misleading.

As a start, consider that Freud himself did not identify the Oedipus story as a myth. On the contrary, although he starts off by calling it "a legend that has come down to us from classical antiquity," he quickly moves to a consideration of the Oedipus story as told specifically in Sophocles' *Oedipus Rex*, a literary text. Freud reinforces this emphasis on literary texts by following his analysis of *Oedipus Rex* with an analysis of *Hamlet*. In other words, the event routinely cited as being the seminal event in the psychoanalytic study of myth turns out not really to be about myth at all.

The failure of modern commentators who discuss the psychoanalytic study of myth (hereafter: PSM) to care much about the distinction between myth and literary texts – or about the distinction between myths and dreams, myths and folktales, myths and clinical narratives, etc. – flows easily from the fact that these distinctions have routinely been blurred by psychoanalytic investigators themselves (starting with Freud). Indeed, I will be arguing that the very logic of psychoanalysis requires that these distinctions be blurred and that this helps to explain why the PSM has

* I would like to thank Sam Clark, Michael Gardiner, Robert Paul and Robert Segal, as well as all the participants at the Beyond Freud conference organized by Jacob Belzen, for making informed and insightful comments on earlier drafts of this chapter.

M. Carroll
University of Western Ontario, London, ON, Canada
e-mail: mcarroll@uwo.ca

always had a limited appeal to those interested in myth. Still, I am getting ahead of the argument that I want to develop. So: let's start at the beginning, move forward along the different paths taken by scholars in the PSM tradition, and then look back on what has been done with a critical eye.

The Beginning

In *The Interpretation of Dreams*, Freud used literary texts like *Oedipus Rex* and *Hamlet* mainly as pedagogic devices. These stories were important, in other words, because they would have been familiar to educated readers and could be used to illustrate his core hypothesis about dreams, namely, that dreams represent the disguised fulfillment of unconscious wishes. What made these two particular stories especially useful to Freud was that the unconscious wishes being expressed in each were (he argued) the two wishes that even then were becoming central to this thinking, namely, the young child's sexual desire for the mother and the corresponding hostility towards the father that this engenders. Contrasting *Oedipus Rex* with *Hamlet* also provided Freud with a way of demonstrating how these same two oedipal wishes could be disguised to a lesser or greater degree.

Oedipus Rex and *Hamlet* aside, there are only sporadic references in *The Interpretation of Dreams* to stories that Freud's readers would have regarded as myths per se. He did use the story of Kronos and Zeus to (again) illustrate his argument about oedipal hostility. But in the end, read by itself, there is little in this early work that would have suggested to readers that the study of myth was, or would be, central to the emerging discipline of psychoanalysis.

Nor did Freud himself build much on his early analyses of myth. On the contrary, Freud himself migrated from the study of myth specifically to the study of religion generally and here, at least initially, he developed an argument quite different from the "wish fulfillment" argument he used in analyzing dreams and myths. Thus, in *Totem and Taboo* (1913/1953), he posited that at some time in our prehistoric past, a band of brothers had risen up and killed their autocratic father in order to gain sexual access to their mothers and sister. Although their guilt over their parricide led these brothers to establish the incest taboo and so to repress the very sexual desires that had given rise to their rebellion, the unconscious memory of that primal parricide – Freud argued – was passed from generation to generation. He then argued that this unconscious memory, and the guilt it produced, continued to shape religious ritual and belief in each succeeding generation. The argument advanced in *Totem and Taboo* became the theoretical substratum for his extended analysis of Israelite religion (and Christianity) in *Moses and Monotheism* (1939/1964), his last major work. The emphasis on the role played by "guilt" in these later arguments is perhaps what most distinguishes these arguments from the earlier "wish fulfillment" argument he had used in studying dreams and myth (where "guilt" plays no role in the process described). Freud would return to a "wish fulfillment" argument in studying religion in *The Future of an Illusion* (1927/1961a), but there his concern was with the process by which we construct our image of God, not our myths.

Yet even though the study of myth was, in the end, not at all central to Freud's own work, the approach to myth pioneered by the (very) early Freud did give rise to a number of continuing traditions.

The Scholarly Study of Myth – Disciplinary Cocoons and Interpretive Enclaves

In a recent survey of several books on the study of myth, Northup (2006) makes three points that are worth repeating here. First, the last 2 decades have witnessed an explosion of popular interest in myth (which Northup dates to Joseph Campbell's "Power of Myth" series on PBS in the late 1980s) and this has in turn promoted an increased scholarly interest in myth. Second, the study of myth has attracted scholars from almost every academic discipline. In Northup's words

> The bibliography of serious examinations of myth issued in recent years is extensive, intriguing – and confusing. [For example] one recent review (...) highlighted the extraordinarily interdisciplinary nature of books on myth studies, as reflected in the roster of scholars covered in the new series of books on myth theory edited by Robert Segal. (...) Frazer the classicist, Buber the theologian, Jung the psychoanalyst, Levi-Strauss the structuralist, Frye the literary critic, Eliade the phenomenologist, Cassirer the philosopher, and Campbell the comparative mythologist (...) to [which] we could add Girard the anthropologist, Müller the linguist, Boas the folklorist, Dardel the ethnologist, and so on, until someone has chimed in from virtually all the humanities and social sciences. (Northup, 2006, p. 5)

But Northup's third point is that this multi-disciplinary in interest in myth has not resulted in interdisciplinary insight mainly because the scholars involved have been unwilling to step outside their disciplinary cocoons to draw upon the work of other scholars. The net result: the study of myth today is fragmented into a number of self-contained scholarly enclaves that have little or no interest in communicating with one another. It happens, however, that at least four of these scholarly enclaves are associated with the psychoanalytic tradition.

The Core Divide – Freud Versus Jung

It is conventional in commentaries that aim to provide an overview of the scholarly study of myth to suggest that the core divide among psychoanalytical investigators is the divide between Freud and Jung. Certainly, in general commentaries of this sort, Freud and Jung are the figures discussed most extensively in the sections devoted to the psychoanalytic tradition, and if other psychoanalytic theorists are discussed at length, it is usually because of a tie to Freud or Jung. This formula, for example, is evident in Robert Segal's *Myth: A Very Short Introduction* (2004b).

Thus Segal begins his "Myth and psychology" chapter by suggesting that "in psychology two theories have almost monopolized the [study of myth]: those of the Viennese physician Sigmund Freud (1856–1938) and of the Swiss psychiatrist

C.G. Jung" (p. 91) – and then goes on to discuss the work of each man at length. The two other theorists who are discussed most extensively in this chapter, however, are Otto Rank and Joseph Campbell, mainly because, Segal suggests, Rank was to Freud what Campbell was to Jung (which seems to mean that Rank and Campbell were both popularizers).

This same tendency, to summarize work done in the PSM tradition using a "Freud versus Jung" contrast, is also evident in Doty's massive *Mythography* (2000). Overall, Doty reviews a great many more theorists than is possible in Segal's brief guide but psychoanalytic arguments are covered in chapters 6 and 7, and the chapter titles here – "Myth on the psychoanalytical couch: Freud and beyond" and "The imaginal, archetypal turn: Jung, Hillman and further beyond" – make clear what becomes apparent when reading the chapters themselves, namely, that here again the central contrast being posited in the PSM tradition is a contrast between Freud and Jung. A final example of this tendency – to focus on Freud and Jung when presenting an overview of the PSM – can be detected, I think, in Thomas Sienkewicz's (1997) annotated bibliography of theoretical approaches to myth given that his brief summaries of particular articles and books in the psychoanalytic tradition inevitably associate the author(s) involved with either Freud or Jung.

But if we grant (with most commentators) that Freud and Jung laid the theoretical foundation for the PSM, what is the nature of that foundation? As a start, it is important to take note of what Freud and Jung had in common. First, as Robert Segal (2003a) has pointed out, both theorists clearly rejected the view of myth that was prevalent in the nineteenth century, which was that myth was somehow "false." For Segal, this nineteenth century view is most of all evident in the theories developed by Edward Tylor and Sir James Frazer, who saw myth as an attempt by primitive peoples to answer questions that are today answered (and answered better) by science. But Segal's characterization is also an appropriate way to characterize the work of Max Müller, whose theory of myth, as Durkheim (1913/1915) long ago pointed out, was at least as popular as the theories developed by Tylor and Frazer. Müller, whose special concern was the mythology of Indo-European cultures, argued that myths arose when elaborate metaphors about nature were (mistakenly) taken literally by Indo-European peoples.

What Freud and Jung also had in common is that they replaced the "myth as false" view with the view that myths are linked to the unconscious. Yet though Freud and Jung were alike in establishing a relationship between myth and the unconscious, they differed in regard to the nature that relationship. Freud's original view has already been presented: myths, like dreams, reflect the disguised fulfillment of unconscious wishes. And of course within the logic of Freud's analysis, these unconscious wishes are disguised because they are unacceptable to the conscious mind. Freud's approach, in other words, forces us to analyze myths in order to confront what we do not want to confront. Jung's view of myth is quite different: for him, encountering myth is a far more positive experience. Segal captures the difference here well:

> Unlike Freudians, Jungians have taken myth positively from the outset. For them, the unconscious expressed in myth is not a repository of repressed, anti-social drives but a storehouse of innately unconscious archetypes that have simply never had an opportunity at realization

(...) The function of myth is less that of release, as for Classical Freudians, than that of growth, as for contemporary ones (...) Jungians see myth as a means of cultivation of the inner world. (Segal, 2003a, p. 606)

According to Jung, myths do this (cultivate the unconscious inner world of an individual and so promote psychological growth) by providing images onto which people can project the archetypes in their unconscious. These unconscious archetypes, in turn, are predispositions that are part of the human experience in all cultures across all historical periods.

But if the PSM began in the two approaches pioneered by Freud and Jung, what has happened since? In the case of the Jungian tradition, it would seem that the answer is "not much." Jung's work has of course generated a great deal of critical commentary; even so, my sense is that the core approach pioneered by Jung is still central to the Jungian tradition in myth studies. Basically, what investigators in this tradition do is what Jung did: tease out the relationship between the images found in myth and the archetypes with which these images resonate (I will have more to say about Jungian analysis later in this essay). The case of the Freudian tradition is quite different.

Classical Freudians and Ego Psychology

Both Robert Segal (2003b, 2004a) and Dan Merkur (2005) have written accounts of the Freudian tradition in the study of myth and both authors suggest that two major schools of thought developed. First, in the immediate aftermath of Freud's work, the study of myth was taken up by a number of investigators who accepted and elaborated upon Freud's core argument, namely, that myths, like dreams, could be seen as reflecting the disguised fulfillment of unconscious impulses and desires associated with childhood experiences. The key names here are Karl Abraham, Otto Rank and Géza Róheim (more on Róheim later).

Rank (1922/2004), for example, in his work on hero myths (which still has wide visibility in the study of myth) argued that there was recurrent pattern to these myths and that this pattern could be interpreted and explained using the theory that Freud had used to interpreted and explain dreams. In particular, Rank argued that these myths should be seen as deriving from "the family romance" described by Freud (involving the young child's hostility for the father and desire for the mother) and so were constructed using the same processes disguise and wish fulfillment that Freud had detected in studying dreams.

What happened next is that analysts working in the ego psychology tradition took an interest in myth. Segal focuses on the work of Jacob Arlow when discussing this tradition; Merkur too sees Arlow as being important but also discusses the work (on myth) of Abram Kardiner and Clyde Kluckhohn.

The core of the ego psychology approach to myth is that myths provide a number of ready-made defense mechanisms that can be used in a culture given the typical experiences in that culture. In Merkur's summary of this tradition

Kluckhohn's suggestion that myths function as prototypes for the formation of defense mechanism that are typical of each culture was widely adopted by both anthropologists

> and psychoanalysts [and here Merkur inserts a large number of citations, including works by Fred Eggan, Weston La Barre, Jacob Arlow, Bryce Boyer and Derek Freeman]. Howard L. Cox (1948) provided a tidy summary of the theory the defensive function of mythology. "Myths (...) become institutionalized because they give type answers to type problems. Thus, they come to take on the nature of an anxiety allaying device." (p. 86)

On my reading, Merkur's reconstruction of the ego psychology tradition veers too much toward the implicit suggestion that Freud's original wish fulfillment approach to myth was supplanted the ego psychology approach. Segal, more correctly I think, emphases that Freud's original framework continues to be used by many scholars. The example that Segal holds up for special attention is Alan Dundes (1934–2005).

Dundes was a folklorist whose academic appointment was in a department of anthropology. Over the course of his career he brought a psychoanalytic perspective to bear on a range of folkloric and anthropological topics, including folk sayings, folktales, children's games, cultural practices like the couvade and the potlatch, urban legends, etc. – and myth (for an overview of Dundes's work, see Carroll, 1993, 2005). Indeed, one of his most well-known articles, published at the very beginning of his academic career, was his article on the Earth-Diver myth (Dundes, 1962). In the Earth-Diver myth, variants of which are found in a great many North American Indian societies, a male Culture Hero has a number of animals dive to the bottom of primeval ocean to secure a bit of sand or mud. Most animals fail, but eventually one succeeds in bringing a bit of sand or mud to the surface and from this bit of sand or mud dry land forms. Adopting a classic Freudian perspective, Dundes argued that the Earth-Diver story is an anal birth fantasy that gratifies a wish to give birth that is found in the male unconscious. Decades later he would use the same argument to explain Middle Eastern Flood myths, including the two versions found in Genesis (Dundes, 1988, p. 177). Flood myths, he argued, gratified male birth envy by destroying the old order of things "through a urinary flood and re-creating the world and man through anal means, that is, by manipulating mud or in a more desiccated version: dust".

Gananath Obeyesekere is someone else who has studied myth using a classically Freudian perspective and whose work is well-known. Like Dundes, Obeyesekere borrows mainly from the early Freud, and in particular – and very explicitly; see Obeyesekere (1990) – from the arguments Freud advanced in *The Interpretation of Dreams*. More so than most other theorists in this tradition (including Dundes), however, Obeyesekere allows for an especially complex interaction between the cultural symbols that appear in myth and ritual and the unconscious of particular individuals. Thus, he argues, there are always a variety of cultural symbols in any society. Some, however, are "personal symbols" (his term) that have been shaped over time in a very direct way by the unconscious concerns associated with some small subset of the population. But others are what Obeyesekere calls "collective representations" and these typically are associated with group rituals of one sort or another. Collective representations have usually been brought into line with prevailing cultural traditions and so cannot easily be re-shaped to suit the life experiences of particular individuals. Even so, Obeyesekere argues, some connection – however tenuous – between collective representations and the unconscious concerns of particular individuals can often be detected in interviews with members of the culture involved.

For Obeyesekere one result of all this is that the same myth can mean quite different things to different individuals and different groups within the "same" culture and the same underlying unconscious elements (involving, for example, oedipal wishes and tensions, a favored theme with Obeyesekere) can come to be connected with seemingly quite different myths in different cultures. Much of Obeyesekere's reputation, at least in the area of myth studies, rests upon his use of this general framework to develop detailed analyses of myths and rituals drawn from Hindu India and from his native Sri Lanka.

Finally, Wendy Doniger has also studied myth, Hindu myths in particular, using a fairly straightforward Freudian approach. In her analysis of the explicit sexuality that is common to many Hindu myths, for example, Doniger (1993/1999) suggests that these myths reflect the gratification of the same infantile oedipal desires discussed by Freud. The only difference, she argues, is that in Hindu mythology these desires are less disguised than is the case in the Western materials considered by Freud, which include – for Doniger (p. 299) – the "Oedipus myth" [sic].

For commentators like Segal and Merkur, then, two separate approaches to myth grew out of Freud's early work on myth and continue today: one based on Freud's original "wish fulfillment" argument and the second associated with ego psychology. A case can be made, however, that a third approach developed from Freud's work as well.

Medusa as Good Mother – The Object Relations Tradition and Myth

As far as I know, no one has yet provided an overview of an "object relations approach to myth" in the way that Segal and Merkur have provided an overview of the Freudian/ego psychology approach to myth. Likely this is because the number of studies utilizing an object-relations perspective on myth is relatively small. Still, such studies do exist. Consider, for example, the three essays that Vanda Zajko and Miriam Leonard selected for the "myth and psychoanalysis" section of their *Laughing with Medusa: Classical Myth and Feminist Thought* (2005).

The first essay in this section, by Rachel Bowlby, develops a critique of Freud's view of the Castration Complex that involves, among other things, a critique of his use of myths about Kronos and Zeus in trying to legitimize that view. The next two selections, however, by Vanda Zajko and Griselda Pollock, are quite different. Zajko is concerned with the story of Achilles, at least as that story appears in various literary texts. In analyzing these texts, she (to cite the editors' own Introduction, p. 14) "uses a Kleinian model of identification to understand the transhistorical power of myth." Pollock, after some initial remarks about Virginia Woolfe and the Classical scholar Jane Harrison, merges a discussion of the work of artist Bracha Ettinger with a discussion of the character of Antigone in Sophocles's text. Pollock's argument is dense, but in the end what she emphasizes is the universal experience of "matrixial co-subjectivity" (p. 116), which the editors more prosaically describe (p. 14) as "an unconditional bond to the maternal other." Here again, then, although Pollock does not cite Melanie Klein's work directly, there seems that emphasis on the pre-oedipal tie to the mother that is a hallmark of the object relations tradition.

Brooke Hopkins's (2001) analysis of the Christian Resurrection story is another (and far more straightforward) example of how the object relations perspective can be used to study myth. Hopkins explains the "lasting appeal" of the Resurrection story by arguing that because the Gospels associate Jesus with stereotypically feminine traits (like patience and nurturance, love), the figure of Jesus functions as a maternal imago. Under this interpretation, the horrendous physical assault on Jesus's body resonates with the unconscious residue of the destructive urges that each infant directs against the mother in fantasy. The fact that Jesus survives these assaults (through the Resurrection) becomes linked to what, in D.W. Winnicott's theory, is a critical event in the development of all infants: the realization that the mother (as object) survives the infant's fantasy attacks without retaliating. For Winnicott, this realization is critical because it lays the foundation for the capacity to love the other (see Hopkins's article for the full argument here).

Is the object-relations tradition likely to become more important in the PSM than is currently the case? If I had to speculate, I would say "probably not." The reason is that the object relation tradition's emphasis on the child's relationship with primary objects and with transitional objects (in the Winnicottian sense of that term) has proven to be especially useful in understanding the way in which individuals construct their image of God and their relationship with God. This is most evident in the work of theorists like, say, W.W. Meissner and Ana-Maria Rizzuto (1979). But while this focus on "God images" and "your relationship with God" promotes a concern with religion generally, or at least a concern with those religions (like those associated with the Judeo–Christian–Islamic tradition) that emphasize a powerful God, it leads away – I think – from a concern with specific myths that may have little to do with a powerful God.

In summary, then, it would appear that there are four distinct traditions concerned with the PSM: the original formulations developed, respectively, by Freud and Jung, and the two traditions associated, respectively, with ego psychology and object relations theory. Of course it hardly seems surprising that investigators working within these four well-established psychoanalytic traditions might, at least occasionally, turn their attention to myth given that both Freud and Jung studied myth. Nevertheless, the fact that particular psychoanalytic studies of myth are so tightly identified with one, but only one, of the major traditions in psychoanalysis has had, and continues to have, has functioned (or so I now want to argue) to limit the use of psychoanalytic reasoning in studying myth.

Self-Limiting Structural Constraints

There are two interrelated constraints that are each an inherent part of the PSM tradition and that function to limit the influence of this tradition. The first of these is this: by tying myth to the unconscious, all psychoanalytic investigators blur the distinction between myth and all the other things that are seen as being shaped by the unconscious. In the psychoanalytic tradition, in other words, it is difficult to separate out the study of myth as a privileged area of study that is completely separate from the study of dreams, the study of humor, the study of everyday life, etc. Related to this is a second constraint: embracing some particular psychoanalytic argument about a particular myth entails embracing a theory of the human personality that is universally applicable and that must inevitably affect how you view a wide range of social and psychological phenomena. These two constraints make the PSM qualitatively different from most other approaches to myth.

To take a simple example: some time ago Jane Harrison (1912) argued that the story of the sword-battering Kouretes who protected the infant Zeus from his father Kronos is modeled on male initiation rituals in early Greek culture. Whatever the fate of this argument in Classical Studies, it is still one that I find moderately convincing. And yet, while embracing this interpretation might (at best) make me a bit more sympathetic to arguments in the "ritual theory of myth" tradition, it hardly requires embracing a theoretical worldview that predisposes me to adopt a certain perspective not just on myth, but also on dreams, folklore, family dynamics, everyday life, etc. By contrast, this is precisely the sort of all-compassing perspective that I must accept if I give any legitimacy whosoever to a psychoanalytic interpretation of some particular myth.

The fact that psychoanalytical interpretations of myth are bound so tightly to theoretical structures that have implications far beyond the issue of myth per se allows us to explain a number of patterns. As a start, it helps to explain why there is so little dialogue even among investigators working within the psychoanalytic tradition. For example, consider how Raya Jones (2003, p. 622) explains why Jung's view of myth has not proven to be popular with most psychologists:

> Jung's account of mythmaking and myths – the process and the product is inseparable from his theory of archetypal configuration of the psyche ... If we reject his hypotheses about the psyche, there seems little reason to study myth. He needs to convince us about his model of the psyche in the first place – and by and large, most psychologists are not convinced.

Jones's specific point is that because most psychologists do not accept Jung's theory of the human personality, they do not accept his interpretation of particular myths. But of course the more general point is that because any psychoanalytic interpretation of a particular myth is tied to a some particular theory of the human personality, scholars who regard that theory as superseded by the theory to which they have become committed (say, in the course of their own analysis or their own clinical practice) will be disinclined to accord legitimacy to that interpretation.

But perhaps more importantly, the fact that particular psychoanalytic interpretations of myth are bound up with an immense theoretical structure that has implications that go far beyond the study of myth helps to explain a second pattern as well: why some of the most prominent scholars working in the PSM tradition have failed to attract students. Consider two cases already mentioned in connection with the classical Freudian tradition in the PSM: Géza Róheim (1891–1953) and Alan Dundes.

Leaders Without Followers

As mentioned earlier, Róheim is routinely identified as one of the more important figures in the PSM tradition following Freud. Merkur (2005), for example, devotes an entire chapter to Róheim's work, and concludes with this glowing judgment:

> In the area of myth, Róheim's contributions were fundamental. He replaced Freud's incoherent speculations about the primal horde with a methodologically tenable concern with child development. He insisted on a universal biological basis to the human psyche, but [...] brilliantly recognized that distinctive child-rearing techniques in different cultures each produce distinctive culturally shared traumas, the consequences of which may be found in myth. (p. 47)

Segal (2003b, pp. 148–149) also singles out Róheim for special attention among the classical Freudians, mainly because Segal sees Róheim as having anticipated some of the views on myth reached by ego psychologists. Nor would it be difficult to other psychoanalytic investigators concerned with myth who have similarly expressed a high regard for Róheim's work (see for example Morales, 1988). Taken at face value, then, all this would seem to imply that Róheim was an important figure in the study of myth. And yet if "important" here means his work was influential, then the truth is much the opposite of what the accounts by Segal and Merkur might otherwise seem to suggest.

Alan Dundes addressed the issue of Róheim's influence in his "Introduction" to an edited collection of Róheim's essays:

> Just how were Róheim and his voluminous writings regarded by anthropologists and folklorists? The sad truth is that Róheim's numerous applications of psychoanalytic theory to anthropological and folkloristic data may be said to have fallen generally on deaf ears (...) Most young anthropologists and folklorists [today] have never even read anything by Róheim and they remain totally ignorant of his unique contribution to the serious study of symbolism and traditional behavior. (Dundes in Róeim, 1992, p. xvi)

While Dundes gives many reasons for Róheim's lack of influence (his writing style, the fact that he published in obscure outlets, etc.), it was, Dundes suggests, the nature of his audience that was the critical thing. In introducing one of Róheim's essays in that book, Dundes wrote

> "Róheim's staunch advocacy of a Freudian approach to folktales is still worth reading, especially since the majority of folklorists continue to reject such an approach out of hand."

I must add that Dundes himself felt clearly that his own career in anthropology and folklore resembled Róheim's. In a later essay he would say: "Despite my best efforts over the past three decades, I seem to have failed to convince my colleagues or students of the utility of [the psychoanalytic] approach" and in that same essay would quote an unnamed colleague as suggesting that he was "a leader in the field without any followers." (Dundes, 2002, p. xi)

As far as I know, neither Róheim nor Dundes ever speculated at any length on why their work on the PSM had had so little influence on their anthropological colleagues. And yet, I suggest, their lack of influence can be seen as a consequence of the two structural constraints mentioned earlier: the fact that the logic of psychoanalysis blurs the distinction between myth and a range of other phenomena and the fact that any psychoanalytic argument, no matter how much it may be focused on some particular myth, is tied to universalistic theory of the human personality. To accept an analysis of some particular myth developed by Róheim or Dundes, in other words, would require accepting an immense theoretical structure that has something to say about just about everything that anthropologists typically study. Given that most anthropologists are not in the first instance committed to psychoanalysis, no single analysis, no matter how well-argued, is ever going to be sufficiently convincing so as to justify a gestalt shift like that.

A Final Puzzle

In his own commentary on Dundes's work, Robert Paul (2003) has advanced an explanation of Dundes's non-influence in anthropology that is different from the one suggested above. Paul – who is both an anthropologist himself and a practicing analyst and someone who has written on myth (see Paul, 1996) – points out that in treating patients an analyst usually works very slowly, moving from "surface to depth" before advancing interpretations about the unconscious. The reason for proceeding in this way is to overcome the resistance and defensive reactions that must inevitably be activated when anxiety-provoking elements are brought to consciousness. This is why analysis can require years. The problem faced by someone like Dundes, then, Paul continues, is that in a publication there is no opportunity to lay the sort of careful groundwork over a long period of time that is associated with analysis. The net result is that readers who do not already embrace psychoanalytic reasons are likely to summarily reject a psychoanalytic argument that forces them to confront the possibility that something familiar to them is associated with something anxiety-provoking.

Paul's argument strikes me as perfectly reasonable, and I see it as complementary to the argument I developed in the last section, at least as regards investigators (like Dundes) who adopt a fairly straightforward Freudian approach in studying myth. Still, the opposite of Paul's "people will summarily reject what their conscious mind doesn't want to hear" argument is "people will accept what they do want to hear" – and this leads us directly to the final puzzle in the PSM tradition: the unlikely but undeniable popular success of the Jungian approach to myth.

Jung and Campbell – Psychic Improvement Through Osmosis

It seems fair to say that the Jungian approach to myth has captured the popular imagination more than any of the other perspectives considered here. This seem especially true if we grant that Joseph Campbell, whose books are still being reissued and still selling well 2 decades after his death, has long been associated with the Jungian tradition. But why has the Jungian approach proven to be so popular?

Certainly, it is not because Jung is easy to understand. On the contrary, his work often borders on the incomprehensible. In saying this, I am hardly saying something new; Jung himself said much the same thing, though in a more positive way. Thus, in a letter written in 1952, and cited by Gerhard Adler (1983, p. 18), Jung wrote

> The language I speak must be ambiguous, must have two meanings in order to be fair to the dual aspect of our psychic nature. I strive quite consciously and deliberately for ambiguity of expression because it is superior to unequivocality and reflects the nature of life.

And even Jung's admirers have tended to say the same things, though perhaps in more circumspect language. Thus Walker (1995) tells us that Jung's remarks on myth were "baffling and outrageous" (p. xi) and that the "road leading from [Jung's] world of the collective unconscious to the world of mythology is a rocky one" because "[Jung's] thought proceeds through intuitive leaps, not logical progressions" (p. 3). Even earlier, James Hillman acknowledged (and explained away) the unsystematic nature of Jung's writing in this way:

> [Freud] made revisions because he had a kind of systematic theory. Jung didn't revise anything. He built on it, he didn't have a critical mind in that sense. Freud comes from a different tree than Jung. Jung comes from a Romantic tree, from a Neoplatonic tree, from a Gothic tree. Freud comes out of an Aristotelian kind of thinking, with a rational, empirical angle. (Hillman, cited in Segaller and Berger, 1989, p. 43)

This is not to say that Jung's work on myth cannot be systematized; clearly that is precisely what, say, Steven Walker (1995) does in his book on Jung in the series edited by Robert Segal. The point simply is that the popularity of Jung's theory with the general public cannot be explained by saying that Jung wrote in an accessible style.

So what does account for Jung's popular success? Likely there are several reasons here, but two in particular stand out. The first involves something very concrete: Jung's approach to myth lends itself easily to presentations that rely heavily on the visual. More simply: there are always lots of pictures in popular books in the Jung/Campbell tradition. The reason for this is that for Jung myths function to allow individuals to project archetypal images in their unconscious onto images found in the external world; as a result it is never difficult for people working in this tradition to find images, drawn from a variety of different cultures, which can be said to be illustrative of "universal" archetypes. Thus, for example, the various essays in *Man and his Symbols* (Jung, 1964) typically contains one or more pictures per page, each accompanied by captions like:

> The "anima" is the female element in the male unconscious (...) This inner duality is often symbolized by a hermaphroditic figure, like the crowned hermaphrodite, above right, from a 17th century alchemical manuscript. (p. 30)

> Often the Self is represented as a helpful animal. Top left, the magic fox of Grimm's fairy tale (...) Bottom, the heroic dog once popular in American films and television, Rin Tin Tin. (p. 206)

A similar emphasis on pictures and images that can be connected to archetypes is found in Jung's *Symbols of Transformation* (Jung, 1956) and Campbell's best-selling *The Power of Myth* (Campbell and Moyers, 1988). In modern cultures permeated by an emphasis on the visual, the effortless use of visual images by authors working in the Jung/Campbell tradition almost certainly adds to the popular appeal of their work.

But the Jungian approach to myth is popular for another reason as well: notwithstanding the ambiguity that pervades Jung's theoretical work, he advances at least one message that is easily understandable and appealing to people living in the West. That message is this: immerse yourself in the myths of more primitive cultures (and if you mix and match myths from different societies scattered across time and place, so much the better) and you will become a better person. Unlike Freud, then, who forces us to confront (in myth) what we do not want to confront, Jung's approach to myth offer the promise of encountering something we very must want to encounter.

In Jung's work, this emphasis on the importance of primitive myth to people living in the modern West emerged most forcefully after his visits to Taos Pueblo and Kenya, respectively, in the 1920s. Thus in discussing these visits and their impact on Jung, Walker tells us that "Jung noted two excellent reasons for studying the mythology of primitive cultures. First, the study of primitives cultures (...) enables us to glimpse our own cultural shadow (...) Second, primitive myths are alive in our psyches. The voice of the unconscious may speak to modern human beings through very unmodern myths!" (Walker, 1995, p. 137), and: "The other great benefit of studying primitive cultures lay for Jung in the paradoxical discovery that primitive myths could speak to him on a most intimate, personal level" (p. 138).

This same emphasis on primitive myths "connecting" with people in an intimate way and making them the better for it is also found in the works of Joseph Campbell and explains, I think, why Campbell is so often associated with Jung despite their differences.

As Robert Segal has so often pointed out, Campbell himself was always at pains to say that he was not a Jungian even though he admired Jung's work. Nevertheless, Campbell, if anything, outdid Jung in promoting a "myth makes you better" message. Segal captures the contrast between Campbell and Jung here nicely:

> Jung considers myth neither necessary nor sufficient for human fulfillment. Whenever myth is used, it should be used with therapy, which is an indispensable supplement, not alternative, to it. [By contrast] myth for Campbell contains all the wisdom humans need. They need only learn to interpret it. They need never venture beyond it. (Segal, 1990, p. 260)

And certainly, in his *Power of Myth* conversations with Bill Moyers, Campbell was very clear in specifying that myth achieved these beneficial effects by virtue of the "connection" that it established between you and the rest of humanity both now and in the past:

> MOYERS: Someone asked me "Why are you drawn to these myths; What do you see in what Joseph Campbell is saying?" And I answered, "These myths speak to me because they express which I now inside is true." (...) Does that come from the ground of my being, the unconscious that I have inherited from all that has come before me?
>
> CAMPBELL: That's right. You've got the same body ... that Cro-Magnon man had thirty thousand years ago. Living a life in New York City or (...) in the caves, you go through the same stages of childhood, coming to sexual maturity [etc.]. Whether I'm reading Polynesian

> or Iroquois or Egyptian myths, the images are the same and they are talking about the same problems. (Campbell and Moyers, 1988, p. 37)

In the end, then, the Jung/Campbell perspective on myth (especially the latter) is appealing because it offers people a simple procedure (i.e., confront and understand myth) for establishing a relationship with all creation, past and present, that works to their personal benefit. And what makes all this especially appealing, at least to modern Western audiences, is the fact that the sort of mystical experience promised by the Jung/Campbell approach to myth is, to borrow now from William Parsons (1999), "unchurched."

Unchurched Mysticism for Moderns

The starting point of Parsons's (1999) analysis of mysticism in modern societies is the "oceanic experience" that Freud discussed in the first chapter of *Civilization and Its Discontents* (1939/1961b). The oceanic experience had been brought to Freud's attention by his friend Romain Rolland, who had suggested (to Freud) that this experience was the origin of religion rather than the processes that Freud had described in his *The Future of an Illusion*. Paraphrasing Rolland, Freud (1930/1961b, p. 64) tells us "it is a peculiar feeling which he [Rolland] himself is never without [and] which he would like to call a sensation of 'eternity', a feeling of something limitless, unbounded – as it were, 'oceanic'." Freud himself went on to dismiss Rolland's oceanic feeling as a residue of the child's pre-oedipal attachment to the Mother.

Parsons himself, however, rejects Freud's interpretation as too simplistic. For Parsons, Rolland's experience of the oceanic feeling was the end product of a process, occurring over many years, in which Rolland drew upon transitory experiences of unity with nature and merged these with a number of intellectual traditions with which he was, or became, familiar (including Spinoza's philosophy, the Hindu mystical tradition, etc.). But more important (for our purposes) Parsons suggests that Rolland's oceanic feeling is the cornerstone of a type of "unchurched" mysticism that is unconnected to any religious tradition and which for that reason appeals to people living in secularizing and pluralistic Western cultures. In other words, because the "unity with all creation" promised by unchurched mysticism derives from psychology, not religion, it is a type of mysticism that will be especially appealing in modern societies that increasingly value rationalism and science and devalue religion.

The central premise of the Jungian approach to myth, namely, that immersion in primitive myth will establish a connection between you and all humankind, is promising us precisely the sort of unchurched mystical experience that Parsons is discussing. And indeed, as Parsons makes clear, many of those (Rolland aside) who promoted unchurched mysticism in the early twentieth century saw an affinity between this type of mystical experience and Jungian psychology. In the end, then, the Jungian approach to myth is popular with the general public because (unlike the Freudian approach to myth), it holds out to modern Western audiences the promise of a scientific (well, quasi-scientific) method of experiencing the sort of oceanic feeling that modern intellectuals (like Rolland), who have distanced themselves from organized religion, have found so appealing.

Whither the Psychoanalytic Study of Myth?

At the moment, I don't see that the PSM is going to change very much over the short term. At best, the Jung/Campbell approach to myth will continue to be more popular with the general public (at least the educated middle class) in modern societies than other psychoanalytic approaches; at worst, the popularity of this approach was a middle class fad that will fade just as many of the New Age philosophics of the 1960s and 1970s have faded. Practicing analysts committed to one or the other of the mainline traditions in psychoanalysis will continue to toss off the occasional analysis of a myth because, well, that's what analysts have been doing since Freud. These analyses will be read by those already committed to the theoretical perspective involved and ignored (if noticed at all) by the vast majority of social scientists who might otherwise have an interest in myth but who are unwilling to take on the gestalt shift in perceiving the world that psychoanalysis requires.

Bibliography

Adler, G. (1983). Introduction. In M. Tuby (Ed.), *In the wake of Jung: A selection from Harvest* (pp. 9–21). London: Coventure.

Campbell, J. & Moyers, B. (1988). *The power of myth*. New York: Doubleday.

Carroll, M. P. (1993). Alan Dundes: An introduction. *The Psychoanalytic Study of Society, 18*, 1–22.

Carroll, M. P. (2005). Tribute to Alan Dundes (1934–2005). *Religion, 35*, 118–124.

Cox, H. L. (1948). The place of mythology in the study of culture. *American Imago, 5*, 83–94.

Doniger, W. (1993/1999). When the lingam is just a good cigar: Psychoanalysis and Hindu sexual fantasies. In T. G. Vaidyanathan & J. J. Kripal (Eds.), *Vishnu on Freud's Desk* (pp. 279–303). Delhi: Oxford University Press.

Doty, W. G. (2000). *Mythography: The study of myths and rituals*. Tuscaloosa, AL: The University of Alabama Press.

Dundes, A. (1962). Earth-diver: Creation of the mythopoeic male. *American Anthropologist, 64*, 1032–1051.

Dundes, A. (1988). The flood as male myth of creation. In A. Dundes (Ed.), *The flood myth* (pp. 167–182). Berkeley, CA: University of California Press.

Dundes, A. (2002). Preface. In A. Dundes (Ed.), *Bloody Mary in the mirror: Essays in psychoanalytic folkloristics* (pp. vii–xiii). Jackson, MI: University Press of Mississippi.

Durkheim, E. (1913/1915). *The elementary forms of the religious life: A study in religious sociology* (trans. J. W. Swain). London/New York: Allen & Unwin/Macmillan.

Freud, S. (1900/1953). The interpretation of dreams. In J. Strachey (Ed.), *The standard edition of the complete psychological works of Sigmund Freud. Vols. 4–5*. London: Hogarth.

Freud, S. (1913/1953). Totem and taboo. In J. Strachey (Ed.), *The standard edition of the complete psychological works of Sigmund Freud. Vol. 13* (pp. 1–161). London: Hogarth.

Freud, S. (1927/1961a). The future of an illusion. In J. Strachey (Ed.), *The standard edition of the complete psychological works of Sigmund Freud. Vol. 21* (pp. 1–56). London: Hogarth.

Freud, S. (1961b). Civilization and its discontents. In J. Strachey (Ed.), *The standard edition of the complete psychological works of Sigmund Freud. Vol. 21* (pp. 57–145). London: Hogarth.
Freud, S. (1939/1964). Moses and monotheism. In J. Strachey (Ed.), *The standard edition of the complete psychological works of Sigmund Freud. Vol. 23* (pp. 1–137). London: Hogarth.
Harrison, J. E. (1912). *Themis: A study of the social origins of Greek religion*. Cambridge: Cambridge University Press.
Hopkins, B. (2001). Jesus and object use: A Winnicottian account of the resurrection myth. In D. Capps (Ed.), *Freud and Freudians on religion* (pp. 230–240). New Haven, CT: Yale University Press.
Jones, R. A. (2003). Jung's view on myth and post-modern psychology. *Journal of Analytical Psychology*, *48*, 619–628.
Jung, C. G. (1956). *Symbols of transformation*. New York: Harper Torchbooks.
Jung, C. G. (Ed.) (1964). *Man and his symbols*. New York: Doubleday.
Merkur, D. (2005). *Psychoanalytic approaches to myth: Freud and the Freudians*. New York: Routledge.
Morales, S. C. (1988). Géza Róheim's theory of the dream origin of myth. In L. B. Boyer & S. A. Grolnick (Eds.), *The psychoanalytic study of society* (pp. 7–28). Hillsdale, NJ: The Analytic Press.
Northup, L. A. (2006). Myth-placed priorities: Religion and the study of myth. *Religious Studies Review*, *32*(1), 5–10.
Obeyesekere, G. (1990). *The work of culture: Symbolic transformation in psychoanalysis and anthropology*. Chicago, IL: The University of Chicago Press.
Parsons, W. B. (1999). *The enigma of the oceanic feeling*. New York: Oxford University Press.
Paul, R. A. (1996). *Moses and civilization*. New Haven, CT: Yale University Press.
Paul, R. A. (2003). Review of Blood Mary in the Mirror by Alan Dundes. *American Imago*, *60*(4), 545–549.
Rank, O. (1922/2004). *The myth of the birth of the hero: A psychological exploration of myth*. Baltimore, MD: The Johns Hopkins University Press.
Rizzuto, A.-M. (1979). *The birth of the living God: A psychoanalytic study*. Chicago, IL: University of Chicago Press.
Róheim, G. (1992). *Fire in the Dragon and other psychoanalytic essays on folklore*. Princeton, NJ: Princeton University Press.
Segal, R. A. (1990). *Joseph Campbell: An introduction*. New York: Penguin.
Segal, R. A. (2003a). Jung's very twentieth-century view of myth. *Journal of Analytical Psychology*, *48*, 593–617.
Segal, R. A. (2003b). Psychoanalyzing myth: From Freud to Winnicott. In D. Jonte-Pace (Ed.), *Teaching Freud* (pp. 137–162). Oxford: Oxford University Press.
Segal, R. A. (2004a). Introductory essay. In O. Rank (Ed.), *The myth of the birth of the hero: A psychological exploration of myth* (pp. vii–xxiii). Baltimore, MD: Johns Hopkins University Press.
Segal, R. A. (2004b). *Myth: A very short introduction*. Oxford: Oxford University Press.
Segaller, S. & Berger, M. (1989). *Jung: The wisdom of the dream*. London: Weidenfeld & Nicolson.
Sienkewicz, T. J. (1997). *Theories of myth: An annotated bibliography*. Lanham, MD: Scarecrow.
Walker, S. F. (1995). *Jung and the Jungians on myth*. New York: Garland.
Zajko, V. & Leonard, M. (Eds.) (2005). *Laughing with Medusa: Classical myth and feminist thought*. Oxford: Oxford University Press.

Psychoanalysis Meets Buddhism

The Development of a Dialogue

William B. Parsons

Psychological interpretations of Buddhism are more comprehensive than one might initially think. This "dialogue," or at least attempts at such, has been a subset of the broader psychology and religion movement since the latter's inception in the late nineteenth century. Indeed, the history of this specific dialogical enterprise has incorporated multiple models and engaged multiple types of Buddhism. To name but a few, even a cursory survey of the past century reveals that theories classified as Jungian, humanistic/transpersonal, empirical/experimental, neurocognitive, existential, behavioral and what can be called "general psychotherapeutic" have all engaged what they consider to be the psychological import of Buddhism (e.g., Boss, 1965; Molino, 1998a; Nauriyal et al., 2006). The relation between these latter studies and psychoanalytic ones is complex as nonpsychoanalytic studies (notably evident in Jungian and transpersonal studies) often employ psychoanalytic concepts in eclectic ways.[1]

Given this complexity, some initial comment concerning parameters is in order. First, we shall confine ourselves to specifically psychoanalytic studies of Buddhism.

[1] There is no question that of these various attempts it was Jung, particularly in the early decades of the twentieth century, who did the most to promote the encounter between depth-psychology and Buddhism. As Daniel Meckel, one of the leaders in the scholarly analysis of the transmission of eastern ideas through the figure of Jung notes (personal communication): "There is no disputing the fact that Jung played a major role as interpreter of Asian religious traditions to popular and academic audiences in Western countries. As I mention in the first page of my introduction to *Self and Liberation*, the best-known translations of Asian texts were initially received by the western public in books with commentaries by Jung. These include Evans-Wentz' translation of *The Tibetan Book of the Dead*, and D. T. Suzuki's famous *Introduction to Zen Buddhism*." Meckel goes on to note that it was the very success of Jung's project, alongside the initial bitter divide between Jungians and Freudians, that helped to limit specifically psychoanalytic encounters with Buddhism. After all no psychoanalyst, at least in the immediate decade after Freud, wanted to be linked to Jung and his notion of a spiritual dimension to the unconscious.

W.B. Parsons
Rice University, Houston, TX, USA
e-mail: pars@rice.edu

J.A. Belzen (ed.), *Changing the Scientific Study of Religion: Beyond Freud?*

Second, by "psychoanalysis" it is understood that while Freud was its undisputed founder, the history of its theoretical development is hardly uniform, incorporating more than a few models of the mind and therapy (e.g., classic drive theory, ego psychology, Neo-Freudian theorists, object-relations theory, Self psychology, intersubjectivity). Third, it bears emphasizing that Buddhism also evinces a complex history of change, which behooves one to pay attention to the specific type or school of Buddhism, as well as meditative technique, is being engaged. Finally, in order to facilitate analysis, we shall divide the history of the dialogue into three periods: 1880–1944; 1944–1970; 1970–2007. Each period will be prefaced with brief summaries of the general cultural and academic atmosphere within which the relevant psychoanalytic theorists and their Buddhist respondents operated. The overall aim is not to provide an encyclopedic summary and analysis of every study. Rather, we shall confine ourselves to those studies which define a trend, an issue, or a notable development within a particular historical period.

Since the studies catalogued below are often quite diverse in their approaches and conclusions, it is good to keep in mind, for purposes of organization and orientation, three general themes which pervade the literature. First, all the studies under consideration view both Buddhism and psychoanalysis as healing enterprises composed of definitive understandings of personhood, explicit existential aims, and suggested mental techniques for realizing those aims. There is, of course, great variance as to how these studies view the accuracy and success of the respective healing enterprises. At one end of the spectrum lies the Buddhist claim that full enlightenment is possible and that psychoanalytic models of the mind are limited while, at the other end, that psychoanalysis is not only the superior interpretative tool but one which can safely cast doubt on the more extreme Buddhist claims of total liberation. The studies below fall at both extremes, but mostly somewhere in between. Second, the two healing enterprises are the product of different cultures. The problems in communication and understanding that the cultural element presents is no small factor, and one finds that it affects the various representatives of both healing enterprises to some degree. Third, there is a definite development in the dialogue. As cultural obstacles are surmounted, as eastern religions saturate and grow in western soil, and as advocates of both healing enterprises gain not only theoretical but existential familiarity with each other, a new synthesis begins to emerge – one which, in its most contemporary form, amounts to a psychoanalytic advocacy of personhood and development which, if not Buddhist in the traditionally doctrinal sense, nevertheless reflects a marked turn towards legitimating spiritual experiences and states.[2]

[2] In this paper I will argue that the dialogue between psychoanalysis and Buddhism has been growing, and that most of this dialogue has taken place in recent decades. Just a cursory glance at the publications in this dialogue bears this out. My graduate research assistants – Nate Carlin and Ann Gleig of the Rice University Religious Studies Department – report as follows: "When we ran the keywords 'psychoanalysis and Buddhism' in the catalogue of the library of the University of Chicago, we found 35 titles, two of which were published in the 1945–1970 period, and 33 of which were published in the 1971-present period. Harvard's library turned up 42 titles – one in the 1880–1944 period; five in the 1945–1970 period; and 36 in 1971-present period. Similar results are found when we used Princeton Theological Seminary's mega-database EBSCO Host, which

1880–1944 – Initial Encounters

Up to the eighteenth century the engagement with Eastern religions in Europe and North America was sporadic and piecemeal, informed primarily through the auspices of missionaries, business enterprises, travel and trade. However by 1880, when the psychology of religion was beginning to establish itself as an intellectual discipline, the gradual dissemination of Eastern religions in the West was well under way in a variety of venues. With respect to academia, chairs in oriental studies and comparative religion were housed at Ivy League schools and the University of Chicago, and comparative religion was well represented at central European institutions, including the University of Vienna, the academic home of Freud. A generation of scholars (e.g., Rudolph Otto, Friedrich Heiler, Max Müller, Paul Deussen, Leopold von Schroeder, Sylvian Levi) and interested laypersons (Paul Carus, Edwin Arnold) as well as accessible translations and comparative studies (e.g., Müller's classic *Sacred Books of the East*, Otto's *Mysticism East and West*) became instruments for sustained informed inquiry. On the wider cultural scale the impact of the East was insured through the auspices of philosophers, poets, and various social mechanisms (e.g., Nietzsche, Schopenhauer, Emerson and "The Dial," Henry Steel Olcott, Madame Blavatsky and the Theosophists), visits from Eastern holy men (e.g., the Hindu saint Swami Vivekananda, the Zen master Soen Saku, and Yogananda – crowned by the World's Parliament of Religions in Chicago in 1893) who secured societies and institutions (e.g., the Vedanta Society) for the proliferation of their meditative techniques, and a social base of Asian immigrants (approximately one million strong) who carried with them their eastern forms of worship (Parsons, 2001; Tweed, 1992; Clarke, 1997; Fields, 1992; Versluis, 1993; Schwab, 1984; Tweed and Prothero, 1999).

Much of this impacted the psychology of religion, as both the exemplars of Hinduism and Buddhism, as well as their western sympathizers, were all too quick to frame eastern religions as commensurate with the scientific enterprise. In central psychological works of this era (and here one could include works by William James, R.M. Bucke, Joseph Marechal, Carl Jung, and James Bisset Pratt) one finds

---

can simultaneously search 30 some databases including Academic Search Premier, ATLA Religion Database, and PsychINFO. The strength of such a powerful database of EBSCO Host is that it can find virtually every recent article on any given topic. A weakness, though, is that it is not as comprehensive when researching topics that were written prior to, say, 1980. Another weakness is that such databases often do not include book chapters. A third weakness is that a given search is subject to the time that the search is conducted. It's possible, for example, for there to be glitches in one of the databases that EBSCO Host is using, so a search on one particular day could yield different results a month later. In any case, with all of these limitations noted, the basic argument bears out in terms of number of publications of articles as well. When we ran the keywords 'psychoanalysis and Buddhism' we got 231 entries: 7 from 1880–1944; 15 from 1945–1970 and 209 from 1971-present. When we ran the keywords 'psychoanalysis and spirituality,' we got 120 hits: 1 from the 1800–1944 period, and 119 from the 1971-present period. When we ran the keywords 'psychoanalysis and mysticism,' the picture looks a little different. In the 1880–1944 period, there were 25 hits: 38 hits for the 1945–1970 period and 134 hits for the 1971-present period. This may well be due to the perennial nature of the topic of mysticism in the psychology of religion."

Buddhism framed in terms of introspection, experience, and the therapeutic process. One can also find other, mostly forgotten theorists fond of psychoanalytic methodology who entered this arena in their analyses of Hindu and Buddhist forms of mysticism (e.g., Morel, 1918; Schjelderup and Schjelderup, 1932). However, our purposes are best met by concentrating on three figures – Sigmund Freud, Franz Alexander, and Joseph Thompson – whose interpretative efforts set the basic parameters for subsequent psychoanalytic theorizing about Buddhism.

The Freudian Legacy

There is no evidence which suggests that Freud had anything more than a passing interest in and cursory knowledge of Buddhism. He wrote almost nothing which directly engaged Buddhist thought and practice. Nevertheless, Freud being Freud, what little reference he did make to Buddhism, or that has been linked (even if erroneously) to Buddhism, has had a substantial impact on subsequent psychoanalytic theorizing on the topic.

Contemporary psychoanalytic studies of Buddhism, when referring back to Freud, have seized on Freud's interpretation of the famous "oceanic feeling" as the foundational element of his interpretation of Buddhism (Epstein, 1995). As this understanding has it, Buddhist meditation aims at the experience of nirvana, an episodic experience of oceanic unity interpreted as a regression to the developmental phase of primary narcissism, the implication being that such a regression is defensive, a way of disclaiming the task of individuation and the vicissitudes of external reality, fate and social engagement. Certainly there is some truth to this in the text of *Civilization and Its Discontents* (where Freud offers his thoughts on the oceanic feeling). Freud explicitly says, for example, that the oceanic feeling, while itself a neutral psychological phenomenon, is taken up by institutional forms of religion and used for defensive purposes and religious consolation. But it is also here, upon a closer inspection of the text in the context of Freud's correspondence with Romain Rolland, the man responsible for Freud's interpretation of the oceanic feeling, that one finds in this assumed and rarely questioned view of Freud outright errors and misreadings of the text – misreadings which have perpetuated unsubstantiated, and now mythical, views about Freud's interpretation of the oceanic feeling and, by extension, of Buddhism, while impeding the unearthing of Freud's more positive views concerning episodic mystical "experience" (or mystical "intuition").

It stands to reason that a correction of the received view is important, if only to set the historical reconstruction of the psychoanalytic encounter with Buddhism on a secure historical foundation. A complete deconstruction of the received view along with extensive supporting evidence has been undertaken elsewhere (Parsons, 1999), so here we will rest content with presenting its basic conclusions. Briefly put, the correspondence between the two men began in 1923 at Freud's initiative, lasting until the latter's death and covering a broad array of topics. The debate over the nature and interpretation of the oceanic feeling began in 1927 when Freud, who admired Rolland particularly for his artistry (Rolland won the Nobel Prize for literature in 1915) and ethics (Rolland was dubbed the "conscience of Europe" for his public stance against anti-Semitism and attempts to broker dialogue at the outset of the Great War), sent him *The Future of an Illusion*. Rolland's response, in a letter dated December 5, 1927, became the impetus for the two men's debate over the nature of the oceanic feeling. An analysis of their debate reveals that Rolland and Freud had two very different conceptions of religion and two very different cultural agendas.

For Freud religion was always that of the common man – an understanding which was western, assumed institutionalized patriarchal forms of socio-cultural power, and whose normative expression was centered in the monotheistic "mighty personality" of an exalted Father-God. In *The Future of an Illusion* he defiantly chastised those "philosophers" who tried to "stretch the meaning of words" to the point that words like "God" and "religious" ceased to bear any resemblance to the Being worshipped by the common-man. In sending Rolland *The Future of an Illusion*, Freud was implicitly asking Rolland to help him create a social space for his secular cure of souls. Rolland, as one of the cultural elite, was to help Freud in his effort to help assuage the *Unbehagen* in der Kultur.

Rolland, on the other hand, took a stance more reminiscent of Jung. He was born Catholic (in 1866 in Clamency) but left the Church in adolescence due to schooling (at the prestigious Ecole normale supérieure) and the cultural atmosphere of Paris (which he referred to as "deicidal"). Subject to a series of mystical experiences, which, utilizing the nomenclature of comparative religion can be called "nature" (that is, unchurched) mystical experiences Rolland, mourning the loss of his native Catholicism, began to construct his own religion. Set down in essay form in 1888 and dubbed the *Credo Qui Verum*, Rolland produced an essentially mystical and highly individualistic, idiosyncratic document, complete with references to transient "oceanic" mystical experiences, culled from a variety of different philosophical and religious sources, particularly the work of Spinoza. Years later, as a result of the complicity of Catholicism in fermenting the Great War, Rolland, in a state of utter disillusionment, turned eastwards to the figures of Gandhi, Tagore, Ramakrishna and Vivekananda. There, he said, he found anew the mysticism of his youth and a source for the vital renewal of western culture. Rolland was convinced that integrating the resources of East and West was the pivotal task of the future, and he eagerly accepted the challenge of helping to forge a new cultural whole. In so doing, Rolland drew from both the comparative study of mysticism and to psychology where, in turning to Freud, he advocated the creation of an unchurched mysticism, which he called a "universal science-religion" and a "mystical psychoanalysis." It was this "religion," thought Rolland, that would be the salvation of mankind.

Strictly speaking, then, it is apparent that Freud's understanding of the oceanic feeling had nothing to do with Buddhism. His interpretation of the oceanic feeling was, first and foremost, an analysis of Rolland's own unchurched mysticism as detailed in his letter of December 5, 1927. Second, and more importantly, the oceanic feeling was not depicted by Rolland as a transient mystical "experience," nor was it understood by Freud as such. To explore this in more detail, if one looks at Rolland's mysticism with respect to his total corpus, one finds that he distinguished between his transient nature mystical experiences and the developmentally later state-like oceanic feeling. There was, in effect, a rudimentary therapeutic rendering of mysticism in which episodic experiences of unity played a role in a wider "process" view of the development of mystical sensibilities. Rolland's transient nature mystical experiences contained an implicit teleology. Initially serving to "render the veil," they further enjoined one to a lifelong ethical and existential struggle which could (although not necessarily) culminate in the more permanent state-like oceanic feeling. In his letter to Freud of December 5, 1927, Rolland described the oceanic feeling as a primordial religious datum, an essentially contentless feeling of the eternal, confessed that he was familiar with the feeling, and referred to it as a "constant state" (a fact echoed by Freud in *Civilization and Its Discontents*, where Freud says Rolland was "never without" the oceanic feeling). To be sure, the notion of a mystical "state" is not unheard of to the theologian or to the comparativist. For example, St. Teresa's notion of "spiritual marriage" is a mystical state framed as the apex of the spiritual life, prepared for by a host of episodic mystical phenomena (including locutions, visions, and transient unitive experiences with God). Turning to Hinduism, one can point to the Hindu sage Sri Ramana Maharshi, who distinguished between two related mystical phenomena: *nirvikalpa samadhi* and *sahaja samadhi*. The former is understood to be a transient mystical experience and is compared to the episodic lowering of a bucket into a well. *Sahaja samadhi*, on the other hand, is understood as a more advanced mystical phenomenon. Indeed, it is the denouement of the mystical path, being described in terms of a river being merged into an "always present" feeling of a limitless, eternal ocean.

Without arguing for exact equivalence, if one had to point to which mystical phenomenon in the comparative study of mysticism that Freud was analyzing when he took on the enigma of the oceanic feeling, it would not be the transient oceanic experiences of unity emphasized by William James, which some psychoanalysts trace to one particular form of Buddhist meditation, namely, the stages of jnana (concentration techniques), but the more advanced, state-like Hindu *sahaja samadhi*. The ethical and existential dimensions of Rolland's personal elaboration of oceanic feeling were lost on Freud, who treated the oceanic feeling as a psychological appendix, a *preservation* of (but not *regression* to, although the preoedipal model could be used, and clearly later was, to interpret *transient* feelings of mystical unity) the stage of primary narcissism alongside the more mature, demarked ego of adulthood. Indeed, it is Kohut's notion of "cosmic narcissism," which is an advanced transformation of narcissism seen as an unusual achievement beyond the bounds of a "normal" therapy, which comes closer to approximating the existential and ethical meaning of Rolland's oceanic feeling.

Freud did, however, address the more familiar transient mystical "experience." But here Freud advocated a very different interpretative model – one that emphasized insight and the similarity between mystical, meditative techniques and psychoanalytic therapy. One finds this model at work in his correspondence with Rolland. In a letter (of July 17, 1929) Rolland wrote to Freud concerning Yoga and the physiology of mystical experiences. In the last paragraph of the first chapter of *Civilization and Its Discontents* Freud, again replying to Rolland, turned away from the state-like oceanic feeling to address the relation between mystical practices and episodic mystical experience.[3] While Freud did not offer a detailed analysis of the latter, he did leave us a telling quotation from Schiller's *The Diver*. The latter is actually quite revealing, the poem being both quite short and very Oedipal. Briefly summarized, it portrays the plight of a lowly page who, on two successive occasions, dives into a feared "whirlpool" (described as an "ocean womb") to retrieve a King's goblet, the reward being the King's daughter and, eventually, the crown itself. The depths of the whirlpool (a term Freud explicitly used to refer to the unconscious) are portrayed as gruesome and the page never returns from his second brave attempt. Certainly the resemblance between the poem and psychoanalytic therapy was not lost on Freud. Interestingly enough, during the academic year 1904–1905 Freud, in a conversation with Bruno Goetz, later poet but then student in the Sanskrit scholar Leopold von Schroeder's class on Indian thought at the University of Vienna, had similarly used Schiller's *The Diver* to speak of the depths of psychic insight present in the "nirvana" of the *Bhaghavad Gita*. The latter had "awful depths" said Freud, and he cautioned the young Goetz to make sure to prepare himself emotionally and intellectually before he undertook the deep psychic surgery described in the Hindu text. This letter indicates that Freud was aware of the debates raging in European Universities about the nature of the term "nirvana." Nirvana as signifying nothingness is, says Freud, "a European misconception (...) it is that which transcends all contradictions (...) It is not (...) sensual enjoyment (...) but the ultimate in superhuman understanding, an ice-cold, all comprehending yet scarcely comprehensible insight. Or, if misunderstood, it is madness" (Parsons, 1999, p. 48). A full analysis of this letter reveals that Freud was not endorsing the ontological views of eastern religions but rather reinterpreting their seminal insights along the line of his emerging theory: nirvana was simply a culturally variant way of expressing insight into the deepest core of the oedipal conflict.

Whether one buys into the integrity of Bruno Goetz's memory and supposed verbatim statements made by Freud or not, it is clear that other letters and texts in the Freudian corpus support a therapeutic rendering of mystical intuition. For example, in a later letter to Rolland, after the latter had sent him his biographies of Ramakrishna and Vivekananda, Freud affirmed that mystical practices could reveal "instinctual impulses and attitudes" which were "highly valuable for an embryology of the soul" (Parsons, 1999, p. 177). One finds a similar interpretative move advocated when one looks at the imagery and linguistic construction of the "psychoanalytic motto" (namely, "where Id was, there Ego shall be"). In describing what

[3] Jeffrey Masson (1984, p. 233ff.) notes that the "other friend" Freud refers to in this paragraph is Friedrich Eckstein (a line of argument followed by the Vermorel and Vermorel (1993, p. 340)). While this may be so, I have argued (Parsons, 1999) that it was Rolland's letter of July 17, 1929 which instigated Freud's reflections on the topic of episodic mystical experience and, additionally, that the figure of Rolland must be included (condensed, as it were) with that of Eckstein in this last paragraph of the first chapter of *Civilization and Its Discontents*. This is so for Rolland's letter speaks of the physiology of Yoga while Freud, writing in reply on July 20, 1929, speaks of Rolland's seeming encyclopedic knowledge – both of which find expression in the paragraph in question.

it is that psychoanalytic therapy does, Freud clothes his remarks in typically poetic terms, speaking of rivers and oceans, of reclaiming land from the sea, and of Faust, Exodus and Genesis. Then, drawing an analogy between psychoanalysis and mystical intuition, Freud remarks that "certain mystical practices" could pierce the usual barriers between the Id and Ego so that one could gain insight into "the depths of the ego and in the id which were otherwise inaccessible" (Parsons, 1999, p. 79). Casting doubt that "ultimate truths" and "salvation" could be had by such a route, he nevertheless went on to say: "it may be admitted that the therapeutic efforts of psychoanalysis have chosen a similar line of approach" (Parsons, 1999, p. 79).

Summing up, one can fairly state that extant understandings of Freud's views on mystical phenomena, which have been liberally extended to Buddhism, have missed the mark. First, most see Freud's view of Buddhist meditation, particularly the kind of episodic oceanic feelings which have been linked to jnana forms of concentration, as consisting of a regression to primary narcissism. While Freud did use the preodipal model, and while that model could easily be adapted to account for episodic mystical experiences, Freud was trying to explain a state-like mystical phenomenon and emphasized what can be called a "preservation" model. In some people the oceanic feeling, a residue from the phase of primary narcissism, was seen to exist as a constant state alongside the more narrowly demarcated ego. It has been further suggested that what for Freud was a psychological appendix was, for Rolland, the end product of a mystical process involving ethical and therapeutic dimensions. From his perspective the oceanic feeling was more like the Hindu *sahaja samadhi*. Kohut's concept of "cosmic consciousness," which he describes as an enduring state and signifies a transformation of narcissism, is a better psychological approximation of what Rolland had in mind. Second, Freud offered a different model for the interpretation of the kind of episodic mystical experiences and insights produced by mystical techniques like Yoga. Such techniques, thought Freud, were like psychoanalysis in that they unearthed, and helped one gain insight into, unconscious content. This line of interpretation, which has been heretofore unacknowledged, presents us with a more positive, therapeutically useful understanding of meditation – one that was certainly seized on by subsequent psychoanalytic theorists.

Alexander's Pathologies

Freud's cursory observations on the therapeutic potential of the mystical element of religion received fuller treatment at the hands of his colleague Franz Alexander. On September 25, 1922, Alexander delivered a lecture in Berlin at the seventh Congress of the International Psychoanalytic Association – a lecture which, first published in the German psychoanalytic journal *Imago* and then, in 1931, in English translation in *The Psychoanalytic Review*, came to be entitled "Buddhistic Training as an Artificial Catatonia (The Biological Meaning of Psychic Occurrences)." Alternately, says Alexander, the essay could have been subtitled "the psychic meaning of biological occurrences." This is so, explains Alexander, with reference to what philosophers would call the "mind–body" problem. Contrary to the extremes of materialism (which Alexander identified with his contemporary Vogt) and idealism (which he linked with Berkeley), Alexander held fast to a psychoanalytic rendering of philosophical positions he ascribed to Spinoza and Schopenhauer: a virtual identity between psychic and biological processes (Alexander, 1931, p. 129).

As the title indicates, it is here that we find a true psychoanalytic pathologizing of Buddhism. There is no evidence that Alexander engaged in the practice of meditative techniques but rather based his understanding of Buddhism purely on the translations and commentaries of his time, notably those by Friedrich Heiler and Hermann Oldenburg. For Alexander Buddhism was a "nihilistic" philosophy, which aimed at the alleviation of suffering through a very specific form of salvific knowledge: that of the origin of life and rebirth (reincarnation). Buddhist meditation (and here Alexander confined himself to not only Theravada Buddhism but, more specifically to jnana [i.e., concentration, calming] forms of meditation to the exclusion of *vipassana* [insight] forms of mediation) worked by concentrating on a variety of objects. It progressed through four stages, each revealing its own level of pathology. Before the first stage was the preparatory stage of moral training, where every vestige of relation to the external world, every "genital, sadistic, oral-erotic, and anal-erotic outlet" must be totally shut down (Alexander, 1931, p. 132). The initial stage of meditation leads to a suppression of thoughts, a masochistic disgust with the body and material reality, and culminates in a state akin to melancholia. In the second stage disgust recedes and is replaced by a more positive attitude towards ego, felt subjectively as being fed by an underground stream of water. This emerging oceanic-like feeling of expansion, also likened by Alexander to an orgasm which is diffused through the entire body (the feeling of being flooded with pure narcissistic libido), is viewed as a regression to schizophrenic catatonic ecstasy. In the third stage apathy replaces bliss and expansion is replaced by detumescence. This is schizophrenic dementia: complete detachment from the world, men and the gods. The fourth stage, which Alexander, following Heiler, sees as a quantitative expansion of the third stage, is a condition of mental emptiness, pure being, absorption, and uniformity. It is in this stage that we find nirvana. It is also here we find the seminal salvific knowledge of (and hence freedom from) the trials of birth, death and rebirth. Psychoanalytically rendered, Alexander, in accordance with his philosophical position of the identity of the biological and mental, reasons that nirvana can only signify a regression to the stage of intra-uterine life: "Nirvana is the condition [i.e., regression to] in the mother's womb" (Alexander, 1931, p. 136). Since in the womb one finds conditions ranging from a formed fetus to the beginning of embryonic development, Alexander posits the stage of nirvana could conceivably contain the biopsychic knowledge of the conditions of birth. Buddhist mediation is a reverse tracing of the stages of development through multiple pathologies, culminating in the intrauterine knowledge of the process of birth. As to how this is possible, Alexander reasons that just as Freud saw in the Christian myth of the Fall the dimly perceived phylogenetic knowledge of the "primal deed," so too in Buddhism do we have, through the deeply regressive form of psychic surgery known as meditation, the dimly perceived knowledge of the origin of birth, presented in the disguised and distorted doctrine of reincarnation.

For Alexander, then, Buddhism was indeed an attempt at therapy. He posited that Buddhism, like psychoanalysis, was an attempt at the therapeutic alleviation of suffering, and that its techniques entailed, also like psychoanalysis, a narcissistic withdrawal into the self. However, unlike psychoanalysis, Buddhism never sought reconciliation between instinctual demands and external reality, but rather a total break and abandonment of the external world. The aim of its therapy was costly and a new model for nirvana and mystical salvation was introduced: regression to intra-uterine existence. In contrast to Freud and Rolland, both of whom had thoughtful reflections on the relationship between psychology, religion, ethics and society, Alexander was quick to criticize Neo-Buddhist European scholars of his day like Leopold Ziegler, who held hope that Buddhism could effect a social whole. For Alexander Buddhism was a narcissistic-masochistic religion incapable of generating a practical social ethic. This ran contrary to the aims of the "transference" religion of Christianity, which was based on the Father and aimed at regulating the affective relations between peoples. The most positive element of Alexander's critique is also the most incredible: that the deeper regression fostered by Buddhist techniques could lead to knowledge about conditions of birth. This is in one sense a variation on Freud's view that mystical intuition could be valuable for an "embryology of the soul." But even here Freud was careful to note that even such knowledge, in the wrong hands (that is to say, absent a psychoanalytically trained therapist), would be useless for adaptation to the external world. Ideally, regression should be in the service of the ego. But according to Alexander, Buddhist regression is in the service of Thanatos.

Alexander's pathologizing of Buddhism has come to represent the general orientation of the early psychoanalytic studies of Buddhism. Certainly other psychoanalytic tracts of this time, notably Ferdinand Morel's 1918 work *Essai sur L'introversion Mystique* (which actually prefigured Alexander's stress on regression to the intra-uterine state) can be found which tout an unadulterated pathologizing of Buddhism. A line can be traced through these early studies up through mid-century studies (e.g., Lewin's link between ecstasy and mania [see Lewin, 1961]) and to the present era (e.g., the work of Jeffrey Masson [see Masson, 1980]). Properly decentralized and relativized this approach has its value, notably evinced by the many contemporary researchers sympathetic to Buddhism who have utilized it to sift out what they see as pathological elements mixed in with the more adaptive, therapeutic and even soteriological elements of Buddhist practice (see Engler, 1986; Rubin, 1996; Epstein, 1995).

Tom's Therapies

Alongside the unadulterated pathologizing of Buddhism among these early studies is another strand of psychoanalytic reasoning which emphasizes the more adaptive, therapeutic aspect of Buddhism. This adaptive rendering of Buddhism is paradigmatically exemplified in an essay by an obscure Chicago psychoanalyst, Joseph

Thompson, who wrote under the pseudonym of Joe Sun Tom. Thompson made his views known in a small essay, entitled "Psychology in Primitive Buddhism" which, found in the pages of *The Psychoanalytic Review* in 1924, prefigured Freud's analysis of the oceanic feeling. The article is marred by generalizations and a total absence of citations. We are left wondering what sources informed Tom's understanding about Buddhism. What we do know is that Buddhism, for Tom, was but a culturally distinct therapeutic enterprise which parallels yet prefigured the insights of psychoanalysis. Thus it is that Tom thinks that both systems aim at the alleviation of suffering and attainment of wisdom, and use introspection and insight to attain their goals: "There are far more affinities between the Buddhist philosophy and Freudian psychoanalysis than exist between the latter and any other system for aiding humanity to attain the goal of increased energy intake, conversion and output (...) the aim of both is identical" (Sun, 1924/1998, p. 11). That said, Tom goes on to create a laundry list of affinities between the two therapeutic systems. Both systems stress the centrality of desire and misguided desire, and both cure through adaptation to external reality. Mediation is akin to free association, and the Buddhist eight-fold path is essentially a cure through sublimation. Thus "nirvana" is not to be explained by "the mechanism of repression but by the most deliberate conscious sublimation" (ibid., p. 6). While cursory, the "adaptive," therapeutic view of Buddhism advocated by Tom is historically important, subsequently being developed by figures like Karen Horney and Erich Fromm.

Summing up, in looking back over this era of the psychoanalytic encounter with Buddhism, one arrives at a few central, expected conclusions. First, psychoanalytic interpretations of Buddhism were limited by the then state of comparativist studies. The latter, from the perspective of contemporary Buddhology, was marred by incomplete and at times misleading translations, as well as by a neglect of the richness and complexity that constitutes the many extant Buddhist schools and practices. Psychoanalytic appropriations of such literature did not distinguish between types or schools of Buddhism, much less the variety of meditational techniques and their associated aims. Similarly, psychoanalysis had almost no contact with the comparative study of mysticism or, for that matter, with any sophisticated form of cultural analysis and contextualization (which has become a central partner in contemporary psychoanalytic studies of eastern religions and cultures). Additionally, there was no direct encounter with Buddhist practitioners, lamas and masters, and there is no evidence that any psychoanalysts of this era ever experimented with meditative techniques, much less knew of their variety – an "insider" dimension significant in that such existential experience, as we shall see, has become a crucial element of contemporary psychoanalytic studies. With respect to the psychoanalytic understanding of Buddhism, then, one can rightly conclude that it was secondhand, a form of armchair ethnography. With regard to its interpretative forays, it is clear that they were rooted in classic drive theory, espoused a psychological universalism, and evinced a reductive agenda which, lacking an appreciation of Geertzian thick descriptive activity, can be accused of harboring the prejudices of orientalism and eurocentrism. One cannot, then, really speak of a "dialogue" being present in this early period. That being said, the psychoanalytic contribution to Buddhist studies from this era was not negligible or irrelevant. Issues like the nature and meaning of mystical intuition, the adaptive therapeutic benefits and pathological elements of Buddhist practice, the similarities and differences between Buddhism and psychoanalysis and the relation of Buddhism to the social order were all issues which played a role in the bona fide "dialogue" to come.

1944–1970 – The Zen Files

In the decades after the Great War one can point to at least three general, inter-related factors which served to change the relation between psychoanalysis and Buddhism to one of friendly, productive engagement. One of these factors was the development in psychoanalytic theory as found in the advances of Neo-Freudians, the resources of ego psychology, and the stirrings of insight into the developmental line of narcissism and object-relations. The latter have proved to be more favorably disposed towards religion than classic drive theory. A second development was the dramatic social, political and cultural changes that occurred in America during the 1950s and 1960s. One can characterize these decades as evincing a liminal quality. To wit: there was a general disillusionment with the social, political, economic and religious institutions of the time. Reigning forms of Christian morality and doctrine were attacked in favor of theologies attacking heteronomy and espousing the death of God. Multiple forms of therapy were widely disseminated, some promoting the ingestion of entheogens and sexual experimentation. This was a richly creative time that gave rise to Aldous Huxley and Timothy Leary, the beatniks and the hippies, the civil rights movement and anti-war sentiments, The San Francisco Zen Center and the Esalen Institute. It looked to the East for cultural resources, touted Gandhi and the Dalai Lama and, most important for our purposes, came to idealize eastern religions, especially Zen Buddhism. Indeed, the dialogue between psychoanalysis and Buddhism of this period was a full-fledged Zen affair.

A third development was the slow psychologization of Asian culture, particularly Japan. As is well known, Freud was constantly trying to insert psychoanalysis into western culture through various devices: his cultural works, relationships with those in socially prominent positions, and institutionalization of his therapeutic enterprise. Freud's ambitions went beyond Europe, engaging those who might serve his cause in the East. As early as 1909, Girindrasekhar Bose had been practicing a variant of psychoanalysis, and his decades long correspondence with Freud eventuated in the establishment of the Indian Psychoanalytic Society in 1922. When Bose sent Freud a lovely ivory statuette of the God Vishnu in 1931, Freud responded that it would be placed on his desk, there to remind him of the "proud conquests it [psychoanalysis] has made in foreign countries" (Vaidyanathan and Kripal, 1999, p. 3).

Freud's engagement with Bose is by now well known. Lesser known, but entirely relevant for our purposes, is his engagement with Japan. We know that the early history of Japanese psychiatry was heavily influenced by the German schools, to which many Japanese flocked for graduate study, and American schools like John

Hopkins and G. Stanley Hall's Clark University. However, by 1919 a psychoanalytic monograph (*The Study of Sexuality and Psychoanalysis*, by Yasusaburo Sakaki) had appeared. By 1930 most of Freud's works had been translated into Japanese, a journal (*Seishinbunseki*, the Tokyo Journal of Psychoanalysis) had been formed, and psychoanalysis was being taught at major Japanese universities. The establishment of the Japanese Psychoanalytic Society was relatively late, being formally accepted by the international psychoanalytic body in 1955. One of the earliest students of psychoanalysis, Kiyoyasu Marui, converted during a stay in the United States, later met with Freud, was supervised by Ernest Federn, and ended up teaching psychoanalysis at his native Tohoku University. Marui's student Heisaku Kosawa similarly met with Freud (he loved the "sitting Buddha in front of the bookshelf" in Freud's study [Blowers and Chi, 1997, p. 118]), underwent analysis with Richard Sterba and was supervised by Ernest Federn (see Blowers and Chi, 1997; Roland, 1988).

Kosawa established an important correspondence with Freud that bears an uncanny parallel with that of Bose. Like Bose, Kosawa was sympathetic to religion, and it was in Buddhist texts (the *Nirvana Sutra* and the *Kyogyoshinsho*, a Pure Land text of the thirteenth century Japanese priest Shinran Shonin) that Kosawa found evidence for a culturally constituted alternate nuclear complex that he termed the "Ajase Complex" (Blowers and Chi, 1997, p. 119). The latter, fully explored in a paper sent to Freud and eventually published as "Zaiakuishikino nishu" ("Two Types of Guilt Consciousness – Oedipus and Ajase") in the Tokyo Journal of Psychoanalysis in 1935 emphasized, over against the primacy of Oedipus, the themes of matricide, guilt and reparation. Freud was predictably cool to this idea but, as was the case with the generations of Indian clinicians after Bose, later psychoanalysts were to make the notion of alternate, culturally constituted nuclear complexes central to their work (Roland, 1988, pp. 78–79).[4]

While several other figures and events dot the historical landscape of the development of psychoanalysis in Japan, the most important for our purposes is the figure of Akihisa Kondo. Kondo, who came out of this matrix, and who was to become one of the more respected clinicians in Japan, decided to go to the United States in the late 1940s for postgraduate training. Kondo was initially wedded to Morita therapy (which was heavily influenced by Zen) but once in America, he decided to train at the Karen Horney Institute in New York City. It was there that he befriended Horney and Erich Fromm. Horney relied heavily on Kondo for her ruminations on the relation between psychoanalysis and Morita therapy, and Kondo became the central link between Fromm, Horney and D.T. Suzuki, the most illustrated Buddhist figure of that time (Roland, 1988, p. 77). Like Kondo, Suzuki's Zen was hardly unpsychological. It was not the monastic, heavily ritualized and doctrinal Buddhism of previous centuries. During the Meiji period (1868–1912), Japan

[4] Freud was, however, enamored of the observation made by another Japanese psychologist, Yabe Yaekichi, that Freud's thoughts on the death instinct (or "nirvana principle") would be well received by a culture which, being infused with Buddhist values, would like the notion of life as tending towards death (Blowers and Chi, 1997, p. 121). It is touching to find that Kosawa's gift to Freud, a portrait of Mt. Fuji, still graces one of the walls of his house in London.

had undergone a phase of rapid modernization and westernization. It responded to corruption within Buddhist ranks and general enlightenment critiques of religion with a "New Buddhism" which was nonsectarian, universal, socially engaged, eminently rational and in tune with science and philosophy. Soen Shaku, one of Suzuki's teachers, was heavily involved in the dissemination of the new Buddhism and had engaged western thought, making his way (as noted in the previous section) to the World's Parliament of Religions in 1893. Suzuki was also heavily influenced by western figures, prominently Paul Carus (who critiqued the materialism and agnosticism of science, the institutional irrationality of religion, and held that the truths of science and religion could eventually be squared) and the writings of William James (particularly his focus on experience as central to religion and mysticism). The latter was easily linked with Suzuki's fondness for the "Kyoto School" (exemplified in the works of Kitaro Nishida) and it's rendering of Buddhism as consisting in an unmediated mystical experience. In his turn to the West Suzuki presented a Zen which had been shaped by western psychological influences. A better match for a culture disillusioned with institutional religion and gravitating towards psychology and existential experience could not be found (see Sharf, 1995). In sum, then, several factors colluded to create a more favorable soil for the growth of "dialogue": the "psychologization" of Japan, of Zen, of the principle (western-influenced) social representatives of that tradition, and a western "liminal" culture looking for a psycho-mystical therapeutic regimen.

The First Wave – Horney, Fromm and Suzuki

Karen Horney's eclectic brand of psychoanalysis and personal turn to the mystical and religious suited her well for dialogue with Zen. Morvay, for example, argues that "Horneyan psychoanalysis (...) defined itself as an existential/phenomenological-based self-psychoanalytic system [which] introduced a truly holistic, optimistic, humanistic, and spiritual style of psychoanalysis [and] foreshadowed the transpersonal and humanistic psychologies of today" (Morvay, 1999, pp. 26–27). Horney's abiding interest in the mystical can be gleaned in the fact that she read Huxley's *The Perennial Philosophy* every night for the last 4 years of her life. It is not surprising, then, that Horney cited Suzuki and Zen as early as 1945 in her book *Our Inner Conflicts*. It was through the auspices of Kondo and two of her patients, Cathy Crane Bernatschke and Cornelius Crane, that she met with Suzuki in the winter of 1950 while the later was on a lecture tour in New York City. It is possible that Horney began meditating under the tutelage of Suzuki at that time. Her encounter was followed by a summer tour through Japan and Zen monasteries with Suzuki in 1952, just 2 months before her death (see Morvay, 1999; Westcott, 1998).

Despite this short amount of time with actual Zen practitioners, Horney assimilated a good deal of Zen thought into her own psychologizing. Primary among the latter are her concepts of the Real Self and Wholeheartedness. For Horney the Real Self is that inner core which is the essential source of self-realization, self-regulation, growth, joy, optimism, and wholeness. If, due to socio-cultural and developmental inhibitors, the expression of the Real Self becomes blocked, the individual suffers from a "basic anxiety" and forms a pseudo self which is kept in place by the twin forces of pride and self-contempt. The therapeutic task consists of being released from the latter two confining forces so that the Real Self can shine through. Wholeheartedness, conceived of as an aim of therapy and ideal for daily living, points towards a person who is entirely absorbed in his or her actions, "operating with all (his or her) faculties while remaining at the same time quite oblivious to [oneself] (...) [one establishes] the highest presence and the highest absence" (Horney, 1998, p. 36). One is emotionally sincere, authentic, and capable of putting all of one's energy and attention into the task at hand.

What is crucial for our purposes is to note how Horney's basic concepts and understanding of therapeutic practice changed with her exposure to Zen. It has been speculated that Horney's initial understanding of the Real Self was in some way indebted to James' articulation of the "spiritual self," that it was "seedlike" in character as something that could and should "grow." But after her exposure to Zen, Horney began to integrate the lessons of "mindfulness" into her theory and practice, so that part of manifesting the Real Self was the capacity to exercise mindful detachment. Mindfulness, in essence, helped cultivate wholehearted attentiveness and absorption. And, over against the seedlike quality of the Real Self was a new formulation of it as being less a "thing" and more a "fluctuating continuum," as Westcott has it, which is ever moving, becoming, and capable of embracing duality (Westcott, 1998). Morvay goes so far as to liken the Real Self to the Buddhist notion of sunyata, insofar as both are "the source of infinite possibility" (Morvay, 1999, p. 34). Wholeheartedness, on the other hand, became exemplified in the Zen aim of being in the here and now – fully focused and without a trace of self-consciousness. Additionally, Horney thought that the mental skills and attributes developed through practicing mindfulness (e.g., focused attention and observation, mindful detachment, self-forgetfulness, a general nonjudgmental attitude) were advances on Freud's "evenly hovering attention" and could be integrated with great results into the therapeutic session. While therapy inevitably engaged the content of experience, Horney began to shift her focus to changing one's relationship to one's experience. Change became conceived of less in terms of striving to be something else and more in terms of simply accepting what one is in the present moment. It is in the acceptance that "change" occurs. It is precisely these elements of Zen, argues Westcott, that prefigure contemporary reformulations of psychoanalytic technique found in psychoanalytic-inclined clinicians engaged in Buddhist meditation and scholarship like Mark Epstein. This makes Horney more pivotal in the history of this "dialogue" than is usually appreciated (see Westcott, 1998).

Suzuki's most formal response to Horney, Fromm and psychoanalysis in general occurred at a conference in Cuerenavaca Mexico under the auspices of the Autonomous National University (and its Department of Psychoanalysis) in 1957. The conference brought together approximately 50 psychologists and psychoanalysts who delivered papers on diverse topics ranging from Sullivan's concept of the Self to the contribution of George Groddeck. But the conference is rightly famous for the lectures of Suzuki, Fromm and Suzuki's colleague and assistant Richard De Martino (later published under the title *Zen Buddhism and Psychoanalysis*). The problem Suzuki encountered was one familiar to all missionary activity, be it east or west: how to communicate religious views in the terminology of the indigenous culture. So it is that Suzuki's writings are suffused with psychoanalytic terminology, tweaked here and there to show its limits and, when the limits became evident, to introduce new terminology that sounded psychological but betrayed a religious, ontological dimension that ran counter to the psychoanalytic tradition.

Suzuki's initial salvo concerned the nature of the unconscious and the Self. Beyond the personal unconscious of Freud, thought Suzuki, lay a deeper unconscious he denoted with respect to several terms: the "cosmic unconscious," the "Unborn," "no-mind" and, most revealing, the "ontological unconscious" (Fromm, Suzuki and De Martino, 1960, p. 49). For Suzuki this entity was "the reservoir of unlimited possibilities" (ibid., p. 14), a deeper Self which was pure subjectivity (likened to a circle with no circumference whose center is found "everywhere and anywhere" [ibid., p. 25]). This Self, or ontological unconscious, was universal but not adequately captured by psychological concepts (e.g. Winnicott's "true self," the undifferentiated self of primary narcissism or the archetypical Self of Jung) for it had ontological significance. The "eye" which accessed it, evident in the experience of satori, was prajna, defined as an intuitive capacity "at once above and in the process of reasoning" (p. 29) through which one sees the "infinite totality of things" (p. 74). The "experience' or apprehension of this Self was not a mere thought or belief, but an event impacting the total personality in which the self, the subject-object dichotomy, and time itself disappeared in an ineffable understanding beyond ordinary human comprehension. All things are seen as relative and moored in the infinite: "the finite mind is rooted in the infinite" (p. 47). Suzuki thought that training was needed to achieve this rare insight and that its effects were discernable. He characterized a process of training in which one could distinguish between mere instinctual existence, a life of reason and instinct characterized by clinging to self and neurosis, and a life after satori where one lives again in the immediate present but with reason uncontaminated by fear and clinging. Such a liberated person displayed discernable behavioral characteristics. They were "artists of life," exhibiting authenticity, "flow" and deep empathy in every act.

In prefacing his point-by-point response to Suzuki, Fromm noted that Zen had afforded him an opportunity to rethink the methods and aims of his brand of "humanistic" psychoanalysis. Fromm noted that the implicit religio-ethical dimension of psychoanalysis, its aim and definition of health, as best contained in the psychoanalytic motto: Wo Es war, soll Ich werden. This aim defined health negatively in terms of the absence of illness. Fromm's reformulation of psychoanalytic theory offered a more positive definition of health as "well being." Moreover, this new aim was similar to the aim of the enlightened Zen monk. Freud's psychoanalytic motto referred to only a localized aspect of the unconscious – that dealing with symptom formation, trauma, instinctual life. Fromm's psychology advocated enlarging the purview to include the "full recovery" of the unconscious and the "total experience of the total man." For Fromm this meant overcoming the split between the socialized personal identity, which varies according to culture, and the "universal" empathic recognition of all potentialities and "identities, all that is virtuous and all vices, within oneself; giving up the illusion of the 'separate ego." It means the "living experience of this universality (...) the experiential realization of humanism" (Fromm et al., 1960, p. 107). He takes Suzuki's notion of the "art of living" as the new ideal – an ideal he takes to be a position not only of Zen but also of that animating a spiritual humanistic orientation. This attitude also has the advantage of overcoming greed, narcissism, and the need to submit to a religious authority. It implies a "change of character," not just an abolition of neuroses, and thus the "more radical aim of a complete transformation of the person" (ibid., pp. 135–136).

In making these claims Fromm went on to address Suzuki's other points. He agreed that the experience of satori was not a regression to primary narcissism. Rather, satori was "the reception of the preintellectual immediate grasp of the child but on a new level, that of the full development of man's reason, objectivity, individuality. While the child's experience, that of immediacy and oneness, lies before the experience of alienation and the subject-object split, the enlightenment experience lies after it" (p. 135). Being enlightened meant being an "artist of life," now rendered as being freed from the regressive pull of the mother and authoritarian rule of the father. It meant having arrived at the full development of reason, overcoming narcissism, creativity, and the immediate, intuitive grasp of reality without "affective contamination." Intuition, in Spinoza's sense, could be made to tally with the psychoanalytic understanding of "working-through" the contents of the unconscious (p. 111).

One cannot help but hear in this give and take echoes of the Freud-Rolland correspondence. Suzuki, like Rolland, was informed by psychology and yet posited a primordial ontological reality which could be accessed through intuitive means. Fromm, like Freud, utilized the "psychoanalytic motto" in order to draw a correspondence between psychoanalytic therapy and mystical practices. The difference between Freud and Fromm lies in the eclectic, humanistic brand of psychoanalysis which made possible a more positive rendering of Buddhism.

Second Wave Theorists – From Fingarette to Kondo

The encounter of Horney and Fromm with their eastern counterparts helped seed a fertile exchange that took root in a variety of venues. New journals, notably *Psychologia* and Horney's own *American Journal of Psychoanalysis*, became legitimate social spaces for the exchange of ideas. A new round of interpretative forays, numerous enough that they occasioned the appearance of review articles, configured new ways of integrating Buddhist and psychoanalytic techniques into the therapeutic enterprise, featured the inclusion of case history material, and legitimated altered states of consciousness as not only beneficial but instrumental to the hermeneutical task. Western cultural soil made sure that this exchange grew rapidly, generating widespread appeal.

The decades after Freud saw the emergence of not only Neo-Freudian theorists like Fromm and Horney but those affiliated with ego-psychology and object-relations theory. Major works like Erikson's *Young Man Luther* (1956/1962) utilized the development of psychoanalytic theory to render a more positive verdict on religious belief, practices and ideation. It is not surprising, then, that one finds similar efforts represented in the new round of psychoanalytic studies of Zen. A paradigmatic ego-psychological study can be found in the work of Herbert Fingarette, who used such advances to promote a simple thesis: Zen was but a culturally relative form of psychoanalysis. But the sophistication and skillfulness of Fingarette's presentation, which utilized a case history (certainly one of the first, if not the first used within psychoanalysis in its dialogue with Buddhism) and a spectrum of ego-psychological terminology, went well beyond previous efforts. Fingarette argued that the paradoxical language of Zen (selflessness, emptiness) was not indicative of pathology or depression but rather a culturally specific use of therapeutic terms which, when properly translated and contextualized in the therapeutic context, had exact analogs in the psychoanalytic clinical setting. What was "lost" in Zen was not the self per se but the "transference self" with its attendant forms of anxiety and intrapsychic conflict. Enlightenment and satori were the product of regressions ("in the service of the ego"), which led to an increase in ego functioning and liberation from neurotic behavior. Harkening back to Freud and Rolland (and, one could argue, prefiguring Kohut's concept of "cosmic narcissism") Fingarette gave adaptive value to preoedipal states as well, arguing that Zen therapy enriched the autonomous ego with the residues of the "oceanic feeling" and a sense of omnipotence tempered by unselfconsciousness (Fingarette, 1965). The psychologist Ed Maupin, banking off Fingarette and ego-psychology, added a stage approach to therapy which prefigured (and bears more than a cursory likeness to) contemporary models which have sought to integrate the developmental arc of psychoanalysis and Buddhism. According to Maupin, Zen was indeed a therapy, which worked via a series of regressed states. In its initial phase, it uncovered and "worked-through" the phase of primary process residue linked to the Oedipus complex. One then had access to the deeper, pre-oedipal fantasies of grandiosity and omnipotence. Once this phase had been managed (with the help of the Zen therapist/master), one then had the internal fortitude necessary to access the intuitive insight contained in satori, which afforded one the experience of wholeness and oneness. Additionally, Maupin introduced the idea of the "trained unconscious." What regression tapped for Maupin were not only developmental vicissitudes but also perceptual and motor abilities registered in the unconscious – abilities waiting to be accessed, developed and utilized. Zen training in archery and the martial arts was a case in point. The latter lead to altered states of "flow" and "supernormal" performances (see Maupin, 1962).

Maupin, who later became interested in (and conducted workshops at) the Esalen Institute, also represents another theoretical trend: the inclusion of psychoanalytic theory as part of a broader, eclectic religious psychology which incorporated data and concepts from eastern religious traditions, existentialism, phenomenology, humanistic psychology, Jungian psychology and the Neo-Freudians. Another good example of this lies in the writings of Harold Kelman, who was deeply influenced by Horney (being Dean of the American Institute for Psychoanalysis), touted theorists like Jung, Boss and Binswanger who were helping build bridges to the East, and traveled to numerous Asian countries to lecture about psychotherapy. Kelman rejected the classic psychoanalytic formulation of a static self in favor of a holistic, dynamic process view and argued, with respect to the analytic session, for the value and inclusion of altered states, of "flow" states, of "now" moments and nonverbal stillness and silence, and an intersubjective role for the analyst. Kelman also introduced the related mystical notions of "communing" and the "pure fact" of the self, both of which suggested a primordial dimension to the self akin to eastern notions of the same (Kelman, 1958, 1959).

The need to expand and transcend extant psychoanalytic theory may well be due not simply to the meeting of Zen and western psychology, but to the mystical experiences of these innovators. In essence, these author's private mystical experience became part and parcel of their generation of universal, public theory. Maupin, for example, speaks of entering into a 3-month long altered state of "witnessing" upon reading Hubert Benoit's *The Supreme Doctrine* (see Kripal, 2007, pp. 152–153) and Kelman's work is sprinkled with accounts of his trance states (particularly during sports related activity) and unitive encounters with nature. This trend of including personal experience as part of theory-building is hardly new, being amply evident in Freud and Jung. For our purposes, it introduces for the first time the element of personal mystical experience as being part of specifically psychoanalytic responses to Buddhism – an element that has become an indispensable and integral part of contemporary psychoanalytic theorizing about Buddhism.

As was the case with Horney, Fromm and Suzuki, one finds a strong Zen response to this new series of psychoanalytic probes into Buddhism. Paradigmatic representations of these perspectives can be found in the essays of two Japanese psychologists: Koji Sato and Horney's old friend Akihisa Kondo (the latter having become the editor of *Psychologia*). Since the time of Horney both camps had agreed that Zen was "like" psychoanalysis and its evenly-hovering attention in that both dealt with the inner world with detachment, observation, and a nonjudgmental attitude. Both Sato (1968) and Kondo, (1952, 1998) pressed the issue of trying to integrate zazen, breathing exercises and mindfulness into the therapeutic encounter, claiming that Zen techniques could lead to a deeper form of relaxation and access to unconscious material. Kondo, in reintroducing the ontological argument advanced by Suzuki, adamantly proclaimed that Zen intuition was one of the deepest functions of the mind, which was capable of being utilized only by a "well-integrated" personality. It enabled one to gain access to the foundational Reality of the Self, which is in reality a "no-Self" seen as a "simple, ever elastic and fully charged potentiality" (Kondo, 1952, p. 12). The Zen practice of "just sitting" in and of itself allowed this deeper self to emerge. Kondo thought that such a view of the self could well be integrated, along with Zen meditational techniques, into the psychotherapeutic enterprise. He gives the example of a patient in therapy, who had also been meditating, who was concerned with the fact of being an illegitimate child. The therapy progressed to the point that Kondo asked finally asked her: "Who were you before you were an illegitimate child?" The patient burst into tears, exclaiming "I am I! Oh, I am I" (Kondo, 1998, p. 64).

1970–2007 – The Flowering of Dialogue

The socio-cultural atmosphere of this period is characterized by an almost predictable accentuation of trends found in the 50's and 60's. For example, one finds an expansion and increase in sophistication with regard to knowledge of eastern religions due to several factors (e.g., the expansion of departments of comparative studies; widespread representation of eastern traditions from indigenous practitioners; an increase in the Asian social base due to the introduction of liberal immigration policies). Along with the widespread availability of scriptures, more accurate translations and trenchant scholarship, multiple schools within Buddhism and their attendant practices (Theravada, Mahayana, Vajrayana; vipassana/mindfulness, koans, visualizations/mantra) have become subject to analysis. Similarly, one finds that the interest in eastern religions from multiple psychological perspectives (e.g., humanistic, Jungian, transpersonal, and experimental-neurocognitive) has become even more pronounced. With respect to psychoanalysis one finds, in addition to the classic, Neo-Freudian, and ego-psychological models of the previous two periods, liberal use of object-relations theory, Self psychology, and intersubjectivity. Finally, and perhaps most important, the psychoanalytic encounter with Buddhism has been driven by an emerging social base which is psychologically informed and hungry for spiritual nourishment – a trend evinced by the widespread growth of retreat centers, weekend workshops, and local centers touting personal growth. Indeed, one consequence of the "liminal" decade of the 1960s was the emergence of a strong religio-cultural strand characterized by the shift away from traditional religion, belief, ideology and bureaucracy to an unchurched, mystical "religion of no religion" (Kripal, 2007) centered around personal experience. The members of this unchurched, modern form of "spirituality," shying away from institutional religion and its association with authoritarianism, mendacity, and dogmatism, have adopted a more eclectic, supermarket approach to religion, synthesizing a multitude of mental practices and constructing a highly private spirituality which is decidedly psychological and holds to a conception of the Divine as innate and within. This modern spirituality, which some see as part of a long unchurched tradition with its roots in the western past (e.g., Unitarianism, Theosophy, Jungian thought, Mesmerism, Transcendentalism, New Thought) is best framed by the pithy statement: "I'm spiritual, but not religious" (Fuller, 2001). It is very much in accord with what Max Weber referred to as "inner-worldly mysticism." Elaborated further by the sociologist Roland Robertson (1978), the inner-worldly mystic is described as a modern form of adaptation to a culture characterized by the rise of capitalism, individualism, pluralism, and various introspective techniques, many of which influenced the baby-boomer generation. Viewed in the context of the capitalistic ethos, inner-worldly mysticism expresses the need to work "in the world" while striving for wholeness and self-actualization. Therapy, yoga, meditation, dietary and exercise programs, and the individualistic, eclectic supermarket approach to religion are part and parcel of inner-worldly mysticism. As Fuller (2001) notes, empirical studies estimate that up to 21% of the current population have chosen to express their religious sentiments in this unchurched, spiritual manner.

It is apparent that this social base has crept into multiple aspects of the practice of analysts and of the therapeutic expectations of analysands. The training analyst Paul Cooper, for example, thinks that there is an undeniable cultural drift in this direction (Cooper, 1998). He draws attention to the empirical fact that many of his analysands understand psychoanalytic therapy as part of their spiritual growth. He also notes that spiritual practices have influenced multiple dimensions of psychoanalytic therapy (e.g., theory, technique, training, supervision). The training analyst Michael Eigen, particularly influenced by Jewish mysticism and Zen, has referred to psychoanalytic therapy as "a psychospiritual journey," arguing that meditative practices and psychoanalytic therapy are not separate but part of an allied process of growth (Molino, 1998a, p. 225). Indeed, the authors who have penned pivotal psychoanalytic studies of this period (e.g., Jack Engler, Judith Blackstone, Paul Cooper, Mark Epstein, Jeffrey Rubin, Jeremy Safran, Harvey Aronson, Nina Coltart, Mark Finn, Anthony Molino, John Suler) reflect a baby-boomer generation socialized into this religio-cultural base. By their own admission many of these authors became attracted to eastern religions (some have doctorates in the field along with their clinical credentials), went on retreats, integrated meditational practices and mystical experiences into their own therapeutic work, and can be classified as "cultural insiders" insofar as they have first hand knowledge of meditational practices and intimate relationships with multiple masters and gurus of various Buddhist schools. Their theoretical and clinical innovations are based as much on personal experience as familiarity with the wisdom of Buddhism and "mystical" dimensions of various religious traditions. These authors, then, wear more than one therapeutic hat: practicing psychoanalysts (who have been analysands) as well as teachers of Buddhist meditation (who have been students of an assortment of Buddhist masters/gurus). The tension between the two has accounted in no small manner for the theoretical and clinical innovations of this period.

Qualifying what follows below with the often used disclaimer that the richness, nuance and diversity of the developments of this period cannot be fully addressed in the confines of shortened space, such developments can be summarized with respect to a few pivotal themes: (1) culture and context; (2) theoretical innovations; and (3) clinical applications.

Culture and Context

Following in the footsteps of early culture advocates like Kosawa (who argued the case for culturally constituted nuclear complexes), many contemporary authors have explicitly addressed the element of culture in the dialogue between psychoanalysis and Buddhism. There is widespread consensus that the two healing enterprises grew up in a different socio-cultural surround and that any true dialogue cannot dispense with a nuanced "how" with respect to the encounter with the Other. Anthony Molino, for example, opens his book with a definition of dialogue taken from the anthropologist Victor Crapanzano, who emphasizes that dialogue between cultures involves both an "oppositional" and a "transformational" dimension – a tension that means that the term "dialogue" implies ongoing mutual influence, an"ever-evolving text" (Molino, 1998a, p. ix). Harvey Aronson, in asking how one can engage the cultural other in a sensitive, respectful manner, seizes on the observations of the social theorist Richard Shweder, who thinks any encounter with "the other" involves four distinct stages: (1) *Thinking by means of the other*, which obliges us to respect the other to the extent that we recognize that they have harnessed truths unavailable or deeply buried in our own culture; (2) *Getting the other straight*, which necessitates an understanding of the internal logic, worldview, and values of another culture as well as the admission that they are relatively true; (3) *Seeing areas where others may have limitations*, which realizes that other cultures, like our own, are incomplete; and (4) *Being aware of oneself in the context of engagement with the other*, which heightens the self-awareness of how one's own culture operates unconsciously, and sometimes in a prejudicial manner, in the encounter with the Other (Aronson, 2004, pp. 35–37). Jeffrey Rubin, noting that the encounter with the other can alternately provoke the defensiveness associated with feelings of superiority as well as the blinders of idealization, warns of the twin poles of "Orientocentrism" and "Eurocentrism." The former is the overvaluation of the healing benefits of meditation, often to the virtual exclusion of the need for psychoanalysis. Eurocentrism, exemplified in early psychoanalytic studies like that of Franz Alexander, is an unjustified reductive treatment of Buddhism. Any attempt at dialogue must be aware of cultural context and avoid the prejudicial pitfalls of Euro or Oriento centrism (Rubin, 1996).

In dialoguing with the Buddhist Other the theme of culture and context also includes the important issues of nomenclature and translation. In the previous period Herbert Fingarette had noted how badly the term "no-self" had been misunderstood, proceeding to offer a proper ego-psychological rendering of that term. The studies of this period agree with Fingarette. A paradigmatic instance is Harvey Aronson's *Buddhist Practice on Western Ground.* Aronson, going well beyond Fingarette's observation that the tem "no-self" is misunderstood and needs to be properly translated into western therapeutic nomenclature, has written extensively on how central terms of Buddhist discourse like "detachment," "anger" and "desire" have been roundly misunderstood by western practitioners, often leading to defensive rather than liberating behavior. For example, with respect to the central teaching of "detachment," Aronson distinguishes between defensive detachment, which is a form of fixation which distances oneself from others and true introspective change, and engaged nonattachment, which does not exclude healthy relationships and engagement, but does require freedom from fixation, excess, and indulgence. It is the latter and not the former, thinks Aronson, which is more faithful to Buddhist teaching (Aronson, 2004, pp. 151–183). The problem is that Buddhist teachers, unaware of the ways in which a teaching may be understood by their western students, as well as the students themselves, some of whom may be looking for religious affirmations of their proclivity to avoid their inner world and problematic relations with others, often collude, if unconsciously, to produce failures in the transmission of teaching.

Theoretical Innovations

If the studies of this period claim that Buddhism is a culturally situated healing enterprise with distinct models of the mind and therapeutic practices, then the next question needing articulation is how to synthesize psychoanalysis and Buddhism. Freud, Alexander and most of the studies of the early period were involved in reductive exercises. Most of the studies of the contemporary period do not exclude the notion that the adherents of Buddhism and its practices exhibit behavior, as is true of any healing enterprise, which can be classified as symptomatic, pathological, and defensive. Jack Engler (1986) for example, notes how teachings like anatta (i.e., no-self) can be used (especially for adolescents and those entering middle-age) to ward off the burden of creating an adaptive identity and rationalize the lack of self-esteem and feelings of emptiness; of how the notion of enlightenment can be cathected narcissistically to cater to the needs of archaic forms of grandiosity; and how student-teacher relationships, transported to western cultural soil, activate debilitating mirroring and idealizing forms of transference. Suler (1993) sees those drawn to meditation as evincing a host of psychological problems, ranging from a fear of autonomy and refusal to assume adult responsibility to issues concerning incapacity for intimacy and passivity/dependency needs.

Joe Sun Tom and most of the studies of the middle period saw Buddhism as a cultural variant of psychoanalysis, an adaptive reading of Buddhism, which presumes that some forms of psychological structure are universal even if the cultural expression of any given healing enterprise is relative. The studies of this period, although more aware of the need for awareness of cultural context and sensitive to issues of distortion than previous periods, also see Buddhism as an adaptive project engaging oedipal and narcissistic themes. Paradigmatic in this sense is the work of Mark Finn (2003) who sees in the texts of Buddhism a culturally disguised rendition of central concepts in the history of psychoanalysis: Oedipus, transitional space, transference. Nina Coltart, who thinks psychoanalysis and Buddhism are "mutually enlightening and potentiating" observes that both processes involve disillusionment and mourning, specifically with respect to dismantling the Winnicottian "false self" (Coltart, 1996, p. 128). Suler (1993) thinks that Buddhist practices are regressions which serve to enhance a healthy, cohesive self.

But what truly distinguishes the studies of this period from those of the others lies in the acknowledgement that Buddhist practice is not simply therapeutic but soteriological; that Buddhism catalogs experiences and states that are outside the borders of existing psychoanalytic theory. How the latter is to be understood and synthesized with psychoanalysis into a more inclusive healing enterprise which is clearly an expansion of psychoanalytic theory yet also different from any existing form of Buddhism then becomes the task at hand. The simplest illustration of the converge of psychoanalysis and a Buddhism that "goes beyond" lies in the early work of Jack Engler (1986), who proposes that psychoanalysis and Buddhism map discrete states of a single developmental sequence, the former describing the lower stages of "conventional" development, the latter the more subtle, spiritual stages of "contemplative" development. In speaking to how these stages relate, Engler is not without recourse to the more pathological treatment of Buddhism, noting that mystical therapies like Buddhism can attract and even exacerbate the condition of those with self-disorders. Such persons are not yet ready for the rigors of meditative life – they are better off with psychoanalytic therapies, which seek to help them "grow" a self. Once a cohesive enough self has developed, one can then engage in meditational exercises designed to gain insight into the reality that there is no enduring self, hence the phrase: "You have to be somebody before you are nobody." The two healing systems, then, are seen to have different aims: psychoanalysis aims to grow a cohesive self while Buddhism aims to realize there is no self. Drawing on studies of meditation which explain how the heightened state of attention and concentration available to meditators allow them to retrace the representational process whereby a sense of self and other come to exist, Engler claims that the insight into no-self literally breaks apart the underlying continuity of self:

> Discovering that there is no ontological core to consciousness or self that is independent and enduring and no stable "objects" of perception (...) no "I" or "thing" enduring across the gap between one construction and arising of the next – this is a profound shock. It is experienced as a free fall into a looking-glass world where, as the Mad Hatter tells Alice, "Things are not as they seem!" It so turns our normal sense of self and reality on its head that, as Niels Bohr once remarked about quantum physics (...) if you don't get dizzy thinking about it, you haven't understood it. (Engler, 2003b, pp. 92–93)

This insight is so profound that it entails an end to suffering altogether – a state, Engler observes, which Freud, and psychoanalysis in general, views as an "ideal fiction." Engler is quick to point out that the insight into anatta is not necessarily a discovery. From the Buddhist perspective, the common-sense understanding that an enduring self exists is an illusion. Indeed, Engler proposes the radical claim that the construction of a separate, enduring continuous self is "a compromise formation with defensive aims" (Engler, 2003b, p. 87). We repress the fact of an unconstructed non-core to existence. If the therapeutic task can be conceived along the lines of mourning, the psychoanalytic encounter with Buddhism now reveals the need to work-through an even deeper level of mourning: that of the existence of a continuous, stable, enduring self. Mark Epstein echoes Engler (apparent in the title of his book *Thoughts without a Thinker*) in suggesting that "Buddhism was articulating a vision of the psyche freed from narcissism" (Epstein, 1995, p. 41) and that we "repress" the insubstantiality of the Self (ibid., p. 48). Epstein argues that the entire ego is not transcended – only the representational components are seen as lacking in any real existence – ego functions (observation, critical thought, recognition and awareness of truth) all remain.

Engler (2003a) has since modified the notion of discrete, hierarchically ordered stages of development noting, via evidence from Rorschach tests, case histories, detailed observations from within American Buddhist communities and anecdotal evidence, that some Buddhist "masters" have exhibited forms of defensiveness and pathology. Subsequent commentators agree, noting that the relation between conventional and contemplative lines of development is complicated and perhaps too thick to untangle. Jeff Rubin, for example, thinks Engler's earlier efforts amount to a "pseudo-complimentary" approach in which "the complexity and multidimensionality of human experience and development is obscured by linear, hierarchical, developmental models" (Rubin, 1996, p. 49). Rather, Rubin argues that the relation between psychoanalysis and Buddhism "is more complex than the existing accounts suggest, forming not a singular pattern of influence but rather resembling a heterogeneous mosaic composed of elements that are – depending on the specific topic – antithetical, complementary and synergistic" (ibid., p. 51). By "synergy" Rubin means that psychoanalysis can help Buddhism investigate unconscious determinants, idealizing transferences, life-cycle difficulties and the like, while Buddhism can help psychoanalysis with non-self centered subjective states and meditational techniques. "Non-self centered subjective states" [e.g., being in love, art, flow states, meditative absorption] are defined as being "open to the moment without a sense of time, unselfconsciousness but acutely aware, highly focused and engaged yet related without fear [...] characterized by heightened attentiveness, focus and clarity, attunement to the other as well as the self, non-self preoccupied exercise of agency, a sense of unity" (p. 69). The view of personhood of psychoanalysis and Buddhism respectively are not better than one another. Rather, they can be mutually enriching: they are "alternating positions of being rather than hierarchically ordered stages" (p. 75). The melding together of psychoanalysis and Buddhism can lead to "a bifocal conception of subjectivity." Rubin sees a new self emerging – a "species-self [...] for whom both individuation and non-self centricity are seen as two interpenetrating facets of what it means to be a human being" (p. 197).

Alternate formulations of the insight into non-self states and their implications for therapeutic trajectories abound. John Suler, for example, formulates non-self states as being close to Bion's notion of "O" ("the archetypic condition of disintegration and catastrophe which underlies being" [Suler, 1993, p. 66]) while Paul Cooper, banking off Ignacio Matte-Blanco's revisionist formulations of the unconscious, argues that Buddhist meditation unearths the deepest dimensions of the unconscious, characterized as the "indivisible mode" where total symmetry prevails: "like Alice in Wonderland" (Cooper, 2000, p. 61). Judith Blackstone (2007) on the other hand, engages Tibetan Buddhist formulations of non-self states and their relation to conceptions of self-other found in intersubjective theory. Blackstone chooses intersubjective theory because it seeks to undermine the illusory distinctions between therapist and client, cognition and affect. She applauds the notion that the therapeutic project is always mutual, involving the interface of reciprocal interacting subjectivities, with the aim of gaining a more flexible and functional organization of personality. However, contra intersubjective theory, Buddhism claims there is a nonorganized self-existing nondual ground which is the basis of all subjectivities and which can be experienced in meditation. It is the experience not of the contents of consciousness but of consciousness itself: an unmodified dimension of subjectivity beyond the self-representations addressed by psychoanalysis. This deep field of nondual consciousness slowly becomes more apparent as we deconstruct the obstacles which keep it from manifesting itself. Psychoanalysis helps this process along, for it deconstructs unconsciously held patterns of behavior and helps us develop more flexible organizations of self. As we do this, the more essential nondual field of consciousness begins to naturally emerge. So while the intersubjective goal of an "expanded repertoire of organizing principles" is not enough, being "far from the spontaneity, openness, and directedness of experience that occurs with nondual realizations" (Blackstone, 2007, p. 29), psychoanalysis can be "reconfigured" to aid in the task of deconstructing the "obscurations" that impede the manifestation of nondual consciousness.

Clinical Applications

In line with earlier theorists like Horney and Fromm, there is general agreement that Buddhist meditation is at the very least a beneficial adjunct to psychoanalytic therapy. One finds that case history material is the rule rather than the exception, and there exist detailed explanations of the various functions meditation plays in the healing enterprise for both the analyst and the analysand. The soteriological aim of Buddhist practice is acknowledged if not affirmed. Mark Epstein, for example, acknowledges that something in Buddhism "reaches beyond therapy, toward a farther horizon of self-understanding that is not ordinarily accessible through psychotherapy alone" (Epstein, 1995, p. 130). Meditation permeates the inner world so thoroughly that "no aspect remains available for narcissistic recruitment" (ibid., p.134). Epstein goes on to speak of how jnana forms of meditation expand the spatial view of self and can lead to nonpathological oceanic experiences. Mindfulness, the practice of "bare attention," deals with temporality, allowing us to be in the moment with fluidity, spontaneity and "flow." He even acknowledges how Buddhism in its more extreme forms can lead to the cessation of suffering altogether. Vipassana gets us to explode the notion of a substantial self – that is, of emptiness. Self is seen to be "a metaphor for a process we do not understand, a metaphor for that which knows (...) It is enough (...) to open to the ongoing process of knowing without imputing someone behind it all" (p. 155). For Epstein Buddhism goes farther than psychoanalysis by asking who the "I" is behind feelings of narcissistic emptiness and rage. In asking us to acknowledge the relativity of the narcissistic emotions it lessens the import and centrality of such feelings. The shift from identifying with reactive emotions to looking at the foundational "I" which lies behind those feelings and is often identified with it "... is the most important contribution Buddhism has to offer to the world of psychotherapy" (p. 220).

On the other hand, if Buddhist practice is generally seen by these authors as being more conducive to the more extreme forms of insight into emptiness, there is also general agreement that psychoanalysis has a better grasp of the origins, subtleties and vicissitudes of developmentally based behavioral patterns. Particularly with respect to deep, narcissistic deficiencies (e.g., Balint's "basic fault," Kohut's archaic structures of narcissism) it is psychoanalytic therapy, and not Buddhist teaching and practice, which is the superior healing enterprise. However, if one puts the two extremes of accessing anatta and treating severe narcissistic disorders aside, the major studies of this period mostly focus on the integration of psychoanalytic and Buddhist practice, and on how the practice of mindfulness helps the traditionally conceived analytic process move forward. Along these lines it is relevant to note that the patients who are the subjects of case histories are part of the normal set of analysands who happen to meditate and not enlightened masters of the tradition.

One focus of inquiry is how the practice of meditation (mindfulness, vipassana, jnana) affects the analysand in both positive and negative ways. Epstein (1995) conceptualizes the benefits of meditation as falling along the traditional Freudian conception of the analytic process as consisting of "remembering, repeating, and working through." The key is the development of an internal atmosphere of calm and of strengthening the ego's capacities of observation and concentration. Cultivating the internal atmosphere of "holding" emotions, of the move from "emotional reactivity" to "nonjudgmental awareness," creates the space necessary to allow remembering and working through to work. It can even facilitate the memory of deep hurts like Balint's basic fault, although traditional psychoanalytic therapy is recognized as being better equipped to heal it. Several case histories (e.g., Rubin, 1996; Cooper, 1999; Engler, 1986) detail how meditation facilitates free association and access to unconscious content, and how it has multiple constructive and destructive functions in therapy. Meditation can lead to a reduction in self-recrimination, deautomatized states, an increased ability to be reflective and manage affect, an increased awareness of habitual patterns of behavior, and aid in the deconstruction of self-representations and "false-self" orientations. But it can also be used in the service of defensiveness, justify a lack of assertive behavior, activate depersonalized states, and exacerbate self-disorders with its aims of perfection, detachment, and passivity. Meditation can be further problematic, if not utilized with psychoanalytic therapy, if unearthed unconscious content is simply observed (as meditation advises) and not worked-through.

With respect to the position of the analyst, multiple studies agree that meditation can cultivate the capacity for self-observation, increase empathy, listening skills and evenly-hovering attention, further helping one become more sensitive to transference and countertransference issues and the value of altered states in the analytic session. In describing this heightened state of awareness, attention, and empathy, Nina Coltart relies on Bion's concept of "O," described as "a state which I see as being "unthought-out" involving a quality of intuitive apperception of another person's evolving truth" (Coltart in Molino, 1998b, p. 177). Epstein (1995) agrees, noting the value of Bion's advocacy of being in the therapeutic encounter without "memory," "desire" or preconceptions, simply letting the "now" of the session unfold.

Concluding Reflections

Within contemporary academia the term "religion," while understood to be necessary and functionally useful, has nevertheless been subject to intense scrutiny and debate. There are notable figures who have uncovered the term's hidden assumptions, fought for its qualification, offered substitutions, even called for its dismissal (Smith, 1963). In any event, when Freud wrote about religion, he entered these debates in a clear and forthright manner. For him the only "deserving" definition was the "common's man's" understanding of religion – an understanding which was western, assumed institutionalized patriarchal forms of socio-cultural power, and whose normative expression was centered in the monotheistic "mighty personality" of an exalted Father-God. In *The Future of an Illusion* he defiantly chastised those "philosophers" who tried to "stretch the meaning of words" to the point that words like "God" and "religious" ceased to bear any resemblance to the Being worshipped by the common-man (Freud, 1927/1964). The sociologist Philip Rieff, who has taken a sustained interest in the success of psychoanalysis, suggests a peculiarly Weberian line of reasoning as to why psychoanalysis, and its critique of religion, was so successful. As is well known, Weber cast the world Catholicism built as magical and enchanted, populated by a host of saintly intermediaries to God. The latter, alongside the church and confessional, gave the believer a psychological release from guilt and anxiety over salvation. The emergence of the Protestant tradition and its attendant social type, the inner-worldly ascetic, sheared the world of such magical releases (Weber, 1958). Faced with the twin theological doctrines of predestination and salvation, with only scripture and conscience as conduits to God, the Protestant, more anxious, and guilty relative to his fellow Catholic, was particularly ripe for psychoanalytic therapy. The success and widespread appeal of Freud was in part due to the ability of his psychology, whose theory and practice focused on the *uber-ich*, guilt and anxiety, to address the psychological world of the inner-worldly ascetic. Culturally speaking, then, classic Freudian psychoanalysis fits hand-in-glove with inner-worldly asceticism (Rieff, 1990). In this regard it is relevant to note that while Catholics and those believers in other religious traditions, as well as their scholarly representatives (e.g., Hans Kung, Mircea Eliade) took to dialogue with psychoanalysis, the most creative, popular, and powerful form of the dialogue between depth-psychology and religion during the mid-twentieth century was that between psychoanalysis and Protestant theology, the predominant issues being the nature of sin, determinism, freedom, guilt and the "heteronomous" God (Jonte-Pace and Parsons, 2001).

This essay has argued that the driving engine behind the encounter between psychoanalysis and Buddhism is, sociologically speaking, that social base comprised of what Weber called inner-worldly mysticism. The term which best characterizes the orientation of this base is "spirituality." While most evident in the last few decades, one can argue that the unchurched, eclectic, psychological and mystical characteristics of spirituality are present not only in the figure of Romain Rolland but also in the dominant figures of the immediate post-war period. Indeed, one could say that the majority of the studies of the contemporary period deserve to be labeled as part of an emerging "psychoanalytic spirituality" (Parsons, 2007). Insofar as the driving social base behind the psychoanalytic encounter with Buddhism does not seem to be diminishing, one can continue to look forward to an increased sophistication in dialogue between these two related healing enterprises.

Bibliography

Alexander, F. (1931). Buddhistic training as an artificial catatonia. *Psychoanalytic Review, 18*(2), 129–141.

Aronson, H. (2004). *Buddhist practice on western ground*. Boston, MA: Shambhala.

Blackstone, J. (2007). *The empathic ground: Intersubjectivity and nonduality in the psychotherapeutic process*. Albany, NY: State University Press of New York.

Blowers, G. H. & Chi, S. Y. H. (1997). Freud's Deshi: The coming of psychoanalysis to Japan. *Journal of the History of the Behavioral Sciences, 33*(2), 115–126.

Boss, M. (1965). *A psychiatrist looks at India*. London: Wolff.

Clarke, J. J. (1997). *Oriental Enlightenment*. London: Routledge.

Coltart, N. (1996). *The Baby and the Bathwater*. Madison, CT: International Universities Press.

Cooper, P. (1998). The disavowal of the spirit: Integration and wholeness in Buddhism and psychoanalysis. In A. Molino (Ed.), *The couch and the tree* (pp. 231–246). New York: North Point.

Cooper, P. (1999). Buddhist meditation and countertransference: A case study. *American Journal of Psychoanalysis, 59*(1), 71–86.

Cooper, P. (2000). Unconscious processes: Zen and psychoanalytic versions. *Journal of Religion and Health, 39*(1), 57–69.

Eigen, M. (1998). One Reality. In A. Molino (Ed.), *The couch and the tree* (pp. 217–230). New York: North Point.

Engler, J. (1986). Therapeutic aims in psychotherapy and Buddhism. In K. Wilber, J. Engler & D. Brown (Eds.), *Transformations of consciousness* (pp. 17–52). Boston, MA: Shambhala.

Engler, J. (2003a). Being somebody and being nobody: A reexamination of the understanding of self in psychoanalysis and Buddhism. In J. Safran (Ed.), *Psychoanalysis and Buddhism* (pp. 35–80). Boston, MA: Wisdom.

Engler, J. (2003b). Reply: Can we say what the self 'really' is? In J. Safran (Ed.), *Psychoanalysis and Buddhism* (pp. 86–100). Boston, MA: Wisdom.

Epstein, M. (1995). *Thoughts without a thinker*. New York: Basic Books.

Erikson, E. H. (1956/1962). *Young Man Luther*. New York: Norton.

Evans-Wentz, W. Y. (Ed.) (1960). *The Tibetan Book of the Dead*. London: Oxford University Press.

Fields, R. (1992). *How the swans came to the lake*. Boston, MA: Shambhala.

Finn, M. (2003). Tibetan Buddhism and a mystical psychoanalysis. In J. Safran (Ed.), *Psychoanalysis and Buddhism* (pp. 101–114). Boston, MA: Wisdom.

Fingarette, H. (1965). *The self in transformation*. New York: Harper & Row.

Freud, S. (1927/1964). The future of an illusion. In J. Strachey (Ed.), *The standard edition of the complete psychological works of Sigmund Freud. Vol. 21* (pp. 5–57). London: Hogarth.

Fromm, E., Suzuki, D. T., & Martino, R. de (1960). *Psychoanalysis and Zen Buddhism*. New York: Harper.

Fuller, R. (2001). *Spiritual but not religious*. New York: Oxford.

Horney, K. (1998). Free associations and the use of the couch. In A. Molino (Ed.), *The couch and the tree* (pp. 35–36). New York: North Point.

Jonte-Pace, D. & Parsons, W.B. (Eds.) (2001). *Religion and psychology: Mapping the terrain*. New York: Routledge.

Kelman, H. (1958). Communing and relating, Part 1. Past and current perspectives. *American Journal of Psychoanalysis*, *18*(1), 77–98.
Kelman, H. (1959). Communing and relating, Part 3. Examples: General and clinical. *American Journal of Psychoanalysis*, *19*(1), 73–97.
Kondo, A. (1952). Intuition in Zen Buddhism. *American Journal of Psychoanalysis*, *12*, 10–14.
Kondo, A. (1998). Zen in psychotherapy: The virtue of just sitting. In A. Molino (Ed.), *The couch and the tree* (pp. 58–64). New York: North Point.
Kripal, J. (2007). *Esalen: America and the religion of no religion*. Chicago, IL: The University of Chicago Press.
Lewin, B. (1961). *The psychoanalysis of elation*. London: Hogarth Press.
Masson, J. (1980). *The oceanic feeling*. Dordrecht: Reidel.
Masson, J. (1984). *The assualt on truth*. New York: Farrar, Straus & Giroux.
Maupin, E. (1962). Zen Buddhism: A psychological review. *Journal of Consulting Psychology*, *26*(4), 362–378.
Meckel, D. & Moore, R. (Eds.) (1992). *Self and Liberation*. Mahweh, NJ: Paulist Press.
Molino, A. (1998a). *The couch and the tree*. New York: North Point Press.
Molino, A. (1998b). Slouching towards Buddhism: A conversation with Nina Coltart. In A. Molino (Ed.), *The couch and the tree* (pp. 170–182). New York: North Point.
Morel, F. (1918). *Essai sur l'introversion mystique*. Geneva: Albert Kundig.
Morvay, Z. (1999). Horney, Zen and the real self: Theoretical and historical considerations. *American Journal of Psychoanalysis*, *59*(1), 25–35.
Müller, M. (1897–1910). *The Sacred Books of the East*. Oxford: Clarendon Press.
Nauriyal, D. K., Drummond, D. S., & Lal, Y. B. (2006). *Buddhist thought and applied psychological research*. New York: Routledge.
Otto, R. (1926/1932). *Mysticism East and West*. London: Macmillian.
Parsons, W. B. (1999). *The enigma of the oceanic feeling*. New York: Oxford.
Parsons, W. B. (2001). Themes and debates in the psychology-comparativist dialogue. In D. Jonte-Pace & W. B. Parsons (Eds.), *Religion and psychology: Mapping the terrain* (pp. 229–253). New York: Routledge.
Parsons, W. B. (2007). Psychoanalytic spirituality. In J. Winer & J. Anderson (Eds.), *Spirituality and religion: Psychoanalytic perspectives* (pp. 83–97). Catskill, NY: Mental Health Resources.
Rieff, P. (1990). *The feeling intellect*. Chicago, IL: The University of Chicago Press.
Robertson, R. (1978). *Meaning and change*. New York: New York University Press.
Roland, A. (1988). *In search of self in India and Japan*. Princeton, NJ: Princeton.
Rubin, J. (1996). *Psychotherapy and Buddhism*. New York: Plenum Press.
Sato, K. (1968). Zen from a personological viewpoint. *Psychologia*, *11*, 3–24.
Schjelderup, H. & Schjeldrup, K. (1932). *Über drei Haupttypen der religiösen Erlebnisformen und ihre psychologische Grundlage*. Berlin: De Gruyter.
Schwab, R. (1984). *The oriental Renaissance: Europe's rediscovery of India and the East, 1680–1880*. (trans. G. Patterson-Black & V. Reinking). New York: Columbia.
Sharf, R. (1995). The Zen of Japanese nationalism. In D. Lopez (Ed.), *Curators of the Buddha: The study of Buddhism under Colonialism* (pp. 107–161). Chicago, IL: University of Chicago Press.
Smith, W. C. (1963). *The meaning and end of religion: A new approach to the religious traditions of mankind*. New York: Macmillan.
Suler, J. (1993). *Contemporary psychoanalysis and eastern thought*. Albany, NY: State University Press of New York.
Sun, J. T. (1924/1998). Psychology in primitive Buddhism. In A. Molino (Ed.), *The couch and the tree* (pp. 3–11). New York: North Point.
Suzuki, D. T. (1964). *Introduction to Buddhism*. New York: Grove Press.
Tweed, T. (1992). *The American encounter with Buddhism, 1844–1912: Victorian culture and the limits of dissent*. Bloomington, IN: Indiana University Press.
Tweed, T. & Prothero, S. (1999). *Asian religions in America*. New York: Oxford University Press.

Vaidyanathan, V. J. & Kripal, J. (Eds.) (1999). *Vishnu on Freud's desk*. Delhi: Oxford University Press.

Vermorel, H. & Vermorel, M. (1993). *Sigmund Freud et Romain Rolland: Correspondance 1923–1936*. Paris: Presses Universitaires de France.

Versluis, A. (1993). *American transcendentalism and Asian religions*. New York: Oxford University Press.

Weber, M. (1958). *The Protestant ethic and the spirit of capitalism*. New York: Scribner.

Westcott, M. (1998). Horney, Zen and the real self. *The American Journal of Psychoanalysis*, 58(3), 287–301.

Hinduism and Psychoanalysis

Encounters at the Crossroads of Psyche, Culture and the Religious

Daniel J. Meckel*

Dimensions of the Encounter

Students of psychoanalysis and Hinduism alike recoil from any monolithic characterization of their subject area. Those familiar with *the* psychoanalytic tradition know it to embody multiple and often contradictory perspectives and techniques; those who study "Hinduism" know that its great and diverse histories leave scholars puzzling over its unity – the very name of "Hinduism" was imposed by outsiders upon India's vast array of people and religious traditions. Indeed the encounter of Hinduism and psychoanalysis, not even 100 years old, has itself many incarnations – too many to address in a single overview, so at the outset of this historical essay I must limit my focus to certain realms of the encounter and trust that to explore any one will afford some sense of the whole.[1]

I will consider a handful of theories that have defined the historical course of the psychoanalytic study of Hindus and Hinduism. These theories reflect the major emergent perspectives within psychoanalysis – classical and Kleinian models, object relations theories and the psychologies of the self – and certain corresponding and salient issues – Oedipal dynamics and Hindu sons, the nature of self and ego in cultural context, and the place of genuine mystical experience within psychic processes. As a way of characterizing and evaluating the plurality of approaches in

* I wish to thank Ana-María Rizzuto and Heinz Henseler for their close critical readings of the initial version of this paper. Thanks also to Michael Carroll, James DiCenso, Diane Jonte-Pace, Dan Merkur, Bill Parsons, Edward Shafranske, Jeffrey Kripal, Bradley Park and Jacob Belzen for their thoughtful comments.

[1] To piece together a more comprehensive history of Hindu-psychoanalytic encounters, see Akhtar (2001, 2005), Kripal (1999, 2000), Parsons (1999, 2000). The present essay draws inspiration from each of these works though I am especially indebted to Akhtar for his informative and insightful work on the history of psychoanalysis in India.

D.J. Meckel
St. Mary's College of Maryland, St. Mary's City, MD, USA
e-mail: djmeckel@smcm.edu

the psychoanalytic study of Hindus, I suggest that it is useful to be mindful of three hermeneutics that are engaged, in varying measure and context, within *all* psychoanalytic thinking. I refer to them in this paper as "dimensions" because they signify distinct forms of analysis or interpretation that are found within any single psychoanalytic study of Hinduism, and because each one privileges a different dimension of human nature; one stressing the universal machinations of psyche, another the interpretive and imaginative processes of meaning-making, and another the influence of ultimate and irreducible realities to which I refer here as the "mystical" or "religious."[2] Allow me to name and define each dimension briefly.

The *explanatory-reductive dimension* includes naturalistic and causal accounts of experience and behavior based on assumptions of universal features of the human psyche, described in such terms as a dynamic unconscious, biological drives, internalization, self-structure, projection, etc. The *cultural-interpretive dimension* includes efforts to think through the worldviews of others, assuming that human beings must be understood in light of their activities and capacities as meaning-makers – interpretive beings who engage and construct the world imaginatively through the fluid symbolic media of given cultures. The *religious-integrative dimension* acknowledges ultimate and/or sacred realities which inform human psychical life. It maintains critical receptivity to others' notions of such realties and strives through dialogue to integrate aspects of these realities into a theory of mind.[3]

It is clear that classical drive theory privileges explanatory-reductive thinking, while its cultural-interpretive assumptions are less obvious (see Ricoeur, 1974, 1970). Post-Freudian object relations theories, from Klein to the present, offer structural theories of psyche (explanatory-reductive) but stress intersubjectivity and so grant more significance to cultural-interpretive processes in psychical life (see Kakar, 1985). Perhaps it is least obvious that all major psychoanalytic thinkers have integrated religious or quasi-religious ideas in their thinking, in that all work with more or less implicit assumptions of ultimacy (see Browning, 1987).

[2] My orientation draws from the field of Religion and Psychological Studies and reflects its interdisciplinary concern to relate and integrate explanatory, interpretive, and religious (or quasi-religious) approaches to the mind. As a sub-discipline of religious studies, Religion and Psychological Studies emerged in the 1950s from the engagement of Jewish and Christian perspectives with the twentieth century psychologies. The field has became increasingly responsive to the engagement of non-western traditions with the psychologies (and neuroscience).

[3] I intend for these hermeneutical categories to be recognizable to anyone familiar with the history of the psychoanalysis of religion, and to help focus my essay on the ways in which psychoanalytic thinking is (or isn't) responsive to Hindu cultural and religious diversity. For insightful considerations of this question within a broader treatment of the encounters between psychoanalysis and religion in the field of Religion and Psychological Studies, particularly with respect to the mystical traditions, see the work of William Parsons (1999). Parsons' categories of "classical", "adaptive" and "transformational" inform my own hermeneutical triad but differ in certain respects. Specifically, his category of the adaptive refers to a given theory's implicit assessment of the adaptive value of religious life, whereas here my dimension of cultural-interpretive applies to thinking that privileges interpretation in mental life and assumes that psychical organization is in significant measure culturally relative. Also informing the present essay is Jeffrey Kripal's (1999) characterization of the Hindu-psychoanalysis encounter, which is organized according to Richard Shweder's (1991) typology of "thinking through cultures."

I turn now to the psychoanalytic study of Hinduism, from Freud to the present, to explore the ways in which a set of influential ideas have explained, interpreted, and drawn inspiration from Hindu lives. I move roughly in chronological order through three kinds of studies, punctuating each with a brief case study or "interlude" drawn from my own ethnographic or clinical work, for the purpose of illustrating and problematizing the issues and approaches described here.

Foundational Studies: Ganesha and the Castrated Hindu Son

It is best to start with Lord Ganesha – the pot-bellied, effeminate and elephant-headed Hindu god who is, in fact, the Lord of Beginnings. An abundance of scholarly reflection from within and outside the disciplines of psychoanalysis addresses the deep psychological significance of the Ganesha mythology.[4] These myths are replete with unmistakeably oedipal themes such as violent confrontation with the father, competition and conflict with the brother, erotically charged adoration of the mother, and yes, castration. In one popular narrative, Ganesha competes with his virile brother Skanda for mother Parvati's affections and the promised reward of a mango. The competition is a race around the universe. Skanda sets off on his peacock vehicle, which is far swifter than Ganesha's tiny mouse. Skanda quickly circles the entire cosmos but finds that he is nevertheless defeated by his brother. This is because Ganesha, whose mother is his universe, circles only her. In doing so, Ganesha pleases Parvati exceedingly and so wins his mother's mango. When Skanda challenges him for it, Ganesha bites into the mango, breaking off one of his tusks. In another well known myth, Ganesha confronts his powerful father, Lord Shiva. Having been created by Parvati from the dirt of her own body, Ganesha stands guard over the entryway to her inner chamber. When Shiva returns and attempts to enter, father and son are entirely unaware of one another's identity. Ganesha refuses entry to his father and in response Shiva decapitates him. When Parvati responds with fury, Lord Shiva restores the boy with the head of an elephant, complete with trunk.

Classical psychoanalytic readings of this particular Ganesha narrative plunge headlong into the realms of murderous oedipal hatred, precarious immersion in the mother, and searing unconscious fears of paternal retribution. Ganesha represents the pre-oedipal Hindu boy whose profound and problematic immersion in the mother leaves him unable to navigate the realm of the father and, by extension, of all male authority. So he remains ever in maternal orbit and submits wholly to father, offering up his masculinity. Accordingly, foundational psychoanalytic studies of India establish castration, maternal identification, and subservience as the hallmarks of the Hindu male psyche. And yet, it is significant that the very first

[4] Psychoanalytically attuned anthropologists, Indologists and historians of religion have long recognized Oedipal dimensions of the tales of Ganesha. See Courtright (1985), Goldman (1978), Ingham (1996), Kakar (1978), Leach (1972), Obeyesekere (1990), O'Flaherty (1973).

Indian pioneer in the psychoanalytic study of Hinduism *revises* psychoanalysis to such an extent as to render Oedipus unrecognizable; that is, by non-Indians.

Girindrashekhar Bose (1886–1953) is the "mother and father" of psychoanalysis in India. From the state of Bihar, he trained as a physician at Calcutta Medical College, graduated in 1917, and later received the Doctor of Science degree in psychology, the first such degree to be awarded in India. In 1921 he founded the Indian Psychoanalytic Society and published his book *Concept of Repression* (1921). Bose' revisionist ideas, put forth in this fascinating work, were the initial focus of a longstanding correspondence with Freud himself, extending from 1921 to 1937. Note that Bose' early psychoanalytic activities and his definitive writing occurred before the correspondence, thus the earliest psychoanalytic ideas to emerge within India did so independently of Freud's direct personal influence. The result, writes psychoanalyst Salman Akhtar, was an *Indianized* psychoanalysis.

> Interestingly, Bose, while highly influenced by Freud's theories, had actually created an Indian psychoanalysis with separate, distinct theoretical notions. He was committed to the integration of traditional Indian philosophy with the Western notion of unconscious processes. (Akhtar, 2005, p. 8)

In this "Indian psychoanalysis," Bose defined the nature of the wish in intersubjective terms and stressed identification with a *truly perceived* other as a fundamental psychical aim (ibid., pp. 4–5). He developed a theory of opposite wishes, according to which any given conscious wish will always have its unconscious opposite. The desire to love, for example, is accompanied by a desire to be loved, the wish to harm by a desire to be harmed (ibid., p. 4). The conflict between two simultaneous and opposite wishes is pathogenic but can be resolved when the unconscious wish is satisfied through identification with an object (i.e., a real person) demonstrating the same wish. In this process of identification (which, as Akhtar notes, anticipates aspects of later relational theories), the true subjectivity of another is apprehended. In addition to these innovations, Bose revised and relativized the theory of the Oedipus complex, based on a conception of a multi-layered and dual-gendered psyche. In "The Genesis and Adjustment of the Oedipus Wish," he claims boldly that normal male development in Indians *does not* produce Oedipal hatred or castration anxiety. Instead, it entails normal identification with the mother and an unconscious desire to be female and bear a child by the father.

Considered in light of the hermeneutic dimensions outlined above, this early appropriation of psychoanalysis in India exhibits *all three dimensions*. Bose' revised psychoanalysis is an explanatory-reductive framework that, he felt, was uniquely suited to Indian patients. Thus he recognized fundamental differences in psychic functioning attributable to cultural differences. Further, his theoretical notions of the intersubjectivity of desire and the developmental aim of true object relations clearly reveal a religious-integrative dimension of his work – they are firmly rooted in a Hindu worldview. Historian Christiane Hartnack (1999) reports that Bose studied Sanskrit texts for their psychological theories and consulted Hindu *pandits* in his efforts to understand those theories. He wrote several essays on traditional Hindu psychology and published his own translation of Patanajli's *Yoga Sutras*. In keeping with his own Hindu intellectual heritage, Bose believed that the individual is not *in essence* separate from others; nor is he fundamentally conflicted, internally or in relation to the outside world. Instead, writes Hartnack, Bose saw the individual as "potentially united with other human beings, animals, plants, and nature" (1999, p. 87). These psychoanalytic perspectives are fully intelligible only within a Hindu framework.

How did Freud respond to Bose and his reformulations? One might characterize his response with reference to a gift that Bose sent to Vienna in 1931 on the occasion of Freud's 75th birthday – a small statue of Lord Vishnu, made of wood and ivory. The statue took its place on Freud's desk among the growing collection of tiny antiquities that he would occasionally contemplate as he worked. From an optimistic and dialogical point of view, one might be tempted to see this curious scenario of Vishnu standing before Freud (while the latter composes some of the foundational texts of psychoanalysis) as the beginning of a conversation that would evolve in time into true dialogue. From a less optimistic point of view, one might recognize that the Hindu deity was grouped with a collection of unlikely desk-mates from around the world and, with them, stood for Freud as merely another emblem of the universal, instinctual life of the psyche.

Freud offered warm appreciation to Bose for the gift, saying in a letter that the statue would assume "a place of honor on my desk." He then added that "As long as I can enjoy life it will recall to my mind the progress of Psychoanalysis [,] the proud conquests it has made in foreign countries ..." (Ramana, 1964). This response illustrates Freud's primary interest in Bose' work. He was moved by the expansion of psychoanalytic ideas into South Asia, yet entirely unmoved by any of Bose' revisions. As Hartnack concludes, "in the end, Freud remained disinterested in true intercultural exchange that went beyond a confirmation of his own expansionist strivings" (1999, p. 101). For the purposes of the larger psychoanalytic enterprise, the first glimmerings of dialogue and theoretical reformulation based on the cultural-interpretive sensibilities of Girindrashekhar Bose were soundly ignored, and would be for decades to come.

From around the time of the establishment of the Indian Psychoanalytic Society and its affiliation with the International Psychoanalytic Association (begun in 1922 with the help of Ernest Jones), small numbers of Indian analysts in Calcutta pursued a lively psychoanalytic discourse on Indian culture and society, and the treatment of Indian patients. They practiced and trained at the Lumbini Park Mental Hospital (opened in 1940) and established *Samiska*, the official English-language journal of the Indian Society. Though their influence extended neither to Indian popular imagination nor to the larger psychoanalytic world, their native familiarity with Indian cultures allowed for psychoanalytic explorations of India that were unencumbered by the tendency to exoticize or pathologize (Akhtar, 2005, p. 11). Additional study of this early enclave of Indian psychoanalysts might reveal continuities with the thinking and clinical practice of contemporary Indian analysts and their patients, furthering the agenda of revision grounded in the cultural and religious sensibilities of India.

After independence, enthusiasm for psychoanalysis waned markedly in India. This, says Akhtar (2005) reflected a general reaction against the British colonial influence upon psychoanalytic studies, evident in the tendency to portray Indians as infantile or inferior (for examples, see Berkeley-Hill, 1921; Daly, 1930). Also, psychoanalytic antagonism toward religion alienated many Indian intellectuals, most of whom identified themselves with an Indian religious worldview in some way (Akhtar, 2001; Kakar, 1994, 1995; Mehta, 1997; Roland, 1988; Sinha, 1966).

It wasn't until the early 1950s and the work of G. Morris Carstairs that the psychoanalytic study of Hindu personality development would regain momentum within and beyond India. In fact, over the following three decades, India became the focus of an abundance of psychoanalytic thinking and debate among analysts, anthropologists, and historians of religion worldwide. Two of the foundational developmental theories to emerge during this period are Carstairs' theory of the "crackdown" in male development and Kakar's notion of the "maternal enthrallment." Each theory privileges the reductive-explanatory; yet each embodies a dialectical tension between the explanatory and the interpretive. In Kakar's case, this tension would initiate a deepening exploration of the place of culture in psyche, and later the integration of mystical dimensions in works that effect a balance of the hermeneutical triad (Kakar, 1991).[5]

Carstairs laid the foundation for most of the psychoanalytic work on India that followed. Born of missionary parents, he lived in India until age 9. He later trained and practiced as a physician and psychiatrist, followed by some training in social anthropology at Oxford and at Columbia University. Carstairs returned to India in 1949 as part of an ethnographic team under the direction of anthropologist Gitel Steed. Working independently in Mewar, Rajasthan, Carstairs generated multiple case studies on which he later based his foundational work, *The Twice Born: A Study of a Community of High-Caste Hindus* (1957). Here he offered an influential analysis of Hindu personality formation in men, at the center of which is what is now known as the "crackdown" theory.

Carstairs identified two common and pathogenic elements of Indian childhood experience which account for what he considered to be a predominance of dependency needs and passivity in Hindu men. The first is a pattern of highly overindulgent maternal care combined with its periodic interruption owing to cultural prohibitions against an Indian mother's display of affection for her child in the presence of the mother-in-law. The second is the sudden and traumatic severance of the Indian boy's prolonged and intense attachment to his mother. This traumatic event typically occurs in the second year when, as a result of the father's renewed claim on the mother or because of the birth of a sibling, the boy is thrust into the realm of the father. The effect of this sudden change is to shatter, far too abruptly, the boy's pre-Oedipal sense of omnipotence and domination, and to leave him unprepared for the world of men. This pivotal experience, wrote Carstairs, constitutes "a catastrophic

[5] After publishing multiple psychoanalytic studies of Indian lives, culture and society, Kakar shifted to writing largely fiction. Given that his theoretical work moved in the direction of integrating mystical insights, we might imagine that the novel has proved for him an especially well suited medium through which to explore the psyche more fully (see Kakar, 2000, 2003).

reversal of the infant's blissful situation" (1957, p. 160) and a devastating rejection by his "loved and dominated mother" (ibid., p. 158).

Drawing on the ideas of Melanie Klein, Carstairs identifies what he believes are common *nuclear phantasies* in Indian infancy. These *phantasies* develop in response to the ominous experience of unpredictable, "mysteriously dangerous" maternal care, and form the basis of adult Hindu modes of responding to the world – the "Hindu modal personality" (ibid., p. 156). For Carstairs, the crackdown reinforces the child's unconscious splitting of the maternal object into good and bad, and establishes in the Hindu boy a state of mind characterized by Klein as the "paranoid-schizoid position." Though Carstairs never refers to the concept explicitly, it informs his writing throughout. Constituted by projections of these early experiences and by the child's own aggressive and retaliatory impulses and imperious nature, the bad maternal object is revengeful, dangerous, bloodthirsty, and demanding.

Carstairs is now one of many to engage notions of unconscious splitting in the analysis of Hindu goddess mythology. In the Hindu pantheon, benevolent, nurturing and maternal goddesses such as Lakshmi, Sarasvati, and Sita contrast starkly with the dangerous, warlike, and terrifying forms of Durga and Kali. Goddesses of the first type are commonly married and, as a result, their inherent power (*shakti*) is controlled. Goddesses of the second type are unmarried and thus uncontrolled. As a result, their divine rage, power, and heat is released into the world, often to the initial benefit of the world but then turning into a cosmic threat. Carstairs focuses on the terrifying forms of the goddess and relates them to what he identifies as pervasive ambivalence toward women on the part of Indian men. The ambivalence is grounded, he believes, in the unconscious combination of adoration and horror toward the maternal part-objects. The most common unconscious strategy by which a boy placates the split-off, bad mother is through total submission and symbolic self castration.

Carstairs also makes comparisons between Indian and Western childhood experience. He claims that a child in Western societies does not typically undergo such severe and sudden frustrations in its attachment to mother. The child is thus better able to reintegrate the good and bad into a whole maternal object that will receive the child's aggressive impulses without permanent disrepair. The result is a more stable and integrated state of mind, defined by Klein as the "depressive position" (also implicit in Carstairs' India-West comparison).

The Twice Born gives us the first major psychoanalytic portrayal, since Bose, of Indian men. It establishes the notion of the castrated Hindu son – a Ganesha complex, as it were – which many later works will incorporate, including Phillip Spratt's *Hindu Culture and Personality* (1966), in which Spratt draws uncritically on the crackdown theory to characterize the "Hindu narcissistic personality type" and the "passive homosexual attitude" of Indian men.

Undoubtedly the richest and most comprehensive psycho-analyses of male development and Indian families are found in the works of Indian analyst Sudhir Kakar. Raised in India, when Kakar turned to psychoanalytic training in Frankfurt in 1971, he had already received advanced degrees in mechanical engineering and economics (from universities in India, Germany, and Vienna). Viewed as a whole – and to date he has written 16 works of non-fiction and four novels – Kakar's writings integrate psychoanalytic, cultural and religious perspectives with unrivalled erudition and nuance. His first major volume, *The Inner World: A Psycho-analytic Study of Childhood and Society in India* (1978), has become the cornerstone of all psychoanalytic work on India, and pivotal in the history of Indological studies.[6] It is brilliant in its application of analytical perspectives (primarily the psycho-social theories of his mentor, Erik Erikson) to Indian and Hindu material, and contains richly descriptive comparisons between psychoanalytic and Hindu worldviews.

For example, in his presentation of "the Hindu world image," Kakar outlines the meaning of "fusion" for Hindus as it relates to the concept of *moksha* – the notion of ultimate liberation from the cycle of death and rebirth, based on monistic assumptions of ultimate oneness or identity of human being with the infinite. Such Hindu notions, as we have seen, informed Bose' Indianized psychoanalysis. Kakar is reluctant to reduce the notion of *moksha* and its associated mystical and ecstatic states of consciousness to Freud's "oceanic feeling," which hearkens back to a psychologically undifferentiated, omnipotent phase of early childhood experience. Rather, he invokes Erikson in cautioning against the "originological fallacy" which would collapse the mysticism of Vedanta and the yogic state of *samadhi* into their presumed psychological beginnings. Kakar also compares the Hindu ideal of the four life stages (*ashramadharma*) to Erikson's eight stages, noting what he takes to be convergences rather than collapsing one in to the other. He does the same with notions of time and destiny. Such comparisons make up the first part of *The Inner World* and express a rich cultural-interpretive dimension of Kakar's approach to the Indian psyche. For the greater share of the book, he retains these rich descriptions while pursuing a primarily explanatory-reductive agenda of applying psychoanalysis to Indian, particularly Hindu, lives and culture.

In this work, Kakar does not pursue a revised psychoanalysis but applies the theories within a highly sympathetic evocation of Hindu life. Interpretive and explanatory moments in *The Inner World* combine but never harmonize. The result is a creative tension between psychoanalytic and Hindu sensibilities – a tension embodied in the person of the author himself. For example, Kakar describes the book as a reconnaissance of his own Indian origins, and he speaks of the inner confrontations shared by Indians who have spent long periods of time in Europe and the United States:

> I have learned to recognize in myself and in other 'modern' Indians the phases of violent rejection and passionate extolling of all things Indian. For this is one of the ways in which this confrontation manifests itself, as the ego attempts to integrate experiences at different points of the life cycle, to try somehow to bring the Indian 'background' and the Western 'foreground' onto a single canvas. (Kakar, 1978, p. 13)

---

[6] Historian of Religion Jeffrey Kripal writes that "... it can be said without too much exaggeration that there are two kinds of texts in the twentieth-century study of Hinduism: those written before Kakar's *The Inner World* (1978), and those written after it. The book is so important because it is here that Kakar sets out a developmental model that would come to define – either positively or negatively – virtually every study that followed" (Kripal, 2001, p. 256).

How does Kakar understand male development in India? To answer this question we might first consider the influence of Carstairs and Erikson. We have looked at Carstairs' theory of the crackdown in a boy's life. By comparison, Erikson describes early experience in Indian families in less traumatic terms. In *Gandhi's Truth: On the Origins of Militant Nonviolence*, Erikson stresses a "diffuse" quality of emotional attachments in extended families, issuing in a characteristic and "abiding nostalgia for fusion" in Indian men (1962, p. 42). He notes the absence in joint Hindu families of the intense and focused relations of the Oedipal triad (a characteristic of *nuclear* families) and suggests that within such diffuse affective relations, Indian boys commonly do not resolve the Oedipus conflict. As a result,

> [M]any live always dependent, expectant, demanding, sulking, despairing, and yet always seeking the fusion which affirms, confirms, fulfills. Such an expectance of reunification by fate *can*, in turn, lead to an utterly passive sense of non-responsibility as an individual, and to a waiting for salvation by some form of re-immersion. (Erikson, 1969, p. 43)

Erikson thus sees blissful immersion and psychological fusion as a pervasive quality of joint family life. The most psychologically significant aspect of early family experience in the lives of Indian men is thus not trauma (a la Carstairs) but the lack of it. Without a mounting and focused aggression toward the father, a boy is never adequately motivated to redirect his Oedipal desires and sufficiently internalize the father, so as to form a superego.

Like Erikson and Carstairs, Kakar recognizes that for Indian boys, early childhood is typically steeped in maternal indulgence, and that the effects of this indulgence will reverberate throughout the rest of his life. Distinctively, however, he argues that the experience of maternal indulgence impacts a boy's psychological development *not* because of its frequency and intensity or because of irregularity or diffusion of affect; but rather because an Indian mother's care is erotically charged. Maternal care becomes eroticized for several reasons, the foremost being the mother's sexual dissatisfaction. Typically, a young woman looks to the birth of male children for status and self-esteem in traditional Indian society, while concurrently suffering a lack of intimacy with her husband during the initial years in his family. Other factors contribute to her dissatisfaction, including extended post-partum restrictions on intercourse and confinement to female quarters; but the primary cause is the husband's distance (a result of his ambivalence over sexual intimacy). In response, the young mother attempts unconsciously to fulfil her erotic needs through her male child.

The mother's eroticized ministrations are overwhelming to the boy. In defense, he forms an unconscious split between the "good mother" who fully gratifies his every wish, and the "bad mother" who poses a threat to his still unstructured ego. The boy idealizes and identifies with the (good) mother, producing the so-called "maternal enthrallment." In terror of her threatening aspects, he renounces his masculinity and so escapes the threat of her sexuality.[7] The result is passivity, dependence and a

---

[7] Kakar thus de-emphasizes the effects of "spoiling" and argues that it is maternal eroticism that gives rise to a boy's dependent and submissive nature (1978, p. 87).

life-long, deep-seated ambivalence towards women. Later the cycle is perpetuated when his ambivalence centers around his own wife, contributing to distant marital relations and causing the wife to turn to her sons for happiness, self-esteem and erotic fulfilment.

In later childhood, says Kakar, male passivity and dependence are further anchored by the boy's traumatic separation from his mother and his abrupt entry into the world of men (Carstairs' "crackdown"). Thrown suddenly into this world, writes Kakar, an Indian boy seeks desperately for the vivid masculine voice – the "Oedipal alliance" – that he requires for the firm establishment of a superego; but he finds only distance in adult men. In the absence of a guiding male figure, the boy further identifies with his mother and adopts finally a position of "feminine submission towards all elder men in the family ... [and] a passive-receptive attitude towards authority figures of all kinds" (Kakar, 1978, p. 134). In keeping with Erikson's emphasis on emotional diffusion, Kakar describes an Indian boy's experience of the world of men in terms of a hydra-like collective, rather than a set of distinct and dyadic relationships.[8]

Finally, for Kakar, the traditional joint family both shapes and is shaped by these psychological dynamics. With its interdependent relations and close forms of personal engagement, the joint-family offers the Indian male a kind of nurturance that echoes his earlier experience of mother; while its hierarchical relations of authority address his narcissism and need for structure:

> In the Indian family, the hierarchical ordering of relationships, and their durability, even timelessness, provides some fulfillment of the individual's lifelong need for external authority figures; the maternal mode of family care salvages some of the continuity between the individual's early and later experiences, while the emphasis on the primacy of relationships seeks to counteract the individual's narcissistic orientation and self-absorption which, if unchecked, would seriously undermine social stability and cooperation. (Kakar, 1978, p. 139)

The theories of Carstairs and Kakar are now foundational to the study of Hindus and Hinduism. Each privileges the reductive-explanatory in formulating the unconscious effects of joint family life and Indian mothering on Hindu personality formation and Hindu religious life as a whole. Each gives us a picture of Indian psycho-sexual development that is resonant with a view of Ganesha as the emasculated son. Passivity, submission to male authority, and ambivalence toward women are Indian men's psychological trademarks. A Hindu boy preserves his vital connection with the good maternal object by means of splitting and an unconscious renunciation of his masculinity. Motivating this symbolic castration is, for Carstairs, an early trauma that amplifies a boy's innate aggressions, which in Kleinian style are projected into the bad mother. For Kakar, it is maternal eroticism that threatens the boy's fragile ego and causes the maternal split.

---

[8] This might account, for example, for the psychological significance of the abduction of Sita, wife of Rama, by the ten-headed demon king Ravana in the Hindu Epic *Ramayana*.

Case Interlude: Vikram Bleeds for His Father

The village of Anidasu is located in Garhwal, the western division of the hill state known as Uttaranchal. Garhwal forms part of the Himalayan range that runs from Kashmir to Assam.[9] Villagers of Anidasu engage in subsistence agriculture and animal husbandry; many of them sell buffalo milk. The village has neither road nor electricity, and its young men are increasingly drawn or sent away from the village to the nearby town to earn, often with limited results. I lived between Anidasu and town for two years of field research, beginning in 1994, and have returned many times since. The first two of my three case studies in this paper, Vikram and his father Ludar, come from this village.

Vikram is 26 years old and married with a 3-year-old son. The eldest of four brothers, he resisted his wedding arrangements but his father Ludar insisted. Vikram acquiesced but immediately following the wedding he left his new wife in the village and took a job in town. Afterward he came home only once every two or three months. "Whenever I go the village," he said, "I begin to feel very strange." Inevitably his visits resulted in angry confrontations with his father. Such confrontations were not new and had, since childhood, often followed a particular sequence in which father would scold and Vikram would respond by inflicting injury upon himself. For example on one occasion he struck himself in the head with a metal potholder. His father would then typically respond by withdrawing into isolation from the rest of the family, feeling guilt for having "caused" his son's injury. The family, especially Vikram's mother, would respond with anger against the father.

At 26, Vikram reported that he continued to feel "strange" at home and was still prone to hostile confrontations with father. Nevertheless, in town he felt isolated from his family and acutely sensitive to his responsibilities toward them. Having become the primary earner for the family, he was ambivalent over their dependence on him – this included his father, who reported intense feelings of sadness and disorientation whenever Vikram was away. "He tells me," said Vikram, "that he thinks constantly of me and worries about how I am doing. But I think that all he cares about is the money I make."

On one occasion, Vikram was enraged to learn that the household had been temporarily without adequate provisions but had not sent him a request to send anything. He went directly to the village and angrily confronted his father. "Everyone depends on me in this house," he said, "and one day I am going to destroy it." Vikram's circumstances worsened when he began to drink heavily after his wedding. He drank with friends and often paid for their alcohol and for their food. When once his younger brother Surbhir scolded him for drinking, spending, and fighting with his father, Vikram replied by saying "you don't talk [i.e., 'explain'] to me and I won't

[9] This mountainous and primarily Hindu area is known all over India as a *devbhumi* (literally "region/soil of the gods") and has great significance in the history of Hinduism as a holy region. It is referred to in the Vedas, Shastras, and the Puranic texts (the *Skanda Purana* describes the geography of the region in detail). Uttaranchal contains some of the most important Hindu pilgrimage sites in India, attracting thousands of Indian pilgrims every year.

talk to you. I am doing my own work and you do yours. Talk to me again and I'll kill you." In more desperate moments, Vikram would sometimes say "I have no family; no father and mother, no wife, no brothers, no son. I am alone."

Once during the wet season, Vikram's employer took him to South India for an extended period of time. For months his family did not hear from him, until finally an urgent letter arrived from him requesting that they copy and distribute it to everyone in the village. In the letter, he reported that Jakh-Devta, the dominant god in the village, had come to him in a dream and said that if the village did not repair his temple and then perform puja in the precise way specified, Jakh-Devta would destroy the village and everyone in it. Vikram wrote:

> The fate of Anidasu worsens day by day as everyone moves forward in life and away from our village. Brothers, if you want to foster the future of your children then make the village into one group and think together. Our village's circumstances are getting worse and Lord Jakh-Devta is very angry that this is happening. Lords Bir and Nag Raja are angry as well, as are the Five Pandavas. All of the gods and goddesses are angry and this is why things are getting worse. Brothers, these very gods and goddesses have corrupted all of our minds. Now in the village, one person does not watch out for the other and people are filled with bad intentions. You must join together and make the decision to go to an oracle (to determine the divine source of the troubles). And brothers, you must repair all of the temples. I will help you (with money) from here. This letter will be given to everyone to read. Brothers I think of you all the time. It is very hot here. Do not think that this letter is a joke. I have simply written the truth.

Some months later Vikram returned to his work in town, and to drinking with his friends. He said nothing more about the dream or the god's commands. Once when Vikram returned home late from an evening with friends, his father was there and began to scold him for "pouring out" his money everywhere. Vikram flew into a rage and shouted at Ludar, "what do you want from me? Do you want blood?" He then seized a knife from the kitchen and, standing in front of his father, slashed open his fore arm, bleeding profusely and permanently crippling his hand.

Reflections

One might approach Vikram's brutal self-injury as an act of emasculation or submission through symbolic self-castration; one might also make sense of it within a Hindu cultural framework as an effort to re-establish his masculinity through his father. I will explore each approach (the first explanatory-reductive, the second cultural-interpretive).

Vikram recounts a long history of heated encounters with father, generally ensuing in some form of self-directed violence on the son's part. In oedipal terms, he harms himself in response to the terrifying possibility of paternal retaliation for his violent feelings toward father. In pre-oedipal terms, as per Kakar (1978), it is the boy's vital connection with a nurturing mother that is preserved in exchange for his masculinity, including the phallic expression of his own aggressive impulses. To confront the father is, unconsciously, to threaten the maternal connection. Thus anger toward father evokes intolerable fears of paternal retribution, but even more primitive terrors of abandonment or annihilation based in early experience of a split off and "bad" maternal object. In addition, it is significant that the father is thought to be essential (at least symbolically) to the cohesion of a family structure, the same structure that restricts and channels a boy's impulse expression, provides him with a moral compass, compensates for a fragile sense of self, and protects him. Unconsciously, to attack the father is to threaten the family (whose mode of care, says Kakar, is essentially maternal). Confronted by his father, Vikram's violent self-injury is thus an unusually pronounced enactment of an otherwise common unconscious strategy of symbolic self-castration. And even though he submits overtly to the father, ultimately and more profoundly he submits to the mother.

A maternal mode of care is also found at the village level. Vikram's dream seems to express deep anxieties evoked by extended separation from both family and village. He fantasizes the disintegration and destruction of the village – tantamount unconsciously to his own destruction, as his own sense of inner cohesion and stability rests in the stability of the collective. In both the dream and his letter to the village, a pantheon of local deities represents the collective of male elders who oversee the village and can preserve or destroy it, just as Vikram's father oversees the integrity of the family. Vikram enjoins the entire village to re-establish itself as a whole through worship of the gods, in which divine blessings are attained though submission and sacrifice.

Why are the gods angry? Vikram claims that it is because of selfish and divisive actions on the part of the villagers, actions that lead to the neglect of the whole community, including its superior and nurturant figures, and its future generations. In this scenario, the villagers represents Vikram's own independent and impulsive strivings, linked to neglect of his family, his father, and his child. In the letter he disavows any such strivings by asserting that the villagers' selfishness comes not from within themselves but from above, as it is the gods who have corrupted their minds. Psychologically, then, the only viable response to anxieties of separation and abandonment, to aggressive impulses toward the father, and to the dangers of his own harmful initiatives, is total submission.

These psychoanalytic speculations illustrate an explanatory-reductive hermeneutic and draw on some of the foundational studies described above. I do not offer them as the best or most definitive, but wish only to illuminate the difference and tension between explanatory-reductive and cultural-interpretive approaches to our case. The latter will seek to understand Vikram through the Hindu perspectives that inform his worldview, as well as the ways in which Vikram engages and interprets them. Accordingly, rather than understanding his act of self-mutilation as symbolic castration, we can see it as a plea for paternal reciprocity, through which the young man might ultimately be empowered rather than emasculated. I will elaborate on this briefly, in light of a few Hindu conceptions and practices.

India's Hindu ontologies stress that no human being can survive or grow in vitality or influence if he/she lacks connection with a superior source of benevolence and nurturance.[10] Hindu sciences emphasize the importance of many kinds of superior connections: astrology asserts the supreme influence of celestial bodies, and Ayurvedic medicine attests to the influence of higher and pervading substances such as *kapha* (literally "phlegm") in the body and its quality of *sattva* ("goodness") in the brain. Popular Hindu texts such as the *Bhagavad-Gita* and the *Ramayana* advocate devotion to superior, divine figures whose beneficial influence is passed down from above, as when a worshipper receives back the purified remnants of offerings (*prashad*) that were offered "up" to a deity, or when a disciple touches the feet of his guru, signifying that from the very lowest part of his master comes goodness that is superior to what is highest in him. These high-low relations of giving and receiving entail the transference of essential qualities such as power (*shakti*), purity (*pavitrta*), goodness (*sattva*), knowledge (*gyan*) and understanding (*samajh*). The effects or influences (*prabhav*) of parents and elders "fall" onto their inferiors who, as a result, are raised up above others on whom their enhanced influence might then fall.

Accordingly, Anidasu villagers believe that they benefit most in life by remaining within such relations, not by somehow "coming out on top" but by weaving themselves ever more tightly into the reciprocal relations of give and take (*len-den*) that constitute family and village life. They believe also that disorder, carelessness, and disunity within village communities, families *and persons* are related to the absence of superior influence – i.e., of "big people" (*bare aadmi*) or "explainers" (*samjhanevale*) – to whom people listen and whom they fear. Even these elders acquire their own "greatness" in reciprocal relations with higher, nurturing, and powerful (and so potentially destructive) beings, such as gurus and gods. In the absence of their divine influence, the result is disorder and disharmony.

Within Vikram's own Hindu worldview, well-being and development require reciprocity with such higher sources of benevolence and blessings. And yet, the long history and extremity of Vikram's self-punitive actions suggest that he perceives no such reciprocity with his father. Instead he sees himself as depleted through giving "up" or "pouring out" without receiving anything in return. In the heat of an argument in which he feels deeply shamed, he gashes open his own fore arm and bleeds profusely for his father, as though making a blood-sacrifice in the face of a god's anger and disapproval.

Thus, according to the explanatory-reductive, foundational theories in the psychoanalytic study of Hindu India, we see Vikram's self-mutilation as an instance of symbolic self-castration. It signals a developmental failure. He is, effectively, the castrated Hindu son. According to a cultural-interpretive approach, we see

---

[10] While the present section focuses on the importance of superior-inferior connections in Hindu culture and society, it is important to note that Western scholarship on India has tended to overemphasize hierarchy, often to the exclusion of other salient dimensions. See Gloria Raheja's *The poison in the gift: Ritual, prestation, and the dominant caste in a North Indian village* (1988) for a more balanced and indigenizing village ethnography. Also see Sarah Lamb (2000) for a multidimensional ethnography of North Indian family interrelations.

Vikram's self-mutilation as an exaggerated example of a *normative* pattern of filial submission. It is a desperate developmental effort to re-establish his masculinity.

Indigenizing Studies: Hindu Families/Hindu Selves

The early 1900s saw the wholesale importation of Western social science in colonial India. Writing and researching in the spirit of development and modernization, and amidst disciplinary concerns for scientific respectability, many Indian social scientists uncritically adopted Western theories and their standards of individual and familial welfare, while bracketing or rejecting their own intellectual and cultural histories as sources of insight about human behavior and experience. Describing the effects of this upon psychology in India, Durganand Sinha writes of the "mindless borrowings from the West that have made the discipline futile and sterile," and of an aura of "foreignness" and "unreality" that psychology in India acquired (1990, p. 47).

From the 1950s to the present, Indian psychologists and sociologists have turned increasingly to their own cultural histories and contemporary issues in order to develop testable hypotheses, models, theories, and forms of practice. Most remain committed to a scientific epistemology and empirical methods while adopting research topics of relevance to India, such as the psychological dimensions of poverty, psychological factors in agro-economic development, health practices, population control, caste and social structure (Sinha, 1990, p. 45). Scientifically conservative thinkers re-examine and modify Western theoretical frameworks in order to make them more relevant to India, while more radical ones reject Western frameworks and return to Indian intellectual history for guiding models and principles (Sinha, 1990, p. 45). "Psychology has to go native if it is to be creative and relevant to society," proclaims one Indian psychologist (Mukherjee, 1980). Accordingly, some have looked to the forms of authority and interdependence within Indian joint families or in the *guru-shishya* relationship for their norms and models of leadership (Sinha, 1980), psychotherapy (Neki, 1973), and mature social relationships (Neki, 1976).

In this same indigenizing spirit, contemporary authors write that if psychoanalysis is to be illuminating and applicable in Indian context, it must be revised to embrace Indian norms of interdependence, authority, and family unity. Anthropologist Gananath Obeyesekere (1990) argues that the Oedipal complex has limited applicability to the familial patterns and religious values of Indian society, in which the nurturing affective ties of the family are preserved through the suppression of individualism and submission to the father. He invites us to imagine Freud "not in Vienna, but in Delhi as an Indian doctor working with Hindu neurotics" and claims that the Sophoclean myth would have little relevance in this context – Freud would have to formulate an Indian complex based on Indian clinical and mythological data (ibid., p. 86), See also Obeyesekere 1984.

In his landmark essay, "The Indian Oedipus," A.K. Ramanujan (1983) shows that in Indian folklore and mythology, the "family romance" entails the flow of desire from mother to son and father to daughter, and of aggression from father to son and mother to daughter-in-law. These reversals of the orthodox Oedipal flow are consonant, says Ramanujan, with the tendency in India to emphasize fulfilment of father and family and the repression of personal independence. Paul Courtright (1985) also writes that Oedipal tensions in Indian families, as reflected in the mythologies of Shiva and Ganesha, are *optimally* resolved through passive submission of the son to the father, the reconciliation of the family, and the subsequent recognition and empowerment of the son. My cultural-interpretive comments on the meaning of Vikram's self-injury echo this indigenous perspective.

These relatively recent efforts to critique and relativize psychoanalytic concepts in view of Indian culture coincide with a renaissance of anthropological interest in cultural conceptions of person and self, and with enhanced awareness of the cultural biases embedded within Western developmental theories of individuation, psychological autonomy, identity, ego and self formation. Some have turned to contemporary, relational psychoanalytic theories in the belief that they establish a deeper place for culture in the psyche and can better accommodate normative forms of interpersonal dependence and less bounded conceptions of self found in non-Western societies. With respect to India, for example, Sudhir Kakar (1985) proclaims the need to "relativize the major analytic concepts" and identifies post-Freudian, object relations theories as especially suited to the task because they imply the early influence of culture upon unconscious images of self and others.[11] Two particularly influential studies of India attempt to cast off the biases of Western individualism and produce contextualized accounts of Indian object relations, self and ego. I will briefly consider each one.

Psychoanalyst Alan Roland, in his volume *In Search of Self in India and Japan: Toward a Cross-Cultural Psychology*, gives us an Indian psyche with a three-part self-structure: the familial self, spiritual self, and individual self. Roland's revisionist psychoanalysis is based on the assumption of radical difference between the Indian's multiple self-experience and the unitary Western self:

> The intrapsychic self varies significantly if not radically according to the social and cultural patterns of societies so civilizationally different. I find that people have a different experiential, affective sense of self and relationships, as well as vastly different internalized world views that give profoundly different meanings to everyday experiences and relationships. (Roland, 1988, p. 4)

Roland stresses the collective, familial and spiritual selves over the private and hidden individual self. The familial self or "we-self," says Roland, is "a basic

[11] Comparing the significance of culture in classical and relational perspectives, Kakar writes: "Besides the dismissal implicit in its characterization as 'later' as opposed to 'early,' culture in the classical theory also suffers from the label of a 'surface' phenomenon and hence being 'superficial,' rather than constituting a part of the 'depth' and hence being more 'fundamental' in the individual's psychic life (...) It is only in the more 'relational' theories ... that culture has an opportunity of appearing in the 'depths'." (Kakar, 1985, p. 444).

inner psychological organization that enables women and men to function well within the hierarchical intimacy relationships of the extended family, community, and other groups" (ibid.). The familial self is symbiotic and reciprocal, functioning in the intensely emotional and interdependent family intimacies where high levels of empathy and receptivity to others are cultivated, and where one's sense of self is shifting and contextual. Roland speaks of "we-self regard" or self-esteem that derives from strong identification with the reputation and honor of the family and other groups, from nonverbal mirroring and from the idealization of elders.

Another effort to formulate a Hindu model of development emphasizes the internalization of "the group" as a measure of psychological maturation in Indian families. In his volume, *All the Mothers are One: Hindu India and the Cultural Reshaping of Psychoanalysis*, anthropologist Stanley Kurtz (1992) explores the ways in which early experience of multiple caretakers in Indian families requires a reformulation of libidinal models of development in Indian males. Impressed by "the sheer amount of time during which the children of [Hindu] joint families were placed in the care of people other than their own parents," Kurtz set about to challenge the "traditional psychoanalytic theory of a dangerously close Hindu mother–child bond" and the assumption that the presence of multiple caretakers has a harmful effect on childhood development. Says Kurtz:

> My claim is that the Hindu child is pushed away by its mother, and pulled toward the larger family group. This stands in sharp contrast to the account of early Hindu childhood put forward by psychoanalytic students of Indian life [in which] the Hindu mother and child are bound in a tight symbiotic union. Since the child is nursed on demand, and since soiling accidents go unpunished, the general stance of maternal indulgence fails to promote the sort of movement toward individuated selfhood that psychoanalysts wish to see. (Kurtz, 1992, p. 37)

In order to escape the individualizing biases of orthodox psychoanalytic studies of India, Kurtz outlines a distinctly Hindu process of early development that he calls "renunciation-on-the-way-to-the-group." He attempts to show that the child is gradually and gently both pushed away by the mother and pulled from her by the family group. As he renounces his exclusive and, by South Asian norms, immature attachment to the mother, a Hindu boy comes first to believe that *all* of the women in the family are really his mother (in what Kurtz calls the *ek-hi* or "just one" phase). In the next stage, which corresponds to the onset of phallic sexuality, a boy is challenged to renounce exclusive and incestuous desires for the mother(s) in favor of the mature satisfactions of immersion into the collective family. This process does not result optimally in an individuated ego, but rather in an "ego of the whole." Thus, Kurtz provides a revised psychoanalytic theory of development in Hindu families, in which a growing child moves optimally toward incorporation of, and into, the group. Using psychoanalysis to explicate a Hindu version of maturity, he thus shows how the extended family environment facilitates, rather than inhibits, maturation.

For Kurtz and Roland, Indian psychological development moves in the direction of "the group" – i.e., away from and, to a significant extent, against exclusive attachments and individuation. This culturally specific line of development, each author assumes, requires a revised conception of ego (Kurtz) or self-structure (Roland) if psychoanalytic theory is to be applicable. While these theories may well be problematic – empirically, psychoanalytically and in their depth of cultural understanding – the two are significant in the history of the Hinduism-Psychoanalysis encounter as revisionist efforts that achieve a balanced dialectic of explanatory-reductive and cultural-interpretive approaches.

Case Interlude: Ludar Singh's Love in the Dark Age of Kali

Ludar Singh is a 55 year old farmer in Anidasu, with four sons, the eldest of whom is Vikram, whose case study is offered above. Ludar volunteered his life story gladly and began with an account of his family losses in childhood. His father died when Ludar was only a year old and soon thereafter his mother abandoned (*chodna*, "threw away, dropped") him in her natal village in order to live elsewhere with another man. Within a year she died as well from disease. Ludar was raised by his maternal grandparents to the age of 12, at which time he was sent from his mother's village to live in his father's family. There his paternal grandfather cared for him like a son but passed away before Ludar's wedding, leaving him with an uncle who was physically abusive and refused care or support of any kind. Left entirely alone to fend for himself, Ludar successfully arranged his own marriage – an unusual occurrence in Anidasu. He learned to work his paternal grandfather's field and managed, with his wife, to produce and provide for a growing family. The history of his trials and determination to survive by his own means, marry and have a family, made Ludar effectively Anidasu's self-made man. Yet for him, as well as for his sons, Ludar's story of going it alone is a story of depletion and irreversible loss of vitality, rather than strength or heroic self-sufficiency.

Ludar saw himself as having been weakened by these early experiences; as having "poured out" his powers. He understood his early losses to have impacted his present psychological and physical conditions as well as his present family relationships. Using a common idiom – one that is nevertheless not to be taken as merely metaphorical – he explained that because he did not "drink his mother's milk," he suffered from shortage and weakness of blood throughout his life. Now he feared old age and decline because, he said, he had been prematurely depleted in childhood and youth. Shortage of blood (*khun ki kami*), he said, also accounted for his general psycho-physical weaknesses and inability to keep peace and maintain coherence in his family. It accounted, for example, for his quickness to quarrel with his wife and to respond with rage to his children when they disobeyed him. Even their disobedience, he said, was a reflection of *his* depletion.

Ludar claimed always to offer but never receive love in his family. He believed that not only his wife but his older sons as well had little or no love for him. He feared that they would not adequately care for him, perhaps even not feed him, when he grew incapable of caring for himself in old age. In fact, because of the general lack of love that he perceived among his sons, he feared that the joint-family household would fall apart after his death, and quite possibly before. As for the younger sons and the grandchildren, Ludar said that he loved them far more than any other father, and that he had, in fact, an unusual capacity to discern a child's inner desires well before it could express them in speech. By comparison, he had doubts about his wife's affections for the younger children and claimed once that she really had little or no love for them at all. Ludar feared that one day they might come to some harm because of her careless neglect; that a child might step into the cooking fire, be trampled by a buffalo or fall from the high mountain trails into the ravine. As evidence of his wife's neglect, Ludar recounted an incident in which she placed the children in the care of her sister (a common practice) so that she could attend a religious festival in town. Ludar encountered her on the trail and became enraged to learn that she, as he saw it, had "selfishly abandoned" the children to pursue her own pleasures. He sent her back directly to the village.

In Anidasu, men's language of love reveals the profound emotional salience of the "whole family." Accordingly, in the indigenous terms and metaphors of their native language, village men more often speak of family as a relatively bounded entity, and of the person as open, mutable, and enmeshed within the family web.[12] Like most Anidasu men, Ludar tended to experience his emotional well being and resilience as constituted within familial relations of cohesion, integration, and reciprocity of care; not through some form of personal completion. For example, he made frequent use of the Hindi verb *manna* in discussing familial love. Often translated into English as "observing," or "obeying," *manna* is also defined in the Oxford Hindi-English Dictionary as "to consider something as such," "to acknowledge [the particular quality of]" and "to hold in respect." I found that Anidasu men use *manna* to describe an essential kind of love among family members that is characterized not only by respect and obedience but also by differential awareness (*hosh*, *samajh*) of each person's qualities and place, and a corresponding order and integration of these multiple qualities and roles within the complex whole.

For Ludar, it was precisely the absence of this sort of love, and a corresponding collapse of sustaining distinctions in his household, that characterized the present and degenerative cosmic era, the *kalyug*. "In the *kalyug*," he said, "all become one," meaning that the distinctions between people are collapsed. He made the additional and striking claim – inconsistent with his own life narrative – that because there were such distinctions, love, and respect when he was a boy, his childhood must not have taken place in the *kalyug*:

> I don't know how long ago it began, but at the time [of my childhood] it must not have been the *kalyug*. I was observant (*manna*) of everything: this is my paternal grandfather, this is

---

[12] Many ethnographic studies suggest that rather than thinking of themselves as "individual," Indians conceive of their bodies, minds, and personalities as "permeable" and inseparably entwined in a "web" or "body" of family attachments (Inden and Nicholas, 1977; Lamb, 1993, 2000; Marriott, 1976, 1980; Trawick, 1990). Accordingly, they often seem to value the dissolution of personal boundaries in family relationships (Trawick 1990, pp. 242–243), the development of multiple and contextual identities (Marriott, 1980; Ramanujan, 1989), and ranked relations of authority (Derne, 1995; Rudolph and Rudolph, 1976). These studies clearly suggest that interpersonal "enmeshment" (in its Indian sense) and psychological variability are salient and valued features of Indian family life.

my mother, this other person is my father's younger brother, this is so-and-so, this is so-and-so. There was *prem* over everyone. Now there is no love at all over anyone. My family doesn't observe love at all (*ye to prem bhi nahin mante*). [But when I was a boy] I observed everything and everyone [properly]. I observed the gods, and things were exactly as the gods said. But now it is the *ghanghor* (muddy, terrible) *kalyug*. In the Ramayan it is written that when the *kalyug* comes, the cow will eat feces and pandits will speak lies. Human beings will not understand each other, and there will be no feelings of love (*prembhav*).

Reflections

Ludar's infancy and childhood were marked by multiple traumatic losses, beginning with his mother, as well as by dislocation and physical abuse. We might expect that now, many years later, as he approaches the inevitable incapacities and dependencies of old age, his anxieties about aging are amplified by memories of early trauma. Further, Ludar's sense that his love is unreciprocated by his children and wife, and that they do not, in fact, even love one another, is also likely fueled psychologically by such memories.

In keeping with Roland's and Kurtz' emphases on early object relations and self- or ego-formation, we will consider Ludar in terms of object relations theory, and particularly the notion of "object constancy." Broadly speaking, object relations theories describe the ways in which early, primary interrelations are internalized as lasting mental representations or "imagos" of self and other that populate the individual's inner world and exert an influence upon cognitive and emotional processes throughout life. Many theorists believe that one's internalized relations are continually "reactivated" or "used" as a means of maintaining inner equilibrium, especially in the face of severe stress or trauma.[13] Many also believe that internalized objects are not fixed and unchanging but are modified throughout life, in reaction to new experiences and changing circumstances (Greenberg and Mitchell, 1983, p. 14). "The very pressure of living," writes psychoanalyst Ana-Maria Rizzuto, "makes us rework, over and over again, consciously and unconsciously, the memories of those we encountered at the beginning of our days" (1979, p. 7). "Object constancy," in this context, refers to the constant and whole quality of an emotionally sustaining internal object.

Accordingly, we might plausibly claim that Ludar Singh experiences himself as unworthy of love and unsuited to his duties as the "big person" and cohesive force of the family because he lacks an internalized and constant maternal object; and that, instead, his internal objects have inconstant and even persecutory qualities. And yet, our claims to this effect are based on notions of optimal caregiving that are specific to non-Indian cultural settings. Given the common experience of multiple caregivers

[13] Psychoanalyst Otto Kernberg describes object relations as follows: "In broadest terms, psychoanalytic object-relations theory represents the psychoanalytic study of the nature and origins of interpersonal relations, and of the nature and origins of intrapsychic structure deriving from, fixating, modifying and reactivating past internalized relations with others in the context of present interpersonal relationships" (Kernberg, 1976, p. 56).

(i.e., "all the mothers") in Indian childhood, we are forced to reconceptualize the nature of internalized objects in Indian context. Further, given that commonly held, Hindu perceptions of the world see it as, by nature, fluid and ever changing, we must also explore the applicability of the notion of "object constancy" in Indian cultural settings.

Psychoanalysts tend to define object constancy, and thus successful personality development, in terms of the qualities of *the* maternal object, the primary care giver, in relation to her child. But in the sociocentric contexts of Indian culture, child care and joint family life,[14] we might can think of the early family matrix as a kind of *composite object*; for as we saw in both Vikram's and Ludar's case, the collectivities of family and village are emotionally salient in waking life, fantasy and dreams. If we revise the psychoanalytic notion of the primary object so as to include the "whole family" (*pura parivar*) or a composite of caregivers, we must also reconceptualize the nature of object constancy. Doing so could sensitize the analytic observer to culturally specific unconscious entities and their impact on conscious experience – for example Ludar's perceptions of his family as unloving and unreliable, or his distressing sense of its fragility and imminent collapse (a sense expressed in Vikram's dream of village disunity and destruction).

As was true of Vikram's violent act of submission to his father, Ludar's fears about family disunity and abandonment are exaggerated instances of common concerns among Indian villagers (in this case, the elderly). Social factors contributing to anxiety about old age and dependency include the near total reliance of aging parents upon their children for survival. Cultural factors – of primary concern in the present, cultural-interpretive reflections on object constancy in India – include Hindu conceptions of the world and time itself.

Hindu notions of *kala*, or time, contribute to the experience of family attachments as shifting, fragile and unreliable. Hindu time is cyclical; and according to the great cycle of ages (*mahayuga*) we are in an age of disintegration and disorder among people and gods, a time in which proper knowledge of *dharma* (duty, order) is nearly absent. The orthodox formulation of the cycle of ages begins with a time of spontaneous righteousness and moral certainty and ends with chaos and degeneration. This is represented in the image of a cow (itself representing *dharma*) who stands on all fours in the first age but loses a leg in each successive one. By the fourth and present age, the *kalyug*, human beings (and their families) find themselves in unstable circumstances indeed. Along with *kala*, other essentially Hindu concepts create a backdrop of universal disequilibrium against which villagers such as Ludar perceive themselves and their most cherished attachments as fragile and transient. These concepts include *samsara*.

Most non-Hindus are familiar with the word *samsara* and know it to refer to the doctrine of reincarnation; yet in India it has multiple meanings. *Samsara* refers to the cycle of death and rebirth, to be sure, but in common usage it also refers to "the world" and connotes the world's unstable and changing nature. *Samsara* can be

[14] For more on the distinction between sociocentric and egocentric cultures, see Shweder and Bourne (1984).

translated literally as "flowing together" or "confluent motion" and so is comparable to the word *jagat* – also meaning "the world" but more literally "that which moves." It signifies, then, a universal context of disequilibrium.[15] Further, many Hindus use the term *samsara* to refer to "family" as a web of attachments that are cherished and yet discarded at the end of this life. And yet, even within this life, joint family households are known for their ongoing cycles of growth, instability and fragmentation. As its members grow in number, the family becomes increasingly diverse and potentially unstable; differential relations of love that are crucial to keeping this fragile whole in balance become strained and can easily break.

A cultural-interpretive approach to inner objects and their relations to mature self-experience in Hindu families must engage this fluid cosmology of *samsara* and the disintegrative course of time implied in the concept of *kala*. These notions create a backdrop of universal flux and flow. Reductive-explanatory theories of ego- or self-formation, internalized objects and object constancy, must also take into account these and other cultural conceptions if they are to be adequate to Indian experience. Ludar's use of "minding" or *manna* with respect to familial love, for example, emphasizes the plurality of relational modes and self-experiences within Hindu joint family life, and suggests that some experiences of love (*prembhav*) are constituted in forms of interpersonal differentiation and order within a cohesive hierarchy – a hierarchy that includes divine as well as human beings. Other forms of love might be constituted in forms of unbounded self-experience and the absence of interpersonal distinctions (see Trawick, 1990). Each constellation of love-experiences suggests the possibility of distinctive and uniquely Hindu forms of internalized object relations.

Integrative Studies: Eroticism and the Mystical

Integrative studies engage what I am calling a religious-integrative hermeneutic in the psychoanalytic study of Hindus: a self-critical engagement and integration into theory of religious dimensions of psychical life. Parsons refers to integrative theories in the field of religion and psychological studies as "transformational" and defines them as granting "metaphysical legitimacy to the religious claim of accessing a transcendent realm beyond the reaches of developmental determinism" (1999, 2000, p. 246). He identifies several such theories within psychoanalytic history, including Lacan's notion of the "Real," Bion's concept of "O," Kohut's notion of "cosmic narcissism" and, one might add, Jung's notion of the "psychoid archetype." Parsons also notes that today, increasing numbers of contemporary psychoanalytic writers are willing to engage and selectively integrate conceptual, practical, and moral aspects of Asian religions into their work:

[15] E.V. Daniel (1984) describes many ways in which Tamil villagers seek equilibrium in how they eat, where they live, when they make decisions, who they marry, who they worship, etc., all set within a world characterized by disequilibrium.

> No longer are Buddhist and Hindu categories of self, development and maturity unreflectively reduced to the implicit value orientations underlying psychological categories. A respect for the interdisciplinary hurdles which must be navigated to insure a bona fide, nonreductionistic dialogue between equal and different ways of configuring self, development and maturity has begun. (Parsons, 2000, p. 246)

Jeffrey Kripal's scholarly and appreciative study of the nineteenth century Hindu saint Ramakrishna Paramahamsa illustrates the dialogical nature of a religious-integrative hermeneutic. In *Kali's Child: The Mystical and the Erotic in the Life and Teachings of Ramakrishna* (1995), Kripal attempts to merge psychoanalytic and mystical perspectives. He recognizes the presence and impact of unconscious factors such as libido, repression, and splitting in Ramakrishna's remarkable person and life history; and he relates these to an irreducible, transcendent or formless dimension of the saint's mystical states (ibid., p. 20). These integrative efforts are most apparent in Kripal's notion of "the erotic":

> [The erotic refers to] a dimension of human experience that is simultaneously related to both the physical and emotional experiences of sexuality and to the deepest ontological levels of religious experience. (Kripal, 1995, p. 23)

With the category of the "erotic," Kripal effects a balance of the three hermeneutics. His notion of the erotic is explanatory, as it functions according to the libidinal economy of psychoanalytic drive theory. It is interpretive, as its phenomenological qualities and sought objects are distinctively Hindu; and the erotic is integrative, as its wellsprings transcend person and biology. This balanced, three dimensional concept of the erotic is at the heart of Kripal's exploration of the saint's famous first vision of the goddess Kali.

Kripal gives evidence of Ramakrishna's early homoerotic longings in the saint's apparent discomfort with his male gender as a boy and his practice of dressing as a woman, as per the ideology of Krishna devotionalism in which the devotee yearns for the divine love as the milkmaids do for Lord Krishna. Kripal also suggests the possibility of sexual trauma caused by young village women who adored the boy and worshipped him as an image of Krishna the divine lover. Their eroticized attentions, Kripal suggests, might themselves have triggered some of Ramakrishna's early dissociative trance-states, for these states effectively allowed Ramakrishna to escape the women and their worship of him (Kripal, 1995, p. 58).

Ramakrishna experienced unusual psychological states from age seven, the time of his father's death. But at the age of twenty, after suffering the departure of his brother (another father figure), he succumbed to a desperate desire for the vision and blessing (*darsana*) of the goddess Kali. In the intensity and pathos of an extended period of yearning for Kali, says Kripal, Ramakrishna became like an infant who cannot see, or be seen, by his mother (ibid., p. 62). Drowning in his prolonged "anxious desire" for Kali's *darsana*, Ramakrishna finally reached for her sword and moved to decapitate himself when at last the goddess intervened. As a young man, Ramakrishna's suicidal attempt at self-decapitation was driven, Kripal believes, by an unbearable shame for his homoerotic desires – the same "anxious desires" that were later directed toward his young male disciples. These desires, says Kripal, were both a longing for God and for sexual experience with a man. Together they produced the initial "erotic crisis" that became the paradigm for Ramakrishna's entry into ecstatic states:

> Ramakrishna's attempted suicide and consequent experience of Kali, in other words, can be understood *both* as a genuinely religious experience driven by mystical longing (...) *and* as a desperate attempt to put an end to his tormenting shame fueled by his homoerotic longing (...) the later, it seems, somehow triggered the former – *an erotic crisis led to a mystical experience*. (Kripal, 1995, p. 77)

Kripal looks closely at the symbolism of Kali's sword in order to understand the intrapsychic and religious development of the saint. Ramakrishna, he writes, was ultimately able "to turn Kali's sword into Krisna's flute." In his first vision, the unconscious meanings of Kali's sword revolve around shame and self-decapitation/castration; yet in his later years, his homoeroticism found more apt symbolic expression in the mythology of Lord Krishna, for it gave rise far less to feelings of shame and self-annihilation than to joy and genuinely religious ecstasy. Thus we must see Kripal's central hermeneutic as religious-integrative, for he redefines the erotic not merely as libido but as a religious category and so integrates a psychoanalytic and mystical perspective on equal terms and in dynamic relation to one another.

Case Interlude: Sushmita and the Third Eye of God

Sushmita is a twenty-year old woman of Indian descent from a middle-class Sikh family in the United States. Her parents immigrated from Trinidad in their mid-twenties and Sushmita was born and raised in Chicago along with a younger brother and sister (two and four years younger, respectively). She is unusually thoughtful and bright. She has long black hair and often wears carefully torn and patched jeans; her ears and lower lip are pierced.

Sushmita's early memories revolve around grade school, where she recalls being the victim of unfair treatment by one teacher in particular who "didn't like Indians." She also recalls favoritism on the part of her parents and grandparents toward her brother, to which she responded, she says, by rejecting her femininity and viewing herself as a male. She wore boys' clothing and played on male sports teams, "as though to somehow transform my gender." She recalls being teased and feeling socially isolated in school, sometimes refusing to go.

Between the ages of nine and eleven, Sushmita began having dreams in which she found herself in "a parallel world governed by vampires." These were highly erotic dreams in which she was often chased by one especially dangerous vampire. The dreams came as often as three times a week, she said, and they confused and frightened her, because she had no way to "rationalize" them.

At age thirteen Sushmita shocked her parents by suddenly cutting off her long Sikh braid and highlighting her hair. Around the same time she was drawn into the local Goth sub-culture and began wearing black combat boots, miniskirt and chains, and listening exclusively to heavy metal music. She rejected her Sikh friends and refused to go to the Sikh temple or attend Indian parties. Sushmita became fascinated with Wicca, joining a group of witches and a high priestess (all much older); she also became interested in Buddhism and "all sorts of mysticism." She now interprets her Goth and new age pursuits as an intentional barrier that she placed between herself and her parents and as a denial of her own Indian identity. "I was rejecting my Indian skin by covering it with a much darker, western symbol of black," she said. To her peers, she became "a person to fear. They saw me as someone they would never understand and left me alone."

Meanwhile, she said, her parents' marriage reached a crisis point. Her mother suddenly "wanted a divorce, not only from her husband but from her children as well." The mother did not divorce her husband, however, largely because he was suffering from a debilitating illness. She was apparently feeling trapped in her circumstances and was in "the throes of menopause," Sushmita claims, and so began to vent her anger and frustrations on her children, at times becoming physically abusive. It was like "the ultimate rejection from my family," she said. "I felt entirely disowned and spent a lot of my time out of the house with a group of friends who weren't exactly the best influence for me." By early high school age, she had also begun cutting and occasionally burning her self.

At age fifteen, Sushmita had what she now understands as a pivotal experience in her life. She was out in an open field, smoking pot with a group of friends. She looked up at one point and saw a break in the clouds which immediately made her think of God's third eye. A bright ray of sun came from the eye and she suddenly felt as though it could see into every aspect of her – "every part of me that had never been noticed before and every part of my life that was ugly and hidden (...) I felt it penetrating deep within myself." It was as though the light were extracting each piece of her life and "re-piecing everything together so that there were gaps and overlaps or discontinuities and parts that didn't make sense." Terrified, she ran toward home but on the way, she said, "I slipped into an open pond and cut myself on a thorn bush," so that when she arrived home he was caked in mud and badly scratched. Feeling as though she had lost control of her body, she threw off all of her clothing and ran naked to her mother, asking her mother to bathe her "the way she did when I was a child." As her mother bathed her in the shower, Sushmita begged forgiveness for having cut her hair, for becoming a Goth, and for causing her parents so much distress. She also promised to respect her parents if she survived this terrible experience. Her mother soothed her, assuring her that she was a good daughter, and slept next to her that night and each night for several months, during which time her mother threw out all the trappings of Sushmita's Goth culture – her books, posters, CDs and clothing.

After this terrifying experience, Sushmita lost her appetite and ate next to nothing; she also developed severe insomnia. During this period she felt a pervasive sense of unreality – that people and relationships were not real and "that the entire world was an illusion. This realization hit me as soon as I felt the third eye inside of me." She had severe panic attacks in school and at social gatherings, prompting her mother to send her to "a series of psychiatrists, psychoanalysts and a hypnotherapist," with little change. Eventually the mother decided to visit a Hindu astrologer who was a friend of the family and in fact thought to be related through distant ancestors from India. The astrologer, Sushmita said, knew everything about her family and its history. After interviewing them and consulting Sushmita's astrological chart, he instructed her to "feed the birds" and perform a salutation to the sun every day, while her mother was to perform a daily prayer.

Eventually, Sushmita began having dreams of snakes covering her entire body. Instead of evoking terror, however, the feeling tone of these dreams was one of calm and comfort. In them, she said, "I would become completely at ease and any anxiety I had would be lifted off from me." She described the dreams to her mother, who immediately produced an image of Lord Shiva that had been stowed away, out of sight of the father, who ridiculed Hindu polytheistic beliefs and practices. Her mother said that the snakes were a sign of Lord Shiva's protection. Sushmita then took an interest in Lord Shiva and began painting images of him and writing poems about him. The dreams continued, including one that she describes as a "lucid dream," in which she battled a liege of sea demons. In the dream, she said, "I made all the decisions Shiva would make while battling the demons. During the battle I could feel my life force gaining energy as every thrust of my arms with swords would penetrate into their core." She also began to chant a Shiva mantra that is believed to protect the devotee from death and release her from danger and disease.

By the time Sushmita turned seventeen, life had improved. She struggled less with anxiety, her relations with parents were better and she had reconnected somewhat with her family's Sikh religion. Sushmita had also replaced cutting with body piercing and began to recognize and pursue some of her own bisexual impulses. Sushmita began wearing colorful clothing again and in fact decided to bleach and dye her hair a bright "fire-truck red" which she kept for almost two years, before going to college. Presently, she continues to see herself as a devotee of Shiva and has had at least one vision of him in which Shiva entered her bedroom and lay down next to her, embracing her until morning.

Reflections

Sushmita's vision of God's eye occurs amidst the turbulent resurgence of sexual impulses in adolescence, and within a context marked by both familial discord and identity confusion. The latter is based in significant measure on her experience as a second-generation Indian immigrant to America; she likes to refer to herself as an "ABCD" – American Born Confused Desi (Indian). She first experiences her own sexual impulses as persecutory and unconsciously represents them through images drawn from Western mythology, namely vampires. Her dreams of being pursued by a deadly yet erotic vampire suggest that she unconsciously experiences the act of intercourse as one of violent depletion, something that would take her life away. In addition to these issues of identity and sexuality, Sushmita's accounts hint at the possibility of early trauma from physical abuse by her mother and distance (at best) from her father. The effects of such early trauma may also include experiences of neglect or abandonment with the birth of her younger brother when she was age two.

In psychoanalytic terms, we find multiple borderline features in Sushmita's case: precocious eroticism linked to primitive fears and persecutory images at age nine, later expressed in a terrifying experience of penetration and fragmentation by a divine gaze; polymorphous expression of erotic impulses by age fifteen, acted out through bisexual relations and colourfully symbolized in bright clothing and red, *fire truck* hair; a florid imaginative life within which she occasionally loses her sense of the "as if" nature of her dreams and visions; and unconscious, defensive splitting, evidenced in polarized dream images of good and evil, and in the division between idealized perceptions of mother and an abiding though ominous fascination with the dark and blood-thirsty maternal goddess Kali.

Despite the borderline features of her case, however, Sushmita's life narrative reveals significant and progressive changes in symbolization and corresponding improvements in her inner and outer life. Whereas Sushmita initially symbolized her unconscious inner world through the media of vampires, she eventually shifted to symbolic forms that drew upon a mythological repertoire of snakes, gods and goddesses, from the Indian side of her life and relationships. Sushmita had chosen to distance herself from her parents and the Indian community, and so had rejected a source of shared symbols. This symbolic distance was made greater by her independent tendencies as an American teenager, and by her mother's abusive actions and the marital discord at home. The distance began to collapse with the overwhelming vision at age fifteen. To be sure, the vision was initially, for her, meaningless – disorienting, violently sexual, uncontrolled, and exposing of her own filth – an irruption of primary process. Further, immediately following the vision, she was infantilized and drawn into merger with her mother (bathed like an infant, stripped of the trappings of her social identity, kept with mother each night). And yet, the eye of her vision soon came to be, and perhaps was from the beginning, the third eye of Lord Shiva. This divine eye articulates with a symbolic world within which Sushmita could give expression to, and so help integrate, her inner turbulence and locate her experience intelligibly within her own familial and Indian relational contexts.

Shiva's third eye is fully elaborated in the popular mythology. Lord Shiva uses his third eye to destroy *Kama*, the god of desire who threatens Shiva's ascetic practice. This insures Shiva's mounting potency (gained through long periods of asceticism) which will eventually be released into the world when Shiva shifts (or is seduced) from his asceticism into an actively erotic mode. Shiva is cyclically an ascetic and a householder; he is destructive of sexual passion for the sake of ascetic withdrawal and yogic meditation, and then actively indulgent in it for the sake of the world. Further, Shiva is linked in many myth cycles to the fierce and maternal goddess Kali. This array of Hindu symbolic forms to which Sushmita turned (or returned) after her initial vision, functioned intrapsychically to give name and expression to terrifying and otherwise inaccessible unconscious realities – polarized, penetrating, wildly destructive – and so facilitate their integration into consciousness. At the same time, these Hindu forms helped her to reintegrate her subjective world into a shared world of religious symbols within her family and community (particularly among the women).

Ultimately, embracing a Hindu symbolic, though initially motivated by pathological and primitive psychic realities, may have opened Sushmita to new and irreducibly religious dimensions of experience. We can thus approach Sushmita's case through the same religious-integrative hermeneutic engaged by Kripal in his study of Ramakrishna. Sushmita's overwhelming vision of God's third eye evolves into an engagement with Hindu mythology that is not merely sexual but "erotic" in Kripal's sense of a dialectic of sexuality and religious experience. For Ramakrishna, says Kripal, early sexual trauma gives rise to dissociative states and trances that are the foundation to later mystical technique and religious ecstasy (*bhava*). A pathological condition connected to deep feelings of shame gives rise to religious virtuosity and genuine mystical experience that is founded in but irreducible to those feelings. Similarly, though in less illustrious context, Sushmita's erotic crisis gives rise to vitality of devotional love and a religiosity that, for the time being, sustains and stabilizes her inner and outer worlds.

But intrinsic to such a religious-integrative hermeneutic is the problem of identifying an authentically mystical or otherwise religious dimension of experience and distinguishing it from its psychological underpinnings. The question applies equally to the lives of ordinary people such as Sushmita and extraordinary individuals such as Ramakrishna, Mohandas Gandhi, St. Augustine and Martin Luther. Psychoanalytic biographies of these historical figures might more easily convince us of the unconscious foundations of religious experience than of its authenticity. And yet, as we have seen, a religious-integrative hermeneutic seems to appear and reappear even in the foundational writings of psychoanalysis. Perhaps this is in response to a dimension of psychical life that would otherwise go unacknowledged.

Concluding Thoughts

In this essay I have given an historical overview of some of the definitive ideas that have shaped the encounter of Hinduism and psychoanalysis. In the process, I have highlighted three dimensions of psychoanalytic thinking about Hindu lives and religious phenomena. Each of these dimensions – the explanatory-reductive, cultural-interpretive, and religious-integrative – entails a discrete hermeneutic that is appropriate to distinctive aspects of psychical life. Historically, we see a sequential shift in emphasis from foundational studies that privilege explanatory-reductive thinking, to indigenizing studies that stress cultural-interpretive approaches, to integrative studies that acknowledge religious or mystical dimensions of the inner world. The sequence alone is not a sufficient measure of "progress" in the encounter, for a given study or theory might stress one hermeneutic to the exclusion of another. Each hermeneutic generates its own kind of valuable perspectives, however incomplete. An explanatory-reductive approach constitutes psychoanalysis, in Kakar's words, as the "iconoclastic discipline *par excellence*, especially wary of our most cherished beliefs and the unexamined convictions we carry with us from our cultural and individual pasts" (Kakar, from Vaidyanathan and Kripal, 1999).

The cultural-interpretive insures consideration of the variability of life forms and imaginative worlds that human beings create and live in. And a religious-integrative approach generates awareness of ultimate dimensions of psychological life, as well as the religious horizons of any given orientation to the mind. The most valuable overall approach to the encounter of Hinduism and psychoanalysis will stress not just one of these hermeneutical dimensions; it will seek a balanced and dynamic interaction of all three.

References

Akhtar, S. (2001). Psychoanalysis and India. In B. Erwin (Ed.), *The Freud encyclopedia: Theory, therapy, and culture* (pp. 275–276). New York: Routledge.

Akhtar, S. (Ed.) (2005). *Freud along the Ganges: Psychoanalytic reflections on the people and culture of India*. New York: Other Press.

Berkeley-Hill, O. (1921). The anal-erotic factor in the religion, philosophy, and character of the Hindus. *International Journal of Psycho-analysis*, *2*, 306–338.

Bose, G. (1921). *Concept of repression*. Calcutta: Sri Gouranga Press.

Browning, D. S. (1987). *Religious thought and the modern psychologies: A critical conversation in the theology of culture*. Philadelphia, PA: Fortress.

Carstairs, G. M. (1957). *The twice born: A study of a community of high-caste Hindus*. Bloomington, IN: Indiana University Press.

Courtright, P. (1985). *Ganesha: Lord of obstacles, lord of beginnings*. Oxford: Oxford University Press.

Daly, C. D. (1930). The psychology of revolutionary tendencies. *International Journal of Psycho-analysis*, *11*, 193–210.

Daniel, E. V. (1984). *Fluid signs: Being a person the Tamil way*. Berkeley, CA/Los Angeles, CA: University of California Press.

Derne, S. (1995). *Culture in action: Family life, emotion, and male dominance in Banaras, India*. Albany, NY: State University of New York Press.

Erikson, E. H. (1969). *Gandhi's truth: On the origins of militant nonviolence*. New York: Norton.

Goldman, R. P. (1978). Fathers, sons and Gurus: Oedipal conflict in the Sanskrit epics. *Journal of Indian Philosophy*, *6*, 325–392.

Greenberg, J. R. & Mitchell, S. A. (1983). *Object relations in psychoanalytic theory*. Cambridge, MA/London: Harvard University Press.

Hartnack, C. (1999). Vishnu on Freud's desk: Psychoanalysis in colonial India. In T. G. Vaidyanathan & J. J. Kripal (Eds.), *Vishnu on Freud's desk: A reader in psychoanalysis and Hinduism* (pp. 81–106). Delhi: Oxford University Press.

Inden, R. B. & Nicholas, R. W. (1977). *Kinship in Bengali culture*. Chicago, IL: University of Chicago Press.

Ingham, J. M. (1996). Oedipality in pragmatic discourse: The Trobriands and Hindu India. *Ethos*, *24*(4), 559–587.

Kakar, S. (1978). *The inner world: A psychoanalytic study of childhood and society in India*. Delhi: Oxford University Press.

Kakar, S. (1985). Psychoanalysis and non-western cultures. *International Review of Psycho-analysis*, *12*, 441–448.

Kakar, S. (1991). *The analyst and the mystic: Psychoanalytic reflections on religion and mysticism*. Chicago, IL: University of Chicago Press.

Kakar, S. (1994). Encounters of the psychological kind: Freud, Jung, and India. In L. B. Boyer, R. M. Boyer & H. F. Stein (Eds.), *Essays in honor of George A. De Vos* (pp. 263–272). Hillsdale, NJ: Analytic Press.

Kakar, S. (1995). India. In P. Kutter (Ed.), *Psychoanalysis international: A guide to psychoanalysis throughout the world.* (Vol. 2, pp. 16–122). Stuttgart/Bad Cannstatt, Germany: Frommann-Holzboog.
Kakar, S. (2000). *The ascetic of desire: A novel of the Kamasutra*. Woodstock, NY: The Overlook Press.
Kakar, S. (2003). *Ecstacy: A novel*. Woodstock, NY: The Overlook Press.
Kernberg, O. (1976). *Object relations theory and clinical psychoanalysis*. New York: Aronson.
Kripal, J. (1995). *Kali's child: The mystical and the erotic in the life and teachings of Ramakrishna*. Chicago, IL: University of Chicago Press.
Kripal, J. (1999). Hinduism and psychoanalysis: Thinking through each other. In T. G. Vaidyanathan & J. J. Kripal (Eds.), *Vishnu on Freud's desk: A reader in psychoanalysis and Hinduism* (pp. 438–452). Delhi: Oxford University Press.
Kripal, J. (2000). Re-membering a presence of mythological proportions: Psychoanalysis and Hinduism. In D. Jonte-Pace & W. Parsons (Eds.), *Religion and psychology: Mapping the terrain* (pp. 254–279). New York: Routledge.
Kurtz, S. N. (1992). *All the mothers are one: Hindu India and the cultural reshaping of psychoanalysis*. New York/Oxford: Columbia University Press.
Lamb, S. (1993). *Growing in the net of Maya: Person, gender, and life processes in a Bengali society*, Ph.D. dissertation, University of Chicago.
Lamb, S. (2000). *White saris and sweet mangos: Aging, gender and body in North India*. Berkeley, CA: University of California Press.
Leach, E. R. (1972) Pulleyar and the Lord Buddha: An aspect of religious syncretism in Ceylon. In W. A. Lessa & E. Z. Vogt (Eds.), *Reader in comparative religion: An anthropological approach*, 3rd edition. (pp. 302–313). New York: Harper & Row.
Marriott, M. (1976). Hindu transactions: Diversity without dualism. In B. Kapferer (Ed.), *Transaction and meaning: Directions in the anthropology of exchange and symbolic behavior* (pp. 109–142). Philadelphia, PA: ISHI.
Marriott, M. (1980). *The open person and interpersonal fluidity*. Washington, DC: Association for Asian Studies.
Mehta, P. (1997). The import and export of psychoanalysis: India. *Journal of the American Academy of Psychoanalysis, 25*(3), 455–471.
Mukherjee, B. N. (1980). Psychological theory and research methods. In U. Pareek (Ed.), *Psychological theory and research methods*. Bombay: Popular Prakashan.
Neki, J. S. (1973). Guru-Chela relationship: The possibility of therapeutic paradigm. *American Journal of Orthopsychiatry, 43*, 755–766.
Neki, J. S. (1976). An examination of the cultural relativism of dependence as a dynamic of social and therapeutic relationships. *British Journal of Medicine and Psychology, 49*, 1–10.
Obeyesekere, G. (1984). *Medusa's hair: An essay on personal symbols and religious experience*. Chicago, IL: University of Chicago Press.
Obeyesekere, G. (1990). *The work of culture: Symbolic transformation in psychoanalysis and anthropology*. Chicago, IL: The University of Chicago Press.
O'Flaherty, W. D. (1973). *Asceticism and eroticism in the mythology of Shiva*. Delhi: Oxford University Press.
Parsons, W. B. (1999). *The enigma of the oceanic feeling*. New York: Oxford University Press.
Parsons, W. B. (2000). Themes and debates in the psychology-comparativist dialogue. In D. Jonte-Pace & W. B. Parsons (Eds.), *Religion and psychology: Mapping the terrain* (pp. 229–253). New York: Routledge.
Raheja, G. (1988). *The poison in the gift: Ritual, prestation, and the dominant caste in a North Indian village*. Chicago, IL: University of Chicago Press.
Ramana, C. V. (1964). On the early history and development of psychoanalysis in India. *Journal of the American Psychoanalytic Association, 12*, 110–134.
Ramanujan, A. K. (1983). The Indian oedipus. In L. Edmunds & A. Dundes (Eds.), *Oedipus: A folklore casebook* (pp. 234–261). London: Garland.

Ramanujan, A. K. (1989). Is there an Indian way of thinking? An informal essay. *Contributions to Indian Sociology*, *23*(1), 41–58.
Ricoeur, P. (1970). *Freud & philosophy: An essay on interpretation*. New Haven, CT/London: Yale University Press.
Ricoeur, P. (1974). A philosophical interpretation of Freud. In D. Ihde (trans.), *The conflict of interpretations: Essays in hermeneutics* (pp. 160–176). Evanston, IL: Northwestern University Press.
Rizzuto, A.-M. (1979). *The birth of the living god: A psychoanalytic study*. Chicago, IL/London: University of Chicago Press.
Roland, A. (1988). *Search of self in India and Japan: Toward a cross-cultural psychology*. Princeton, NJ: Princeton University Press.
Rudolph, L. & Rudolph, S. (1976). Rajput adulthood: Reflections on the Amar Singh diary. *Daedalus*, *102*, 145–167.
Shweder, R. (1991). *Thinking through cultures: Expeditions in cultural psychology*. Cambridge, MA: Harvard University Press.
Shweder, R. A. & Bourne, E. J. (1984). Does the concept of the person vary cross-culturally? In R. A. Shweder & R. A. LeVine (Eds.), *Culture theory: Essays on mind, self, and emotion* (pp. 158–199). Cambridge: Cambridge University Press.
Sinha, D. (1990). Appropriate indigenous psychology in India: A search for new identity. In S. Iwawaki, Y. Kashima & K. Leung (Eds.), *Appropriate indigenous psychology in India: A search for new identity* (pp. 38–48). Amsterdam/Lisse/Berwyn: Swets & Zeitlinger.
Sinha, J. (1980). *Nurturant task leader*. New Delhi: Concept.
Sinha, T. C. (1966). Development of psychoanalysis in India. *International Journal of Psycho-analysis*, *47*, 427–439.
Spratt, P. (1966). *Hindu culture and personality: A psychoanalytic study*. Bombay: Manaktalas.
Trawick, M. (1990). *Notes on love in a Tamil family*. Berkeley/Los Angeles, CA: University of California Press.
Vaidyanathan, T. G. & Kripal, J. J. (1999). *Vishnu on Freud's desk: A reader in psychoanalysis and Hinduism*. Delhi: Oxford University Press.

The Paternal Metaphor Revisited in Post-Freudian French Religious Psychoanalytic Anthropology*

René Devisch

Before addressing the topic of the multilayered function and meaning of the father figure in the religious perspectives of the Yaka of southwest Congo,[1] section "Freud Among Francophone Africanists" will explore some relevant theoretical avenues offered by both the social anthropological and the significant post-Freudian francophone literature in the traditions of Devereux and/or Lacan. These readings

* The research, which began in 1971, among rural and urban Yaka has been carried out in collaboration with the Africa Research Centre, renamed as the Institute for Anthropology in Africa, at the Katholieke Universiteit Leuven. I acknowledge with gratitude financial support in the past from the Belgian National Foundation for Scientific Research, the Research Fund – Flanders, the European Commission Directorate-General XII, and the Harry-Frank Guggenheim Foundation, New York. The research was and is carried out in collaboration with my colleagues at the IMNC (Institut des Musées Nationaux du Congo), as well as the CERDAS Research Centre at the University of Kinshasa. There is almost no psychoanalytical perspective dealt with in this paper that has not been scrutinised in a dialogue with Claude Brodeur, philosopher and psychoanalyst in Montréal (and 20 years my senior), pursued since the early 1990s. At the Belgian School of Psychoanalysis, colleague-psychoanalysts have, since September 2002 in the very witty ambience of our monthly seminar on Culture, bodiliness and the unconscious, shared their inspiring views and radical questions regarding the matrixial, borderlinking art and dreaming, gender-specific initiation and healing. I thank Peter Crossman for his editorialship.

[1] My thematic perspectives and theoretical questions stem from three forms of anthropological experience in a great diversity of cultural and social milieus in Africa: firstly, by way of extended fieldwork among the Yaka of southwest Congo, in the Yitaanda settlement of 12 villages in Northern Yaka land, from 1971 till 1974; and annual research stays since 1986 of some 3 weeks or more among the Yaka and Kongo people concentrated in some of Kinshasa's townships; secondly, for some 6 weeks in 1988, I was fortunate to assist in the finalisation of an in-depth religious anthropological research among Guji-Oromo pastoralists to the south of Awasa in south-Ethiopia; and thirdly, in situ supervision of doctoral researchers led me to locations in nine African countries (to suburbs of Cairo in Egypt and of Douala in Cameroon, to rural western Congo, northern Ghana, southwestern Kenya, southeastern Nigeria, northwestern Tanzania, KwaZulu Natal in South-Africa, northwestern Namibia) and to the Druze communities in northern Israel.

R. Devisch
KU Leuven, Leuven, Belgium
e-mail: René Devisch@ant.kuleuven.be

J.A. Belzen (ed.), *Changing the Scientific Study of Religion: Beyond Freud?*

demonstrate a recent psychoanalytically acknowledgeable attention to a local people's particular intercorporeal, intersubjective and transworldly shaping of self, unconscious fantasy, emotion and social commitment. Conversely, such attention echoes the anthropologist's very flexible observational participation in the life of the host community, in a manner evocative of the transferential process that develops between a psychoanalyst and an analysand. Section "The Yaka Religious Sensibility for the Weave of Things and the Augural" will set out my own combination of a culture-sensitive, endogenous anthropological approach and aspectual psychoanalytically informed interpretation of the domain of the religious among the Yaka. Apart from the (post)missionary sphere of influence, the Yaka religious composing with the life world comprises a four part framework, without, however, any reference to some personalised Divinity or single Supreme Being. There is, first of all and with regard to public life, a general ordering and societal legitimisation of knowledge, behavioural patterns and institutional tasks, centred on ancestral agencies. Second, dreamwork as well as the performing of mediumnic divination and of healing or transition rituals including sacrifices, all develop on the community level a multifaceted exchange with both ancestors and cult spirits. Third, one encounters in the familial domain a profound though more diffuse and informal, mediumnic and augural sensitivity to the (in)auspicious resonance function of the bond with the primordial matrixial source of all life and common fate situated in the womb of the earth. Fourth, we note the individual perversion of the mentioned religious attitude through fatal witchcraft and sorcery – a topic that will not be dealt with in this paper. Section "The Agnatic Ancestors, Matricentred Filiation and the Maternal Uncle" will focus primarily on the bilineal kinship structure of the extended family among the Yaka. Patrilineal descent as determinative of a person's social identity is being combined with the matrilineal filiation of physical life and destiny to the individual. I argue that it is the maternal uncle, and not the father, who in the name of matrilineal filiation authoritatively gives witness to the religiously enforced Order of the Ethical Law and the local version of the incest prohibition as the minimal intersubjective ordering. Drawing on the preceding, section "Transworldly Phallogocentric Symbolisation and Matrixial *Signifiance*" summarises the glaring difference among the Yaka between encompassing, religiously-tuned and phallogocentric symbolisation processes on the one hand, and on the other the more fragmentary and diverse augural sensibility to transworldly matrixial *signifiance* or emerging meaning production.

Freud Among Francophone Africanists

The dialogue between anthropology and psychoanalysis among French-speaking scholars has dealt primarily with the (inter)subjective and culture specific ways in which the gendered subject is formed and constitutes itself in the multilayered processes of production and (possibly intercultural) exchange of experience, recognition and knowledge. These are preferably approached in the reciprocal articulation of kinship relations and economic, political and religious implications, or also in the multifaceted and passional expression of sexuality and of the interpersonal and intersubjective sharing of life, affects, aspirations, cultural and religious horizons of meaning that mobilise emotions or commitment in the conjugal, parent–child or brother–sister relations (Godelier and Hassoun, 1996; Muxel and Rennes, 1989). Both disciplines have, in increasing measure, recognised homologous mechanisms at work in the culture and the psyche of individuals. Offering complementary perspectives, they have approached these mechanisms primarily in terms of the normative (re)construction of identity as well as in relation to the often seriously disruptive process of becoming in the intercultural contexts of migration. Their fields of view intersect in the socially pregnant spheres of family and filiation, gender differentiation and inter-generational relations, ethno-social identity and *métissages*, formation of symptoms and the experience of illness, resentment or revenge and accusations, and in the process of defining what is normal and abnormal.

Sigmund Freud has in the main taken a critical scientific outlook with regard to the largely unconscious psychodynamic development and domestication of human nature. He approaches this last in its resonance with social relations and culture, and among these especially history and religion. Many of Freud's evolutionary postulates have become untenable, in particular his biologistic and psychogenetic recapitulation proposing a parallel between onto- and phylogenesis. In contrast, Freud's perspective on childhood and deep unconscious motivation in the subject-in relation to the parent and other primary kinship figures, at least as an heuristic approach rather than a conclusion, appears to have been one of his more enduring contributions to the (post)modern self-understanding offering moreover possibilities for relevant cultural comparison (cf. Flax, 1990; Obeyesekere, 1980).

Bronislav Malinowski was perhaps the first within the field of anthropology to take a critical distance from Freud's universalistic theses regarding childhood. Already in Freud's time and based on his study of the matrilineal Trobriands in the northeastern islands of Papua New Guinea, Malinowski (1929) proposed that the Oedipus complex, focussed on the father–son relation and centred on patrilineality, cannot be seen as universal. Although Malinowski may have been wrong to reject the psychic Oedipus dynamic on the basis of social data alone, he nonetheless laid bare a blind spot in Freud's all too narrow and naturalistic scope. Freud only had an eye for the father–child (in fact, father–son) relation within a naturalistic model of the Oedipal trangulation, and this only in and from the perspective of the European and semitic patriarchal, cognatically organised, family structure (Nandy, 1995, pp. 81ff.; see Godelier's view, below). This father–son model also underscores Melford Spiro's (1982) thesis aimed at refuting Malinowski's denial of the Oedipal dynamic among the Trobriands. Malinowski shows how among the latter, the maternal uncle functions as the authoritative figure par excellence in relation to the child, and it is primarily within the brother–sister relationship that the basic drives are being socialised and symbolised. Moreover, anthropologists such as Margaret Mead, Anne Parsons, Gilbert Herdt show how more relevant it is to focus on the mother–child relation within the great variety of familial and normative organisations of the basic relations and socialisation.

Up until the work of Claude Lévi-Strauss, the Durkheimian *Ecole sociologique* dismissed any attempt at dialogue with psychoanalysis as irrelevant. In his attention to the structural play of duties, loyalties tensions and communications between the various positions in the elementary kinship structure, between shaman-healer and client, or even between the *dramatis personae* in Sophocles' Oedipus myth, Lévi-Strauss (1958) initially appeared to have been marking out a field of interest in common with Freud. In the event, Lévi-Strauss' Kantian-rationalistic reading of the non-conscious cognitive logic that governs the human spirit in its symbolic and social production (including the incest prohibition) led to a profound divergence with Freud. More seriously, Lévi-Strauss (1958, pp. 183–203, 206–226) inverts the so-called scientific yet ethnocentric pretensions of Freud, and treats psychoanalysis as a western culture-specific technique or ethnotherapy whose functioning he sees as homologous with Amerindian shamanistic techniques. Lévi-Strauss (1958, pp. 239–242) proposes, just as Paul Ricoeur (1970, pp. 208–209) was later to do, that Freud's hypothesis in *Totem und Tabu* postulating a primordial culture-founding patricide, was nothing more than a science-like myth or a mythopoetic variant on an original Greek andro- and patricentric myth of Oedipus. Moreover, Lévi-Strauss demonstrates that the incest prohibition cannot have sprung out of some *Ur*-patricide, yet itself constitutes the social principle or mechanism par excellence that pushes each generation to maximise marital exchange (Lévi-Strauss, 1958, pp. 56–62); within his structuralistic equivalence of culture and the rule of exchange, Lévi-Strauss focusses only on the inter-generational prohibition against incest and is not concerned with the brother–sister incest (prohibition).

Among francophone studies, we find in the work of Lina Balestriere (1998) a more recent and fresh presentation of Freud's psychoanalytic hermeneutic and theory formation. Drawing in part on her clinical experience and a broad review of the literature, she deepens the Freudian approach (and, in the process, the Lacanian metaphorical perspective as well) to the father- and mother-figure functions.

It was George Devereux (1978, 1980)[2] and Jeanne Favret-Saada (1977), rather, who clarified the significant research and theoretical implications of the complementary, psychoanalytic and anthropological, approach. In the anthropological encounter, such as they see it, transference and countertransference spur the researcher on to question him- or herself with regard to the place of the question (for help, information, insight, respect, intercultural recognition) and the transactional circulation and intrusion of affects in the researcher and the host group.

[2] My essay unfortunately cannot deal with Devereux's fundamental contributions to complementary psychoanalytical and anthropological perspectives on human experience (Devereux, 1978) and on the inextricable interrelationship between culture (religion) and psyche, cultural values and unconscious symptom formation. These perspectives are too important to be dealt with in a sketchy manner. Yet, inasmuch as I have opted to take Lacan's work as a reference, I am at a loss as to how to make the leap from there to Devereux's major contribution on the intercultural scientist's self-deceptive countertransference of desires and resistances, on the scientist's own biases and blindness. Devereux also brilliantly brings out how much a disturbed person may witness to culturally induced anxiety, repression and the like. In his major work (1980, chapter 10), Devereux lists the characteristics of Occidental civilisation that tie in with, and hence produce, schizophrenic symptoms. This analysis leads him to assert that schizophrenia is the privileged "ethnic psychosis" of modern western industrial society.

Tobie Nathan and his group have, from the early 1980s, been developing unique forms of ethnopsychoanalytic therapy in line with both Devereux's complementarist approach to the homologic processes in psyche and culture as well as with Didier Anzieu's (1984, 1985) work on the unconscious in the group and on the skin-Self (*le Moi-corps*) (Nathan, 1986). Their clinical work with patients from non-western countries at the Centre George Devereux at the University of Paris Nord is rather unique (Streit, 1997). It is an attempt towards integrating, in a culture-sensitive way, both the patients' mother tongue, culture-specific aetiology and meaning of symptoms, as well as their personal and deeply kin-related experience of distress, often expressed in a religious idiom. Most debated by his colleagues (Corin, 1997) are Nathan's aims as a therapist to endorse an illocutionary position (Nathan, 1994) and to re-anchor the immigrant patients within their primordial culture. The problematic question here is: what equips and legitimates the foreign therapist in seeking to re-anchor clients in their primordial cultural coding, which is both non-conscious and allegedly at work in their – in part religiously informed – perception, sensorium and identifications?

The School of African Psychopathology at the open-door Fann hospital of social psychiatry in Dakar, Senegal, is centred around Henri Collomb's (1967) culture-sensitive views. Its work entails radical innovations in the psychiatric practice in West Africa in the aftermath of colonisation which had criminalised numerous local therapeutic practices. Practitioners at Fann follow a somewhat Lacanian tradition, inasmuch as they situate the patient within the symbolic order of language and culture in search of strengthening the patient's ability to symbolise his or her conflictive experiences and fantasies. The pioneering sensibility for the patient's discourse or voice and for transference, in this postcolonial awareness of racial wounds and cultural rights, as well as the incipient theorising of cultural dimensions to the psyche and pathology, lead to re-organising the hospital setting and protocol, and to foster a genuine caring function on the part of the family as well (Ortigues et al., 1967). Houses in the local village style are being built in the courtyard of the psychiatric unit in order to host the family members who accompany the patient. Andras Zempleni (1977), who as a member of the Dakar School incisively deals with folk 'psychiatric' systems, tells us that the above-mentioned sensibility in particular aims to unblock the patient's religious signifiers. These comprise, for example, the patient's possession by ancestral spirits or states of bewitchment or cursing, as understood in terms of his or her complex lineage structured world and life course.

It was in this same intercultural and interreligious context that, in the wake of colonisation, husband and wife Marie-Cécile and Edmond Ortigues broadened their psychoanalytic attention to focus as well on the various narratives, gestures and horizons (clinical, aetiological, familial and religious; those of sorcery and the practice of marabous; as well as of conflicts between tradition and modernity); these were, notably, elements that emerged in the *lay therapy management group* in relation to a quest for mental health care at the Fann hospital and to the questions and points of view of the patients themselves. In this, their approach broke with that of plying the patient with intrusive questions soliciting responses of whose function – to lay bare unconscious mechanisms – the subject remained unaware. The latter style, then, characterises the psychoanalytic work among the Dogon in Mali by Paul Parin et al. (1966). The majority of Ortigues' 178 patients, all male, with whom their book deals, belonged to the closely related Wolof, Lebou or Serer societies that, in part due to the influence of Islam over the last 5 centuries, have juxtaposed their matrilineal foundations with patrilineal principles. Their book, *L'Oedipe africain* (1966), echoes the research of other members of the Fann group (inventoried by Collignon, 1978). The case studies they recorded intend to demonstrate that the reference to the 'father' (who is at times the genitor, at others the social father or family head) takes a central place in virtually every case, even in those concerning children raised by the maternal uncle or those who have not known their genitor. Nevertheless, the father appears only as a link in the lineage and as a marker with regard to the subjects belonging to a particular age grade. Here, as Daniël Schurmans (1972) also shows, interpersonal rivalry tends to involve mainly 'brothers' while at the same time aggression sublimated by the law of familial solidarity takes the form of persecutional interpretations of sorcery and cursing. Speaking more recently of their work in a multicultural context, and particularly of the central problem of transference in an intercultural encounter, Edmond Ortigues (1996) reveals the extent to which his clinical sensitivity acquired in Dakar and his attention to alternative subjectivities has continued to inspire his plural psychoanalytic listening in France.

In their assessment of the book *L'Oedipe africain*, Gilles Deleuze and Félix Guattari (1972, p. 201) argue that an oedipal triangulation is still to be found there. In a new and expanded edition of their book, Edmond Ortigues, (1984, p. 278) expresses his agreement on this point. This revised edition omits the original chapter 2, which was the most Lacanian-inspired section of that work. Without resolving it, their book points to the problem of the normative occidental model of the rational and autonomous self; yet the Ortigues nevertheless acknowledge that they are unable to provide a theoretical explanation of the culture-specific psychodynamic underscoring both the sociocentric or relational self and the fatal effects of a conflict in the family and fearing a witchcraft threat coming from one's parents, as was encountered at Fann. This last question regarding the persecutional logic is very much the one also debated, in the local west- and central-African traditions, by Ellen Corin and Gilles Bibeau (1980). The question of determining whether the Oedipus complex is only an interpretative model, rather than a structuring psychodynamic common to all cultures – in other words, whether the Freudian model of sexuation and Oedipal triangulation can legitimately be applied outside of bourgeois occidental culture (or the Viennese context of Freud's time) – has led to a century of controversy. Alice Bullard (2005, p. 183) draws the following conclusion on the discussion regarding the limitations of the Freudian model of the Oedipal complex: "The revisionist debates over the Oedipus complex revolve around the theme of human universality versus cultural particularism. Because of the Freudian Oedipal complex is believed to lie at the root of the symbolic process it is generally thought to make its presence felt throughout the culture. According to this view, folk beliefs, myths, prominent stories, erotic attractions and life patterns all reflect the Oedipal imprint." But this namely in culture-specific ways, I would add to her last statement.

Paul Riesman (1986) offers a most comprehensive survey of the early anthropological and psychodynamic studies on the person in Black Africa. In *L'enfant du lignage*, Jacqueline Rabain (1979) depicts phenomenologically the experiences of both parents and children (from weaning to initiation in an age grade at the age of 6) in Wolof society, and how they respond to cultural codes of care and sharing, (self)control and transparent living with other children, adults, ancestors and the world of spirits. Echoing, on his behalf, the postulate of a cultural management of the socially produced subject, such as the patrilineal Bamileke of northwest Cameroon perceive it, Charles-Henry Pradelles de Latour, (1991, 1995) has developed an 'ethnopsychoanalytic' interpretation, inspired by Lacan, of the cultural unconscious. His attention centres on the imaginary with regard to kinship that instils in the subject an aspiration to an indefinite yet mobilising difference and intersubjectivity. The subject, such as Lacan was led to define it, is not the subject of representation (following, for example, a binary or persecutional logic of self/other, inclusion/exclusion and so on) nor the auto-governing self of depth psychology. In the Lacanian perspective, the subject appears essentially in the symbolic play that allows it to explore its difference within an imaginary that one might call a borderlinking space (in Ettinger's, 2006 terms). This is an imaginary that unfolds in the play of transference and of re-articulation, each time slightly differently, of the deeply embedded unspoken, and one which forms the basis of the ternary logic internal to the intersubjective discourse of the subject. Pradelles de Latour thus draws particular attention to symbolic play in which the subject involves itself, susceptible to overcome a symbolic lack, a non-relation, and especially bivalence. This last at once mobilises origin and end, life and death (as does the sorcerous mother), agent and object (while being exposed to plants that are both curative and toxic), or cause and effect (like the abominable that evokes terror). The terms of this symbolic play, which are culturally specific and express in the banal signifiers of quotidian life, readily instruct us on the specifically cultural regulation of desire.

The Bamileke subject profiles itself in the border space between its interior motivations (such as desire or hunger for *jouissance*,[3] or its anguish, based on a logic

---

[3] Lacan sees a tensional relationship between jouissance (a notion evocative of the Freudian concepts of *Genuss*, *Wunscherfüllung*, *Befriedigung*) and desire (longing, the Freudian libido), the vital erotic, and symbolisation. Freud and Lacan define the human being, in particular the male, as moved by an unceasing flux of energy and a never fulfilled longing in the unconscious to fully savour experience through ever heightening one's enjoyment, even to a discomforting peak, as may occur in the sexual act. Indeed, to be able enduringly to satisfy one's desire, paroxysm must be kept at a distance. The unceasing longing, which can never be voided by the awareness and acceptance of one's condition of lack, springs from the erogenous zones at the bodily orifices. A core of this longing or desire resists symbolisation, yet may vent itself in its imaginary expression through dream-images, ideals, fantasies, phantasmatic and visionary artistic or ecstatic creativity. Repressed desire may discharge itself in a symptom, complaint, lapses or mistakes, and hence in dreamwork or creative metaphorisation. The (possibly repressive) sociocultural institutions or power, on the one hand, and the Order of the Law, on the other, may mobilise the suppression of lack and longing, or their transcendence, in verbal-cultural creativity.

In the 'phallic jouissance' (enjoyment that, in particular in the male, eshews castration), there is no longer any distancing, and thus neither representation, symbolisation, nor true relation with the

of all or nothing) and the pressing call to social responsibility. It thus profiles itself between identities such as daughter (within her filiation group) and wife (within her residential group and familial group by marriage), or again between imaginary debt (governing in explicit ways the agnatic relations between father and son) and symbolic debt (with regard to the father of the wife's mother, called the life giving *ancêtre de derrière* or 'backside ancestor'). This symbolic debt qualifying the matrimonial alliance can be extrapolated onto any political or religious function which is constituted solely by the coupling of difference and reciprocity. It is reaffirmed, for example, in each offering or sacrifice presented to the 'ancestor behind' in the event of illness or misfortune. Indeed, such offerings establish an asymmetric reciprocity and an intergenerational hierarchisation between the givers and receivers of the woman (and thus of the life that she transmits to her children); they thus evoke the symbolic law of reciprocity that at once founds and presupposes the incest prohibition. Through the intervention of the 'backside father' and under his symbolic law, the father and brothers relinquish the gratifying presence of respectively his daughter or their sister (whom they in principle might be tempted to assimilate), and cede her as a potential spouse following the logic of exchange. It is, therefore, the 'backside ancestor' who is the representative of the law of differentiation and exchange at the levels of filiation, matrimonial alliance and consanguinity.

Turning somewhat later to the matrilineal society of the Péré in northwest Cameroon bordering southeast Nigeria, Pradelles de Latour (2005) showed that, in this group, there was no differentiation between consanguinity and filiation: one's belonging to a filiation group is transmitted solely by the mother to her children within the matrilineage.[4] The maternal uncle has the power (*potestas*) of life and death over his nephews and nieces: he is the guarantor of their belonging to the matrilineage and of their well-being. He is nonetheless an ambivalent and potentially persecutional figure: coming from the same womb as the mother of his nephews and nieces, it is possible for him to resort to a dual and conflictive, even incestuous or sorcerous relation in their regard, and thus abuse or reject them. The uncle, however, is himself subject to a superior institution, namely the symbolic order defining the plus and minus, the positive and the negative (or the paternal metaphor or Order of the Law, in Lacanian idiom). This is the guarantor of both difference and the ideals of exchange as well as of the sanctions that are invoked in the case of any perversion of this exchange. For his part, the father retains the *auctoritas* as the competent educator who teaches the child both to direct his or her life and to win independence as well as to insert him- or herself in the network of exchanges. There is therefore

Other (sex). The subject is, in the jouissance, emptied out to the point of merging with the object. Lacan speaks of an impossible jouissance, as when the difference between libido and death drive collapses in an undirected anxiety or cancerous emptying out of self, or in an obsession, illusion or perversion that withdraws from the Order of the Law. It is a kind of horror-jouissance. The concept is akin to that of the Real, *Das Ding*: such jouissance is impossible and destructive, yet goes on to fascinate.

[4] I have come across Pradelles de Latour's work only after having finished my reading of the father and mother figures and functions among the Yaka, as set out in section "Transworldly Phallogocentric Symbolisation and Matrixial *Signifiance*".

a clear separation between, on the one hand, the function of guarantor of the Order of the Law (assumed for the subject by the maternal uncle), and, on the other, the function of engendering. Genitor and child share neither flesh nor blood ties, nor are they held to belong to a common group. There is, moreover, a clear distinction between sexual jouissance (such as is shared by genitor and genitrix) and the Order of the Law (to which the maternal uncle is witness).

In *Meurtre du père, sacrifice de la sexualité* (Godelier and Hassoun, 1996), social anthropologist Maurice Godelier,[5] in dialogue with the psychoanalyst Jacques Hassoun, links the socialisation of sexuality and desire, and thus the relation between subjects (in primordial time), with the problematic of sacrifice or the suppression of the a-social, undomesticated dimension of sexuality. The social person cannot but be a split, divided, being. Godelier proposes, in the manner of an axiom, that this suppression is co-originating with the imposition of a sexual division of labour and of familial relations of consanguinity, marriage and descent. Ontologically speaking, the human being would have begun to produce society (namely kinship, economic and political relations, articulated in cultural diversity) before fashioning homo- and/or hetero-sexuality, experienced along with age in a masculine or feminine manner. In order to live together, the human being would have formed a capacity to act on his or her own sexual nature along with the more basic ability to transform, materially and intellectually, nature into society and culture (ibid., pp. 28–32). Human, and especially feminine, sexuality, which is ostensibly both biological and social, continues to be a ventriloquism for the social. The Freudian hypothesis that the murder of the *Urvater* and the incest prohibition are constitutive of society, as well as the Lacanian association of the Order of the Law with the father function, are, according to Godelier (p. 11) too closely bound up with the Judeo-Christian intellectual heritage.

Godelier published his magnum opus *Métamorphoses de la parenté* in 2004. In contrast with Lévi-Strauss' study *The Elementary Structures of Kinship* (originally published in 1949), which deals with the unconscious cognitive logic underlying the array of kinship structures, Godelier's work takes historical-contextual, social and symbolic practices as his point of departure. His approach starts from a double challenge. First, how to understand the phobic distinction between the sexes as developed by a great number of peoples of the New Guinea Highlands, such as the Baruya among whom Godelier lived for 3 years as an anthropologist? During adolescence, and taking the solitary cassowary as their alter-ego, the young men 'conceive' and 'harden' themselves, in an autogenerative manner, as warriors in 'the unspoiled order of physical (subsocial and subcultural) life'. They achieve this through institutionalised and repeated practice of sodomy with peers, namely 'those who have had no (emasculating) sexual relations with women' (the founders of regenerative, rather than autogenerative, culture and sociality). Some of the

[5] Following university degrees in philosophy, psychology, letters, political economy and anthropology, Godelier worked for some time with Lévi-Strauss as an assistant researcher before carrying out anthropological fieldwork among the Baruya in the Papua New Guinea Highlands. He delegates the human sciences on the National Science Committee in Paris.

neighbouring peoples have instead institutionalised fellatio between classificatory fathers and sons, as was earlier the case with the practice of very selective headhunting (Herdt, 1982). Conjugal sexual relations are engaged in only very furtively, with great anxiety and always in improper spaces and moments. Senior men compensate for waning virile and generative capacities by organising aggressive-ostentatious or rivalling potlatch feasts of extreme asymmetrical gift-giving. More specifically, one by one they expend the whole of the year's agricultural production (all the tubers and often 100 or more hogs) on a single feast for the local population of several hundred people. The implicit challenge in such an act is one-upmanship: 'you do it better; try to surpass me'.

Godelier's second challenge at the start of his study is the mutation, observed in the West since the 1970s, in the role of the family and familial relations, which no longer form the foundation of society (itself a product of the nation-state and the thoroughly capitalistic economy). One notes – in ways evocative of the matrilineal family such as among the Pèrè, depicted above after Pradelles de Latour – the dissociation between the rights that the hetero- or homosexual couple both share perhaps temporarily, on the one hand, and on the other the enduring and equal responsibilities of the legal parent or social reproducer. This last development points to the so-called 'parenting equality' or *parentalité* in western society now marked by today's imperative of equality and cut loose from the traditional gendered authority roles and hierarchy between the father and mother.

In his worldwide comparison of seven major kinship systems (Sudanic, Australian, Dravidian, Iroquois, Crow-Omaha, Eskimo, Hawaian) among the some 10,000 known societies across the globe, Godelier (2004) undermines many ethnocentric presumptions and offers an extremely relativising perspective on fatherhood and kin. He attempts to describe and compare the main practical differences in kin bonds and relations of power worldwide, over the generations and within the scope of the reproduction of the larger societal, cosmological, religious, and imaginary systems (covering aspects of life, aptitudes, behavioural patterns, values, ideals, myths, fantasies, psychic forces). In order to do so, Godelier has selected the following variables for consideration: (1) reproduction, consanguinity, affinity and filiation (in the knowledge that only 39% of societies are cognatically organised, as in the West, with the nuclear family linked together through matrimonial alliance, descent and consanguinity via both the men and the women, centred around the individual and approached from the individual's perspective); (2) matrimonial alliance and parenting equality, including the sexual reproduction without acknowledging the genitor, father or husband, like in Na society in the Chinese Himalaya where kinship centres on mothers and the maternal uncle; (3) residence; (4) kinship terminology; (5) perceptions concerning reproduction (including the substances that 'make up a child') in a socially accepted manner; in the majority of cases with more vital partners – sometimes also non-human – than a genitrix and a genitor; (6) a minimal and indispensable governing structure, including sexual taboos (in the recognition that the incest taboo is not universal or can have very diverse meanings).

Two other scholars who have shed light on the subject are portrayed in sections "The Yaka Religious Sensibility for the Weave of Things and the Augural" and "The Agnatic Ancestors, Matricentred Filiation and the Maternal Uncle" of this paper; these are, namely, Jacques Lacan and Bracha L.Ettinger[6] whose work is inspired by Lacan. As Markos Zafiropoulos (2003) has demonstrated, Lacan himself leaned very heavily, at least in his early period, on the work of Lévi-Strauss.

The Yaka Religious Sensibility for the Weave of Things and the Augural

In rural-based Yaka society numbering some 350,000 people in the Southwest of Congo, in the vast expanse of the Southern savannah on the Angolan border, the domestic and public day-to-day life scene of great – and in the last decades increasing – scarcity is undoubtedly marked by their modes of production as hunter-gatherers and small-scale subsistence farmers. Their autochthonous space-time patterns are barely affected by the small inroads of a cash economy. Here, literacy is by no means a mutational force. If, for the last 60 years, half of the youngsters could enjoy a few years of elementary – though very rudimentary – school education in the rural area, nothing like books, newspapers or informative text is available in the region other than the Bible. The well-educated few are all migrating to urban opportunities. The stability of the male–female, hence marital, relations is very much linked to the gender hierarchy and division of labour regarding the social order, itself a core constituent of the imaginary with regard to the gender 'division of sexual labour' or gender role in the conjugal reproductive sexuality. The women are responsible for subsistence agriculture and the daily nourishment and upbringing of the family, while the hunt, palaver, hut-building and migrant labour – the last in the aim of purchasing clothing, tools and other means of production – form the most highly-praised domains of male 'production'. Since the 1960s many Yaka, among them certainly all those who done secondary education or further, have emigrated to Kinshasa. There, most of the by now half a million Yaka grouped in several suburban slums lead a precarious existence.

Individual development and familial or societal organisation, at least insofar as the rural Yaka are concerned, are inseparable from that culture's cosmocentric orientation. Fatherhood, motherhood, upbringing, agriculture, hunting, palaver, and the range of daily livelihoods give both expression and form to a vital world system in which wovenness (*-kuba*),[7] sense of balance (*-niinga, niingisa*), amiability (*kitoko*),

---

[6] Having worked for many years in Paris, Bracha L. Ettinger has recently moved to Tel Aviv. Ettinger (2006) offers an attentive reading and critique of some of Lacan's later teachings (see note10). Next to Griselda Pollock (2006), Paul Vandenbroeck (2000, pp. 237–274) and René Devisch (2007), essays regarding her theoretical work are offered in Ettinger (2000) and the special section on Bracha L. Ettinger: "Memory, representation and post-Lacanian subjectivity" of *Theory, Culture & Society* 21 (2004) no 1. See moreover: http://www.metramorphosis.org.uk/.

[7] Regarding the terms rendered in ki-Koongo, the prefix ku-, wu- of the infinitives is replaced by the hyphen.

vitality (*mooyi*), zest for life (*kyeesi*), honour and shame (*tsoni*) together constitute the interpersonal and transworldly building blocks of a cosmo-genesis and a meaning-bearing cosm-et(h)ic. Distinct from the (Lunda) ruling class, the Yaka commoners, like many other Bantu people, seek to disclose the world as a womb (*ngoongu*) and a weaving (*kuba*). They lay themselves open to whatever may come as a life- and meaning-bearing drama of forces and more or less favourable versus unfavourable *events* (*maambu*) and *messages* (*bikuma, n-samu*), rather than as a set of *facts*. Public discourse gives little attention to the aspect of 'the will' in individual behaviour, yet accentuates rather the extent to which authoritative consultation, good words, negotiation, solidarity and ritual practice 'make life'. The pliability of culture and of society is here a given, and stands in shrill contrast with our western stereotypes with regard to 'traditional' cultures and their alleged mimetism.

Our attention is directed here primarily to the 'weave' (cf. *religare*) of things, as much in the play of movement, bordercrossing and borderassertion, and even more to layered processes of bondedness and resonance, over against dissonance and disruption. It concerns the weave of things within the rhythm of the daily trajectories of the sun – the communal sun-clock – as well as within the cycles of the moon, seasons and generations. Yaka patterns of thought trace each form of life ordering and common fate, all woven into each other, back to a central source of life located in the womb of the earth (*ngoongu*). It is here that unceasingly spring up and resource the major streams of life, namely the rivers, the sun and the rains. The sun is seen as a mass of water rising up from the Kwango River, of which the entirety of Yakaland forms the watershed, and sets itself up in the firmament; when heating up and boiling, it may spill over in rain and manifest itself as a rainbow over Kwangoland. Non-christianised Yaka have developed no indigenous concept of god nor, for that matter, a hierarchical or patriarchal worldview or thought structure. Nor have they integrated the notion of nation-state or its consequences into their views. However, their life world is not one to be understood along some rhizome-thinking, to be possibly understood in lines with Gilles Deleuze and Félix Guattari (1980). The cosmic, social and interhuman life streams are woven and intertwined as fields of orderedness and bondedness, in a braiding of forces and meanings. Rituals celebrate this as a resonance between people and their life world; between the past, the present and the future. Cults, spirits, ancestors and healer-priests strongly contribute to this borderlinking. They weave these spheres together with the reproductivity of birth and the arts of cooking, the hunt, agriculture, smelting and smithery, all in the cycles of rotting, yeasting, germination, growth and flowering, burning and melting, boundary-waning and -linking, negotiation and authoritative speech. As I have worked out in a former study (Devisch, 1993), the rhythm of the drum and dance, weaving and fabric, cooking and fermentation, the branching of the tree and migration journeys, the cycles of the moon and vegetation, and above all reproductive sexual communion, pregnancy and the mother–child bond, all offer central metaphors and structuring principles.

In Yaka society good health and social recognition are the product and the being of intercorporal, intersubjective and interworldly entwining and weaving. According to divinatory aetiology, a person is formed (*wuka muutu*) in the play of multiple and many-layered sensory, sexual and verbal weaves and contexts. As I will demonstrate, moral rules and moralising discourse arise only when health and social problems occur, for these amount to a tear in the fabric. The weave that constitutes and confines the individual, intertwines the latter into multiple exchanges of life, affect, emotion and knowledge between agnatic and uterine kin, between people and the extrahuman or invisible worlds (ancestors and spirits as well as the efficacy of ritual and witchcraft), between the subject and his or her ever-shifting situational life world. This latter is coloured by his or her age, gender, marital status, involvement in physical and social reproduction, and public or social roles and status. Yaka culture regards these exchanges as a life-supporting weave that is both intercorporal and intersubjective and binds together the spheres of body, self, family and life world. Inasmuch as the (urban) Yaka consider health and quality of life to be the product of good family bonds (including good neighbourly and professional bonds), poor health is ascribed to problems between kin (neighbours or colleagues). Translated in dialogue with the ideals of a western bourgeois ethos, the becoming a subject in Yaka society is not so much a crafting, an improving or a wording of self-knowledge, self-discipline and guilt-feeling against the longings of one's desire. It essentially is an (inter)corporal, (inter)subjective and cosm-et(h)ic process of styling of *co(n)naissance*, desire and self-awareness. The French notion of *co(n)naissance* (literally, co-birth, but colloquially referring to experiential knowing and insight) offers an insightful linguistic rendition of this sensuous, emotional, hence 'fleshy' (cf. Merleau-Ponty, 1964) intercorporeal and dialogical sharing of knowledge and co-implication of subjects and their life world.

Like many other Bantu, the Yaka have not developed their own system of writing, and literacy remains a marginal phenomenon. Reality, therefore, is not approached as an open book or as a script that is translated or comprehended through representations, nor is it held to be a working ground towards technocratic progress or an eschaton, as in the western-modern or Judeo-Christian vision. Here the religious impregnates the intersubjective worlds of meaning. Indeed, broadening our scope, it appears how much for three quarters of humanity, corporeality and spirituality, visible and invisible worlds, the realms of the living and the ancestors, are seamlessly integrated in the here and now – as might be manifested in the pulsing borderlinking between the glow of a fire and its penetrating organic scent; in the spread of a contagious enthusiasm between a few individuals and the group; or in the merging of the abrupt counterrythm of the dance drums and the collapse of the medium into trance. In non-literate milieus in many African countries, and more briefly in Afro-Brazilian culture, I have met people who in my presence addressed themselves – in whispers, adjuration, alliteration play, song or archaic language, exclamations, incantations, oaths, or glossolalia – to an ancestor or some extrahuman presence in their lives whom they experienced as an inner message or a power that precedes and supports them in life. It appears to me that non-literate people can hardly be said to abstract their experience through representation (that is, in a symbolised imaginary) projected onto the mental screen of a text (e.g., biblical, theological, pastoral, liturgical, moralising) or an analog-figurative (religious) art picture that lends itself to deciphering and critical distancing (in what in Lacanian terminology amounts to a 'phallic' process, one of affirmation or negation, tangling or untangling, confounding and demystifying, contrasting or isolating). While suspending the distinction between the affective and the conceptual, these forms of language play, extending into dramatic arts and fields of vision (including multisense or synesthetic playing on suggestibility in entrancement, induced hallucination, dreaming, spirit possession, affective identification), they moreover offer ways to unveil the unsayable and untouchable, which alike the invisible may hint at both the cunningly unsettling spirit world, the epiphanous ancestral world, hence the uncanniness of witchcraft. All this is looked at in the (intersubjective and transworld) borderzones of communal rejoicing, dreamsharing, maternal caring, holistic healing, embodying the spirit in trance-possession, alike in the ecstatic gift of glossolalia or in mediumnic divination.

Among the Yaka, just as among many other societies in Central Africa, ancestral religion has kept itself quite aloof from the process of Christian or Muslim missionary *métissage*. In the Yaka ancestral religious system, there is no message of salvation, divine revelation, or gnostic spirituality, nor is there an appeal to a sinful and needy humanity to form a church-like community. Alongside the phallogocentric drive for order in relation to the ancestral world, the religious attitude comprises a mantic sensitivity to the extra-human and augural, as well as to numinous portents of misfortune and life-threatening signs, that appear in the folds of the life world and everyday human existence. In other words, for the Yaka, the religious numinous breaks through namely in the ritually orchestrated, borderlinking and performative experiences. Trance possession, attributed to cultic or ancestral spirits (who induce clairvoyance and psychotic-like self-surpassing) receives a ritual form in the afflicted person by way of an eruptive experience of agony, orgasmic self-conception, auto-gestation and rebirth each flowing into the other (Devisch and Brodeur, 1999, pp. 97ff.). In the communitarian experience of death and bereavement, the local life-world appears to fall into the grip of enigmas and metastases of the Real and the flux of *jouissance*, or of the excess of the 'non-dead' and the inaccessible. Mourning transits from the night of the life world, or the eclipse of culture and the ethical, to the gradual dawn or rebirth of the community and the ethical (ibid., pp. 203–222). Augural signs allow for the local community's celebration of its life-bearing transition; these might be a collective hunt-held in anticipation of a full moon or a new season, the end of a mourning period, or at the conclusion of an initiatory seclusion in an intense interaction with the tutelary spirits. The transition ritual celebrates the passing from the night (the dark, dangerous, fearful, gloomy, haunting, malefic, menacing, threatening) to the dawn's oracular presaging of the day-time world (vatical, visionary, premonitory, propitious). Dream, among the Yaka, is a privileged medium of contact with the deceased, the agnatic forbears and the primordial uterine source of life in the womb of the earth and provides access to their force-field spanning the division between life-giving, fortune-bearing and auspicious energies, on the one hand, and inauspicious, misfortune-bearing powers on the other. Like the vacillating shadow, the Yaka religious experience manifests itself in the liminal space between appearance and disappearance, presence and absence; it is a flashing experience (*une expérience clignotante*: Laplantine, 2003, p. 30), requiring a sensitivity to the 'between', the 'neither nor'. A person's shadow or double (*yiniinga*) offers a borderlinking metaphor for the religious. The root meaning of *yiniinga* would indicate an object that constantly swings from one side to another, like the shadow of a leaf blown about by the wind. While seeking attachment to something new, it attempts to detach itself from yet another object. As a verb, *-niinga* denotes the skillful balancing of an object on the head. It may also designate the movement of a rolling log. *Yiniinga* therefore stands for rotation or transition, such as between light and darkness, the visible and the invisible, and implies transitional or borderlinking capacity. It is primarily used to refer to a person's 'shadow' or 'double', and by extension to a potentially numinous quality.

The Agnatic Ancestors, Matricentred Filiation and the Maternal Uncle

Blood Relations and Filiation, via Fathers and Mothers, Are Doubly Unilineal

The father function orders in linear fashion through 'division', that is, through distinction on the basis of observable difference; it 'supervises' (that is, orders along *scopic*, visual, lines) intergenerational and sociocentric identity.[8] This ordering develops parallel to the matrilineal weaving of the uterine and life-regenerating vitality and the common fate.

Physical fatherhood (*yitaata*) is delegated by the forefather to the adult male. *Khoondzu ye ngolu*, literally, the erectile quality of the spinal column and the vigorousness, tonicity and force or muscularity of the limbs, tap from the ancestral life force. These terms also refer to the power of resistance a father must possess in order to be able to counteract any witchcraft attacks that might befall his offspring. The highly praised attribute of erectility is symbolised, among other objects, by the chiefly knife. (In the Yaka imaginary, virile erectility stands in sharp contrast with the receptive and enfolding female body, which ideally exhibits soft and rounded forms.) In the Yaka cultural representation of the body, fatherhood comprises the transmission, in the semen, of the patrilineal ancestral life force (*ngolu*) via the

[8] The Yaka view of the human subject contrasts with the North-Atlantic bourgeois ethos situating identity in the individual's inner core that stems from the inner self's zeal for interiorisation, self-mirroring self-centredness, introjection and projective identification. The Yaka, except for the Christianised and educated members of the second or later generation(s), do not subscribe to the Christian or Enlightenment distinction between nature and culture, or between mind and drive in the individual's 'heart' (namely in his or her inner and self-scrutinising comprehension, or anxiety-ridden and self-suspicious conscience). Unlike modernist philosophy, the Yaka do not associate the maternal with nature, instinct or carnality. And in their view, the village space (hata) literally means a space "cut out" of, and thus part of, the more encompassing forest realm (n-situ). In other words, for the Yaka society is an integral part of the larger environment, or, translated in modernist terms, culture is a part of nature.

fontanel, skull and backbone and, in coitus, to the hard, bony parts (and erectility) of the agnatic descendants. For the man, the transmission of life is a process of yeasting (the male equivalent of the female process of cooking). Sexual drive and *communion* relinks the process of decomposition, elicited by genital scent, with the renewal of life in an auto-generative process of yeasting (*fula*) that binds the forefather-genitor with the descendant. The virility of the sexually reproductive man is praised for its *khoondzu* or erectility and bodily muscularity, which in fact denote the presence of the erectile life force in the spinal column and cranium of the genitor.

Parenthood (*-buta baana*, literally, the making of children) is associated with weaving (*-kuba*) in which the virile contribution is symbolised by the shuttle that rhythmically weaves together, in the fabric, the feminine warp and the male woof. Actual sexual relations are, rather, spoken of in terms of *-biindasana maalu*, literally the mutual solicitation to participate in the entwining one another's legs. In this same reciprocality the Yaka subject is structured as a never-fading weave and a borderlinking quest. One's identity is primarily sociocentric, just as a stitch is bound together with innumerable other stitches in order to form a fabric: the bonds linking subjects are multilayered and plural. (Funeral rituals, just as healing rituals that are based on rites of passage, produce a reverse mirror image of what physical and social reproduction, *mboongu*, signifies. Funeral rituals always aim, literally, to cut the deceased loose from the family and society and, as a consequence, either to invest him as a forefather with a clear bonding function, or to fold the deceased mother back into the primal womb of the earth and contribute to recycle it, much like a seed or a tuber, in a movement of infoliation or invagination.)

Several important distinctions are spontaneously made between physical and social fatherhood. First, the *taata meenga* (literally, the father through blood) or physical father is namely the one who enjoys the rights *in genitricem*. In other words, he is the one who "opens and shuts the door (of the dwelling or of the vagina)" and transmits bony or skeletal erectility to the foetus. The physical father is seen to be one and the same with the socially-recognised spouse of the genitrix (even if he is not the biological father of the newborn as a result of impotence or extramarital relations on the part of the mother). However, should the mother's spouse, his older brother and the family head all fail to claim physical fatherhood, this role will then be conferred on the mother's older brother (thus the maternal uncle of the newborn child) on condition that the mother's spouse or his older brother himself accept, conversely, the role of maternal uncle. In other words, the uncle becomes father on condition that the father takes on the role of uncle.

Second, *taata*, the classificatory social father, is the family head or the elder in the patrifiliation within the extended family, or exceptionally the genitor's older brother provided he has paid the bride price and given the necessary gifts. It is he who maintains the sense of family among his descendants and guarantees the social identity of each of the members, even more, perhaps, than seeking – as is the maternal uncle's task – to promote their good health and solicit their ethical commitment.

Third, the term *pfumwakaanda* indicates the head of the patriclan made up of closely related patrilineages that fall primarily under the responsibility of a Lunda dynasty (Devisch and Brodeur, 1999, pp. 49–51). The referential term *pfumu*, head, is most often accompanied by the name of the location of the ancestral shrine. Members of the same extended family or patriclan live in the same neighbourhood or in adjoining settlements. The average Yaka village – promoted into a unity and given a locality name by the colonial administration – comprises some 15 or more nuclear families grouped in three to six relatively autonomous extended families or distinct lineages. The head of the patrilineage is by definition the 'embodiment' (in his bones, semen, or in his peace-making and socially reproductive or emancipating rhetoric) from the local patrilineal descent group (*yikhanda, yitaata*). Life force (*khoondzu ye ngolu*, including the male qualities of resilience, resistance and power), social rights and identity are passed on by the father through patrilineal descent, which is traced back to the founder of the group. Neither the father nor the family head pass on a family name. The father unites his descendants with the force of the ancestral-agnatic life stream in each of the descendants as well as in the transmission of kinship and political structures and institutional behaviour: marrying and burying, deliberating and judging, hunting and managing land, blessing and where required cursing, binding together and unbinding.

Fourth, the most originary and binding father function is seated in this patriarchal life-giving power, for both life-giving and inflicting or averting evil of the father-founder and the agnatic life-stream flowing down the generations from forefather to genitor and progeny. Among the Yaka, as among the neighbouring peoples of western Congo and eastern Angola, the agnatic founder-ancestor is compared with or depicted by particular perennial natural phenomena. This could be the rock where a spring gives birth to a river that carries away the rains in that region. Here the rock stands for a primordial space–time (*muyitsikhulu*) and is made culturally present by a 'stone block' that portrays, in a localised form, the mythic-historical time of 'in the beginning', an incessant and unceasing origination of the complete, immortal and inalienable primordial potency. Similarly, the founder-ancestor could be depicted by the ceaseless movement of sap that rises to feed the cluster of palm nuts in the old palm tree at the *zuumbu* or the dwelling place of the founder-ancestor (such trees can live for more than 100 years).

It is the founder-ancestor of the patrilineage who makes the destiny, aspirations and insisting desire of his descendants meaningful, and connects them with the Name-of-the-Father (a Lacanian notion explained below) as a vector of an abstract symbolic order. This is to say that the founder-ancestor bears the function of the ultimate bond and ultimate signifier without signified, a sort of ultimate moebius knotting or braiding together (*nkata*) of the phallic function (as differential element and mobiliser of the search for meaning). But simultaneously, the Name-of-the-Father function fails to unveil and enfold the meaning of the sheer fortuitous, the absurd, or the unknowable which resists the group's meaning grids. That function is moreover unable to respond to the subject or the group sucked into anxiety or in deep pain. Family or clan heads ensure the 'presence' of the agnatic forefathers in the form either of evergreen trees or fully grown forked branches from this tree, a species known for its very hard white wood. The mythical clan or lineage founders, of Lunda and therefore allochthonous origin, are represented by the erection of a *bindzandza* shrine in front of the home of the clan head. This comprises an outer fence enclosing evergreen *n-yoombu* trees. The clan's agnatic life stream is generated by fermenting palm wine, the sacrifice of blood and the booty of the hunt. In this metaphor of the tree, the ancestors are situated at the level of the roots, the trunk and the rising and fermenting sap. The (male) descendants, who live in the same neighbourhood, are perceived as making up the leafy roof, following the image of the hut roof and the husband who "crawls over the conjugal bed." The sacrifice and the fermentation are a borderlinking and transformative moment between life and death, the living and the ancestor: both effectuate a transition. The ancestor shrine, called *ndzo makhulu*, dedicated to the autochthonous Kongo forefathers, consists of a miniature hut of some 70 cm high and width. Against the back wall some six or seven bone-hard wooden blocks from a mature tree, in the form of a fork are erected in a row. The ancestral bond is created by spitting the chewings of a tonic kola nut on the blocks while reciting the lineage genealogy and the multiple titles of the chiefs.

-*Hoya n-samu kunduumba/kuluziingu*, literally, speaking the message at the grave/the place of enduring life (together with the libation of palm wine, a blood sacrifice or the offering of some consciousness-enhancing hemp), serves to renew this segment of the society in the sharing of reproductive life force between forefather and descendant. The lineage head constitutes his father function as a re-generating of the father function of the founder-ancestor. This is no patricide against the primordial father (the Yaka have no monotheistic patri-religion, nor any form of monocentric father figure), but rather a reawakening (incited by incantations – such as the one below – pronounced on the ancestral grave) of the common fate of the group (notwithstanding the threat of possible perversions through jealousy, rivalry and fighting over titbits). Such regeneration re-mobilises here and now the daily processes of giving and receiving, binding and loosening. In other words, access to the symbolic ancestor is made not by way of an unequivocal signifier but via an ambivalent and potentially perverse relation. The following incantation, uttered on the ancestral grave of subregional Chief Taanda Kapata (and which I recorded in September 1990 in Yitaanda village), testifies to this.

> I am of chiefly blood. Unto you, my rulers, I do come. Do not ignore me because I am not dressed as tradition decrees. Out of Lunda we come, descendants from Zikuta and Nzofu. Arch-ancestor Khapheela Kaangu, keeper of the hunting rights. Your strength I pass on. I plant my sword in you. Praise to you, descendants of Kapheela Kaangu, keepers of the hunting rights. Accept the palm wine and the hemp that I bring you. Those that wish me evil will say that I came to the grave to plot my revenge. Ancestors, keep an eye on them. May my assailant break his neck for I have done no man any wrong.

The Matricentric Filiation of Mooyi – Uterine Artery and Weave, or Life-Regenerating Vitality and Common Fate in Complicity

In the daily tasks of survival around the home, in the fields or on the path to or from home when collecting food, firewood or water, Yaka grandmothers,

mothers, girls and small children spontaneously develop among themselves a flood of contacts and cooperation. These relations rarely appear to be forced, strained or frustrating. Moreover, this flood, it seems to me, incites the group spontaneously, good-humouredly and willingly to feelings of attentive care for each other, affective bonding and self-evident sharing. One seldom sees a woman working alone (except perhaps in her field), or without a child in her lap or on her arm or back – an infant is never left alone.

Seen from the subject, it is through the mothers and grandmothers in the polygynous extended family or large household that he or she is literally incorporated, into an intercorporal and intersubjective ravelling of multi-layered sensory and verbal weaves. These unfold in the sharing of table and bed, in the exchange of 'life-regenerating vitality and common fate' (*mooyi*), affect, emotion and practical knowledge. This ravelling or knotting process develops along the lines of a cyclical, rather than diachronic, time frame, that of the women's and seasons' cycle. Seen from the group's perspective, it is in and around the main family settlement that this fabric binds together, in the here and now, agnatic descendants and their married-in spouses, the visible worlds and the invisible or extrahuman fields of the ancestors, spirits and forces that may be life-threatening but also healing. The anchor point of the Yaka subject is socio- and cosmocentrically formed in the differing contextual practices of exchange and inter-animation (mutual enlivening). The skin, bodily 'cavities' and vital organs (in particular the hollow bones, the heart, liver, and womb – cf. infra), the articulations of the limbs and a person's senses constitute the heavily laden junctures on which all connections and exchanges with others and with the visible and invisible worlds are projected.

Yingudi, motherhood, is the essential participation in the cyclical self-renewing uterine or motherly life source in the womb of the earth/world, or the womb of all life (*ngoongu*). Parturition is perceived as a protrusion (an exfoliation or exvagination) of the womb. The bride is by definition the one who, with the blessing of both her parents, transmits the uterine fertility received from her mother and the parental dwelling "along the path leading through the savannah to the conjugal home." In compensation for the handing over of this fertility to the husband's family, a bride-price is offered and divided up between her paternal family, her mother and the three generations of uncles. Conjugal sexual relations are licit only after this has taken place and after the bridegroom's family has performed, for this purpose, the ritual of addressing the lineage ancestor and "opening the life artery" at the newly constituted hearth.

The uterine life source is symbolised, in the ancestral shrine and in the healing cults, by a clump of *pheemba* or bright white kaolin. This porcelain clay is mythically associated with the womb of the earth and the site where the moon regenerates itself during the day before rising once again at twilight or in the night. This kaolin, along with other *regalia*, is handed over to the new lineage head and placed in the care of his first wife. (In the context of healing, the novice therapist achieves his full status as healer when his initiator shares with him some of the kaolin he himself was given by his master at the time of his initiation.) Gynaecological anomalies, considered to occur at the level of the womb of all life (*ngoongu*), are in a homeopathic way turned against themselves in the fertility shrine, *lukobi*. Both the fertility shrine and the kaolin stored there, may not be seen by the eyes of the uninitiated. The uterine bond that ties the subject to his or her mother and her maternal relatives is a blood tie with the uterine source of life. This is not seen to be one and the same with the nameable ancestors or with the heroic or primordial culture-founders. It is an unnameable and cyclically self-regenerating source of life situated in the womb of the earth, and cosmologically (rather than geographically), associated with the source of the Kwango River that drains Yaka land of its rains. Drawing on the maternal source of life and the life artery, the mother transmits the 'soft' parts of the body to the child: organs, blood, innate physical traits and individual talents or deficiencies (*yibutukulu*).

Foodstuffs, produced and prepared by the mother, regenerates the blood that transforms itself into mother-milk. Women prefer to eat either foods grown or collected in or close to the earth or produced from the palm nut (tubers, beans, fish, rodents, chicken, palm oil ...), comestibles that are ideally soft, sweet, juicy and cool according to the humoral classification. For the bride, the qualities of ideal beauty are depicted by her corpulent body and rounded forms, which also forebode great fertility. The mother is the custodian of the hearth (*n-kwa ziku*), where she cooks the meals in the conjugal dwelling. This confers authority on her domestic space, and on her the role of setting the boundaries of agnatic heat in the home, limiting it to the home: the three hearth stones and the cooking pot are to the cooking fire as female to male, or as boundedness and closure to male separation or division.

The matrilineal bonding with the mother, her mother and the maternal grandmother with the uterine life artery and source of life, is also put forward in the narratives handed down to married mothers from generation to generation. The tree, with its roots, base, trunk, and top, symbolises the uterine link with the source of life (Devisch and Brodeur, 1999, p. 53). This life source bubbles up and bulges out in multiple transitions in daily or ritual life in the well-bounded female space of the main dwelling, the paths to and from the home of origin and the family's fields, the bush, the spring and the initiation hut. One thinks of brooding birds laying eggs, or the palm blossoms that, after producing an abundance of palm sap, go on to develop into a cluster of palm nuts. Similarly, the processes of motherhood and child-bearing, healing, mediumnic trance and initiation, as well as the act of cooking, baking of pottery, or the rhythm of the heartbeat or a drum come to mind. The clairvoyance of the diviner concerns a trans-world, borderlinking capacity to voice the Ordering Efficacy of the primordial life-stream and the uterine flow and weave of life and the common fate. Rather than referring to an ability for extrasensory perception, the Yaka see this clairvoyant capacity more as a mediumnic one, for the diviner being the medium of the spirit world tied to the uterine life flow communicating through him or her.[9] All these phenomena offer exceptional ties, gliding boundaries

[9] Among the Yaka, divination and its clients see the otherworldly realm as underpinning the this worldly social-symbolic order and holding the key to the individual's ability and good or bad fate (Devisch and Brodeur, 1999, pp. 93–117). Yaka cosmology underscores people's sense of the world and human life as fundamentally in-appropriable. It is an order of the world and human

or borderlinking potential between the realms of the visible and the invisible, living and becoming, death and rebirth, the *Unheimliche* and the *Heimliche*, formlessness and permanent change, or deficiency and surfeit.

Conversely, there are a number of manifestations of the folding-back of this life source behind a scaffold of hierarchy, opposition, exclusion, including hereditary illness or handicap, misfortune, fatal curse or sorcerous vengeance. Serious afflictions such as blindness, deafness, motoric handicap or insanity can, according to the Yaka, point to a disturbance in the basal and essential unity with the maternal life source. Anything that can harm someone's life and the multi-layered fabric on which it depends is, in Yaka aetiology, approached in terms of theft or witchcraft (Devisch, 2005). In the run-up to a healing ritual, it is the task of the therapist to tame the most pernicious symptoms and influences of witchcraft or of a vindictive cult spirit, and to bend these negative dimensions back against themselves self-destructively. This action literally takes the form of a judicial process against the origin of the affliction. The effects of the illness are hereby 'bent back' into signs of rehabilitation, prosperity and recovery. The cult figurine, which is initiated together with the patient, captures or embodies the origin of the illness (referred to as *fula*) of the patient or his or her handicap, whereby the affliction is homeopathically bent back into a means of healing and a sign of rehabilitation and happiness. Ill and growth, the negative and the new, the abject and the sublime, the invisible and the visible do contaminate one another at the gliding border, not so much of exclusion of the one by the other, but of a shared linkage with the unnameably known. The latter is being evoked by the heartbeat, the visionary trance, the sacrifice, the gasping for breath. This gliding border in the life world, in interpersonal transaction, alike in an energy-arousing ritual, draws on the paradoxical or bipolar corporeal experience of agony, orgasm, pregnancy, birth giving or trance. That what resists naming is the shadow (*yiniinga*) of what overcomes you. The shadow hides behind the visible, the nameable. It sticks to the image but withdraws from its naming in words, and its seizure through the gaze. It can only be reached at a potent in-between space.

Mooyi, denoting the uterine life artery and weave, or the life-regenerating vitality, is a substantive that is usually employed in the plural form. The uterine life artery and weave is no localised or reified substance, nor is it male or female. It is the fabric that, in a very singular way, unfolds within the maternal line (*mooyi ku yingudi kakala*). The uterine life artery feeds the intimate affective capacity in each person, enabling them to touch and affect each other existentially (whether this be to inspire or to discourage), and to commit themselves to the corporal and shared fate between humans and their source of life. *Mooyi*, in the terms of Bracha L. Ettinger

life depicted as being constantly emerging, though versatile, capabilities, like the never-failing transition between day and night, sun and tempests, life and death, satiety and hunger, or goodness and evil in each of us. In the case of a lasting disempowerment or affliction (insoluble conflict, disaster, exceptional loss, lack of income, chronic illness, misfortune, threat of death, or difficult decisions concerning the foundation of a home, marriage or divorce, or migration opportunities), Yaka people in uncertainty may call upon the clairvoyant capacity of a mediumistic or shamanic diviner (who may be male or female) to lay bare the cosmological and social issues bearing on the problem.

(see note 7), is a matrixial, borderlinking and (trans-)subjectivising affective force sustaining one's commitment to life and compassionate rapport.

Kyeesi or lust for life (whose meaning is more accurately rendered by the terms respectively in german and dutch, *Geist-Trieb* and *geest-drift*) is an essential sensory and cheerful feminine borderlinking capacity of *mooyi*. It is an intersubjective field of co-vibration or -resonance, a matrixial encounter-event, a co-emergence and composition of traces and waves of jouissance between myself and the other with whom I live, such as between co-initiates or table- and bedmates. It is a metabolisation of mental traces for and in each other. The conjugal pair, their housemates or coinitiates influence or share in each other's vitality, cheerfulness and hope through corporal contact, commensality, the intimacy of the home, mutual sharing and intimate chatting (and, as initiation songs tell, in the case of the married couple, through the giving and receiving of one another's loving and desiring gaze, arousal through and from each other's bodily scent, and playful touch in 'entwining legs').The life artery rises up in breath, blood, sensuality, the senses, vitality and life-regeneration. The lust for life that mounts in the life artery inspires and weaves through the whole of (inter)corporeality. It causes the individual to surpass his or her boundaries in hunger, virile life force (*ngolo*, *khoondzu*), and lust for life, in conjugal *communio* as well as in each ritual act that aims at the stirring up and transmitting life.

Efficacy of the Law of Minimal Intersubjective Ordering – Avuncular, Rather than Patricentric

The functions of maternal uncle, granduncle and great-granduncle mediate between the visible and invisible worlds, between ethical diligence and ludic disregard for norms. It is not the father but the uterine filiation (*yikheetu*, *yimaama*, *yingudi*) that, notwithstanding the intense corporal sharing of fate with the motherly life artery, opens the subject primarily to exchanges or encounters with descent groups outside of his or her own patrilineage or patriclan, as well as to the matrixial transworldly resonance and borderlinking. This sharing of fate is not localised in any biography, history or geography, but rather at the border between this-worldly and the otherworldly. The mother is, socially speaking, through uxori- and patrilocal marriage always perceived as a stranger or the 'unthought known' (namely one who realises inter-domestic branching and weaving, as well as intergenerational intercorporeality beyond the already existing and the predetermined) in the extended home of her husband; in the same way, her mother and maternal grandmother each provide the differential and borderlinking trait in their respective extended families and homes.

The maternal uncle, addressed as *ngwakhasi* or *ngwasi* – literally, male mother – has a distinguishing and mediating function. "The maternal uncle is, to the generation that precedes us, the *sole* male ascendant whose identity we may be certain" (Martens, 1975, p. 168). "One should note (…) that since the mother is the first space of identification, the 'opposite sex' in relation to any child – whether girl or boy – is always that of men" (ibid., p. 171). In this avuncular function he assists in transforming the signifiable (alliance, physical motherhood) into a signifier (of simultaneous alliance and filiation), as well as into a signified (namely the highly singular relations, always subordinated to the Ordering Efficacy of the Law, of brother and sister, mother and child, husband and wife). Before he can enter into the function of uncle, he is first the representative of the bride-givers and therefore the one who gives his sister in marriage to the bride-takers, in exchange for the brideprice and the compensations that follow throughout her life inasmuch as she gives birth and raises up children in the house of her spouse. Further, the uncle is the one who hands his nephew or niece over to the initiator, and thus places him or her in the matrixial frontier or the primordial transsubjective or liminoid zone of the initiation cult. His approval is required for each existential passage in the life of a nephew or niece, such as marriage or migration.

The maternal uncle impersonates the border function and the singular mediation of both alliance and filiation as well as of the desires of his sister, her husband and their children (Devisch, 1993, pp. 92–131). It is within this context that he refers to the Ordering efficacy of the Law (*k'amba*: see below), namely of the unavoidable reciprocalness, the boundedness-in-difference or the difference-in-boundedness. The maternal uncle splits apart the imaginary of the mother–child dyad and blood bond (the 'all', given the predominance of an ethos of reproduction in the Yaka worldview) by means of the singular – symbolic-imaginary – logic of the matrilineal filiation (the 'not-all'). The uncle ever represents the singular in the dyad: he is a reminder that only the several children from one and the same mother can claim the same and thus singular matrilineal filiation in which the Law is in vigour. The maternal uncle is the function in relation to which the enjoyment of the mother–child relation, like the husband–wife relation, structures itself. In his capacity as brother of the mother, he represents the unavoidable evidence of the incest taboo for the mother, her husband and their children – as I shall set out below in a paragraph on 'the Order of the Law'. He simultaneously presents himself positively as the uncle of her children, or, as the giver of the bride in relation to the husband of his sister, he speaks as the one who watches over the fertility and well-being of his sister and her offspring; negatively, he speaks as the one who reminds one of the incest taboo. For the Yaka, incest is held to be equivalent to an (agnatic) life stream that swallows its own foam, or even flows backwards back to its source. This is the way in which the incest taboo is understood to apply to father and daughter, mother and son, or brother and sister, whose relations are regulated by stringent rules of respect and avoidance.

Expressed in the Lacanian idiom, the bride takers perceive the uncle above all as the split being (*l'être clivé*), because of his role as the disturbing Other or, perhaps better, as *object a* under the sign of a voracious desire, a greedy if not vengeful yearning. Moreover (and returning to the Yaka perspective), he appears simultaneously in a joking relation and behind the mask of a potentially vengeful witch-craving in relation to the same children, namely his nephews and nieces. Within the joking relation, he makes erotic allusions with regard to his nieces and through furtive touch assesses the dimensions of their breasts and hips. Strictly speaking, the possibility of sexual intimacy between maternal (grand)uncle and (grand)niece, or between grandparent and grandchild, is not seen as abhorrent incest, but does demand a family council – in the presence of the granduncle and great-granduncle – for the purpose of restoring the family structure.

To place the relation in positive and hypothetical terms, the uncle (and above all the cleavage and asymmetry in his double manifestation) assists the young mother in articulating her desires with regard to her child as 'something beyond', as 'what might happen', as a shifting point between an ordering efficacy of the Law (the unavoidable, minimal 'normalising' or ordering structure) and the unfulfilled, the as yet unknown possibilities for growth, in the diagonal trajectory between acceptance of fate and one's aspiration, between daring and angst.

The imaginary uncle figure appears negatively – seen from a Lacanian perspective – as the enigmatic mask of the longings of the Other, the field par excellence where the subject seeks protection from cleavage, from angst, and against the strange and structural character of the *object a* (*object cause*, or the *initium* of desire). It is precisely in this element, in the admittedly differing and partly enigmatic *présence* the uncle has in the desires of the mother and her child, that the maternal uncle, it appears to me, does the work of a father function and at the same time makes it superfluous. He refashions the Name-of-the-Father function into Father-of-the-Name (giving), which, by and for the mother, articulates a paradoxical function of simultaneously knotting and splitting ('splitting-into-one-another', cf. sinthome) of the Lacanian symbolic and real.[10]

Leemba is in the Yaka view the reference term for uncle and etymologically signifies the one who brings to rest, softens, but also loosens or castrates. In this sense the uncle is a mediator or borderlinking between genders and between bride givers and takers as well as between the generations, in function of their reciprocal desires vested in *mooyi*, namely the life artery, weave and common fate in the uterine line. Within the marriage alliance and parenthood of his sister and the

[10] Up to 1970, the so-called earlier Lacan develops his phallogocentric focus on the Oedipal dynamic and paternal metaphor (namely, the father figure as foundation of the symbolic order or ultimate signifier without a signified) as well as on the speaking subject engendered by the structure of language, yet embroiled in the mechanisms of representation. From 1970, the so-called later Lacan moves from structural linguistic models to topology and covering such topics as the Borromean rings. He from then on deals foremost with the "Names-of-the-Father" as well with the place of the Real and of jouissance (all posthumously published due to Jean-Alain Miller: Lacan, 1970/2001, 1975–1976/2005). Jouissance always leaves a remainder which cannot be verbalised: the object 'a'. Similarly, the later Lacan's focus is on lalangue and the signifier's indeterminate attachment to and substitution by jouissance. In other words, his new focus is on the sinthome (Lacan, 1975–1976/2005), a neologism depicting the open-ended enactment of symbolic and imaginary *significance*, which is precisely not a call to the Other inasmuch as it is guided by pure jouissance addressed to no one. Around an empty centre, at the very edge of the sayable, the sinthome supports a structural or operatory relationship among subjects, and between subjects and the object world. Religious and political leaders, institutions, artists and literature (one thinks of James Joyce) develop sinthomes in the form of deconstructed ('per-verse' [*père-version* in French] or per-versely oriented) motifs, puzzles and enigmas. The sinthome may effectively foster the audience's attention, while aligning them to 'empty' centres of *significance*. The sinthome remains beyond analysis or interpretation, yet triggers unconscious enjoyment, all the while mobilising and organising crucial orientation, commitment, embodiment and jouissance.

filiation of the child, the maternal uncle binds the Order of the Law (the fundament of exchange) with the order of lust for life or *Geist-Trieb* (*kyeesi*) as a manifestation of *mooyi*. He thus couples the Law to the desiring for a jouissance, expressed in the hunger (*ndzala*) of the father and the mother for esteem (*luzitu*), as well as for self-transcendence towards 'something else'. The Order of the Law comprises in essence the inescapable social prerequisite of reciprocity, of a continuous movement towards 'something just beyond', beyond self-enclosure or being closed in on oneself. The borderlinking capacity of *kyeesi* is then the polar opposite of *kyoosi*, paralysis or shutting in. Moreover, shared lust for life leads to a reciprocally contagious enjoyment (*-mokasana, -nyuukisana, -biindasana maalu, -hoyasana*), while, in contrast, imposition or intrusion or border-transgression (*zuundza, yiluta*) leads to isolation and paralysis of an enjoyment that is closed in on itself (*luhweetu*) or an excessive but exhausting enjoyment (*yiluta*). Being withdrawn or closed in on oneself or emptying out the body and one's life force is the central theme of witchcraft discourse. Paranoid-vindictive witchcraft (*-loka*) unravels the vital fabric of kin and unbinds or stifles life (*-kola*; Devisch, 1993, pp. 146ff., 2005).

In the collective phantasm it is not so much the father figure but that of the maternal uncle that, among the Yaka, is much feared as potentially life-threatening or castrating precisely in his protective gestures with regard to his sisters and matrilineal (grand)nephews and -nieces. It is, moreover, the uncle, and not the father, who sees to it that the marriage partners for his (grand)nieces are legitimate, just as he commands his share of the brideprice and the further compensations for the life that his sister is transmitting and taking care of.

Among the Yaka and in their worldview, the Order of the Law holds the status of *k'amba*, the order of the inescapable, of an assigned fate; the term literally means, 'it is simply evident that…', or, 'is it not so that…?' *-Hoyasana, -diisasana* – namely speaking, eating, living in the reciprocal exchange of shared community, is the core of the Ordering Efficacy of the Law, thus the only sphere to bear binding moral qualifications. The negative of this order is expressed in terms of stealing (*-yiba*), the quintessential notion of 'evil'. This concept covers each life-threatening or ill-intentioned disregard or infringement of the Law of Exchange in the family circle and more specifically in the uterine filiation. It comprises, in particular, incest, illicit sex, thievery and life-threatening or mortal violence, and includes fatal witchcraft. As *Sinnbild* (*zinnebeeld*, in dutch) of the Order of the Law, the white kaolin clay, *pheemba* (under the protection of the family head's First Wife), makes present a primordial matrix ('the archaic m/Other') or a cosmogenetic and moral metramorphosis.[11] It calls up, for the Yaka, the basal metaphysical and ethical axiom, namely the matrixial capacity homoeopathically to turn evil – namely in the forms of disrespect, disregard, breaking down or infringing on the fundamental reciprocity that makes possible the transmission of life – back upon itself. This homeopathic capacity thus restores or reaffirms the order of reciprocity. The kaolin demonstrates the extent to which the Ordering Efficacy of the Law is neither a Law

[11] Bracha L. Ettinger's notion of metramorphosis is a neologism composed out of 'metamorphosis' and 'metra' (the Greek term for womb, uterus).

of the Father nor of any god-the-father figure, but rather what is postulated behind all human engagements. *K'amba* points to the inescapable necessity to shape society such that humans in their unconscious desire, throughout their life course, seek to live and invest in community. It is the maternal uncle who sees to it that the social relations of exchange (and thus the creation of the society) remain mobilised around his sister and her children.

A curse (*n-sasu*, *-sasa*, literally, 'incantation'), if ever formulated within the maternal line, activates the inescapable self-maintenance of this basal order of reciprocity, primarily through the fatal sanction of delict. Infliction of the sanction may result in madness (*-kaluka*), illness or misfortune caused within a *cult of affliction*. This is the institutionalisation of curse and sanction as the preservation of the basal reciprocity in the uterine life source. The Order of the Law ultimately has no other foundation than itself, and is incommensurate with the Christian converts religious guilt ethic of sin (Robbins, 2004) or with some eventual sacralisation of the avuncular relation and the primordial source of life as an all too human quest for vengeance. As I have demonstrated elsewhere (Devisch, 2003), such sacralising '*père-versions*' (Lacan's term; see note 10) occur today in the healing churches of the holy spirit in Kinshasa; they identify the versatile Janus figure of 'the holy spirit-satan' to be the cause both of loving as well as of self-serving and perverse desires.

Transworldly Phallogocentric Symbolisation and Matrixial *Signifiance*

The preceding analysis demonstrates the extent to which the profound attention that the Yaka devote to reproduction, filiation and alliance is directed to the production, enhancement and articulation of meaningful intercorporeity, (inter)subjectivity, sociality and being-in-the-world. In this regard, a glaring difference appears between encompassing, religiously-tuned, phallogocentric symbolisation processes, on the one hand, and the more fragmentary and diverse sensibility to flashes of transworldly matrixial *signifiance*, on the other.

In the patriarchal order and the public scene, the forming of the subject, as well as the authoritative institutional and institutionalising production of meaning and knowledge occur within the explanatory language as the dominant structure of people's (un)consciousness. Institutionalisation and meaning are being produced through processes of distinction or splitting and (metonymic, metaphoric) substitution, rather than of confusing or melting together. The former are directed to bringing about visibility and order, which oppose to the sphere of the incomprehensible or unintelligible, suspicious invisibility and indefiniteness, or the undomesticatable and wildness; this last, for example, typifies the situation both of deep night – particularly around the new moon just before the first glow of dawn, as well as of the so-called impenetrable and opaque forest realm beyond the known hunting grounds (Devisch, 1993, pp. 86ff.). These realms connote menacing negativity and contamination which are to be avoided. In other words, on the public male-dominated scene, the articulation of the imaginary realm is preoccupied with symbolic signification and the domestication of the heterogenous and hybrid elements in the sociocultural reality and the environment. Public palavers conducted by elders, like also rites of passage, seek to halt the entanglement or emptying out of the symbolic by orderfully tapping into and domesticating unconscious imaginary registers; this involves subordinating the shocking to the reconciliatory, the brutal to the refined, the darkness to the public realm of daylight, the helpless to the powerful, or envy to solidarity.

The structuralistic paradigm of Lévi-Strauss, to which the early Lacan is tributary, helps us to situate and map out such an ordering process of meaning production. We are here dealing with the production of meaning on the basis of the complicity of a signifier and a signified, or of signifiers themselves, as well as of the metaphoric transposition of meaning or a metonymic substitution of meaning. In this view, meaning stems from the relation between something that is present and something that is absent, between something in language and something outside of it, or something of this order (or its terms) and something of another order (or its terms). The distinguishing criterion is inspired or instated on the basis of an exogenous indication or element, such as the will to control, the safeguarding of order, negotiability or predictability. Such meaning production is – in Lacanian terms – phallic: its focus is on the binary structuring of verbal or language-like signification. It focuses on multiple significations centred on and in the subject, inasmuch as they are directed to building up social and cultural legitimation within a linear and vertical time–space order in line with the governing canons of meaning and value. According to structuralist thinking, members of a culture espouse the symbolic order and the discourse of the Other (i.e., the given culture): they thereby become entwined in the binary, at times dumb and restrictive, social and cultural constructions and conventions.[12] In Yaka socioculture, for example, children of the same mother are enclosed in a same identification process vis à-vis the mother, one that is guaranteed by the figure of the maternal uncle and the Order of the Law of which his function is evocative. And yet, inversely, the maternal uncle also figures as the instance around which potential negativity in the family may nestle. The phallic mode of meaning production readily lends itself to a sociological theory of religion. In this view, as François Laplantine, (2003, p. 11) aptly puts it, religion is considered secondary, vis-à-vis that what it is not. Religion is there understood as a metaphor: the belief in the ancestral or cult spirits is in fact seen as a belief in society's undisputable or sovereign self-maintenance. To put it another way, in Godelier's (Godelier and Hassoun, 1996) terms, in the perspective of structuralist sociology, religion – like sexuality – appears as a ventriloquism mechanism for the social, in the service of the reproduction of

[12] According to the structuralism of Lévi-Strauss, the only mode of meaning-production of what makes itself present in language or a symbolic system, comes about through splitting, separation, castration. The Other and in particular l'objet a[autre] escapes this binary structuring of meaning in lines with its linguistic model. It is therefore defined as out of reach, lost (such as the m/Other and other lost part-objects) and for which again and again substitutes are to be looked for if one aims to come to meaning-production in language.

social orders inscribed both in human intimacy and in the organisation of the life world.

The matrixial approach of the unreflected knowledge and significance in the fluid borderlinking should not be seen in opposition to the structuralistic perspective, but as complementary to it. According to Griselda Pollock (2006, p. 21), the matrixial *signifiance* or metamorphosis may unfold itself through poetic language that conveys multilayered meaning, or through the "*père-version*" of the conventional discourse's phallicism as effected by way of neologisms, irony, *Sinnbild*. But above all, rhythm, sacrifice, and rites of passage and initiation awaken significance from within the matrixial borderlinking forces. Among the most noteworthy of these are the vital (inter)corporeal functions, such as heartbeat, circulation of blood, menstruation cycle, reproductive sexual union, pregnancy, sharing of the meal, digestion, and above all, breathing and its audibly accelerated or decelerated rhythm. The Yaka ascribe the end of a death agony to the cessation of breathing: life and death are thus bound to breathing. For the Yaka, the invisible (in its numinous or augural dimensions) is the source (namely, the primordial space–time, *ngoongu*, in the womb of the earth) that energises these visible and self-steering vital bodily processes, giving them rhythm and form – such as in the heaving of the chest in breathing, the heartbeat, the digestive process, the menstruation cycle and the development of pregnancy. What is invisible can assist to break open the unspeakable in the visible. In the matrixial view, this ungraspable and ceaseless, hence transcendent, source of life-giving emergence, rhythm, boiling over or yeasting, is a basal organic and autogenerative process: it stems from the life-giving process in *ngoongu*, and is radically endogenous to physical and cosmic life and to whatever elements give colour, scent, rhythm and form to the matrixial cultural life and its development of significance. This latter process is, in the words of Merleau-Ponty (1964) regarding the invisible, a sublime coming out of what is inside, within the human, within the being-in-the-world and the life process. The invisible allows itself to be imagined at the fluid border of what can be seen, in the *yiniinga* or shadow, literally the rotational movement or tipping moment between light and darkness, the visible and invisible, the tangible and the sensual. The *Sinnbild* is akin to a fragmentary organic development of a back and forth movement (as in an up- and downwards movement, or a climbing spiral movement, for example), and the augural capacity emerging between one bundle of signs, significations or words, and another. The *Sinnbild* as sensual and meaning-bearing image carries one reality over onto another, not so much in order to form a coherent whole or to come nearer to the 'lost' (maternal) totality for which one may be longing, but because the (matrixial) reality is not to be grasped through conceptualising or within a conceptual system without having to reduce it. The *Sinnbild* enlivens language from another, complementary experiential world.

The matrixial capacity for borderlinking is primarily heuristically valuable in achieving an understanding of the female and avuncular (inter)subjectivity-as-meeting, of the borderlinking between people or things as well as between the visible and the invisible; it isolates difference not as difference in, for example, superiority and subordination. The matrixial approach offers the possibility of tracing, from within the intimacy of events, the aspects of plurality, strangeness and change processes as well as the paradoxal flowing together of very diverse forms of meaning development and jouissance. The formless white clump of kaolin clay (*pheemba*) is, for the Yaka, probably the matrixial *Sinnbild* par excellence. It symbolises the cosmic primordial womb (*ngoongu*), which remains hidden from view. Above all, this kaolin clay makes present in the group the originary and augural time–space of all life, rising and swelling out of it. Kaolin mediates the plenitude of life, healing and the making whole that is achieved in the fluid border space without pretending at exhaustive symbolisation or ultimate jouissance. In contrast with the monadic effect of the relation of the subject to *object a* (the unsayable in the Other), the matrixial *Sinnbild* couples the subject with a borderlinking 'other force', a force that is outside of the subject yet at the same time present within it. For the Yaka, it is a given that one discovers an/the 'other' in oneself, in and through intersubjectivity, intercorporeality and the transworldly, namely through contact with one's co-habitants, the life world, and the invisible. According to Yaka culture, it is evident that, through intersubjectivity, intercorporeality and the transworldly, namely through contact with the other, that one – in the process of searching for a harmony, an image, a form, or moral, mental or spiritual enhancement (or resonance) – discovers the other in oneself, fellows, the life world or the invisible world. This discovery can be made more concrete in a *Sinnbild* that releases, that can maintain the unsayable, the unnameable, at a verbal and visual distance yet at the same time bring them close in a meaningful imaging, in a quasi oniric *Sinnbild*, often full of ambiguity, (collective imaginary) fantasy and imaginary power. The *Sinnbild*, just like the dream, can fulfil the function of a safety valve to the unconscious. Expressed in the words of Didier Anzieu (1984, p. 57, my translation): "The nocturnal dream is the hallucinatory realisation of the desire; the primary psychic processes appear to be dominant there, despite their imbrication with the secondary processes. In other words, the dream, like the neurotic symptom, is a debate with an underlying phantasm." The matrixial breaks with the linearity of a narrative or of the imposition of social order on disorder or dysfunction, and privileges the other and complementary possibilities of equality-in-difference by way of the art of living, artistic drive, possession and trance, poetic and expressive language, the sensations and affects of music, or the ecstasy of the extrahuman or the spirits.

References

Anzieu, D. (1984). *Le groupe et l'inconscient: L'imaginaire groupal*. Paris: Dunod.

Anzieu, D. (1985). *Le Moi-peau*. Paris: Bordas.

Balestriere, L. (1998). *Freud et la question des origines*. Brussels: De Boeck Université.

Bullard, A. (2005). L'Oedipe africain, a retrospective. *Psychopathologie Africaine*, *42*, 171–203.

Collignon, R. (1978). Vingt ans de travaux à la clinique psychiatrique de Fann-Dakar. *Psychopathologie Africaine*, *14*, 133–323.

Collomb, H. (1967). Assistance psychiatrique en Afrique (expérience Sénégalaise). *Psychopathologie Africaine*, *1*, 11–84.

Corin, E. (1997). Playing with limits: Tobie Nathan's evolving paradigm in ethnopsychiatry. *Transcultural Psychiatry*, *34*, 345–358.
Corin, E. & Bibeau, G. (1980). Psychiatric perspectives in Africa. Part II: The traditional viewpoint. *Transcultural Psychiatric Research Review*, *17*, 205–233.
Deleuze, G. & Guattari, F. (1972). *Capitalisme et schizophrénie 1: L'Anti-Oedipe*. Paris: Minuit.
Deleuze, G. & Guattari, F. (1980). *Mille plateaux: Capitalisme et schizophrénie*. Paris: Minuit.
Devereux, G. (1978). *Ethnopsychoanalysis: Psychoanalysis and anthropology as complementary frames of reference*. Berkeley, CA: University of California Press.
Devereux, G. (1980). *Basic problems in ethnopsychiatry*. Chicago, IL: University of Chicago Press.
Devisch, R. (1993). *Weaving the threads of life: The khita gyn-eco-logical healing cult among the Yaka*. Chicago, IL: University of Chicago Press.
Devisch, R. (2003). Parody in matricentred Christian healing communes of the Sacred Spirit in Kinshasa. *Contours: A Journal of the African Diaspora*, *1*, 171–198.
Devisch, R. (2005). Witchcraft and sorcery. In C. Casey & R. B. Edgerton (Eds.), *A companion to psychological anthropology* (pp. 389–416). Oxford: Blackwell.
Devisch, R. (2007). Intercultural borderlinking, intersubjectivity, and Bantu healing cults. *Medische Antropologie*, *19*, 97–114.
Devisch, R. & Brodeur, C. (1999). *The law of the lifegivers: The domestication of desire*. Amsterdam: Harwood.
Ettinger, B. L. (Ed.) (2000). *Artworking 1985–1999*. Ghent: Ludion/Brussels: Paleis voor Schone Kunsten.
Ettinger, B. L. (2006). *The matrixial borderspace*. Minneapolis, MN: University of Minnesota Press.
Favret-Saada, J. (1977). *Les mots, la mort, les sorts: La sorcellerie dans le Bocage*. Paris: Gallimard.
Flax, J. (1990). *Thinking fragments: Psychoanalysis, feminism and postmodernism in the contemporary West*. Berkeley, CA: University of California Press.
Godelier, M. (2004). *Métamorphoses de la parenté*. Paris: Fayard.
Godelier, M. & Hassoun, J. (Eds.) (1996). *Meurtre du père, sacrifice de la sexualité: Approches anthropologiques et psychanalytiques*. Paris: Arcanes.
Herdt, G. (Ed.) (1982). *Rituals of manhood: Male initiation in Papua New Guinea*. Berkeley, CA: University of California Press.
Lacan, J. (1970/2001). *Autres écrits*. Paris: Seuil.
Lacan, J. (1975–1976/2005). *Le séminaire livre XXIII: Le sinthome* (Ed. J.-A. Miller). Paris: Seuil.
Laplantine, F. (2003). Penser anthropologiquement la religion. *Anthropologie et Sociétés*, *27*, 11–33.
Lévi-Strauss, C. (1949). *Les Structures élémentaires de la parenté*. Paris: Presses Universitaires de France.
Lévi-Strauss, C. (1958). *Anthropologie structurale*. Paris: Plon.
Malinowski, B. (1929). *The sexual life of savages in north-western Melanesia*. New York: Harcourt, Brace & World.
Martens, F. (1975). A propos de l'oncle maternel, ou modeste proposition pour repenser des cousins croisés. *L'Homme*, *15*, 155–175.
Merleau-Ponty, M. (1964). *Le visible et l'invisible*. Paris: Gallimard.
Muxel, A. & Rennes, J.-M. (Eds.) (1989). *Le père. Métaphore paternelle et fonctions du père: L'interdit, la filiation, la transmission*. Paris: Denoël.
Nandy, A. (1995). *The Savage Freud and other essays on possible and retrievable selves*. Delhi: Oxford University Press.
Nathan, T. (1986). *La folie des autres: Traité d'ethno-psychiatrie clinique*. Paris: Dunod.
Nathan, T. (1994). *L'influence qui guérit*. Paris: Odile Jacob.
Obeyesekere, G. (1980). *The work of culture: Symbolic transformation in psychoanalysis and anthropology*. Chicago, IL: University of Chicago Press.
Ortigues, E. (1996). L'influence de l'expérience Africaine sur notre pratique clinique. *Journal des Anthropologues* (Association française des anthropologues, Paris), *64–65*, 87–95.

Ortigues, M.-C. & Ortigues, E. (1966). *L' Oedipe africain*. Paris: Plon.
Ortigues, M.-C. & Ortigues, E. (1984). *L' Oedipe africain*. Paris: Harmattan.
Ortigues, M.-C., Martino, P., & Collomb, H. (1967). L'utilisation des données culturelles dans un cas de bouffée délirante. *Psychopathologie Africaine*, *3*, 121–147.
Parin, P., Morgenthaler, F., & Matthèy-Guenet, E.-C. (1966). *Les blancs pensent trop: 13 entretiens psychanalytiques avec les Dogon*. Paris: Payot.
Pollock, G. (2006). Introduction. Femininity: Aporia or sexual difference? In B. L. Ettinger (Ed.), *The matrixial borderspace* (pp. 1–38). Minneapolis, MN: University of Minnesota Press.
Pradelles de Latour, C.-H. (1991). *Ethnopsychanalyse en pays Bamiléké*. Paris: EPEL.
Pradelles de Latour, C.-H. (1995). Ethnopsychanalyse: Une autre approche du sujet. *Journal des Anthropologues* (Association française des anthropologues, Paris), *64–65*, 97–114.
Pradelles de Latour, C.-H. (2005). *Rites thérapeutiques dans une société matrilinéaire: Le gèrem des Pèrè (Cameroun)*. Paris: Karthala.
Rabain, J. (1979). *L'enfant du lignage: Du sevrage à la classe d'âge chez les Wolof du Sénégal*. Paris: Payot.
Ricoeur, P. (1970). *Freud and philosophy: An essay on interpretation*. New Haven, CT: Yale University Press.
Riesman, P. (1986). The person and the life cycle in African life and thought. *African Studies Review*, *29*(2), 71–138.
Robbins, J. (2004). *Becoming sinners: Christianity and moral torment in a Papua New Guinea society*. Berkeley, CA: University of California Press.
Schurmans, D. (1972). Significations psychodynamiques et fonctions culturelles des interprétations traditionnelles Wolof des maladies mentales. *Psychopathologie Africaine*, *7*, 57–100.
Spiro, M. (1982). *Oedipus in the Trobriands*. Chicago, IL: University of Chicago Press.
Streit, U. (1997). Nathan's ethnopsychoanalytic therapy: Characteristics, discoveries and challenges to Western psychotherapy. *Transcultural Psychiatry*, *34*, 321–343.
Vandenbroeck, P. (2000). *Azetta: Berbervrouwen en hun kunst*. Ghent: Ludion/Brussels: Paleis voor Schone Kunsten.
Zafiropoulos, M. (2003). *Lacan et Lévi-Strauss ou le retour à Freud (1951–1957)*. Paris: PUF.
Zempleni, A. (1977). From symptom to sacrifice: The story of Khady Fall. In V. Crapanzano & V. Garrison (Eds.), *Case studies in spirit possession* (pp. 87–140). New York: Wiley.

Psychoanalytic and Philosophical Inquiries into Religious Subjectivity

James J. DiCenso

The Question of the Subject

My paper explores how modern philosophy of religion and psychoanalytic theory interact on the question of what I call *religious subjectivity*. This is a theme that draws from Freud, and remains consistent with his insights and theories, while also seeking to go beyond Freud's work in some key respects by drawing on a variety of post-Freudian theorists from France. Generally, I will use the concept of religious subjectivity as an encompassing rubric to characterize personality transformations involving enhanced capacity for critical self-reflection, ethical awareness, and other-directedness. My use of the term *subject*, and also the more dynamic designation *subjectivity*, is derived from Jacques Lacan's revised psychoanalytic topographic model, which has had a broad influence among contemporary theorists in a variety of fields. This model has been appropriated in differing ways by theorists such as Foucault and Kristeva, and also parallels Paul Ricoeur's endeavors to conceptualize a progressive, transformative model of the personality in psychoanalytic terms.

Lacan invoked the concept of *le sujet* to thematize the overall psycho-dynamics of the Freudian topography in a way that retained the fissured and conflicting, as well as the interactive and inter-personal features of Freud's model. At the same time, Lacan sought to articulate an over-arching reference point for personal transformation and development that is never directly articulated in Freud's work. Lacan's *subject* expresses an understanding of the person that incorporates the drives or id (Lacan's *real*), the super-ego as well as the interpersonal, linguistic, and cultural influences constitutive thereof (Lacan's *symbolic*), as well as the Freudian ego, of which Lacan strongly emphasizes the narcissistic components under the heading of the *imaginary*, while generally downplaying the reality-testing functions.

Lacan usually defines the subject indirectly and in negative terms by emphatically differentiating this concept from that of the ego. He thus insists that "the ego is

J.J. DiCenso
University of Toronto, Toronto, ON, Canada
e-mail: james.dicenso@utoronto.ca

J.A. Belzen (ed.), *Changing the Scientific Study of Religion: Beyond Freud?*

an imaginary function, it is not to be confused with the subject" (Lacan, 1975/1988, p. 193). While the formation of an ego is obviously a necessary factor in personal maturation, as expressed in Lacan's famous "mirror stage," it also is characterized by a closure and fixating of the personality in the form of a persistent narcissism. Hence Lacanian psychoanalysis rejects post-Freudian attempts to synthesize a focal point for progressive personality formations under the heading of the ego. This is a crucial issue, because Lacan describes the subject as a modality of *reflective consciousness* that is actually blocked and masked by the narcissism of the ego. As he states: "we call the ego that nucleus given to consciousness, but opaque to reflection, marked by all the ambiguities which, from self-satisfaction to 'bad faith' [*mauvaise foi*], structure the experience of the passions in the human subject; this 'I' [*moi*] who (...) opposes its irreducible inertia of pretences and *méconnaissances* to the concrete problematic of the realization of the subject" (Lacan, 1966/1977, p. 15). Here Lacan restricts the form of consciousness associated with the ego to what might be called "perception-consciousness," which he also associates with conformity to predominant social norms. By contrast, the subject is a concept that seeks to articulate that potentially self-reflective dimension of us which appears when the fixity and blockage of habitual identity structures, as informed by social conditioning, is questioned and opened up. In contrast to the "closed" ego, the subject is defined as a dynamic process that is both relational and temporal and by which a more encompassing and self-aware mode of consciousness is cultivated.

My aim here is not to explicate this Lacanian model in detail, but merely to use it as a conceptual reference point for characterizing contemporary psychoanalytic and philosophical approaches to the problem of progressive personality transformation. Lacan's model has the advantage of avoiding the reification of some other post-Freudian models of "the self," including those that elevate the ego to the status of the whole, while yet offering a means of articulating a more inclusive and differentiated developmental frame of reference. Some of the late work of Michel Foucault on the "hermeneutics of the subject" can also contribute to clarifying what is at stake in this discussion of religious subjectivity. Foucault strongly affirms Lacan's contributions in stating: "It seems to me that Lacan has been the only one since Freud who has sought to refocus the question of psychoanalysis on precisely this question of the relations between the subject and truth" (Foucault, 2001/2006, p. 30). Whether or not Foucault is entirely fair in this assessment, he is certainly correct in indicating a quality of truth in the Lacanian subject that cannot be reduced to conformity with external reality. This is precisely *not* the reality testing and social adaptation of perception-consciousness, but is rather a critical capacity to reflect on oneself that is something more like a *spiritual* form of truth. In fact, Foucault himself clearly makes this connection, and he defines the notion of spirituality as follows: "I think we could call 'spirituality' the search, practice, and experience through which the subject carries out the necessary transformations on himself [or herself] in order to have access to the truth" (Foucault, 2001/2006, p. 15). Basically, Foucault differentiates between strictly rationalist philosophical approaches to the subject, whose maxim he characterizes as "know yourself," and more encompassing and transformative spiritual approaches whose maxim is "care of the self." What is most crucial about the latter method is that it turns critical investigation back upon the presumed rational bearer of knowledge, to inquire into the limitations and possible distortions of this subjective modality. As Foucault states: "spirituality... postulates that for the subject to have the right of access to the truth he must be changed, transformed, shifted, and become, to some extent and up to a certain point, other than himself" (ibid., p. 15).

This approach to the truth of the subject as a largely spiritual issue in the sense indicated by Foucault, shapes my understanding of *religious subjectivity*. This capacity for self reflective consciousness, and the associated self-transformation, will be seen to have a strongly ethical component, in the sense that it is impossible without inter-personal relations, and because it can serve to ameliorate the nature of those relations. If we become more conscious of our motivations and desires, and less narcissistic in the pejorative sense of being blindly self-involved and self-serving, we potentially become more capable of other-directed, ethical behavior. For Lacan, the analytic situation is the key vehicle by which the "realization of the subject" (which is of course different for each person), might occur. However, this theme of "becoming other" can be inclusive of multiple conventional religious worldviews and discursive symbolic systems, insofar as these can facilitate the reflective psychological processes involved (through narrative, ritual practice, the cultivation of interior states, and so forth). At the same time, blind adherence to religious doctrines can work to *inhibit* the capacity for reflection and transformation that Foucault calls "spiritual." Hence, the model of religious subjectivity I will explicate is irreducible to the belief systems of any specific tradition, and has affinities with the type of "unchurched" spirituality, or with heterodox "mystical" trends in various religious traditions, as discussed by others in this volume. Each of these rubrics seeks to articulate contemporary concerns with thinking through progressive and "religious" possibilities in human beings beyond the frameworks of traditional inherited religious worldviews and authorities. Finally, as I will now explicate in greater detail, the problem of religious subjectivity forms a bridge between theorists of a more philosophical variety and those with a more specifically psychoanalytic approach, and hence becomes a focal point for inter-disciplinary inquiry.

Some Relevant Historical Background

Before proceeding to a further discussion of how specifically psychoanalytic theories contribute to my theme, I want to outline some relevant issues in traditional philosophy of religion. This will serve to show more clearly how psychoanalytic theory both critiques and extrapolates upon aspects of this tradition, which is certainly one of the explicit and implicit conceptual conversation partners for Freud and much of post-Freudian psychoanalytic theory (particularly those in the French tradition). As modern European theorizing about religion took shape in the eighteenth and nineteenth centuries, certain subtle shifts in the object of inquiry can now be seen to have occurred. This is a time when the disciplinary boundaries between philosophy and psychology, not to mention anthropology and other social sciences, had not yet congealed. Many of the period's inquiries into the nature of religion are therefore highly revealing in this regard, because they seem to necessitate inherently inter-disciplinary or multi-disciplinary approaches to the phenomena – a matter that will also re-emerge in significant ways in more contemporary theories of religion and subjectivity. I want to begin by indicating the manner in which philosophical engagements with religion's postulated objects (God, the soul, an afterlife, and so forth) begin to open up questions of the *nature of human subjectivity* that have a significant psychological dimension, and that also exhibit something of the spiritual concerns I've described. These philosophical articulations of the human, subjective, and especially ethical concerns that seem to underpin religious inquiries establish a key domain in which the interests of philosophical and psychoanalytic inquiry will intersect and interact.

It is a commonplace that modern philosophy, including the philosophy of religion, emerges with Descartes' focus on "clear and distinct ideas" that follow from the positing of his famous "cogito," or "thinking substance" in response to seemingly all-corrosive doubt (Descartes, 1637–1641/1960, p. 92). Focusing on the rational human mind as the reference point for religious truths follows directly from this positing. As Descartes emphasizes: "consequently we must necessarily conclude from all I have previously said that God exists. For even though the idea of substance exists in me from the very fact that I am a substance, I would nevertheless have no idea of an infinite substance, I who am a finite being, unless the idea had been placed in me by some substance which was in fact infinite" (Descartes, 1637–1641/1960, p. 101). This is a rationalist re-formulation of Anselm's ontological argument, wherein the very idea of an infinite being, present in the minds of finite beings such as ourselves, is seen to necessitate the existence of that infinite being. What I want to emphasize is that the "Cartesian moment," as Foucault calls it, shifts the focus of philosophizing about religion in a major way from logically confirming the existence of posited objects, to the question of the subject who knows. However, as Foucault also points out, the Cartesian moment basically discredits what he calls the ancient form of "care of the self" involving critical self-reflection, and it restricts the epistemic approach of "know yourself" to the criterion of "self evidence" (Foucault, 2001/2006, p. 14). In other words, once the rational subject has confirmed the presence of infinite ideas within his or her own mind, no further process of critical self-reflection engendering self-transformation is required.

I will return briefly to these rationalist views. However, in the mainstream of European thought, arguments based on innate ideas of the rationalist tradition gave way to more rigorously empiricist orientations focusing on observable knowledge of the natural world, and these need to be discussed as also bearing on the turn to issues of the subject. In the domain of religious thought, the empiricist approach found its counterpart in deism, natural religion, and the "argument from design." With regard to these views, the impact of David Hume's interventions is inestimable. Hume's work on religion is valuable for my topic because, in criticizing the design argument, he also contributed to a human-centered approach to religion, though in a very different way from Descartes. Hume actually anticipates psychoanalysis in certain respects, insofar as he counters rationalist models by emphasizing the embodied, affective, historically and culturally informed features of human subjectivity and religious belief.

For many theorists who embraced the skeptical and empirical orientations to knowledge that were attendant upon the rise of modern science, Hume's refutations and qualifications of the dominant attempts to weld religious belief and dogma to reason and proof, i.e., the argument from design, were conclusive. Hume illustrated, in ways that are if anything even more compelling in a post-Darwinian universe, that available evidence in the natural world that might be used to argue for a grand "designer" is at best inadequate and equivocal. He pointed out, for example, that "every argument, deduced from causes [God] to effects [an ordered world], must of necessity be a gross sophism; since it is impossible for you to know anything of the cause, but what you have antecedently, not inferred, but discovered to the full, in the effect" (Hume, 1779–1757/1993, p. 18). In other words, the qualities and virtues attributed to the cause or creator of this universe cannot exceed those evident in the creation itself. One cannot logically leap from a flawed universe which, despite its intricacy and beauty, is rife with suffering, imperfection, and injustice on multiple levels, to the positing of a perfect, omnipotent creator. In this vein, Hume continues: "As the universe shows wisdom and goodness, we infer wisdom and goodness. As it shows a particular degree of these perfections, we infer a particular degree of them, precisely adapted to the effect which we examine" (ibid., p. 21). In this way, Hume can reasonably allow for the possibility of *some* form of first cause to this world but, somewhat irreverently, he proposes that this flawed world might be "the work of some dependent, inferior Deity" (a view quite reminiscent of certain forms of Gnosticism), or perhaps, he speculates, "it is the production of old age and dotage in some superannuated deity ... " (p. 71). Elsewhere, Hume proposes another view he thinks better corresponds to observable reality than that of a single omnipotent and beneficent deity. The world, he argues, "is so full of variety and uncertainty, that, if we suppose it immediately ordered by any intelligent beings, we must acknowledge a contrariety in their designs and intentions, a constant combat of opposite powers, and a repentance or change of intention in the same power, from impotence or levity" (p. 139). Although characterized by an irreverent and ironic tone, these reflections illustrate that there is no necessary logical connection between the observable empirical world and the specific characteristics attributed to a creator deity as inherited from the biblical tradition.

These and other such arguments served to pry apart the uneasy alliance between traditional religious metaphysics and the rising influence of empirically based scientific and rational reflection. The ensuing retreat from grand metaphysical speculation will have an effect on a wide variety of subsequent theorists, of whom Immanuel Kant has had the most lasting significance. Kant will follow Hume not only in eschewing metaphysical speculation, but also in turning his analytical gaze toward the subject who engenders the rich panoply of religious and metaphysical conceptualizations and imaginings that have been intrinsic to virtually every known human culture. To stay with Hume a moment longer, however, we also note in his writings on religion a variety of attempts to link the origins and nature of religious systems (including both monotheistic and polytheistic) to a variety of human sources. In his

Natural History of Religion, Hume attempts to trace the formation of "the first religious principles," exploring the questions of "what those principles are, which give rise to the original belief, and what those accidents and causes are, which direct its operation..." (Hume, 1779–1757/1993, p. 134). Like the metaphysical models that might be contrived to explain the complex world we inhabit, so too the *human* sources of religious belief are seen to be *multiple*. At one point, for example, Hume proposes that "the first ideas of religion arose not from contemplation of works of nature, but from a concern with regard to the events of life, and from the incessant hopes and fears, which actuate the human mind" (ibid., p. 139). This theme of the frailty and weakness of human beings, their dependence on an unpredictable world, and the consequent fear, uncertainty, and need for consolation that give rise to religious beliefs, courses through the *Natural History*. Here the more properly "philosophical" concerns with argument, proof, and disproof give way to more complex anthropological and psychological types of reflection about the non-rational bases of, and influences upon religious belief. There is a Freudian quality to many of these analyses, and even the mechanism of "projection," through which these inner needs give rise to the objectified manifestations of religious worldviews, is implied. As Hume states: "There is an universal tendency in mankind to conceive all beings like themselves, and to transfer to every object, those qualities, with which they are familiarly acquainted..." (p. 141). Hume, of course, has little regard for such worldviews founded on the irrational needs and fears of humans, and is quick to point out the gross anthropomorphisms of which they are guilty. "The absurdity is not less," he asserts, "while we cast our eyes upwards; and transferring, as is too usual, human passions and infirmities to the deity, represent him as jealous and revengeful, capricious and partial, and, in short, a wicked and foolish man, in every respect but his superior power and authority" (pp. 141–142). These skeptical and critical reflections are most certainly the core contribution of Hume to theorizing religion, and these approaches to the phenomena remain prominent in Freud's empiricist and psychoanalytic critiques a century and a half later in *Future of an Illusion*.

Nevertheless, other humanistic considerations begin to take shape in Hume's work, and are variably addressed by numerous philosophical and psychoanalytic theorists. There is a sense, only hinted at by Hume, in which apart from the baser and ignoble affective motivations underlying religion, there may also be an affinity between *some* of the concerns of religions and modern attempts at furthering the personal and moral development of human beings. In the *Natural History*, Hume critically remarks on the tendency of religions to privilege superstitious practices and "frivolous observances" that often serve no moral or human purpose or that work against moral betterment. In the course of this critique, he makes reference to "virtue and good morals, which alone can be acceptable to a perfect being..." (p. 179). This is a key, if undeveloped aspect of Hume's thought; that is, the way in which his critiques of religion also serve to shift focus from the literal validity of objectified metaphysical representations to the question of human subjectivity, with the question of a possible *ethical subjectivity* lingering in the background. These ethical concerns are evident in the concluding paragraphs of the *Natural History*, where Hume laments: "Hear the verbal protestations of men: Nothing so certain as their religious tenets. Examine their lives: You will scarcely think they repose the smallest confidence in them" (p. 184). Here, in revealing the scandalous hypocrisy of many traditional believers who mouth doctrinaire platitudes while remaining blind to their own ethical shortcomings, Hume prioritizes the question of the actual ethical betterment, the "inner transformation," as it were, of human beings. To be sure, it remains unclear what possible relation between religion and a humanistic approach to moral progress can really be discerned in Hume. It may be that once the wreckage of unfounded beliefs and superstitious practices is cleared away, a less impeded gravitation toward moral concerns might occur. Or, once this wreckage is cleared away, there may remain something left in religions that might serve to increase our propensity toward becoming better.

Such concerns are given a more fully articulated treatment in Kant, and as this occurs there is an enrichment of the question of the ethical or religious subject (which are essentially one and the same for him, as they are for Emmanuel Levinas in the twentieth century, see Levinas, 1961/1969, pp. 40 and 43). Kant anticipates psychoanalysis in a different way, insofar as he questions the self-evidence of the "objective observer" still assumed by Hume. While this is a massive topic in itself, here I will only make a few brief remarks that set the stage for discussing some of the psychoanalytic contributions to these issues. As we know, in the *Critique of Pure Reason*, Kant undertakes a "Copernican revolution" that directs philosophy to inquire into the faculties whereby the human subject is able to have organized knowledge of the world, and Kant therefore turns away from a naïve empiricist approach that assumes we can know things as they are in themselves. Kant accepts the Humean critique of all speculative attempts to gain knowledge of metaphysical or supersensible realities, and he simultaneously opens up a new problematic of complex, multi-layered subjectivity that is necessarily active in shaping experience of the world.

Although Kant can generally be classified as a rationalist or idealist, he takes issue with the traditional representatives of those schools of thought. So, for example, in the *Critique of Pure Reason*, Kant discusses what he terms the "**problematic** idealism of Descartes," which he describes as "doubtful and **indemonstrable**..." (Kant, 1997, p. 326). Here Kant dismisses the rationalist pretension to derive the existence of God from innate ideas. He accepts the empiricist premises of Hume, and draws the logical conclusion in arguing: "All our cognition starts from the senses, goes from there to the understanding, and ends with reason, beyond which there is nothing higher to be found in us to work on the matter of intuition and bring it under the highest unity of thinking" (p. 387). In other words, while the mind under the faculty of "understanding" necessarily organizes information received through the senses (intuitions), and can independently, through the faculty of reason, postulate ideas, it cannot have knowledge of presumed objects (such as religious and metaphysical ones) that provide no sensory intuitions. Indeed, there can be a pathological quality to metaphysical thinking, as Kant indicates when he states: "One can place all **illusion** in the taking of a **subjective** condition of thinking for the cognition of an **object**" (p. 439). In brief, Kant's work overturns both the rationalist *and* empiricist paths to metaphysical and theological certainty. Kant concludes that "reason accomplishes just as little on the one path (the empirical) as on the other (the transcendental), and that it spreads its wings in vain when seeking to rise above the world of sense through the mere might of speculation" (p. 563).

However, Kant differs significantly from Hume in turning explicitly to the *problem of morality* as an alternate path to metaphysics. Kant notes: "What speculative philosophy could not succeed at, bringing reason out of the field of sensibility to something real outside it, practical reason is able to do, namely, giving an existence that is not sensible (…) This is morality, if one admits it through freedom" (p. 537; Kant's note *a*). Kant's model of ethics differs profoundly from Hume's, in that for Kant ethics is founded on *a priori* moral laws given with our free rational subjectivity, and hence is not derived from experience. Kant summarizes it this way: "Now morality is the only lawfulness of actions which can be derived entirely *a priori* from principles. Hence the metaphysics of morals is really the pure morality, which is not grounded on any anthropology (no empirical condition)" (p. 696). In this way, even as he places rigid restrictions upon what we can *know* though "speculative reason," Kant formulates a revised transcendental subject who is also capable of producing rational norms, i.e., the moral laws of practical reason. Here, as many (including both Nietzsche and Freud) have noted, Kant strips away the pretensions of metaphysical knowledge only to re-instate them by the apparent slight-of hand of postulating a "pure practical reason" that offers a "moral proof" for the existence of freedom, God, and the immortality of the soul.

Two important occurrences accompany this turn to the *moral subject*. First, Kant affirms that it is the human capacity to act autonomously according to universal moral laws that is the essential concern of philosophy, and secondly, he affirms that religion is valuable only insofar as it takes the form of "moral religion." In this, however, Kant's work also poses a fundamental problem. In principle, as autonomous rational beings we should be capable of knowing, and acting according to, a universal moral law (the categorical imperative). In reality, however, even Kant ultimately admits that fallible human beings not only fail to abide by the moral law, but most often seem to have no sense of it at all, instead following a series of lesser, "hypothetical" imperatives based on self-love (see Part One of Kant, 1998). Importantly, when Kant turns to historical religions (or, what he terms "revelation"), his analyses are bitingly critical, and in fact elaborate extensively upon many of Hume's criticisms by adding a number of psychologically oriented critiques along the lines of illusion, delusion, and fetishism.

At the same time, Kant is one of the first theorists to view religious traditions, their writings, symbols, worldviews, doctrines, and so forth, as possible vehicles of human improvement without reference to literally understood metaphysical doctrines. Kant states that "we require an interpretation of the revelation [the historical religious tradition] we happen to have, i.e. a thoroughgoing understanding of it in a sense that harmonizes with the universal practical rules of a pure religion of reason" (Kant, 1998, p. 118, 1968, vol. 6, p. 110). For Kant, religious representations provide no *knowledge*, but rather give concrete symbolic expression to regulative principles (ideas) informing the practical (moral) use of reason. In *Religion*, these issues are condensed into the critical analysis of religious idolatry as inhibiting the cultivation of "moral religion," because the idolatrous fixation on literally understood doctrines inhibits the autonomous application of practical reason. It is in this context that Kant will refer to assumptions of having directly and literally represented the "thing itself," the moral law, in strikingly Freudian terms, as *fetish faith* (*Fetischglaube*) and *delusory faith* (*Wahnglaube*) (Kant, 1998, p. 185; 1968, vol. 6, pp. 193–194). In essence, if historical religions can be purged of their delusions, superstitions, and literalisms, they might serve as symbolic vehicles that assist in actualizing the moral potential already inherent in all persons. They must be subjected to rigorous critical interpretation in terms of the moral law, and then appropriated as culturally-formed guides for the moral subject's pedagogical itinerary. There is a circular element to this approach, in the sense that we find in historical religious symbols the *a priori* moral laws seemingly accessible through pure practical reason. Nevertheless, this circular approach is also potentially dialectical (but not in the systematized form of Hegel), insofar as it understands the need to turn to the universes of language, symbols, and traditions, as a means of furthering self-knowledge. The seemingly solipsistic rational-moral subject, whom Kant postulates on *a priori* grounds, nevertheless would seem to require a detour through cultural (and religious) productions. This detour intersects with a number of major issues, such as the interplay among reason, culture, and history. Most importantly, it calls into question the possibility of clinging to the *a priori*, transcendental subject as a self-contained reference point for ethical or religious subjectivity.

Psychoanalytic Interventions

For various reasons, Kant forms a major reference point for a wide range of contemporary theorists who seek to augment or modify classical rationalistic and disembodied models of human subjectivity. Kant is strategically located in the history of ideas, because he both refutes traditional arguments of metaphysics and rational theology, and opens new avenues to questions of ethical and religious subjectivity. He anticipates psychoanalysis in a certain sense, by inquiring into the constitutive factors whereby the subject is able to know, to will, and to make autonomous ethical choices. He also forms a foil for psychoanalytic and other contemporary inquiries into these issues, in so far as he resolves these questions by re-affirming a noumenal, *a priori*, transcendental subject of morality who is largely unaffected by history and culture.

One recent example of the twofold relation to Kant is found in Pamela Sue Anderson's *A Feminist Philosophy of Religion*. This is a work that incorporates a considerable amount of classical and contemporary psychoanalytic theory to address the limitations of classical philosophy of religion. Anderson's analysis seeks to demarcate the limits of rationalist approaches to religion by disclosing the exclusions built into the supposedly neutral male rational subject that sustains these theories and arguments. This analysis has direct implications for feminist thought, but also takes issue with culture-bound, Eurocentric views, and ultimately has relevance for anyone seeking to move from an abstracted model of subjectivity to one that incorporates the findings of psychoanalysis in both classical and contemporary forms. Anderson begins by questioning and critiquing the assumptions of much standard philosophy of religion right up to the late twentieth century, which posits "the supposed objectivity of the rational, individual, male-neutral subject of western philosophy and theology." Anderson also characterizes this assumed objective subject as "the objective view-from-nowhere, understood in the sense of the God's-eye view..." (Anderson, 1998, p. 36). Anderson's assessment of Kant provides a good sense of why he has continued to intrigue a wide variety of theorists. She notes that "already in the eighteenth century Kant demonstrates the instability of the embodied rational subject and so the instability of coherence. Kant also exposes the lack of correspondence between rationality and reality for any individual embodiment of reason, and, hence, the limitations of human reason alone." At the same time, Anderson pinpoints limitations to Kant's own responses to these problems. For example, following the above comment she also notes the way "Kant employs imagery to achieve the closure of unity of his own philosophical reasoning" (p. 11). Similarly, she later discusses the way in which "Kant's search for objectivity seems bound up with an abstract unitary subject..." (p. 85).

Anderson shows that Kant's contributions actually straddle the disembodied rationalist subject which, as I have shown re-appears in his moral subject, and a more contemporary sensibility that understands the potentially moral (or spiritual, or religious) subject as fallible and as located within specific biographical, historical, and cultural frameworks that can influence and affect both self-knowledge and actions in the world. One might say that thinkers sensitive to these issues seek to retain the latter insights of Kant's work, and retain as well the focus on human moral development as a key religious/spiritual issue, while discarding the remnants of rationalist metaphysics still impacting his thinking. Anderson herself turns to, among others, the psychoanalytic tradition that runs from Freud through Lacan to Kristeva (and which includes Ricoeur as a philosophical conversation partner), as a means both of rupturing the closure and exclusiveness of the male rationalist subject, and in order to formulate more pluralized, other-directed understandings of subjectivity (see Anderson, 1998, pp. 100ff.).

As Anderson notes, Freud anticipates many of the criticisms of traditional philosophy leveled by contemporary psychoanalytically-influenced theorists, and he often positioned his views in relation to general philosophical assumptions concerning the autonomous rational and/or moral subject. As I have illustrated in a previous publication, there are strategic points in Freud's work where Kant's moral subject, who seems to be taken as a paradigm for rationalist philosophers, is sharply differentiated from the psychoanalytic model of the personality (see DiCenso, 2007). For example, in *The Interpretation of Dreams*, the appearance of unconscious immoral desires in dreams is used to qualify Kant's autonomous moral subject (Freud, 1900/1953, p. 68). In this case, the psychoanalytic model is used to critique the one-dimensional subject of rationalism; however, a later criticism moves to developmental and inter-personal issues. In the *New Introductory Lectures on Psychoanalysis*, the chapter entitled "The Dissection of the Psychical Personality" addresses the formation of the super-ego, which Freud equates with "the origins of conscience." Freud mentions the "well-known pronouncement of Kant's which couples conscience within us with the starry heavens (...) as the masterpieces of creation."[1] Freud challenges the metaphysical assumptions behind Kant's proclamation in stating: "The stars are indeed magnificent, but as regards conscience God has done an uneven and careless piece of work, for a large majority of men have brought along with them only a modest amount of it or scarcely enough to be worth mentioning. We are far from overlooking the portion of psychological truth that is contained in the assertion that conscience is of divine origin; but the thesis needs interpretation. Even if conscience is something 'within us', yet it is not so from the first" (Freud, 1932/1964, p. 61). Freud interprets Kant's pronouncement about the *divine* origin of conscience to mean that the almighty father (or father-figure, or parents)[2] is the origin of, and model for the internalized moral agency of the super-ego. Similarly, in "The Economic Problem of Masochism," Freud concludes that "Kant's Categorical Imperative is thus the direct heir of the Oedipus complex" (Freud, 1924/1961, p. 167).[3] In these and other references, Freud's criticisms are directed against tendencies to disconnect a rational ethical subject from the multi-layered, diversified realms of embodied, social-historical existence. These include not only the drives and affects, but also the cultural, linguistic, and parental factors that constellate in both the ego and the super-ego. If Freud undermines the rationalist confidence in God-given conscience, he also awakens us to the need to understand the factors constitutive of conscience and ethical norms, if we are ever to ameliorate them.

The *Weltanschauung* essay of the *New Introductory Lectures* is another place where Freud develops his critical dialogue with philosophers. He attacks all attempts to address questions of the meaning and purpose of life in sweeping, inflexible terms. Here he also emphasizes that the most dangerous "enemy" of empirically-oriented reason is *religion*, which he describes as an "immense power which has the strongest emotions of human beings at its service." It is significant that Freud describes religion as having "constructed a *Weltanschauung*, consistent and self contained to an unparalleled degree, which, although it has been profoundly shaken, persists to this day." In the same vein, Freud makes broad reference to the grandiose claims of "philosophy," which clings "to the illusion of being able to present a picture of the universe which is without gaps and coherent," and which "goes astray by over-estimating the epistemological value of our logical operations..." (Freud, 1932/1964, pp. 160–161). Here philosophy and religion,

[1] Freud is paraphrasing Kant's comments from the conclusion to the *Critique of Practical Reason*. In Kant's words: "Two things fill the mind with ever new and increasing admiration and reverence the more often and more steadily one reflects on them: the starry heavens above me and the moral law within me" Kant, 1996, p. 269 (1968, 5:161).

[2] For an elaboration of the argument that Freud's oedipal model ranges from the father *per se* to an expanded notion of parents, parental figures, and other bearers of cultural norms, see DiCenso, 1999, pp. 23–29.

[3] The Oedipus complex is, of course, the central psychoanalytic trope for articulating the conflicts occasioning the formation of the super-ego.

despite their obvious differences, are each critiqued for their unwarranted extensions of human knowledge to form all-encompassing explanatory "world pictures" or cosmologies, whether based on reason or revelation.

Such comments confirm that Freud is consistent in his model of experimental reason, as applied to the human condition by psychoanalysis, and that he eschews the grandiose claims of both "religion" and "philosophy." Moreover, this critique is also compatible with Freud's model of ethics as requiring an analytical engagement with the full spectrum of faculties and drives constituting the human being, including the regressive, pathological, and irrational ones. In other words, Freud is not necessarily dismissing questions of meaning and ethical advancement, but is rather trying to reframe these in a non-metaphysical, or non-totalized, analytic framework.

Another important attendant issue arises here. Freud is profoundly aware that the "wounding" to the self-esteem of purportedly rational and autonomous beings that psychoanalysis undertakes engenders profound resistances and denials (as it does to this day). This point is encapsulated in Freud's famous account of the way in which "the universal narcissism of men, their self-love, has up to the present suffered three severe blows from the researches of science" (Freud, 1917/1955, p. 139). Here Freud briefly summarizes the displacement of the geocentric universe by Copernicus and Galileo, and the refuting of the human presumption of being essentially disconnected from the animal kingdom on the part of Darwin as the first two major "blows to narcissism." Freud then summarizes his own, preeminent blow to our narcissistic and grandiose illusions as follows: "these two discoveries – that the life of our sexual instincts cannot be wholly tamed, and that mental processes are in themselves unconscious and only reach the ego and come under its control through incomplete and untrustworthy perceptions – these two discoveries amount to a statement that *the ego is not master in its own house*" (Freud, 1917/1955, p. 143). Again, this qualification of the mastery of the ego has profound ethical as well as epistemological implications.

The objects of Freud's critical dissection are usually very clear, taking the form of idealistic models of subjectivity that ignore the complex inter-connections among the various psychical faculties. These idealized models are sustained by the same infantile forces that feed into the reassuring cosmologies of religions: human narcissism and wish fulfillment. These regressive orientations not only sustain worldviews that might be shown to be incorrect, but more seriously they sustain the uncritical smugness and ethical complacency abhorred by Hume. These pathological orientations are culturally informed, that is, sustained by inherited worldviews such as the religious ones, as much as they are the product of individual biography. It is in response to this problem, at once psychological and cultural, that Freud advocates such alternatives as "the psychological ideal, the primacy of the intelligence," and its correlate "education to reality" (Freud, 1927/1961, pp. 48–49). These more scientifically and empirically oriented goals, articulated in *Future of an Illusion*, are complemented by Freud's crucial emphasis on "the love of man and the decrease of suffering" (p. 53) as the progressive ideals of psychoanalysis. As I have emphasized, these and other such reflections show Freud to have wide-ranging concerns with bettering the human condition; his approach is at once psychological and cultural, and it combines self-knowledge with ethical development.

However, beyond these broad recommendations the constructive, progressively oriented model of the human subject offered by Freud is far less easy to discern. This is the case for a number of reasons: Freud's psychoanalytic model evolved throughout his work, even beyond the essential changes categorized under the two main topographies. Additionally, because Freud was quite consistent in rejecting grandiose metaphysical models, or *Weltanschauungen*, he perhaps drew back deliberately from the task of finalizing a psychoanalytic model of the subject. What we inherit from Freud is a dynamic and open-ended interplay of agencies, faculties, mechanisms, all subject to specific modification in relation to the biological, biographical, and cultural particulars of every human life. Indeed, if we are to remain faithful to Freud's insights, we must respect the prudence he exhibited in mapping the possibilities of a transformed modality of subjectivity. This is not to say that the multifarious post-Freudian attempts to clarify and articulate an overarching sense of subjectivity, including those stemming from Lacan, are not valuable, but merely that caution is in order in any effort at relinquishing the dynamic and necessarily unfinished qualities of the Freudian subject.

Contemporary Extrapolations

Having sounded a caveat, it should also be noted that there are various clues in Freud's work that contemporary theorists draw upon to formulate constructive models of subjectivity. Going back to Anderson for a moment, she cites a passage from the *Introductory Lectures*, contemporaneous with the essay "A Difficulty in the Path of Psychoanalysis," that also makes mention of the "three great blows" to human narcissism. In this version, Freud strikingly refers to "human megalomania" as having received its "most wounding blow" from psychoanalysis' displacement of the illusory mastery of the ego. Additionally, and importantly, Freud then offers a "call to introspection" as the necessary response to this blow (Freud, 1917/1963, p. 285; and see Anderson, 1998, pp. 103–104). This call to introspection implies a task of deeper self-understanding, and hence some progressive ethical modification of the personality, as potentially arising from the disavowal of false narcissistic megalomania. Hence, at least implicitly, the "deconstructive moment" undertaken by Freud in relation to classical rationalist and idealized models of the subject also gives rise to a deeper, more dynamic avenue of self-inquiry and self-knowledge.

Another resource in classical psychoanalysis that has repeatedly been mined by contemporary approaches to personality transformation is the indications of linguistic, symbolizing, and representational features in unconscious dynamics. These are also significant because they serve to counteract the seemingly mechanistic portrayals of the non-conscious and non-ego aspects of the subject. Examples of these features run throughout *The Interpretation of Dreams* (and are also constitutive of Freud's approach to symptoms). For example, in discussing the dream work, Freud introduces two important ideas: the links between significant latent thoughts and insignificant dream content connected by chains as in puns and riddles

(Freud, 1900/1953, p. 176), and the related notion of displacement along associated paths (p. 177). Another two key, related features of the dream work, are *condensation* (in which multiple meanings are compacted into a single image), and *over-determination* (in which multiple factors converge in the formation of the dream, pp. 283–284). Freud also emphasizes that in analysis these dense networks of meaning formed through over-determination call for a corresponding process of *over-interpretation* (pp. 279, 353, 523). In another instance, Freud notes that the artificial connections established through the dream work operate along the lines of "associations based on homonyms and verbal similarities . . ." (p. 596). My point in citing these passages is simply to show, as Lacan, Kristeva, Ricoeur, and others have elaborated in their different ways, that the Freudian model of unconscious dynamics is irreducible to a mechanistic or biological one. As Kristeva puts it, "language is not in the unconscious; the unconscious is not language; however, they do not exist independently of each other. (Those tempted to believe in the so-called biological purity of the Freudian unconscious, please take note)" (Kristeva, 1996/2000, p. 39). The quasi-linguistic aspects of the dream work show that problems of meaning and interpretation (*Deutung*) are from early in Freud's work co-present with other more scientifically and biologically oriented models and metaphors (see DiCenso, 2001, for further discussion of this theme).

Many post-Freudian theorists elaborate the way that the interior "otherness" of the personality, the non-ego and non-conscious aspects of the subject, becomes manifest within symbolic resources. In Ricoeur's work, this appears as the famous distinction between energetics and hermeneutics, which are not exclusive but rather complementary approaches to the phenomena of the unconscious. Speaking of Freud's approach to the dynamics of dream work and symptom formation, Ricoeur states: "this dynamics – or energetics, or even hydraulics – is articulated only in semantics: the 'vicissitudes of instincts' to use one of Freud's expressions, can be attained only in the vicissitudes of meaning" (Ricoeur, 1970, p. 6). This grasp of the inter-twining of force and meaning in the encompassing psycho-dynamics that exceed the control of the ego opens the door to a wider understanding of subjectivity.

Lacan places less emphasis on the coherence of meaning than does Ricoeur. Still, a parallel approach to unconscious dynamics appears in his stating that "desire always becomes manifest at the joint of speech, where it makes its appearance, its sudden emergence, its surge forwards. Desire emerges just as it becomes embodied in speech, it emerges with symbolism" (Lacan, 1978/1988, p. 234). This emergence of desire (which unlike the term 'energetics' already brings "instincts" or the drives into the domain of inter-personal relations and meaning) occurs in the form of the polysemy, over-determinations, and the production of new semantic avenues through re-combination and re-contextualization that appear in dreams, symptoms, and other phenomena not arising under the control of the ego. In this respect, Lacan emphasizes that it is not the ego alone, but also the unconscious aspects of personality, that are transformed by language acquisition. As he states: "the unconscious is constituted by the effects of speech on the subject, it is the dimension in which the subject is determined in the development of the effects of speech, consequently the unconscious is structured like a language" (Lacan, 1973/1977,

p. 149). This approach opens an inquiry into the modes of discourse associated with the unconscious, such as representation in images, displacement (related to metonymy), and condensation (related to metaphor). Finally, Kristeva has made a major contribution with her articulation of the distinction between the semiotic and the symbolic. Unlike the symbolic realm constituted by the linguistic forms of cultures, the semiotic is a modality of expressiveness more closely linked to the body, to affects, and psychical energies. The semiotic hence articulates a diversification in our understanding of meaning, and it forms the basis for an interpretive bridge between conscious and unconscious (see Kristeva, 1987/1989, pp. 21–23).

If we now think of subjectivity in terms of the question of how this is related to religion, the issue of the openness or closure of models creates a crossroads of sorts. We can try to "fill the gap" in Freud's thinking by invoking an overarching Self reminiscent of the transcendental models of Kant and Hegel, not to mention closed appropriations of religious models of a soul or higher self, as is most obvious in the case of Jung. By contrast, we can *follow through* on Freud's approach by articulating and thematizing the dimensions of meaningful subjectivity implicit in his work without occluding the critical insights of psychoanalysis. In other words, when studying Freud's writings on religion, ethics, and culture, it is comparatively easy to see how and why Freud seeks to discern pathological formations based on narcissism and wish-fulfillment in these shared *Weltanschauungen*. By contrast, our attempts to articulate Freud's own constructive contributions must always be held in relation to his justifiable skepticism concerning finalized models. Nevertheless, my argument is that there is a very complex relationship between psychoanalysis and philosophical approaches to religion and ethics, and that Freud repeatedly speaks to the work of philosophers such as Kant because, despite profound differences, there remain many shared concerns in the project of psychoanalysis. In seeking to decrease suffering and pathology in human beings, psychoanalysis also contributes to the "spiritual" tasks of modifying our mode of consciousness in order to enhance self-awareness and ethical capacity. Therefore, psychoanalysis, in confronting the abstracted "knowing subject" with the multiplicity of ways in which it is constituted in permeable inter-play with somatic, familial, and cultural factors, provides a key means of furthering the more complex task referred to by Foucault as "care of the self."

To further pursue this line of thought, I will mainly draw from Paul Ricoeur's incomparable attempt to bring psychoanalysis into dialogue with philosophy, which remains the high-water mark of philosophical engagements with psychoanalysis addressing themes of the *question of the subject* and the *question of religion*. Ricoeur's work is the most sustained and coherent attempt to address the potentially progressive aspects of subjectivity indicated by psychoanalysis. Rather than reject or patch over the disruptions to the rational-autonomous subject perpetrated by Freud, Ricoeur tries to push these forward to their logical conclusions in order to yield new constructive insights. Ricoeur's work shares concerns with language, symbols, and with the dynamics of subjectivity extending beyond the agency of the ego with other French post-Freudian theorists such as Lacan, Foucault, and Kristeva, among others, despite their profound and obvious differences (see Roudinesco, 1986/1990, pp. 390ff., for background details on the relationship of Ricoeur and Lacan in particular). Without eliding these differences, I want to draw on Ricoeur's work to synthesize a major theme appearing in attempts to think through the Freudian model in a way that remains faithful to Freud's eschewal of metaphysics and totalizing models, precisely by entering into the "narcissistic wound" Freud opens.

Ricoeur begins his philosophical engagement with psychoanalysis with his now-famous depiction of Marx, Nietzsche, and Freud as the three great modern architects of the "hermeneutics of suspicion." What is crucial here, according to Ricoeur, is that they each share "the decision to look upon the whole of consciousness primarily as 'false' consciousness." Ricoeur further emphasizes that this pervasive doubt has been carried "to the very heart of the Cartesian stronghold," (Ricoeur, 1970, p. 33) in such a way that, as we have seen, the supposedly objective rational subject can no longer be excluded from critical analysis. However, in referring to *false consciousness*, which he also calls the "false Cogito," Ricoeur implies that there is a *true consciousness*, or perhaps something like Foucault's and Lacan's "truth of the subject" accessible through Freud's critique of narcissism. Indeed, this is borne out very rapidly as Ricoeur outlines his view that "consciousness... is a task, but it is a task because it is not a given..." (Ricoeur, 1970, p. 44). Ricoeur's approach does not seek to salvage a traditional core subject behind or beyond the narcissistic illusions dispersed by psychoanalysis. Rather, in positing consciousness as a "task," he embraces Freud's undermining of traditional models and certainties *as the very means* whereby consciousness works toward being liberated from falsity. Here I should note that Lacan quite similarly argues that "the tension between the subject (...) and the ego (...) is the starting point for the dialectic of consciousness" (Lacan, 1978/1988, p. 177). For each thinker, the unconscious is understood not as a blind deterministic force, but as signifying, and as the basis for reflection and hence for a dialectical model of emerging consciousness. Note also how in each case Freud's concerns with the "megalomania" and narcissism of the ego, and his ensuing "call to introspection," are extended into a model that involves dislocating the fixities of the ego within a wider dynamic and reflective process.

Ricoeur is much less polemical than Lacan in confronting the question of the ego, but he also seeks a wider frame of reference for articulating meaningful subjectivity. He argues that "the agencies of the second topography are not so much places as roles in a personology. Ego, id, and superego are variations on the personal pronoun or grammatical subject; what is involved is the relation of the personal to the anonymous and the suprapersonal in the individual's coming-to-be." Having mapped an understanding of the person or subject beyond the hegemony of the ego, Ricoeur then asserts that "the question of the ego is not, indeed, the question of consciousness..." (Ricoeur, 1970, p. 181). Ricoeur employs multiple designations for this wider psychical framework of consciousness, and he is careful, unlike Lacan, to include the rational and reality-testing functions of the ego within this overarching subjectivity. At the same time, he consistently echoes Lacan in differentiating this subject from the ego, and in seeing narcissism as a barrier to wider self-awareness and self-consciousness. As Ricoeur states: "narcissism interposes itself between ourselves and reality; that is why the truth is always wounding to our narcissism"

(Ricoeur, 1970, p. 278). On the same page, Ricoeur links narcissism to the "false Cogito," and in so doing he explicitly brings the psychoanalytic critique of illusion into confrontation with philosophical rationalism, which unwittingly perpetuates a closed model of subjectivity. He further relates the overcoming of narcissism to the task of progressively altering consciousness in ways that enhance our capacity to respond to that which is "other," arising either from the unconscious or in relation to others in the world.

The inclusion of "reality-testing" as a necessary feature in overcoming false or narcissistic consciousness is crucial to the "dialectical" quality of Ricoeur's approach. The movement toward the truth of the subject is not solipsistic; it necessitates an engagement with others and otherness (including cultural and symbolic forms). This understanding of subjective development extending beyond a self-contained model is evident in Ricoeur's explication of the processes of sublimation. Ricoeur argues that "the concept of sublimation has two sides. On the one hand it concerns the set of procedures involved in the constitution of the sublime – i.e. the higher or highest – aspects of man; on the other hand it concerns the symbolic instrument of this constitution of the sublime" (Ricoeur, 1970, p. 488; also see p. 523).This is a point also made by Kristeva; that is, that the internal or psychical processes of sublimation require the mediation of cultural resources thorough human interactions. In Kristeva's words, "language, and nothing else, leads to exteriority" (Kristeva, 1996/2000, p. 57). Hence the dynamic of consciousness extends not only beyond the ego, but also necessarily straddles the realms of psychology proper, human interactions, and the cultural forms that enable and shape these interactions.

In developing the theme of the inter-connectedness of consciousness and other-directedness, Ricoeur argues that "reality-testing is correlative to the *Durcharbeiten*, the 'working through', the hard work aimed at true meaning, which has no equivalent except in the struggle for self-recognition that constitutes the tragedy of Oedipus, as Freud himself tells us" (Ricoeur, 1970, p. 371). Although I cannot develop the point here, this model of striving toward self-recognition not only through inter-personal relations, but through interpretive engagements with the symbolic and linguistic media of cultures and traditions, is a core theme running though Ricoeur's work. In another essay on psychoanalysis, Ricoeur speaks of "pursuing self-recognition through the restoration and extension of the symbolic process in the public sphere of communication." He adds: "in this sense, psychoanalysis pursues in its own way the project of recognition that Hegel placed at the summit of ethical life..." (Ricoeur, 1981, p. 265). Unlike Hegelian thought, however, Freud and Ricoeur share a sense that recognition involves loss and suffering that cannot be recuperated. There may be an advance in self-conscious reflection, but this is never complete, and cannot fully reconcile the conflicts of existence. Therefore, as Ricoeur also emphasizes, "the failure of all theodicies, of all systems concerning evil, witnesses to the failure of absolute knowledge in the Hegelian sense" (Ricoeur, 1970, p. 527). Again, Ricoeur is quite close to Freud in resisting the illusory consolations offered by grand metaphysical schemata that incorporate loss and suffering into a coherent explanatory system satisfying to the rational subject. Instead, the point of a psychoanalytic approach is not to explain away negativity, but to use it to advance the task of reflection and personal maturation. In this respect, Ricoeur does not hesitate to state that “humiliation is itself part of the history of self-consciousness” (Ricoeur, 1970, p. 427). Ricoeur also emphasizes that while psychoanalysis and the Hegelian dialectic of consciousness each involve a “discipline of reflection,” and “a decentering of the home of significations,” the displacement effected by Freud occurs “in the reverse direction...” (Ricoeur, 1970, p. 422). That is, psychoanalysis fosters an encounter with our “past” in the form of developmental vicissitudes, rather than interpreting each moment of existence in a Hegelian manner as graspable within a future-directed process of continual dialectical mediation. The way this “backward looking” movement might assist us in moving toward some unthematized condition of improved intra and extra psychical relations indicates the major theme of the relation between archeology and implicit teleology (Ricoeur, 1970, p. 447).

When Ricoeur argues that “in order to have an *archê* a subject must have a *telos*,” he is not re-instating a traditional Aristotelian ordered universe. His point is that in delving into the constituent elements of the personality, i.e., in undertaking an “archeology” of drive development, object relations, repression, and so forth, psychoanalysis *indirectly opens a broader vista of consciousness and understanding*. That is, consciousness is assisted in moving beyond its present condition of fixity and narcissistic denial, to a “somewhere else.” Reciprocally, Ricoeur emphasizes that “there is no teleology except through the figures of the mind, that is to say, through a new decentering, a new dispossession, which I call spirit or mind...” (Ricoeur, 1970, p. 459). Thus, archeology and teleology are dialectically interdependent. The ends and goals of subjective development, of spiritual truth, are not posited in advance, except perhaps along the broad lines of enhanced reflectiveness and other-directedness. It is only negatively, through the analytic process that “dispossesses the false Cogito,” that the broader subjective horizon Ricoeur calls “self-recognition” might emerge (and here again a parallel with Lacan’s *via negativa* of the dialectic of subjectivity is indicated). Although I cannot adequately develop the theme here, for Ricoeur this self-recognition is also the underpinning for the recognition of the other that is indispensable for ethics. This intertwining of the tasks of engaging the inner and outer “other” is also central to Kristeva’s work, where we find the point succinctly expressed: “Psychoanalysis is then experienced,” she states, “as a journey into the strangeness of the other and of oneself, toward an ethics of respect for the irreconcilable” (Kristeva, 1988/1991, p. 182). In my view, there is a shared concern among these theorists. The task of furthering “consciousness” cannot be reduced to a self-contained or solipsistic project of enhanced awareness in the sense of “perception consciousness.” This would bring it back within the orbit of narcissistic grandiosity. Rather, “consciousness” here means the capacity to reflect on one’s own assumptions and biases, and reciprocally to open oneself more readily to the perspectives, positions, and needs of others. Therefore, the dialectic of consciousness indicates an enhanced other-directedness, and hence an enhanced ethical capacity. It is in this sense that I see it as expanding upon the tradition of religious reflection concerned with improving the relations of human beings among themselves.

Conclusions

While psychoanalysis mounts critiques of the disembodied rationalism of the mainstream European philosophical tradition, it can also be shown to share a number of features with, and to be in dialogue with that tradition. To be sure, there are other areas of interplay between psychoanalysis and, for example modern social theory, or clinical and experimental psychology. However, psychoanalysis can also be grasped as a broadly based hermeneutics of the human condition that seeks to understand subjectivity in dynamic relation with interpersonal and cultural contexts. Thus, while contributing to larger humanistic questions of self formation, ethical development, and meaning, the psychoanalytic project can be reduced neither to social conditioning nor to experimental or physiologically based psychology. Indeed, Freudian and post-Freudian psychoanalysis has a crucial role to play in contemporary reflection insofar as it militates against *both* the abstracted and self-contained speculations of much philosophy and religious thought, *and* the dehumanized, technologized, and corporatized methodologies and models dominant in current social-scientific and natural-scientific approaches to humanity. It is in this way that I understand the interface among psychoanalysis, some strands of philosophy, and religious inquiry. The problem here is not to re-instate the certainties and consolations that accompany traditional religious worldviews, but rather to grasp the potential for human consciousness to become transformed in ways that allow broader, more inclusive, more ethically oriented horizons, as itself a religious or spiritual task.

References

Anderson, P. S. (1998). *A feminist philosophy of religion*. Oxford: Blackwell.

Descartes, R. (1637–1641/1960). *Discourse on method and Meditations* (trans. L. J. Lafleur). Indianapolis, IN: Bobbs-Merrill.

DiCenso, J. J. (1999). *The other Freud: Religion, culture and psychoanalysis*. London: Routledge.

DiCenso, J. J. (2001). Dreams, inner resistance, and self-reflection. In K. Bulkeley (Ed.), *Dreams: A reader on the religious, cultural, and psychological dimensions of dreaming* (pp. 285–294). New York: Palgrave.

DiCenso, J. J. (2007). Kant, Freud, and the ethical critique of religion. *International Journal for Philosophy of Religion, 61*(3), 161–179.

Foucault, M. (2001/2006). *The hermeneutics of the subject* (trans. G. Burchell). New York: Picador.

Freud, S. (1900/1953). *The interpretation of dreams*. In J. Strachey (Ed.), *The standard edition of the complete psychological works of Sigmund Freud, Vols. 4–5*. London: Hogarth.

Freud, S. (1917/1955). A difficulty in the path of psycho-analysis. In J. Strachey (Ed.), *The standard edition of the complete psychological works of Sigmund Freud, Vol. 17* (pp. 137–144). London: Hogarth.

Freud, S. (1917/1963). Introductory lectures on psychoanalysis. In J. Strachey (Ed.), *The standard edition of the complete psychological works of Sigmund Freud, Vol. 16* (pp. 5–182). London: Hogarth.

Freud, S. (1924/1961). The economic problem of masochism. In J. Strachey (Ed.), *The standard edition of the complete psychological works of Sigmund Freud, Vol. 19* (pp. 159–170). London: Hogarth.

Freud, S. (1927/1961). *The future of an illusion*. In J. Strachey (Ed.), *The standard edition of the complete psychological works of Sigmund Freud, Vol. 21* (pp. 5–56). London: Hogarth.
Freud, S. (1932/1964). New introductory lectures on psychoanalysis. In J. Strachey (Ed.), *The standard edition of the complete psychological works of Sigmund Freud, Vol. 22*. London: Hogarth.
Hume, D. (1779–1757/1993). *Dialogues and Natural history of religion*. Oxford: Oxford University Press.
Kant, I. (1968). *Werke*. Berlin: De Gruyter. (Akademie Textausgabe, 9 vols.)
Kant, I. (1996). *Practical philosophy* (trans. M. Gregor). Cambridge: Cambridge University Press.
Kant, I. (1997). *Critique of pure reason* (trans. P. Guyer & A.W. Wood). Cambridge: Cambridge University Press.
Kant, I. (1998). *Religion within the boundaries of mere reason* (trans. A. Wood & G. Di Giovanni). Cambridge: Cambridge University Press.
Kristeva, J. (1987/1989). *Black sun: Depression and melancholia* (trans. L. Roudiez). New York: Columbia University Press.
Kristeva, J. (1988/1991). *Strangers to ourselves* (trans. L. Roudiez). New York: Columbia University Press.
Kristeva, J. (1996/2000). *The sense and non-sense of revolt* (trans. J. Herman). New York: Columbia University Press.
Lacan, J. (1966/1977). *Écrits: A selection* (trans. A. Sheridan). London: Routledge.
Lacan, J. (1973/1977). *The four fundamental concepts of psycho-analysis* (trans. A. Sheridan). London: Penguin.
Lacan, J. (1975/1988). *The seminar of Jacques Lacan, Book I: Freud's papers on technique, 1953–1954* (trans. J. Forrester). Cambridge: Cambridge University Press.
Lacan, J. (1978/1988). *The seminar of Jacques Lacan, Book II: The ego in Freud's theory and in the technique of psychoanalysis, 1954–1955* (trans. S. Tomaselli). Cambridge: Cambridge University Press.
Levinas, E. (1961/1969). *Totality and infinity* (trans. A. Lingis). Pittsburgh, PA: Duquesne University Press.
Ricoeur, P. (1970). *Freud and philosophy: An essay on interpretation* (trans. D. Savage). New Haven, CT: Yale University Press.
Ricoeur, P. (1981). The question of proof in Freud's writings. In J. B. Thompson (Ed. & trans.), *Hermeneutics and the human sciences* (pp. 247–273). Cambridge: Cambridge University Press.
Roudinesco, E. (1986/1990). *Jacques Lacan & Co* (trans. J. Mehlman). Chicago, IL: University of Chicago Press.

Julia Kristeva and the Psychoanalytic Study of Religion

Re-reading "Mourning and Melancholia"*

Diane Jonte-Pace

In his seminal essay "Mourning and Melancholia," Sigmund Freud distinguished between a healthy response to the loss of a loved one, which he characterized as mourning, and a pathological form that he termed melancholia. In this essay, I suggest that the French feminist and psychoanalyst, Julia Kristeva, especially in her works *Black Sun* and *New Maladies of the Soul*, has rewritten Freud's famous essay, especially in regard to the role of religion. I argue that Kristeva's earlier work examines religion in terms of mourning, while her later work interprets religion in relation to melancholia. Where her analysis of mourning shows how traditional theologies structure and symbolize death and loss, her treatment of melancholia shows that cultures and individuals experience melancholia when religion cannot provide the framing narratives for loss. By breaking out of a Freudian binary that associates mourning with health and melancholia with pathology, Kristeva uncovers adaptive, as well as dysfunctional, forms of melancholia. She hints that a constructive and creative path through postmodern, post-religious melancholia can be found, not through religious belief or the experience of the sacred, but rather through the study and interpretation of biblical and religious texts. I begin this essay with a brief introduction to Kristeva's life, career, theory, and approach to religion, before turning to her creative rethinking of Freud's work on mourning.

---

* This paper incorporates material from two earlier essays: "Melancholia and Religion in French Feminist Theory," in W. Parsons, J. Jonte-Pace, and S. Henking (Eds.), *Mourning Religion*, Virginia Press, 2008, and "Julia Kristeva and the Psychoanalytic Study of Religion: Rethinking Freud's Cultural Texts," in J. Jacobs and D. Capps (Eds.), *Religion, Society, and Psychoanalysis: Readings in Contemporary Theory*, Westview Press, 1997. This material is reprinted here with the permission of both University of Virginia Press and Westview Press.

D. Jonte-Pace
Santa Clara University, Santa Clara, CA, USA
e-mail: djontepace@sev.edu

J.A. Belzen (ed.), *Changing the Scientific Study of Religion: Beyond Freud?*

Life, Career, and Theory

Born in Bulgaria in 1941, 3 years before the Soviet takeover in September 1944, Kristeva was raised in a family attentive to music, literature, art, and religion. Because they were not Communist Party members, her family was denied access to the educational system of the privileged "red bourgeoisie." However, she obtained a "double education" (Clark and Hulley, 1990, p. 172) in Bulgaria by attending both the obligatory state schools where she was inculcated with "Marxist orthodoxy" and French schools where, receiving a "francophile and francophone education," she was trained as "an intellectual in the French sense of the word" (Kristeva, 1984, p. 265).

As a graduate student in languages, literature, and linguistics in a Bulgarian literary institute, Kristeva had begun a thesis on the modernist novel when she was offered a doctoral fellowship sponsored by De Gaulle's government in the mid-1960s. She accepted the fellowship, arriving in Paris in the Christmas season of 1965. Enrolling at L'École Practique des Hautes Études in 1966, she began a course of study in linguistics, working with semiotician Roland Barthes, linguist Emile Benveniste, and anthropologist Claude Lévi-Strauss.

She quickly became part of an avant garde intellectual and political community associated with the journal, *Tel Quel*. In addition to Roland Barthes, the *Tel Quel* group included philosopher and deconstructionist Jacques Derrida, historian of ideas Michel Foucault, literary theorist Tzvetan Todorov (also from Bulgaria), and the writer Philippe Sollers whom she later married. These were intellectual iconoclasts whose work centered on language and writing understood as subversive practice – production rather than as representation (McCance, 1988, p. 18). They emphasized a revolutionary "*écriture limite*" as the focus around which "a new theoretical discourse on language as subjective experience was constituted" (Kristeva, 1984, p. 268). Their radical critiques of structuralism and humanism were crucial in initiating the "post-structuralist explosion" in France. Activists as well, they engaged in intense public debate over nationalism, communism, feminism, and the possibilities of revolutionary social change, becoming deeply involved in the Paris demonstrations of May 1968. Thus Kristeva became a central player not only in the arena of radical political activism but also in the avant garde literary and academic communities of Paris at a time of intense social and intellectual ferment.

Even in the early phase of her career in linguistics, psychoanalysis was prominent in Kristeva's work. Her interest in revolutionary forms of speaking and writing led her to seek a theoretical perspective which could attend to subversions of linguistic and social hegemony. Her 1969 publication *Séméiotiké*, for example, offered a method of "semanalysis" involving both psychoanalysis and "semiotics," the theory of the meanings of signs. "The psychoanalytic experience," she later stated, "struck me as the only one in which the wildness of the speaking being, and of language, could be heard" (Kristeva, 1984, p. 275). Kristeva's doctoral thesis in semiotics, *La Révolution du Langage Poétique*, defended in 1973, presented a psychoanalytic theory of the subject through an analysis of poetic texts. She argued that poetic language in the work of Mallarmé and Lautréamont opens to an "Other" which is the corporeal or material body. The publication of the thesis in 1974 led to Kristeva's appointment as professor of linguistics in the Department of Texts and Documents at the University of Paris VII. Kristeva also holds a position as a regular visiting professor at Columbia University in New York in Comparative Literature.

Throughout the early seventies Kristeva was engaged in frequent dialogue with psychoanalytic thinkers and writers, in particular with the French psychoanalyst Jacques Lacan, attending Lacan's famous seminars until 1974. Lacan soon became a friend and an intellectual sparring partner. In an autobiographical essay, "My Memory's Hyperbole," Kristeva acknowledged the significance of Lacan's views during these years for her own work and for the work of others in the *Tel Quel* community: "it was Lacan's insolence in daring to introduce the 'great Other' into the very heart of the speaking structure that propelled us on this course. We were attempting, in our own fashion, to circumscribe the unavoidable necessity of this Other and to analyze its crises, which determine the transformations, the life, and the history of discourses" (1984, p. 270). Thus in the early and mid-seventies, psychoanalysis became more and more central in Kristeva's thinking. She states that "Little by little my semiolotic [sic] mode of thinking (...) expanded to include a truly psychoanalytic approach" (1984, p. 267).

The mid-1970s marked a turning point in Kristeva's life and career, bringing her even more closely into the heart of psychoanalytic theory and practice. After a trip to China in 1974 in the company of Sollers, Barthes, and others (Lacan had hoped to join the group but was unable to do so), Kristeva reevaluated her prior commitment to collective political activism, continuing to affirm her commitment to a politicized analysis of intellectual activity while abandoning an activist stance toward revolutionary social change. In 1976 she gave birth to a child. During this period, like some other French feminists, she began to address the problems of femininity and motherhood. She was trained as a psychoanalyst between 1976 and 1979, not in the school of Jacques Lacan, but rather in the Psychoanalytique de France, an association founded in 1964 when its members split from the Lacanian school (Doane and Hodges, 1992, p. 87). Emphasizing the work of Melanie Klein and D.W. Winnicott, the school was attentive to the interrelationships between self and "object" (or "other"). Since the late seventies, Kristeva's publications became increasingly psychoanalytic, focusing more and more on the psychological understanding of the self and the psychological origins and effects of religious ideas and practices. A prolific writer, she publishes fiction, literary criticism, cultural analysis, art history, epistolary volumes, autobiographical essays, and other genres (Kristeva, 1987b). Psychoanalysis remains a frequent touchstone in her writings. Indeed, I believe that her work constitutes a careful reworking of Freud's major theories.

Kristeva's background in linguistics provides an important foundation for her psychoanalytic theory of the self: She incorporates semiotics and psychoanalysis, emphasizing language or speech as a crucial component of subjectivity. She refers to the self or subject as the "speaking subject" or the "speaking being." But this "speaking being" is never entirely encompassed by language. Affects, drives, and kinesthetic awareness of the physical body, for example, are trans-linguistic or pre-linguistic experiences continuously interruptive of the linguistic order.

Nor is the speaking being a unified being. Because of the tension between language and the non-linguistic realms of affect and sensation at the heart of the speaking being, Kristeva refers to the subject as the "*sujet en process*." The double meaning of the French term *en proces*, meaning "in process" or "on trial," is significant. In Kristeva's view, all formulations or expressions of the self are tentative for, first, we are constantly changing, and second, we are constantly judged, evaluated, and tested before the structures of language and society which comprise "the Law." Thus, our subjectivity, "in process" and "on trial," is never unified or monolithic. Kristeva explains: "As speaking beings, always potentially on the verge of speech, we have always been divided, separated from nature (...) We are no doubt permanent subjects of a language that holds us in its power. But we are subjects in process, ceaselessly losing our identity, destabilized by fluctuations in our relation to the other, to whom we nevertheless remain bound by a kind of homeostasis" (1987a, pp. 8–9).

Kristeva describes this destabilization inherent in the "subject in process" in terms of two "orders": the symbolic and the semiotic. The "symbolic order," a term Kristeva borrows from Jacques Lacan, is the space of language, culture, morality, and society. The symbolic describes a social system that requires renunciation of desires and acceptance of cultural and linguistic meanings. In Kristeva's view, the symbolic is constantly disrupted by "the semiotic," "a psychic modality logically and chronologically prior to the sign, to meaning and to the subject" (1987a, p. 5). The semiotic can take many forms. It emerges in art, music, religion and literature, in rhythm, color, ritual, and poetic language. It emerges in emotion, pain, and pleasure. And it appears in dreams, symptoms, and psychosis. The pre-linquistic or trans-linguistic processes of the semiotic – pre-oedipal and pre-linguistic in origin – are initially structured and directed in relation to the mother's body. They are "archaic traces of the links between our erogenous zones and those of the other, stored as sonorous, visual, tactile, olfactory, or rhythmic traces" (p. 9). Kristeva's ongoing project, evident in her work over three decades, has been to trace the effects of the semiotic upon the symbolic order – the strange or alien upon the familiar – within culture, history, and the individual psyche.

For Kristeva (and Lacan) the symbolic order expresses "*le nom du père*," the name of the father. The aural ambiguity of the French word *nom* is significant here. *Le nom* ("the name") is aurally indistinguishable from *le non* ("the no"). The symbolic order is thus a patriarchal social order articulating the name of the father, the law of the father, and the forbidding "no" of the father. The semiotic, on the other hand, represents a challenge to the patriarchal symbolic order. The semiotic interrupts and displaces the order of language based on paternal authority by means of ruptures in syntax, rhythm, and semantic coherence.

Does Kristeva idealize the semiotic? Some of her writings portray the semiotic as an enlivening, enriching, transformative, revolutionary realm, somewhat reminiscent of Winnicott's "transitional space" (1971), within which language can open itself to the playful, poetic, or creative. Kristeva's work on the semiotic in the context of avant garde literature and art, her analysis of the semiotic in religious faith and mystical experience, and her location of the origins of the semiotic in a space "metaphorically suggesting something nourishing and maternal" (1987a, p. 5) exemplify this sense of the semiotic as a benign maternal territory. However, she also has a clear sense of the other side of the semiotic, such as its expression in psychopathology, fascism, misogyny, and in the "horror" expressed in religious rituals which, through sacrifice, separate the sacred from the profane (1982). The semiotic is important as well in her understanding of mourning and melancholia in relation to religion.

What is Kristeva's view of religion? Kristeva is neither a critic nor a defender of religion but rather an interpreter of its effects, especially its absence in culture and psyche. Her own words provide an indication of the complexity of her experience and evaluation of religion. "I am not a believer," she asserts in *In the Beginning was Love*. "I recall having been born into a family of believers who tried without excessive enthusiasm perhaps, to transmit their faith to me." In adolescence, she recounts "I knelt before the icon of the Virgin that sat enthroned above my bed and attempted (unsuccessfully) to gain access to a faith that my secular education did not so much combat as treat ironically or simply ignore" (1987a, pp. 23–24). If Kristeva's secular Bulgarian education ignored religion, the larger political structures in Bulgaria nearly negated it. Religion was suppressed throughout Eastern Europe, functioning underground as a realm of possible freedom from totalitarian authority. Kristeva notes that "the experience in Bulgaria permitted me at once to live in an extremely closed environment (...) to understand the weight of social life, and at the same time, to try to find the small spaces of freedom, which include, for example, the arts, the interest in foreign languages, even religion" (in Clark and Hulley, 1990, p. 172; see also Edelstein, 1992, p. 47).

Some of her critics attack Kristeva for what they see as an excessively sympathetic or "sentimental" stance toward Christianity (Doane and Hodges, 1992, p. 73). Feminist deconstructionist Gayatri Spivak challenges Kristeva as an "apologist for Christianity" (1988, p. 264) and literary theorist Ann Rosalind Jones critiques Kristeva's interest in religion and romantic love on the grounds that neither have "been alternatives to women's subordination; they have been the ideologies through which that subordination was lived" (1984, p. 70). In my view, however, Kristeva takes neither the stance of believer and defender nor that of secular critic and attacker. Rather, she assumes an analytic or hermeneutic perspective, showing how religion functions as a "polylogic" or multivocal discourse in psyche and culture. She demonstrates that, in certain contexts like the Bulgaria of her youth, religion offers a space of possible freedom, while admitting that in other contexts religion expresses a hegemonic structure of patriarchal monotheism which "represses women and mothers" (1986a, p. 18) or a horror of the "abject" originating in a primal abhorrence of the mother (1982). Moreover, she explores the absence of religion and its effects on psyche and culture: the liberatory or adaptive dimensions of religion, its repressive or oppressive elements, and the effects of its loss. Her approach is neither apologetic nor critical – it is analytic.

I have argued previously that Kristeva's oeuvre can be seen as a systematic re-writing of Freud's major works on religion: *Powers of Horror* reworks *Totem and Taboo* by seeking the origins of culture in matricide and the abject instead of patricide and incest; *In the Beginning was Love* represents a revision of *The Future of an Illusion* by reinterpreting illusion as a "glorious" fiction that nevertheless "gives an accurate representation of the reality of its subjects' desires" (Kristeva, 1987a, p. 11); and *Strangers to Ourselves* echoes *Civilization and its Discontents,* asking how it is possible to live in culture and community given the inevitability of xenophobia and aggression. I have also found evidence that Kristeva's analysis of the sources of anti-Semitism in abjection in *Powers of Horror* explicitly echo Freud's speculations on the same topic in *Moses and Monotheism* (Jonte-Pace, 1997, 2001). In each case I showed that Kristeva integrates contemporary perspectives into her reading of Freud on religion. Interweaving Freudian, Lacanian, object-relational, and post-structuralist perspectives, she incorporates a focus on gender, maternity, the problems of women in patriarchal society, and the enigma of the subject as "speaking being"(Jonte-Pace, 1997, p. 248). She constructs an approach that makes a significant contribution to the psychoanalytic theory of the origins and effects of religious practice and discourse in human culture. Her integrative approach has had a significant scholarly impact well beyond the psychoanalytic community. Her work is widely read in feminist studies and religious studies, post-structuralist theory and critical theory, and in psychoanalytic circles.

In this essay I suggest that Kristeva's *Black Sun* and *New Maladies of the Soul* represent an explicit application of "Mourning and Melancholia" to religion. Kristeva draws a connection between Freud's work and her own, taking Freud's text as her point of departure in *Black Sun.* She states, "I shall examine matters from a Freudian point of view (...) bring[ing] out from the core of the melancholy/depressive composite (...) a common experience of object loss and of a modification of signifying bonds" (Kristeva, 1989, p. 10). And she contrasts Freud's complex explanation of mourning and melancholia in 1917 with words he had written just a year earlier "to the psychologist, mourning is a great riddle" (Kristeva, 1989, p. 98). Her re-reading of "Mourning and Melancholia" represents an exploration of that "great riddle." She inquires into the intersections of loss, grief, and religion, in part, by charting terrain that Freud did not fully explore: the relation of the maternal to loss and death.

As noted above, Kristeva is part of a group of scholars known as French feminists whose work has become increasingly significant for the psychoanalytic study of religion in recent decades (Crownfield, 1992; Joy et al., 2002a, b; Kim et al., 1993; Reineke, 1997). Although "French feminism" is a contested term, the following description is widely accepted: The French feminists include a group of theorists working in France and focusing on gender, most of whom are indebted to (but critical of) the psychoanalytic work of Jacques Lacan, and most of whom have been affiliated with the *Psych et Po* (*Psychanalyse et Politique*) movement that emerged in Paris in the aftermath of the social and political protests of 1968 (Joy et al., 2002a, pp. 1–7). In addition to Julia Kristeva the group includes Luce Irigaray, Hélène Cixous, Catherine Clément, Monique Witting, and others. While there are common themes and concerns in the work of these theorists, there is also great diversity in their approaches. They do not constitute an ongoing "movement" per se. Yet collectively they have constructed a "vocabulary and direction for a detailed and complex analysis of religious institutions" (Joy et al., 2003a, p. 9).

Let us briefly survey the view of mourning and melancholia in the writings of some of Kristeva's psychoanalytic conversation partners, namely Freud, Cixous, and Clément. Freud's essay of 1917 differentiated two approaches to loss. Mourning, he argued, proceeded through several steps: a period of conscious experience of loss, a period of deep grief, and a phase of recovery. Mourning, in other words, was a successful encounter with loss. Melancholia, on the other hand, he described as a more problematic response, involving unconscious conflicts and, frequently, an entrapment in grieving or an inability to mourn.

Memory is important in Freud's understanding of how mourning and melancholia work. Supported by cultural rituals and structures, memory assists in the "working through" of loss and grief. The process is "carried out bit by bit" as the lost object is remembered and the affect associated with it is transformed: the "memories and expectations by which the libido is bound to the object" are recalled, "hypercathected," and gradually "detached" (Freud, 1914/1958). When the work of memory and mourning is complete, "the ego becomes free and uninhibited again" (Freud, 1917/1957, p. 245). In melancholia, however, the process of remembering and working through is disrupted. The ego cannot achieve the desired freedom but is imprisoned in (or by) trauma. We cannot remember, or we cannot stop remembering (c.f. Homans and Jonte-Pace, 2006, p. 8).

Freud specified that mourning and melancholia emerged not only "in reaction to the loss of a loved person" but also in reaction to the "loss of some abstraction ... such as one's country, liberty, an ideal" (Freud, 1917/1957, p. 243). And he suggested that grief could have a collective expression as well. Whole cultures could experience a sense of loss; whole cultures could grieve, mourn, or experience melancholia. Thus, according to Freud, mourning and melancholia are both psychological and cultural, individual and collective. And, as Freud hinted and others have pointed out more explicitly, these cultural "abstractions" or "symbolic losses" often include religion (Homans, 2001; Jonte-Pace, 2001; Mitscherlich and Mitscherlich, 1975; Santer, 1990). Peter Homans (2001), for example, has argued that Freud experienced a powerful sense of the loss of religious community and common culture, and that the successful mourning of that "symbolic loss" led him to introspective insights into his own mental processes. Those insights in turn, Homans argues, led to the ideas that constitute psychoanalysis.

Helen Cixous and Catherine Clément (1986) have drawn upon Freud's understanding of mourning and melancholia to ask important questions about religion, gender and culture in the modern world. In their view, depression (closely related to melancholia) is a widespread experience in the modern industrialized West due to the ubiquity of alienation, injustice, and suffering. In contrast to hysteria, the dominant symptom of the nineteenth century, depression, "our own contemporary symptom," is a product of "social mobility, technological advances, women's emancipation, and the breakdown of the sacred" (Clément and Kristeva, 2001, p. 172). Mourning is necessary for curing melancholia or depression. For both theorists, religion, in the form of mysticism, initiation, trance, ecstasy, or "writing" (which for Cixous, is a form of mysticism) is what makes mourning possible, leading to a cure. These mystical or sacred experiences "allow for a renegotiation with both loss and destructive traces, and a return to life" (Joy et al., 2003a, p. xxiv; Hollywood, 2003). Ideally depression "precedes a rebirth" and can be compared to "an initiation": it has positive possibilities, including an entrée to the sacred as well as transformative, life-enhancing experiences. It is "the only rite of initiation remaining for industrialized countries" (Clément, in Clément and Kristeva, 2001, p. 147). But mourning, according to Clément and Cixous, is difficult today precisely because of the paucity of rituals through which depression can be resolved. Under these conditions depression often lingers and becomes deeply melancholic. In Clément's words, "the void of the sacred becomes lost in a chasm and rebirth does not come about" (Clément, in Clément and Kristeva, 2001, p. 147).

Amy Hollywood, a Religious Studies scholar and interpreter of the French feminists, discusses Clément's and Cixous's interest in mourning and mysticism. For both, she suggests, the work of mourning is related to the work of encountering death; for both, mourning is "perhaps inevitably religious." According to Clément, mysticism is "a way of encountering and working through death that enables a return to life." Similarly, for Cixous, a "mystical mode of writing (is) a way to apprehend and resolve loss, particularly that brought about by the death of the other" (Hollywood, 2003, p.148). Cixous speaks of the "(w)rites of mourning." She points to the "necessity of catharsis particularly for women who need to mourn both religious and political losses" (Joy et al., 2003a, p. xxiv). Both insist, as Hollywood points out, that mourning is a "particularly crucial task for women at this point in human history… still so often burdened with the work of mourning and so often the victims of the greatest material and spiritual losses" (Hollywood, 2003, p. 156).

Julia Kristeva's writing on religion, mourning, and melancholia shares a great deal with the writings of Freud, Cixous and Clément (Cixous and Clément, 1986). She has published a collaborative epistolary volume with Clément on the feminine and the sacred (Clément and Kristeva, 2001). And her understanding of the almost transcendent significance of writing echoes Cixous' in many ways. However, her analysis differs in a number of ways from theirs. She is not convinced that mysticism or "the sacred" is inevitably a healing force for depression: mysticism is instead a type of depression or melancholia in Kristeva's reading. She seems to suggest, as I'll show below, that the study of religion, rather than the experience of religion, can serve as a "counterdepressant." She devotes more attention than they to the way that traditional religious symbols can contribute to constructive mourning. Nevertheless, her work extends their psychoanalytic readings – and Freud's – into deeper explorations of both mourning and melancholia in relation to religion. Most significantly, she challenges the assumption shared by Cixous, Clément, and Freud, that melancholia is inevitably pathological. She finds ways that it can be liberating and creative.

Speculating on health and pathology, diagnoses, and therapeutics, Kristeva attends to the role of religion in the origins of mourning and in the study of religion as a constructive way of addressing melancholia in modernity. She suggests that traditional Christianity offered an effective and powerful discourse of mourning and loss. She explores ways that we are all melancholic today, ways that religious symbols, practices, and ideas fail to provide support for the melancholia we experience. She focuses particular attention on the response to the changes or losses associated with religion that accompany modernity. Kristeva's central diagnostic and therapeutic questions focus not only on whether we mourn or are melancholy, but, acknowledging the impossibility of a completed sense of mourning within the context of modernity, whether we can be creatively melancholic or are fated to be defensively unable to mourn. These are our choices, from a Kristevan perspective.

Mourning

Christianity, Kristeva argues, "supplies images for even the fissures in our secret and fundamental logic" (Kristeva, 1987a, p. 42). It is the genius of the Christian construct that it "facilitates perfectly the structural requirements of signification"(McCance, 2003, p. 139). In Kristeva's reading, the crucifixion, the center of Christian theology, doctrine, and liturgy, functions in two ways for believers, and, indeed, for all who are touched by the discourses of the Christian tradition. First, the crucifixion contains a set of symbols that help us negotiate loss and death. Second, the crucifixion articulates the experience of loss and division associated with the origin of the speaking self, the necessary sacrifice marking the developmental shift from preverbal immersion in the maternally linked semiotic (the imaginary) to the realm of the father associated with the entry into subjectivity and language (the symbolic). The crucifixion retraces the birth of the "subject in process" in the separation from the archaic maternal realm.

What does she mean by this? One of Kristeva's interpreters explains: "Christianity has, through facilitating an imaginary identification with the death of Christ, provided a means of bringing death into the symbolic [i.e., into language] or at least it has provided a way for enlarging the imaginary and symbolic means available for coping with death" (Lechte, 1990, pp. 36–37). Christianity embodies the deep sense of division we experience as we are torn from a pre-linguistic state, close to the mother, as we enter the paternal territory of language – in Lacan's terminology, the *nom* or *non du père*. It traces the "essential alienation that conditions our access to language in the mourning that accompanies the dawn of psychic life, the death that marks our psychic inception" (Kristeva, 1987a, p. 41). Christianity thus shapes the psyche, providing structures, symbols, and words for the encounter with loss. It shows us how to mourn by retracing the primary mourning of the mother at the birth of the speaking self. Christ's death and resurrection function as a paradigm for the experience of maternally inflected loss-grief-recovery that constitutes mourning. Kristeva's concern about modernity and melancholia begins with this paradigm and its fragility or absence in the contemporary world.

Melancholia

"Never before in the history of humanity," Kristeva states, "has this exploration of the limits of meaning taken place in such an unprotected manner, and by this I mean without religious, mystical or any other justification" (Kristeva, cited in McCance, 2003, pp. 135–136). The "unprotected" quality of psychic life in modernity is a central concern of Kristeva's. She is particularly interested in the loss of the viability of religious images and symbols and the ubiquity of melancholia in the post industrial west. Her focus is on death, atheism, and the symbol of the Virgin Mother. In her interpretations of the contemporary era she explores how we engage in a discourse of death without a discourse of resurrection. In her analysis of the psychodynamics of atheism, she examines the religious art of the early modern period, tracing the beginnings of the loss of a sense of transcendence, a sense of death without renewal or resurrection, of loss without hope, and of the absence of God. In addition, she directs her attention to the dramatic effects, on women's lives especially, of the loss of the symbol of the virgin mother, a symbolic structure that intricately intertwines sex with death.

In *Black Sun*, Kristeva develops an account of melancholia as post-religious depressive despair. Speaking in the first person, she describes an experience of an "abyss of sorrow," of "not knowing how to lose," of being "unable to find a valid compensation for loss." She concludes that the depressed or melancholic person is often a "radical and sullen atheist" whose atheism is symbolic and semiotic as well as theological: close to a sense of "asymbolia" wherein all meanings are lost (Kristeva, 1989, pp. 3–5). Kristeva's work has commented on the psychology of atheism in a number of texts, always with a critical view. As McCance explains, "for Kristeva, this asymbolic atheist is not just someone who has been stripped of all religious conviction." Rather, it is a kind of "semiotic atheism, a condition where all faith and values are undone, all signs are emptied of their significance, when the promise for meaning of any kind has been revoked" (McCance, 2003, p. 139).

For Kristeva, atheism is a dangerous form of repression. In her small volume on psychoanalysis and religion, *In the Beginning was Love*, she proposes an alternative to atheism: a nondefensive affirmation of religious illusion accompanied by a non-repressive renunciation of faith: "what today's analyst must do, I think, is restore to illusion its full therapeutic and epistemological value. Does this mean restoring value to religion as well? Not altogether… Repression can be atheist; atheism is repressive whereas the experience of psychoanalysis can lead to renunciation of faith with clear understanding" (Kristeva, 1987a, pp. 21–27). Her "renunciation of faith with clear understanding" is less repressive than the strident atheism one finds in some secularist discourse (or in some of Freud's texts) and far less melancholic than the absolute atheism/asymbolia she describes in *Black Sun*. This renunciation of faith is part of the Kristevan path through melancholia that I'll describe shortly.

In an effort to uncover what anticipates today's melancholic atheism and the contemporary absence of a vocabulary for death, Kristeva looks at Hans Holbein's 1522 painting of "The Body of the Dead Christ in the Tomb." Holbein's painting provides an entree into an historical moment of transition to modernity. Painted "on the threshold of the modern, as metaphor of the collapse of the Christian story" (1989, p. 110), the work emerges at a dramatic critical moment of modernity when the transcendent properties of the Christian narrative are threatened. Kristeva describes the painting, emphasizing Holbein's minimalism: the "empty stare (...) the dull blue-green complexion, are those of a man who is truly dead, of Christ forsaken by the Father ('My God, my God, why have you deserted me?') and without the promise of Resurrection" (1989, p. 110). Holbein's bleak Christ, like the Protestant iconoclasm contemporary with it, "with its extreme simplicity of signs" (Lechte, 1990, p. 36) is almost devoid of all affect. Christ is portrayed as dead and alone, with an expression of a hopeless grief. The painting is a vivid representation of melancholia: isolated, affectless, lacking any hint of passion or idealization. There is "no coded rhetoric... to alleviate the anguish induced by the intimation of death. [It is a] representation of the complete absence of affect in signs which characterizes the melancholic's position" (Lechte, 1990, pp. 36–37). This powerful and painful embodiment of melancholia portrays, in Kristeva's words, "a melancholy moment (an actual or imaginary loss of meaning [...] or despair, an actual or imaginary razing of symbolic values including the value of life)." Holbein, she concludes, leads us "to the ultimate edge of belief, to the threshold of nonmeaning" (1989, p. 135).

Theologian Grace Jantzen articulates clearly the question that Kristeva is asking in her work on Holbein: "If we are irretrievably post Christian how shall we as individuals or society, do the death-work that does not go away with the demise of Christendom?" (Jantzen, 2003, p. 123). Kristeva herself does not always insist that we are "irretrievably post Christian": indeed, she finds traces of belief even in the most secular psyche, arguing that "believers (...) amount to almost everyone, in spite of what we might think" (1987a, p. 26). Nevertheless, Jantzen's framing of Kristeva's question is indeed central for our era – and it is related to the question of the mother, for in the Christian narrative and the western unconscious, birth and death, mother and child, the virgin mother and the Christ, are inseparable.

One of Kristeva's most frequently quoted texts, "Stabat Mater," poses a number of significant questions about the fantasy that for centuries upheld the symbolic economy of the West and its underlying grand narrative, the notion of a virgin mother who gives birth to (and mourns the death of) a special son. She articulates "a few questions (...) concerning a motherhood that today remains, after the virgin, without a discourse" (Kristeva, 1986b). What does it mean to lack a discourse of motherhood, to be living "after the virgin"? The concept is rich, complex, and central to Kristeva's thinking. The most significant element is the paradox of virginity and motherhood in relation to sex and death: eternally a virgin, eternally untouched by sex, Mary is also, whether through theologies of "dormition" or "assumption," untouched by death. Traditional Christianity constructs an ideal of the woman who is a sex-less immortal mother: the fantasy functions, in Kristeva's words, to "tame the maternal." Although this idealization of a virginal motherhood has exacted a harsh toll on women's lives for many centuries, it has also nevertheless functioned as a cultural code providing a vocabulary and container for the feminine and the maternal.

The collapse of this symbolism leads to what Kristeva calls the psychic sore of modernity. Like the loss of a discourse of death, the loss of the cultural discourse of the ideal form of the maternal can push us toward melancholia. The draw of melancholia is doubly strong "after the virgin" because of the roots of mourning and melancholia in the loss of the archaic mother at the birth of the self. (Jonte-Pace, 2001). McCance even suggests that the form of Kristeva's text "Stabat Mater" is a subtle echo of the content of "Mourning and Melancholia" where Freud referred to melancholia as an "open wound." The split columns of the essay, she proposes, "oscillate on a symbolic-semiotic borderline, alluding perhaps to Freud's 'Mourning and Melancholia,' the sight of a wound or scar" (McCance, 2003, p. 139).

If, as Kristeva suggests, melancholia is a ubiquitous feature of the contemporary landscape, our entire culture may be in serious danger. "In the flight from dogma and the impossible precariousness of faith," Lechte thus asks, "may we in the west not be risking collective suicide, or at least a symbolic death?" His answer is bleak: "For Kristeva, the answer seems to be Yes" (Lechte, 1990, p. 39). In Kristeva's analysis, the current fragility of religious discourses of death and the maternal does indeed leave us in a melancholic position: "after the virgin," and without a vocabulary for sex and the maternal, and after the crucifixion, without a vocabulary for hope in the wake of death and loss, we are vulnerable or "unprotected" in an unprecedented way. The loss of all possibility of meaning and the inaccessibility of affect are serious risks. And yet, I argue, Kristeva is not despondent; she does not exhibit a defensive "inability to mourn," she does not suffer from an inability to remember or to stop remembering, nor does she argue that this is our condition. Instead she offers tentative responses to this melancholia, suggesting two possible paths within and through the "abyss of sorrow": psychoanalysis and postmodern writing. I believe that she also hints at a third path. She implies that the study of religion is the sort of response to melancholia that may "open up the closure" of melancholia.

I want to describe these Kristevan paths through melancholia, but it is important to emphasize first that Kristeva's sense of an opening beyond melancholia through postmodernism or psychoanalysis is circumscribed, tentative, ambiguous, limited – and, of course, highly intellectual (perhaps even elitist.) Her goal is not to find a final fix or a permanent cure; she does not seek a return to transcendence. Rather, she seeks a way to live with melancholia, to live with ambiguity as "subjects in process, ceaselessly losing our identity" (Kristeva, 1987a, p. 9). She seeks ways to allow melancholia to be creative rather than defensive. She even hesitates to use the term hope: the "ambiguous position of the analyst," she says, "bases itself not on hope but on the fire of tongues." This "fire" is sparked by a self-reflexive, interpretive, meta-cognitive "combustion," a "three-way loop" (Kristeva, 1995, p. 125), involving a hermeneutical stance of reflection upon one's own psychic process.

One path through melancholia named by Kristeva is psychoanalysis. She begins *Black Sun* with a chapter called "Psychoanalysis: A Counterdepressant." Elsewhere she had argued that it is only through psychoanalysis that "we know that we are foreigners to ourselves and it is with the help of that sole support that we can attempt to live with others" (Kristeva, 1991, p. 182). She is clear that the analytic process avoids the nihilism of an excessive rationality: "psychoanalysis viewed as a theory of knowledge of psychic objects is part of the nihilist effort to objectify man's being. Nevertheless (...) the analytic process is first and foremost an unfolding of language prior to and beyond all unification, distantiation, and objectification." In her words, psychoanalysis is the "modest if tenacious antidote to nihilism" (1987a, pp. 60–63).

For Kristeva, another path through melancholia is postmodern writing and literature: she asks whether postmodern "écriture" is the breakthrough many have been waiting for; whether it represents an attempt to open up the closure of melancholia, or, in Freud's words, to close the "open wound" of melancholia. For Kristeva, like Cixous, writing takes on a creative force and a powerful luminosity. Kristeva herself explores this option, attempting to "write in the face of a post Christian enigma or void" with what McCance calls a "borderline writing," a writing that walks the "fine edge of melancholic grief and opens itself to an important other or outside of language." Postmodern writings work close to the "thick film of language ... where moods such as melancholia leave their remains"(Joy et al., 2003a, p. xxiii; see also McCance, 2003).

Kristeva's understanding of psychoanalysis and postmodern writing as potential paths beyond melancholia, I believe, leads her directly into the study of religion. Does the study of religion embody a path through the melancholia produced by religious changes and losses in modernity, a path that allows us to find a way to live and work creatively within melancholia? Kristeva's most explicit remarks on the study of religion and religious texts can be found in a chapter in *New Maladies of the Soul* called "Reading the Bible" in which she reflects on her interest in biblical texts, religious studies, and the interpretive process. She asks "why is it that ever since Freud analytic attention has invariably focused on the sacred, and more specifically, on the biblical sacred?" (1995, p. 123). She cites directly a number of scholars of religion whose work has been important to her – Mary Douglas, Jacob Neusner, and Evan Zuess in the *Journal of the American Academy of Religion* – and she refers explicitly to the discipline of religious studies (1995, p. 116). The essay "Reading the Bible" can be read as a meditation on Kristeva's own longtime interest in sacred texts and their interpretations; it can also be read as a reflection on the study of religion in relation to the "new maladies" (such as melancholia) of modernity.

Kristeva begins the essay by differentiating her own psychoanalytic inquiry into biblical texts from the methods and assumptions more typical in the study of religion. While the discipline of religious studies engages in semiological, structural, and functional analyses, posing questions about "the logic or rhetoric of the text," her own work poses questions about the "linguistic subject of the biblical utterance ... and its addressee: who is speaking in the bible? for whom?" This perspective leads her to the "intra or infrasubjective dynamics of the sacred text" (1995, pp. 115–117). She retraces her own answers to these intra and infrasubjective questions in texts published over several decades: she found the abjection of the mother in the "Levitical rules ("the object excluded from these rules ... is ultimately the mother"); she found the father of personal prehistory in the unrepresentability of God (1995, pp. 118, 122). Her approach, in other words, asks about interpersonal dynamics and unconscious fantasies woven through sacred texts; her analysis creates a hermeneutical space attentive to subjectivity: "interpreting these dynamics would require that we recognize a new space, that of the speaking subject ... who opens himself ... to analyzable spaces" (1995, pp. 117–118).

Although Kristeva differentiates the "intra or infrasubjective" approach of psychoanalytic interpretation from the more typical approach found in the study of religion – the inquiry into the "logic or rhetoric of the sacred text" – those of us who work in the broad field of "Religion and Psychological Studies" or "Psychology and Religion" will recognize the intersubjective and hermeneutic questions she poses. Most of her analysis, in fact, is as relevant to the discipline of religious studies as it is to the field of psychoanalysis: both balance on the tightrope between belief and interpretation, hoping that their analyses will, in her words, "guide them toward the mechanism – if not the enigma – of what is seen as holy" (1995, p. 115).

Kristeva is careful and nuanced in her description of this interpretive tightrope. She states that "Psychoanalytic interpreters are obliged to distance themselves from Faith in the Goddess of Reason as well as from religious Faith" (1995, p. 123). She explains: "Interpretation is an imaginary discourse that serves as truth [and] makes no attempt to hide its status as fiction, as a text"(1995, p. 124). Her words point to the luminosity – even the "combustibility" that we noted earlier – of the interpretive process. She suggests that psychoanalysis is "neither biblical, rationalistic, religious, nor positivist, the place of the analyst is always elsewhere and deceptive (...) This ambiguous position generates an ethics of construction if not of healing" (1995, p. 125).

Kristeva thus encourages – and indeed, her own work embodies – a process of "remembering, repeating, and working through," to use Freud's words, a process "carried out bit by bit," engaging the work of memory and interpretation around religious images, symbols, and practices. This work of memory, Freud argued, is crucial to the work of mourning. Kristeva, with her frequent forays into the history of art and religion, helps us see that it is central as well to the ongoing – or interminable – work of melancholia. For like analysis itself, melancholia is interminable. In modernity we are never finished with the remembering, the grieving, the working through.

Freud's acknowledgement that analysis is "interminable" is echoed by Kristeva in a reference to "the serene delicacy of the never attained end of analysis," which, she says, is "analogous to the logic of the Bible" (1995, pp. 125–126). Kristeva concludes her essay "Reading the Bible" with these words: "We should read the bible one more time: to interpret it, of course, but also to let it carve out a space for our own fantasies and interpretive delirium" (1995, p. 126). With the interpretations that make up our field we acknowledge that religion "can be made into an object of analysis" at the same time that we "admit ... that it conceals something that cannot be analyzed" (1995, p. 115).

The study of religion, in other words, is part of the treatment that Kristeva recommends for cultural melancholia, this "new malady of the soul" so widespread in modernity. Kristeva thus rewrites "Mourning and Melancholia," expanding the analysis into the realms of culture, religion, and gender. In spite of her respect for and careful analysis of traditional religious codes, she does not yearn nostalgically for a return to premodern religious discourses of transcendence, nor does she submit to the fantasy of a "sublime other (who) promises the melancholic absolute meaning – the fantasy of a literalist or fundamentalist absolute" (1995, p. 140). Unlike Clément and Cixous, she does not encourage the experience of the sacred (or religion or mysticism) as a cure for depression and melancholia. Unlike Freud she does not promote atheism, which, as we noted above, she sees as repressive. Kristeva recommends "a renunciation of faith with clear understanding" (1987a, p. 27): neither atheist/secularist, nor religious/ mystical, but rather, open to the play of interpretations, memories, and meanings within melancholia.

Kristeva's work, I believe, challenges the Freudian binary that assumes mourning is adaptive and melancholia pathological. The binary model sees mourning as the completion or resolution of the grieving process, while regarding melancholia as either an inability to mourn or an ongoing entrapment in the grieving process. In connection with memory, as we noted above, we cannot remember or we cannot stop remembering. The Kristevan escape from the binary separates and differentiates these two forms of melancholia: the inability to mourn is the more pathological form, while the ongoing immersion in loss, grief, and memory can be productive, creative, enlivening, and hopeful – at least when it is not, to use the vocabulary of Freud's first essay on religion, an "obsessive act." This is a melancholia involving a sense of both resignation and reclamation, and an acknowledgement that we are all in some sense, melancholy but not despairing, both post-religious and believers still.

Freud's first contribution to the psychology of religion, "Obsessive Acts and Religious Practices," interpreted the repetitions that characterize ritual and obsession as ways in which the body memorializes without remembering. Paul Ricoeur has said that mourning is to memory as melancholia is to repetition without remembering (cited in Homans, 2008). I believe, however, that melancholia, even with its repetitions, can also be a way to remember – and to keep remembering. In this sense "Obsessive Acts" is not unrelated to "Mourning and Melancholia": for Freud, both essays struggle to articulate the riddle of memory and loss. Kristeva shows us how the solution to that riddle lies close to religion.

Thus Kristeva re-reads Freud, rethinking "Mourning and Melancholia" and developing it in the direction of an interpretation of religion and its vicissitudes in modernity. Mourning, melancholia, and religion are inextricably interwoven in her work. Religion gave us a discourse of loss and redemption and showed us how to mourn. The fragmentation of religious groundings in modernity gave way to the "dark sun" of melancholia, a "new malady of the soul." And, although melancholia can lead to asymbolic, atheistic despair (no memories, no symbols), it can also provide the context for a reading, remembering, and reinterpreting of religious texts, not to escape the "new malady," but to pursue the "interminable" project of "remembering, repeating, and working through."

References

Cixous, H., & Clément, C. (1986). *The newly born woman*. Minneapolis, MN: University of Minnesota Press.

Clark, S. & Hulley, K. (1990). An interview with Julia Kristeva: Cultural strangeness and the subject in crisis. *Discourse, 13*, 149–180.

Clément, C. & Kristeva, J. (2001). *The feminine and the sacred*. New York: Columbia University Press.

Crownfield, D. (1992). *Body/text in Julia Kristeva: Religion, women, and psychoanalysis*. Albany, NY: State University of New York.

Doane, J. & Hodges, D. (1992). *From Klein to Kristeva: Psychoanalytic feminism and the search for the good enough mother*. Ann Arbor, MI: University of Michigan Press.

Edelstein, M. (1992). Metaphor, meta-narrative, and mater-narrative in Kristeva's 'Stabat Mater.' In D. Crownfield (Ed.), *Body/text in Julia Kristeva: Religion, women, and psychoanalysis* (pp. 27–52). Albany, NY: State University of New York Press.

Freud, S. (1914/1958). Remembering, repeating, and working through. In *Standard edition of the complete psychological works of Sigmund Freud*. Vol. 12 (pp. 145–156). London: Hogarth Press.

Freud, S. (1917/1957). Mourning and melancholia. In *Standard edition of the complete psychological works of Sigmund Freud*. Vol. 14 (239–257). London: Hogarth Press.

Hollywood, A. (2003). Cixous and Clément. In M. Joy, K. O'Grady, & J. Poxon (Eds.), *Religion in French feminist thought: Critical perspectives* (pp. 145–161). London/New York: Routledge.

Homans, P. (2001). *Symbolic loss: The ambiguity of mourning and memory at century's end*. Charlottsville, VA: Univeristy of Virginia Press.

Homans, P. (2008). Conversations on Freud, memory, and loss. In W. Parsons, D. Jonte-Pace & S. Henking (Eds.), *Mourning religion*. Charlottsville, VA: University of Virginia Press.

Homans, P. & Jonte-Pace, D. (2006) Tracking the emotion in the stone: An essay in psychoanalysis and architecture. *The Annual of Psychoanalysis, 33*, 261–284.

Jantzen, G. (2003). 'Death, then, how could I yield to it?' In M. Joy, K. O'Grady, & J. Poxon (Eds.), *Religion in French feminist thought: Critical perspectives* (pp. 117–130). London/New York: Routledge.

Jones, A. R. (1984). Julia Kristeva on femininity: The limits of a semiotic politics. *Feminist Review,18*, 56–73.

Jonte-Pace, D. (1997). Julia Kristeva and the psychoanalytic study of religion: Rethinking Freud's cultural texts. In J. Jacobs & D. Capps (Eds.), *Religion, society, and psychoanalysis: Readings in contemporary theory* (pp. 240–268). Boulder, CO: Westview Press.

Jonte-Pace, D. (2001). *Speaking the unspeakable: Religion, misogyny, and the uncanny mother in Freud's cultural texts*. Berkeley, CA: University of California Press.

Joy, M., O'Grady, K., & Poxon, J. (2002a). Introduction. In M. Joy, K. O'Grady, & J. Poxon (Eds.), *French feminists on religion: A reader* (pp. 1–12). London/New York: Routledge.

Joy, M., O'Grady, K., & Poxon, J. (Eds.) (2002b). *French feminists on religion: A reader*. London/New York: Routledge.

Joy, M., O'Grady, K., & Poxon, J. (2003a). Editor's introduction. In M. Joy, K. O'Grady, & J. Poxon (Eds.), *Religion in French feminist thought: Critical perspectives* (pp. xv–xvii). London/New York: Routledge.

Joy, M., O'Grady, K., & Poxon, J. (Eds.) (2003b). *Religion in French feminist thought: Critical perspectives*. London/New York: Routledge.

Kim, C. W. M., St.Ville, S. M. & Simonaitis, S. M. (Eds.) (1993). *Transfigurations: Theology and the French feminists*. Minneapolis, MN: Fortress Press.

Kristeva, J. (1982). *Powers of horror: An essay on abjection* (trans. L. Roudiez). New York: Columbia University Press.

Kristeva, J. (1984). My memory's hyperbole. *New York Literary Forum, 12–13*, 261–276.

Kristeva, J. (1986a). *About Chinese women* (trans. A. Barrows). New York: Marion Boyars.

Kristeva, J. (1986b). Stabat Mater (trans. L. Roudiez). In J. Kristeva & T. Moi (Eds.), *The Kristeva reader* (pp. 160–186). New York: Columbia University Press.
Kristeva, J. (1987a). *In the beginning was love: Psychoanalysis and faith* (trans. A. Goldhammer). New York: Columbia University Press.
Kristeva, J. (1987b). *Tales of love* (trans. L. S. Roudiez). New York: Columbia University Press.
Kristeva, J. (1989). *Black sun: Depression and melancholia* (trans. L. Roudiez). New York: Columbia University Press.
Kristeva, J. (1991). *Strangers to ourselves* (trans. L. Roudiez). New York: Columbia University Press.
Kristeva, J. (1995). *New maladies of the soul* (trans. R. Guberman). New York: Columbia University Press.
Lechte, J. (1990). Art, love, and melancholy in the work of Julia Kristeva. In J. Fletcher & A. Benjamin (Eds.), *Abjection, melancholia, and love: The work of Julia Kristeva* (pp. 31–48). New York: Routledge.
McCance, D. (1988). Kristeva and the subject of ethics. *Resources for Feminist Research, 17*, 18–22.
McCance, D. (2003). Kristeva's melancholia: Not knowing how to lose. In M. Joy, K. O'Grady, & J. Poxon (Eds.), *Religion in French feminist thought: Critical perspectives* (pp. 131–141). London/New York: Routledge.
Mitscherlich, A. & Mitscherlich, M. (1975). *The inability to mourn: Principles of collective behavior*. New York: Grove Press.
Reineke, M. (1997). *Sacrificed lives: Kristeva on women and violence*. Bloomington, IN: Indiana University Press.
Santer, E. (1990). *Stranded objects: Mourning, memory, and film in Postwar Germany*. Ithaca, NY: Cornell University Press.
Spivak, G. C. (1988). *In other worlds: Essays in cultural politics*. New York: Routledge.

Index

MIX
Papier aus verantwortungsvollen Quellen
Paper from responsible sources
FSC® C105338

If you have any concerns about our products,
you can contact us on
ProductSafety@springernature.com

In case Publisher is established outside the EU,
the EU authorized representative is:
Springer Nature Customer Service Center GmbH
Europaplatz 3, 69115 Heidelberg, Germany

Printed by Libri Plureos GmbH
in Hamburg, Germany